An Economic Theory of Managerial Firms

The separation between ownership and control has become common practice over the last century, in most medium and large firms across the world. Throughout the twentieth century, the theory of the firm and the theory of industrial organization developed parallel and complementary views on managerial firms. This book offers a comprehensive exposition of this debate.

In its survey of strategic delegation in oligopoly games, *An Economic Theory of Managerial Firms* is able to offer a reinterpretation of a range of standard results in the light of the fact that the control of firms is generally not in the hand of its owners. The theoretical models are supported by a wealth of real-world examples, in order to provide a study of strategic delegation that is far more in-depth than has previously been found in the literature on industrial organization. In this volume, analysis is extended in several directions to cover applications concerning the role of: managerial firms in mixed market; collusion and mergers; divisionalization and vertical relations; technical progress; product differentiation; international trade; environmental issues; and the intertemporal growth of firms.

This book is of great interest to those who study industrial economics, organizational studies and industrial studies.

Luca Lambertini is full professor of Economics at the University of Bologna, Italy. He was previously the Head of the Department of Economics of the same University and member of the Executive Committee of EARIE (European Association for Research in Industrial Economics).

Routledge Studies in the Economics of Business and Industry

An Economic Theory of Managerial Firms

Strategic Delegation in Oligopoly

Luca Lambertini

Routledge
Taylor & Francis Group

LONDON AND NEW YORK

First published 2017
by Routledge

2 Park Square, Milton Park, Abingdon, Oxfordshire OX14 4RN

52 Vanderbilt Avenue, New York, NY 10017

Routledge is an imprint of the Taylor & Francis Group, an informa business

First issued in paperback 2020

British Library Cataloguing-in-Publication Data
A catalogue record for this book is available from the British Library

Library of Congress Cataloging-in-Publication Data
Names: Lambertini, Luca, author.
Title: An economic theory of managerial firms: strategic delegation in oligopoly/Luca Lambertini.
Description: Abingdon, Oxon; New York, NY: Routledge, 2017. | Includes index.
Identifiers: LCCN 2016050415 | ISBN 9781138658349 (hardback) | ISBN 9781315620879 (ebook)
Subjects: LCSH: Oligopolies. | Industrial organization (Economic theory)
Classification: LCC HD2757.3.L359 2017 | DDC 338.601–dc23
LC record available at https://lccn.loc.gov/2016050415

ISBN: 978-1-138-65834-9 (hbk)
ISBN: 978-0-367-66786-3 (pbk)

Typeset in Times New Roman
by Sunrise Setting Ltd., Brixham, UK

This one's for Massimo
Duke knows why

Contents

Figures

Preface

This book is about the nature of the firm seen as a contract between (at least) two subjects, an owner and a manager. As such, the proposed topic is way too large; indeed, as large as the area defined by the combination of oligopoly theory and contract theory. In fact, what I am about to reconstruct is the portion of this area in which contracts delegating firm's control to managers are observable strategic tools in the hands of owners. This will be done after an overview - wide in scope but necessarily short in space - of the theory of the firm as we have acquired it from the debated developed by many outstanding scholars in several directions over the last eighty years or so. Hence, it is correct to say that this volume outlines a theory of the firm, out of many.

The separation between ownership and control has been common practice in most of medium and large firms all over the planet, throughout the last century. Managerialization has acted as a primary factor in fostering the growth of medium and large firms alike, and has significantly contributed to shaping the minds of consumers as well as the structure of the economic system as we see it now.

Currently, the strategies determining the trend and performance of the global economy are determined by top managers acting on behalf of stockholders, who motivate their agents through delegation contracts based on a spectrum of incentives ranging from revenues to sales to market shares, usually combined with profits. After the earliest analysis of the arising of managerial firms in the 1930s, the theory of the firm and the theory of industrial organization developed parallel and complementary views on managerial firms, alternatively based on asymmetric information (as in agency theory and neo-institutionalism) or strategic interaction (as in oligopoly theory).

As I have anticipated above, this book offers a comprehensive exposition of this debate, with a compact but exhaustive overview of the former and a detailed reconstruction of the latter. After a reconstruction of the literatures on transaction cost economics, new institutional economics, agency theory and the theory of the growth of the firm, the proper survey of strategic delegation in oligopoly games sets off with the analysis of alternative incentive schemes in models where managers are in charge of manoeuvring market variables only and then proceeds by considering additional elements such as collusive behaviour, mergers, divisionalization and R&D investment.

The impact of delegation on intraindustry trade and the environment is also illustrated. Finally, a look at the long run implications of managerial incentives is taken in a differential game framework, which establishes a direct connection with the early discussion on the theory of the growth of the firm in the late 1950s and early 1960s. The exposition of theoretical models is accompanied by real-world examples to motivate the formal analysis and corroborate intuition.

Aims and style

The main aim of this volume is to make justice of a literature which has fully developed itself as a subset of the theory of industrial organization but so far, unlike other branches of the same theory (e.g., R&D races and product differentiation), and surprisingly enough, has not acquired a place of its own and has not been given a full-fledged reconstruction. All of this, I would like to stress, has happened the relevance of the topic notwithstanding. A plausible way of outlining the motivation of a book on strategic delegation is the following. Large corporations drive the global economy via managerial decisions, while the majority of industrial organization (IO) assumes pure profit-seeking behaviour. Hence, the task of this book consists in providing a reinterpretation of a range of standard results in the light of the fact that firm's control is generally not in the hand of firm's owners, and this makes a difference. The standard of the exposition, in terms of the mathematics involved, will be in line with that of industrial organization textbooks commonly adopted in graduate courses at the MSc/MPhil and PhD level. Accordingly, the whole book or parts of it can be used in analogous courses in Economics as well as Business and Management. It may also be of interest to researchers, practitioners and policy makers professionally involved in this field.

Structure of the book

The first chapter outlines the origins and evolution of the economic theory of managerial firms since the arising of transaction cost economics in the late 1930s. Then, it illustrates the main features and achievements of models belonging to agency theory and neo-institutionalism, and the managerial motives in the theory of the growth of the firm. Then, a perspective on strategic delegation is also outlined, where strategic incentives mix up with asymmetric information and agency problems.

Chapter 2 is for the layout of the baseline model where firms set either prices or quantities and managers control these market variables. The material of this chapter contains the detailed illustration of three alternative incentive schemes: (i) profits and sales (or revenues); (ii) comparative performance; and (iii) market shares and profits. The analytical exposition and comparison of these alternative approaches will be supported by a geometrical illustration of the impact of delegation in the map of best reply functions in the market stage. Another core issue discussed in this chapter is the strategic value of observable vs unobservable managerial contracts. To complement the theoretical analysis, the chapter also summarises the empirical evidence on the performance of managerial firms. As an up-to-date addendum, a survey of experimental evidence is also provided, as the separation between ownership and control is receiving a growing amount of attention in the area of behavioural/experimental economics.

The topic dealt with in chapter 3 is the following. The coexistence of firms with different objective functions is a long standing issue in the theory of industrial organization, and of course its analysis has crossed the territory of strategic delegation, in the form of the following question: if private firms adopts delegation contracts based on sales or revenues, may a public firm enhance welfare by hiring a manager, and - if so - through which incentive scheme?

Chapter 4 covers two issues of great interest to antitrust agencies: the stability of implicit collusion in repeated games and the incentive to carry out horizontal mergers. This, together with chapter 8, is the most policy-oriented part of the book.

The issue illustrated in chapter 5 is the incentive for firms to vertically integrate and to become multidivisional. The latter aspect has an evident connection with Williamson's M-form. The models exposed in this chapter tell that strategic delegation can indeed be reinterpreted as a form of coordination of a vertical supply chain. The anti- or pro-competitive effects of divisionalization are illustrated in detail.

Chapter 6 investigates the impact of managerialization on innovation incentives. The effects of some forms of strategic delegation are observationally equivalent to those of R&D for process innovation. Moreover, casual observation suggests that short-run profit incentives may well be outperformed by other more forward-looking contracts when it comes to major R&D projects.

An account of this discussion is offered in this chapter, covering process and product innovation, licensing and the make-or-buy decision, i.e., in-house investments vs outsourcing. The theme of chapter 7 is the interplay between managerial incentives and endogenous product differentiation, either horizontal or vertical. This subject matter, intuitively, is closely connected with the material discussed in the previous one. The survey covers several issues, such as the need to increase product differentiation in order to offset the pro-competitive effects of managerialization, and the incentive for owners to delegate product design in addition to market variables.

Chapter 8 covers two aspects closely connected with the core problems of a global economic system: trade flows and pollution/resource extraction.

The analogy between some forms of strategic delegation and corporate social responsibility will also be illustrated in detail.

Surprisingly enough, the dynamic analysis of managerial behaviour and its impact on firms' investment plans and long-run performance has been accounted for very early (in the aforementioned theory of the growth of the firm, dealt with in chapter 1) and then left aside, with very few exceptions which, however, provide many suggestions for fruitful extensions. Hence, this chapter not only summarises this brief discussion but also takes up the task of stimulating its resurgence.

Acknowledgements

This book largely results from the stimulus and encouragement I have received from many friends and colleagues over many years, during which I've been vaguely thinking about the project that has ultimately materialized into the present volume. Among them, I should like to mention Bengt Holmström, whose lectures on agency theory at the University of Bergamo in 1987 when I was a young undergraduate triggered my choice of that theme for my *tesi di laurea*, Paolo Onofri and Gianpaolo Rossini, supervisors of that dissertation for my first degree, at the University of Bologna; and my supervisors during my graduate studies at the University of Oxford, Martin Slater and John Vickers. Additionally, I would like to thank Flavio Delbono, Michael Kopel, Andrea Mantovani and Arsen Palestini for many fruitful suggestions and comments. Needless to say, the responsibility for the contents and any remaining errors or omissions remains with me only. Special thanks to Emily Kindleysides, Andy Humphries, Laura Johnson and the whole editorial team at Routledge/Taylor & Francis, who accompanied me most friendlily and efficiently through this venture, as usual. And then to Monica, who had the patience to grant me work slots off the family time, even in hard times.

1 The theory of managerial firms

Setting the stage

In the neoclassical theory of the firm (or production), the essence of a firm is its technological endowment: essentially, its production function or its cost function. At the (perfectly competitive) general equilibrium, things like firms' size or internal organization do not matter and are not modelled. As stressed by Jensen and Meckling (1976), we encounter countless references to the theory of the firm, while one should more correctly talk about a theory of markets, in which firms adopt strategies usually aimed at profit maximization, their internal structure being blackboxed. That is, the first generation of models describing oligopolistic behaviour (and, in the opposite limits, monopoly or perfect competition), say, between the early 1970s and the mid-1980s, takes the assumption of pure profit maximization as given and investigates its consequences. This amounts to saying that firms are controlled by owners, although this aspect is not explicitly discussed.

All of this does not answer two fundamental questions. (i) What is a firm? And (ii) why firms rather than markets? These questions are intuitively relevant, as casual observation reveals that there are many firms around, whose size, in terms of employment, installed capital or revenues, is almost as large as that of the markets wherein they operate and, not rarely, larger than several countries around the globe.

The prevailing view about the nature of the firms is that they are a nexus of contracts rather than simply a container of technologies (see, once again, Jensen and Meckling, 1976). Consequently, the firm appears to be more easily understood in terms of the contractual and informational constraints it faces, rather then those of a technological nature described in neoclassical microeconomics.

This chapter offers a reconstruction of the debate about the nature of the firm as a set of contracts, from its early days when the matter was understanding the reasons for internalizing transactions into firms replacing portions of markets to its latest developments combining agency theory with oligopolistic interaction. As will become clear in the remainder, the evolution of this debate has a common flavour but is not linear, as the theory of the growth of the firm – initiated in the late 1950s and then abruptly abandoned twenty years later – illustrates.

1.1 Of firms and markets

Although a sense of the diversity, alterity and antagonism between firms and markets already existed (see, e.g., Berle and Means, 1932), the explicit departure from a theory of the firm based upon the efficient use of technology in competitive markets must be credited to Ronald Coase (1937). In Aghion *et al.* (2011, p. 181) words:

> Ronald Coase raised a question that may at first appear naive but in fact turned out to be fundamental: if the market is an efficient method of resource allocation, then why do so many transactions take place within firms? Coase developed verbal arguments for the existence of firms, in particular emphasizing haggling problems in decentralized market transactions, which he thought authority within firms could partly overcome. In other words, firms exist because there are costs to using the price mechanism: prices must become known, bargains must be made, contracts must be written. In his famous essay, Coase (1937) quoted the description of D.H. Robertson (1928, p. 85) that firms are 'islands of conscious power in oceans of unconsciousness like lumps of butter coagulating in buttermilk.'

Coase (1937) offered the first interpretation of the rise of firms as entities agglomerating actions previously carried out in markets. In a way, the story could be told as if 'in the beginning there was the market', an isotropic and perfectly competitive universe of atomistic activities including production and transactions. Then, there appeared clumps or clots altering that homogeneous market landscape. Those clumps where firms internalizing some activities and transactions into complex hierarchical organizations governed by internal rules (contracts) among groups of individuals (owners, managers, workers) with conflicting interests. These hierarchical structures started replacing increasingly larger portions of markets, and the question soon became whether gigantic structures could eventually replace entire markets. Coase's (1937) answer, echoed by the subsequent literature, was that most probably this cannot happen, since the remedy to the transaction costs involved by the market mechanism has an endogenous limit: internalizing transactions entails organizational costs adding up to production ones and making governance more and more problematic as the size of a firm increases. In the end, this form of attrition generated by internalizing an expanding volume of transactions previously entrusted to the market prevents the visible hand of a firm from replacing Adam Smith's (1776, 1976) invisible hand (Chandler, 1962, 1977).

In a nutshell, transaction costs cause market failures which, in turn, create room (and incentives) for the formation of firms, by removing transactions from the market and transferring them into organizations whose growth is then conditional upon their ability to control such transactions at least as efficiently as the market would do.

1.2 U-form vs M-form, and opportunistic behaviour

Williamson (1964, 1975, 1979, 1985, 1986) revisited Coase's (1937) intuition, developing it into the New Institutional Economics. The connection with Coase's

(1937) transaction cost economics is made explicit on several occasions, for example:

> it is not uncertainty or small numbers ... that occasion market failure but it is rather the joining of these factors with bounded rationality on the one hand and opportunism on the other that gives rise to exchange difficulty.
>
> (Williamson, 1975, p. 7)

As in Arrow (1974), the basic idea is that transactions flock into firms as the hierarchical structure of the latter eliminates the need for stipulating and enforcing a mass of contingent contracts. Williamson gives a full-fledged shape to the representation of this mechanism, on the following grounds:

- the market and the firm are alternative instruments that can be used to carry out economic transactions;
- the criterion for assigning a transaction to the market or to a firm is relative efficiency;
- human and environmental factors influencing markets also operate within firms' boundaries.

Environmental factors are *uncertainty* and *small numbers*. Human factors are *bounded rationality* and *opportunism*.[1] Consider first the environmental factors. If anticipating correctly all of the relevant future contingencies affecting a transaction or a chain thereof, possibly protracting over a long time horizon, then a firm may fruitfully replace the market. The same applies if vertical relations are affected by small numbers, in particular, upstream, when vertical relations matter: high degrees of concentration in industries producing crucial inputs or intermediate goods imply the risk of being thrown out of business for downstream firms selling final goods to consumers. Intuitively, this theme is conducive to a theory of vertical integration. As for the human factors, creating and expanding a firm may respond to complexity and the inadequacy of the price mechanism; moreover, the interaction between agents with divergent (or simply misaligned) incentives gives rise to opportunistic behaviour, which, as we shall see in the remainder of the chapter, is an alternative label for moral hazard.

In the New Institutional Economics, the firm is a hierarchical organization. This means that a *leitmotiv* of the theory is characterizing *authority within organizations*. The analysis of this crucial aspect takes place in the form of a discussion about the transition from the U-form (unitary form) to the M-form (multidivisional form). This idea was already present in Chandler (1962) and then it flourished in Williamson (1967, 1975) as well as in Calvo and Wellisz (1978, 1979) and Rosen (1982), among others.

The U-form is usually adopted by young and/or small firms; a single executive office controls several activities (R&D, production, advertising, etc.), each of which is carried out in a single division. The specialization of each division is seen as a way to best exploit possible economies of scale, while the choice of concentrating control in a single office is motivated by the need to avoid effort duplication. However, the adoption of the U-form may involve the typical issues connected with team production (see below).

The M-form arises as a response to the phenomenon of control loss as the firm's size increases. This entails the inability to (i) focus the entire firm on well defined organizational objectives, and (ii) cope with bounded rationality and the informational impactedness going along with opportunistic behaviour. The M-form can be considered as a cluster of small-scale U-forms constituting its divisions, whose activities can be coordinated from an upstream general staff. This involves separating strategic decisions from all of the others; the long-run view of the future of a firm is outlined by the general staff, while any specific actions are delegated to divisions. Any conflicts between individuals or divisions are solved upstream, through selective interventions.

1.3   Asset specificity, moral hazard and vertical integration

Williamson (1971a) and Alchian and Demsetz (1972) open up a new stream of research concerning the nature of the firm, where a key element is the presence of asset specificity producing appropriable quasi-rents, measured by the difference between the value attached to an input when the latter is employed for the specific task for which it has been conceived and the best alternative (Klein *et al.*, 1978). Hence, the rise of long-run relationships (i.e. production activities and – in general – economic transactions) consolidating themselves into a firm can be explained in terms of the use of assets whose nature is specific to that particular set of activities. The typical example of this sort is an irreversible investment in a durable good or a capital input which creates a *lock-in effect*.[2] This creates an incentive towards vertical integration, which is obviously reinforced in the presence of small numbers upstream. The tradeoff between asset specificity on the one hand and the increasing pressure on hierarchical control on the other determines whether the final outcome is vertical integration or not (Williamson, 1985; Riordan and Williamson, 1986).

Another source of the same incentive is the interplay between informational asymmetry and moral hazard (or opportunistic behaviour), leading to the hold-up problem whereby independent upstream firms may well underinvest in the quality of a specific input (Grout, 1984; Joskow, 1985), relying on the fact that contracts are incomplete and the input quality is unobservable before it's too late.

The related literature on property rights (Demsetz, 1967; Grossman and Hart, 1986; Tirole, 1986; Hart and Moore, 1988, Hart and Moore, 1990, *inter alia*) has formalized anew both the issue of contract incompleteness and the incentive to carry out investments in specific assets:

> Contractual rights may be of two types: specific rights and residual rights. When it is too costly for one party to specify a long list of the particular rights it desires over another party's assets, it may be optimal for that party to purchase all the rights except those specifically mentioned in the contract. Ownership is the purchase of these residual rights of control.
>
> (Grossman and Hart, 1986, p. 692)

That is, the advantage of resorting to vertical integration consists of internalizing whatever cannot be specified in detail in a contract. Once again, this strategy may also translate to a strategic advantage when downstream market competition takes place, either because of foreclosure or simply because vertically separated rivals buy inputs at the price prevailing in the upstream market instead of transferring them at marginal cost along the vertically integrated structure.

1.4 What does a firm maximize?

As I have indicated at the outset of the chapter, this is a sort of digression, insofar as it offers a more concrete connection between the aims of firms on one side and the market on the other. As we shall see at the end of this chapter, agency theory has also followed an analogous line, much later than the contributions I am about to illustrate in this section.

Moreover, the point of departure of this literature appears before the New Institutional Economics and, to some extent, can be thought of as a forerunner of the strategic delegation approach emerging in the 1980s. I am referring to the Baumol (1958) model, where the possibility that a firm may maximize long-run revenues rather than profits is considered, under a constraint posed by the attainment of some profit level $\overline{\pi}$. The essence of the model is represented in Figure 1.1.

Curves $R(q)$, $C(q)$ and π represent revenues, total costs and profits of the firm in the long run. The minimum acceptable profit $\overline{\pi}$ is identified by the horizontal line crossing the profit curve in correspondence with the peak of revenues, which of course requires an output larger than the profit-maximizing production level. The dashed line crossing the intersection between revenues and total costs identifies the output at which profits are nil. The argument of Baumol (1958) hinges on the idea that any profits exceeding $\overline{\pi}$ are reinvested in demand-enhancing activities, such as advertising and R&D for product innovation and design, as these

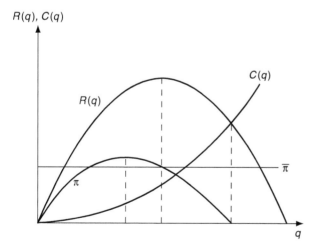

Figure 1.1 Revenue maximization in the Baumol (1958) model.

efforts ultimately expand revenues. This amounts to saying that, in the long run, the minimum profit constraint $\overline{\pi}$ will always bite.

The argument proposed by Baumol (1958) is largely informal – in particular, it doesn't explicitly formalize the connections between market competition and the firm's choice of an objective function differing from profits – but suggestive of a number of deviations from the traditional (neoclassical) view of the firm as a profit-maximizing entity subject to market pressure. Needless to say, it has rapidly triggered a debate which has been fostered also by the emergence of a *behavioural theory of the firm* a few years later (Cyert and March, 1963), in which it is neatly pointed out that a firm gathers groups of individuals with diverging interests, and therefore the observed behaviour of a firm is the result of a process intertwining a manifold of different aims and incentives.

A plausible way of summarizing Baumol's (1958) value added consists of saying that, in this paper, he introduces two key elements interacting with one another: the presence of a constraint and the concrete possibility that firms do not maximize profits. Taking this premise as a departure point, we may easily read anew the wide, but here and there also confusing, debate emerging in the 1960s and easily make full sense of it.

A first plausible extension is indeed an objection to the use of a minimum profit constraint applied to revenue maximization, which is replaced by the opposite view whereby a firm might decide to seek profit maximization under a constraint defined as a minimum volume of sales. As shown by Shepherd (1962) and Osborne (1964), the two procedures are, in general, not equivalent (see also Monsen and Downs, 1963).

A second route explored in the 1970s is close in spirit to the basic idea of agency theory, as it stresses that a manager might maximize her/his own utility, containing several arguments unrelated to profits, under the constraint posed by the market value of the firm (Williamson, 1971b; Ng, 1974; Yarrow, 1976), and also accounting for uncertainty concerning the possibility for stakeholders to intervene to limit managerial discretionality (Yarrow, 1973).

The echo of this debate resonates also in the parallel theory of the growth of the firm, where the central topic, in terms of the subject matter of this book, is the impact of managerial incentives and alternative goals on the long-run performance of firms.

1.4.1   The theory of the growth of the firm

The building blocks of this literature are the contributions of Penrose (1959), Baumol (1962), Marris (1963, 1964) and Williamson (1966). Common to all of them is the idea that managers care for firms' growth over time, whereby it is meant that 'growth' has to do with the dynamics of demand and output or revenues, not necessarily with the profit path. The innovative element characterizing this literature is the relevant role attributed to the *time dimension*.

Its main drawbacks are that (i) the models are not formalized as optimal control problems, so that the time dimension largely remains behind the curtains, and none of these models explicitly cope with the interplay between firms' growth and the structure and intensity of market competition.

The outcome of the stream of research involving Baumol (1962), Marris (1963, 1964) and Williamson (1966) is that the profit path of a managerial firm is conditional upon the intertemporal growth of demand and output; in other words, maximizing growth (or the growth rate) of sales does not maximize profits – although Williamson (1966) in fact claimed that pursuing one goal amounts to pursuing the other, in a model which significantly differs from the others.

Penrose (1959) deserves some additional remarks, as we will come back to it in Chapter 9. In Penrose (1959), the matter is not the identification of managerial objectives and their impact on firms' profits. Managers are assumed to maximize their respective firms' profits, but their activities are subject to endogenous limits imposed by the twin task of managing the firm (pushing its growth rate) and, at the same time, expanding the stock of managerial skills inside the firm. The impact of these factors has become known as the *Penrose effect*, and, in more modern terms, could be thought of as a *diseconomy of scope* affecting the spectrum of managerial tasks and therefore hindering the growth rate of firms. This view has been profitably formalized into a properly dynamic model (Slater, 1980) which has opened a promising stream of research based on the tools of optimal control and differential game theory revisiting ideas at the basis of the initial debate on firms' dynamic evolution.

1.5 Agency theory

The climax of the view of the firm as a contract or a set of contracts is agency theory, in which a principal delegates a crucial activity to an agent. The principal can be the owner (in which case the agent is a manager) or a manager (in which case the agent is a worker). The principal–agent relationship may take place simply in a condition of *hidden action*, by which it is meant that the agent's behaviour is unobserved by the principal, or in a condition combining hidden action with *hidden information*, which implies that the principal cannot reconstruct the motivations of the agent's unobserved behaviour. In both cases, the presence of hidden action entails that the principal faces a moral hazard problem. What follows is a synthetic exposition of the backbone of the literature on agency theory, based on Ross (1973), Mirrlees (1975, 1976, 1999),[3] Harris and Raviv (1979), Holmström (1979), Shavell (1979), Grossman and Hart (1983) and Rogerson (1985b), *inter alia*.

Since the basic elements of the agency game are going to appear again later in the book, I shall describe them in some detail. The simplest version of the model including hidden information describes a game between two players, a principal (owner) and an agent (manager). The owner is risk neutral while the manager is risk averse.

The principal only observes the output and profits of the firm. The game is stochastic, so that the output $q(x, \varepsilon)$ of the firm is determined by the agent's effort x and a stochastic variable ε whose distribution is common knowledge.

Variable ε is the state of the world, and its exact realization is the manager's private information prior to choosing effort x. That is, the agent's awareness about the state of the world is her/his hidden information; consequently, managerial effort is conditional on the state of the world, $x(\varepsilon)$. To grasp the bearing of hidden information in this context, one can simply figure out a situation in which the stochastic variable describes the behaviour of the oil market: the principal observes neither the manager's strategy x nor the realization of ε, so, ex post, if profits are low, the manager may just assert she/he has chosen the optimal effort and impute the unsatisfactory outcome to 'bad luck', in the form of a negative shock hitting the oil market.

Since the principal cannot figure out precisely the relationship between the state of the world ε, effort x and the firm's expected profits $E(\pi)$, the contract offered to the agent is the outcome of the tradeoff between incentive and insurance. That is, it incorporates a compromise between the principal's intention to induce the optimal effort on the part of the manager and the need to come to terms with the latter's risk aversion.

Define as $R(x, \varepsilon)$ and $M(R(x, \varepsilon))$ the firm's revenues and the manager's remuneration, respectively (assuming any other costs away for simplicity, $R(x, \varepsilon)$ can be thought of as profits, gross of managerial remuneration). Consequently, the expected profits are

$$E(\pi) = E(R(x, \varepsilon) - M(R(x, \varepsilon))) \tag{1.1}$$

Moreover, the managerial utility function $U(x, M)$ is assumed to be decreasing in effort x and increasing in remuneration M, and the reservation utility is U_0. Consequently, in order to be accepted by the candidate agent, the contract must satisfy $E(U(x, M)) \geq U_0$, i.e. the expected utility associated with working inside the firm must be at least as large as the certain reservation utility generated by the best outside option.

The equilibrium contract solves the following constrained maximization problem:

$$\max_{M} E(\pi) = E(R(\tilde{x}, \varepsilon) - M(R(\tilde{x}, \varepsilon))) \tag{1.2}$$

subject to

$$\tilde{x} = \arg\max E(U(x, M(R(x, \varepsilon)))) \tag{1.3}$$

$$E(U(\tilde{x}, M(R(\tilde{x}, \varepsilon)))) \geq U_0 \tag{1.4}$$

where (1.3) is the *incentive compatibility constraint*, indicating that the agent will seek to maximize her/his own expected utility, and (1.4) is the *participation constraint* based on individual rationality reflecting the above considerations. The structure of the program (1.2)–(1.4) fully reflects the principal's awareness of the candidate agent's incentives. The solution outlining the equilibrium contract is necessarily a second-best one.

Of course, under full information – implying that x and ε are observable to the principal – the first best can be attained through a contract solving (1.2) under a single constraint posed by (1.4), since if no informational asymmetry is involved, the incentive compatibility constraint (1.3) can be disregarded as it is immaterial. In other words, symmetric information transforms the model into an insurance problem, whose solution instructs the principal to grant the agent full insurance.

In the asymmetric information case, the solution of the principal's problem relies on the so-called *monotone likelihood property*. Let $F(R(\cdot), x)$ be the cumulative distribution function of $R(\cdot)$ over the support $[\underline{R}, \overline{R}]$, with density $f(R(\cdot), x)$, for any given effort x. Higher effort levels stochastically improve the firm's performance: if $\tilde{x} > \hat{x}$, then $F(R(\cdot), \hat{x}) > F(R(\cdot), \tilde{x})$.

Next, suppose the utility function of the manager is separable in remuneration and effort, so that it can be written as

$$U = u(M) - g(x) \tag{1.5}$$

with $u(M)$ increasing and concave in M and $g(x)$ increasing and convex in x. If one writes the Lagrangean function for the constrained optimization problem (1.2)–(1.4) accordingly, the maximand appearing in it is

$$\int_{\underline{R}}^{\overline{R}} [R(\cdot) - M] \, f(R(\cdot), x) \tag{1.6}$$

and the first-order condition with respect to M delivers the following:

$$\frac{1}{\partial u(M)/\partial M} = \lambda \frac{\partial f(R(\cdot), x)/\partial x}{f(R(\cdot), x)} + \mu \tag{1.7}$$

where λ is the multiplier attached to the incentive compatibility constraint (1.3) and μ is the multiplier of the participation constraint (1.4). If the manager can choose effort in a binary set $(\underline{x}, \overline{x})$, $0 < \underline{x} < \overline{x}$, (1.7) can be rewritten in the following form:

$$\frac{1}{\partial u(M)/\partial M} = \lambda \left[1 - \frac{f(R(\cdot), \underline{x})}{f(R(\cdot), \overline{x})} \right] + \mu \tag{1.8}$$

Reading the first-order condition in this form is a lot easier. The magnitude $f(R(\cdot), \underline{x})/f(R(\cdot), \overline{x})$ appearing in (1.8) is the *likelihood ratio*, implying that managerial remuneration increases with the firm's performance, provided higher profits are a correct signal of the intensity of the agent's effort. More explicitly, if $f(R(\cdot), \underline{x})/f(R(\cdot), \overline{x})$ is monotone, then the agency problem (1.2)–(1.4) can be solved by relying on observed profits.

1.5.1   *Moral hazard in teams*

Moral hazard may also commonly affect akin situations in which the firm is modelled as a structure in which a manager is monitoring a group of workers whose efforts enter the production function as input in a non-separable way. This idea dates back to Alchian and Demsetz (1972), who stressed the rise of free riding inside a firm, much the same as in the classical prisoners' dilemma game: if the single agent's effort is not observable, then each agent has an incentive to shirk. The envisaged solution to the incentive problem is to make the monitor the residual claimant over the net profits of the firm, after the distribution of wages to workers/agents.

To illustrate the rise of free riding inside a firm, here I illustrate a simplified version of the model by Holmström (1982). A group of n agents is employed in a firm whose output q is obtained through the production function $q = b \sum_{i=1}^{n} \sqrt{x_i}$, where $x_i \geq 0$ is agent i's effort and b is a positive parameter. Each agent has a utility function $U_i = w_i - cx_i$, where $w_i \geq 0$ is the wage[4] and $c > 0$ is a parameter which, for simplicity, can be assumed to be symmetric across agents. The shape of U_i reveals that agents are work-averse (in particular, in this example, they are affected by a constant work-aversion).[5] If, again for the sake of simplifying the exposition, market price is constant and normalized to one, individual remunerations are the outcome of a sharing rule of the final output. The sharing rule is decided by the principal, who is unable to detect the intensity of each individual effort x_i. Hence, the principal sets $w_i = q/n$ for all output levels at least as high as some given lower bound $\overline{q} > 0$, and $w_i = 0$ otherwise (cf. Groves, 1973). If indeed $w_i = q/n$, the individual utility writes

$$U_i = \frac{b \sum_{i=1}^{n} \sqrt{x_i}}{n} - cx_i \tag{1.9}$$

The Nash equilibrium of the fully non-cooperative game in which each agent i picks the value of x_i that maximizes U_i is delivered by the solution of the following system of first-order conditions:

$$\frac{\partial U_i}{\partial x_i} = \frac{b}{2n\sqrt{x_i}} - c = 0 \tag{1.10}$$

whereby $x^N = b^2/(4c^2n^2)$, where superscript N stands for Nash equilibrium. The resulting individual utility is $U^N = (2n-1)b^2/(4cn^2)$, and the output is $q^N = b^2/(2c)$.

Instead, the Pareto-efficient solution is attained by imposing the a priori symmetry condition upon efforts, $x_i = x$ for all i, and then maximizing the generic U_i (or the collective utility $U(n) = \sum_{i=1}^{n} U_i$) with respect to e. Doing so, one obtains $x^* = b^2/(4c^2)$, yielding $U^* = b^2/(4c)$. What prevents the attainment of the first best outcome is the unilateral incentive to free-ride upon the $n-1$ co-workers by deviating from x^* along the best reply (1.10). Given that the best replies are orthogonal to each other due to the additive separability of production technology and payoff functions with respect to efforts, the optimal deviation $x^D(x^*)$ coincides with the Nash equilibrium strategy x^N. The individual utility resulting from unilateral deviation is $U^D = [1 + 2(n-1)n]b^2/(4cn^2)$, higher than U^N. Hence, the team production game has the structure of a prisoners' dilemma, with a Pareto-inefficient Nash equilibrium at the intersection of dominant strategies.

It is also worth noting that the difference $x^* - x^N$ is nil if and only if $n = 1$, which conveys the trivial message that a team collapsing to a singleton produces the efficient effort and increases monotonically as the team size increases, i.e. $\partial(x^* - x^N)/\partial n > 0$. This finding reveals that the free riding problem is exacerbated by any increase in the number of agents employed in the firm.

The solution proposed by Holmström (1982) consists of the following. The monitor, who is the residual claimant over the firm's profits, designs a contract establishing that each agent will be paid a salary equal to a symmetric share of the efficient output if the latter is achieved, or zero in any other case. That is,

$$
w_i = \begin{cases} \dfrac{q^*}{n} & \text{iff } b \displaystyle\sum_{i=1}^{n} \sqrt{x_i} = q^* \\[2em] 0 & \text{iff } b \displaystyle\sum_{i=1}^{n} \sqrt{x_i} \neq q^* \end{cases} \tag{1.11}
$$

The idea behind (1.11) is the 'Groves mechanism' (Groves, 1973), whereby if a team fails to attain some predetermined result, then the entire team is harshly punished *even if the failure is due to a single member's behaviour*. Although the contract defined in (1.11) puts on every single member the responsibility of the team's collective performance, thereby seemingly forcing all agents to produce the symmetric efficient effort, it is affected by a non-negligible shortcoming, as in principle it implies that the monitor should fire and replace the whole team every time the output falls short of its optimal level. The practicability of this procedure is evidently questionable in real-world firms and organizations, with very few exceptions.[6]

A later resurgence of interest in the rise of moral hazard in teams and the related incentive schemes has highlighted the possible rise of an *incentive reversal* phenomenon (Winter, 2009; Bel *et al.*, 2015; Smirnov and Wait, 2016), consisting of the fact that higher remuneration levels may in fact induce lower effort levels on the part of agents, which has also found confirmation based on experimental evidence (Klor *et al.*, 2014).

1.6 Market competition and incentives

During the aforementioned debate on firms' growth, Manne (1965) and Hindley (1970) introduced the idea that market competition may exert a pressure on managers via financial markets, thereby somewhat aligning their behaviour in the direction of profit maximization. These contributions anticipate an analogous discussion taking place later on in the domain of agency theory, where market factors are seen as plausible instruments to alleviate the agency problem.

In the principal-agent literature, this possibility emerged in Jensen and Meckling (1976), Fama (1980) and Klein and Leffler (1981), taking then a well defined role with Hart (1983), Nalebuff and Stiglitz (1983), Scharfstein (1988a,b) and Hermalin (1992, 1994). In this territory, the endogenous link between market competition and incentive schemes is conceived as follows. Shocks and, in general, states of the world observable to managers but hidden to owners may favour managerial slack. However, common or positively correlated shocks on relevant variables, such as input prices, convey pieces of information which are very relevant from the owners' standpoint: if, in the presence of a common shock, a firm is outperformed by other similar competitors, the implication is that its manager is shirking. This is also important when it comes to mergers and acquisitions, since a bid acquires a signalling value, as illustrated in Scharfstein (1988b).

To make the point, I will briefly illustrate the essential features of the Hart (1983) model. Consider a market where n firms operate competitively; $m \in [1, n-1]$ of them are managerial enterprises, while the remaining $n - m$ are entrepreneurial. The market demand function is $Q(p)$, monotonically decreasing in the price p. Every entrepreneurial firm bears a total cost function $C(q, c)$, where q is the individual output and $c \in [\underline{c}, \overline{c}]$ is the market price of an essential input employed in production. Conversely, the cost function of the typical managerial firm is $C(q, c, x)$, where $x \in [\underline{x}, \overline{x}]$ is managerial effort, and once again $c \in [\underline{c}, \overline{c}]$; i.e. the 'extraction' of the input price is a matter of luck, independent of the structure of the firm.

A relevant assumption about the managerial firm's cost function is that c and L are substitutes, in such a way that the following properties hold:

$$\frac{\partial C(q, c, x)}{\partial c} > 0; \quad \frac{\partial C(q, c, x)}{\partial x} < 0 \tag{1.12}$$

as is the case, e.g. if the cost function is $C = cq/x$. Note that this specification of $C(q, c, x)$ clearly hints at an interpretation of managerial efforts in terms of cost-reducing activities or, equivalently, process innovation.[7]

Let M measure managerial income. The utility function of the representative manager coincides with that typically considered in agency models and might be written explicitly as in (1.10). In general, the manager is a work-averse and income-loving individual, so that his expected utility is

$$E(U) = E(u(M) - g(x)) \tag{1.13}$$

with $u(M)$ increasing and concave in M and $g(x)$ increasing and convex in x.

To ascertain the bearings of market competition on managerial behaviour, it suffices to look at the case in which the managerial contract is such that

$$\begin{aligned} &M \geq \overline{M} \\ &E(u(\overline{M}) - g(\overline{x})) = U_0 \end{aligned} \tag{1.14}$$

where the lower bound to managerial income, $\overline{M} > 0$, is chosen so as to grant the manager her/his reservation utility U_0 in correspondence with the upper bound of the effort range. This guarantees that the principal will never require the agent to produce an effort in excess of $\overline{x}$. Hence, the principal's problem consists of inducing the agent to accept the contract for all states of the world, i.e. for all $x \in [\underline{x}, \overline{x}]$. This amounts to satisfying the participation (or individual rationality) constraint

$$E(u(M) - g(x)) = U_0 \qquad (1.15)$$

always.

Assuming perfect competition, the price is uncontrollable by all firms alike, independently of their internal organization. Hence, any entrepreneurial unit, to which nature has assigned a given $\tilde{c} \in [\underline{c}, \overline{c}]$, will choose q to maximize $\pi = pq - C(q, \tilde{c})$. As for managerial firms, in a hidden action regime it can be assumed that they won't behave as pure profit-seeking entities. To this it must be added that managers observe c, while owners only observe outputs and profits. However, what principals may fruitfully exploit is the distribution $F(c)$ of possible costs (which is common knowledge) and their own rational expectations about the equilibrium price.

The market clearing condition is

$$S(n - m, p^*) + S(m, p^*) = Q(p^*) \qquad (1.16)$$

i.e. the aggregate supply of entrepreneurial firms $S(n - m, p^*)$ plus the aggregate supply of the managerial ones must exactly match market demand $Q(p^*)$ at the competitive equilibrium price p^*.

If shocks (input cost extractions by nature) are not correlated, the owners of managerial firms will impose a profit level such that the contract (1.14) will bite. All managers play $x = \overline{x}$ and are rewarded with $M = \overline{M}$; no room for premia for good performances, as it would be a pure waste of resources. As a result, this version of the model predicts that the industry supply curve will fall short of its first best level (reachable if x is observable), causing a price increase (Hart, 1983, pp. 370–2).

In the opposite scenario in which shocks are perfectly correlated, Hart (1983, pp. 373–5) proves the existence of an incentive equilibrium in which, by virtue of the owners' knowledge of the joint distribution function of input cost c and market price p, every single manager chooses $x = \overline{x}$ and her/his firm's profits coincides with the first best one. This is the consequence of the fact that, thanks to their rational expectations, combined with the perfect correlation across shocks, the owners of managerial firms deduce from the appropriate version of (1.16) that there exists a positive relationship between c and p and use this information to write a contract forcing managers to work flat out as if their efforts were indeed visible to their principals.

The relation between managerial and organizational slack and the structure of the industry or equivalently the intensity of competition has by now acquired a consolidated position in the literature, with many relevant extensions following the seminal papers mentioned above. See, e.g., Schmidt (1997), Barros (1997), Raith (2003) and Baggs and De Bettignies (2007).

Further reading

A summary of most of the material covered in this chapter can be found in the first unnumbered chapter of Tirole (1988) on the theory of the firm; see also Holmström and Tirole (1989). For additional insights on property rights, see Maskin and Tirole (1999a). For more on the alternative objectives of firms, see Solow (1971) and Grossman and Hart (1977). Vertical integration is an evergreen, the related debate being revived perpetually, from Grossman and Hart (1986) to Whinston (2003) and Acemoglu *et al.* (2007, 2010). Relevant extensions of the principal-agent model in different directions can be found in Fama and Jensen (1983), Rogerson (1985a) and Holmström and Ricart i Costa (1986), among many others. An exhaustive overview of the agency theory is in Arrow (1985) and Sappington (1991). For contract theory, ranging also outside the theory of the firm, see Salanie (1997), Maskin and Tirole (1999a, 1999b), Bolton and Dewatripont (2004), Hart and Moore (2007, 2008) and Tirole (2009). For additional research on the interplay between market competition and incentives, see Martin (1993), Senbongi and Harrington (1995), Barros and Macho-Stadler (1998), Graziano and Parigi (1998) and Piccolo *et al.* (2008).

Notes

1 The influence of this discussion reverberates into the parallel debate unravelling at the same time in the administrative sciences (see Simon, 1961, Simon, 1964; Downs, 1967). See also Arrow (1974) on the endogenous limits posed by informational concerns on the expansion and efficiency of organizations.
2 Note that this is the opposite of what is assumed in models related to the theory of contestable markets, where sunk costs are assumed away, i.e. investments are fully reversible (Baumol *et al.*, 1982).
3 The 1999 paper is the published version of the 1975 manuscript, after the Nobel Prize awarded to Sir James Mirrlees.
4 Note that here the choice of using w to denote remuneration implicitly suggests that we are talking about a *salary* paid to a *worker* rather than a remuneration for managerial inputs.
5 The argument and its conclusions would be qualitatively analogous if one assumed instead $q = b \sum_{i=1}^{n} x_i$ and $U_i = w_i - cx_i^2$, in which case the work-aversion would be increasing.
6 One such exception has nothing to do with firms and markets, for sound reasons. The method implied by (1.11) has been traditionally used in armies all over the planet for a long time. Unlike a firm, an army doesn't have to face the replacement issue, and therefore can indeed resort to a mechanism analogous to (1.11) to effectively solve the free riding problem.
7 This view is at the basis of the model proposed by Hermalin (1994), which is contained in Chapter 6.

References

Acemoglu, D., P. Aghion, R. Griffith and F. Zilibotti (2010), 'Vertical Integration and Technology', *Journal of the European Economic Association*, **8**, 989–1033.

Acemoglu, D., P. Aghion, C. Lelarge, J. Van Reenen and F. Zilibotti (2007), 'Technology, Information and the Decentralization of the Firm', *Quarterly Journal of Economics*, **122**, 1759–99.

Aghion, P. and R. Holden (2011), 'Incomplete Contracts and the Theory of the Firm: What Have We Learned over the Past 25 Years?', *Journal of Economic Perspectives*, **25**, 181–97.

Alchian, A. and H. Demsetz (1972), 'Production, Information Costs, and Economic Organization', *American Economic Review*, **62**, 777–95.

Arrow, K. (1974), *The Limits of Organization*, New York, Norton.

Arrow, K. (1985), 'The Economics of Agency', in J. Pratt and R. Zeckhauser (eds). *Principals and Agents: The Structure of Business*, Cambridge, MA, Harvard Business School Press.

Baggs, J. and J.-E. De Bettignies (2007), 'Product Market Competition and Agency Costs', *Journal of Industrial Economics*, **55**, 289–323.

Barros, F. (1997), 'Asymmetric Information as a Commitment in Oligopoly', *European Economic Review*, **41**, 207–25.

Barros, F. and I. Macho-Stadler (1998), 'Competition for Managers and Product Market Efficiency', *Journal of Economics and Management Strategy*, **7**, 89–103.

Baumol, W. (1958), 'On the Theory of Oligopoly', *Economica*, **25**, 187–98.

Baumol, W. (1962), 'On the Theory of the Expansion of the Firm', *American Economic Review*, **52**, 1078–87.

Baumol, W., J. Panzar and R. Willig (1982), *Contestable Markets and the Theory of Industry Structure*, New York, Harcourt Brace Jovanovich.

Bel, R., V. Smirnov and A. Wait (2015), 'Team Composition, Worker Effort and Welfare', *Intenational Journal of Industrial Organization*, **41**, 1–8.

Berle, A. and G. Means (1932), *The Modern Corporation and Private Property*, New York, Macmillan.

Bolton, P. and M. Dewatripont (2004), *Contract Theory*, Cambridge, MA, MIT Press.

Calvo, G. and S. Wellisz (1978), 'Supervision, Loss of Control, and the Optimal Size of the Firm', *Journal of Political Economy*, **86**, 943–52.

Calvo, G. and S. Wellisz (1979), 'Hierarchy, Ability, and Income Distribution', *Journal of Political Economy*, **87**, 991–1010.

Chandler, A. (1962), *Strategy and Structure*, Cambridge, MA, MIT Press.

Chandler, A. (1977), *The Visible Hand: The Managerial Revolution in American Business*, Cambridge, MA, Harvard University Press.

Coase, R. (1937), 'The Nature of the Firm', *Economica*, **4**, 386–405.

Cyert, R. and J. March (1963), *A Behavioral Theory of the Firm*, Englewood Cliffs, NJ, Prentice-Hall.

Demsetz, H. (1967), 'Toward a Theory of Property Rights', *American Economic Review*, **57**, 347–59.

Downs, A. (1967), *Inside Bureaucracy*, Boston, Little, Brown.

Fama, E. (1980), 'Agency Problems and the Theory of the Firm', *Journal of Political Economy*, **88**, 288–307.

Fama, E. and M. Jensen (1983), 'Separation of Ownership and Control', *Journal of Law and Economics*, **26**, 301–26.

Graziano, C. and B.M. Parigi (1998), 'Do ManagersWork Harder in Competitive Industries?', *Journal of Economic Behavior and Organization*, **34**, 489–98.

Grossman, S. and O. Hart (1977), 'On Value Maximization and Alternative Objectives of the Firm', *Journal of Finance*, **32**, 389–402.

Grossman, S. and O. Hart (1983), 'An Analysis of the Principal-Agent Problem', *Econometrica*, **51**, 7–45.

Grossman, S. and O. Hart (1986), 'The Costs and Benefits of Ownership: A Theory of Vertical and Lateral Integration', *Journal of Political Economy*, **94**, 691–719.

Grout, P. (1984), 'Investment and Wages in the Absence of Binding Contracts: A Nash Bargaining Approach', *Econometrica*, **52**, 449–60.

Groves, T. (1973), 'Incentives in Teams', *Econometrica*, **41**, 617–31.

Harris, M. and Raviv, A. (1979), 'Optimal Incentive Contracts with Imperfect Information', *Journal of Economic Theory*, **20**, 231-59.

Hart, O. (1983), 'The Market Mehanism as an Incentive Scheme', *Bell Journal of Economics*, **74**, 366–82.

Hart, O. and J. Moore (1988), 'Incomplete Contracts and Renegotiation', *Econometrica*, **56**, 755–85.

Hart, O. and J. Moore (1990), 'Property Rights and the Nature of the Firm', *Journal of Political Economy*, **98**, 1119–58.

Hart, O. and J. Moore (2007), 'Incomplete Contracts and Ownership: Some New Thoughts', *American Economic Review*, **97**, 182–86.

Hart, O. and J. Moore (2008), 'Contracts as Reference Points', *Quarterly Journal of Economics*, **123**, 1–48.

Hermalin, B. (1992), 'The Effects of Competition on Executive Behavior', *RAND Journal of Economics*, **23**, 350–65.

Hermalin, B.E. (1994), 'Heterogeneity in Organizational Form: Why Otherwise Identical Firms Choose Different Incentives for Their Managers', *RAND Journal of Economics*, **25**, 518–37.

Hindley, B. (1970), 'Separation of Ownership and Control in the Modern Corporation', *Journal of Law and Economics*, **13**, 185–222.

Holmström, B. (1979), 'Moral Hazard and Observability', *Bell Journal of Economics*, **10**, 74–91.

Holmström, B. (1982), 'Moral Hazard in Teams', *Bell Journal of Economics*, **13**, 324–40.

Holmström, B. and J. Ricart i Costa (1986), 'Managerial Incentives and Capital Management', *Quarterly Journal of Economics*, **101**, 835–60.

Holmström, B. and J. Tirole (1989), 'The Theory of the Firm', in R. Schmalensee and R. Willig (eds), *Handbook of Industrial Organization, Amsterdam*, North-Holland.

Jensen, M. and M. Meckling (1976), 'Theory of the Firm: Managerial Behavior, Agency Costs and Capital Structure', *Journal of Financial Economics*, **3**, 305–60.

Joskow, P. (1985), 'Vertical Integration and Long Term Contracts', *Journal of Law, Economics and Organization*, **1**, 33–80.

Klein, B. and K.B. Leffler (1981), 'The Role of Market Forces in Assuring Contractual Performance', *Journal of Political Economy*, **89**, 615–41.

Klein, B., R. Crawford and A. Alchian (1978), 'Vertical Integration, Appropriable Rents, and the Competitive Contracting Process', *Journal of Law and Economics*, **21**, 297–32.

Klor, E.F., S. Kub, E. Winter and R. Zultan (2014), 'Can Higher Rewards Lead to Less Effort? Incentive Reversal in Teams', *Journal of Economic Behavior and Organization*, **97**, 72–83.

Manne, H. (1965), 'Mergers and the Market for Corporate Control', *Journal of Political Economy*, **73**, 110–20.

Marris, R. (1963), 'A Model of Managerial Enterprise', *Quarterly Journal of Economics*, **77**, 185–209.

Marris, R. (1964), *The Economic Theory of Managerial Capitalism*, New York, Fee Press.

Martin, S. (1993), 'Endogeneous Firm Efficiency in a Cournot Principal-Agent Model', *Journal of Economic Theory*, **59**, 445–50.

Maskin, E., and J. Tirole (1999a), 'Unforeseen Contingencies and Incomplete Contracts', *Review of Economic Studies*, **66**, 83–114.

Maskin, E. and J. Tirole (1999b), 'Two Remarks on the Property-Rights Literature', *Review of Economic Studies*, **66**, 139–49.

Mirrlees, J. (1975), 'The Theory of Moral Hazard and Unobservable Behaviour: Part I', mimeo, Nuffield College, University of Oxford.

Mirrlees, J. (1976), 'The Optimal Structure of Incentives and Authority within an Organisation', *Bell Journal of Economics*, **7**, 105–31.

Mirrlees, J. (1999), 'The Theory of Moral Hazard and Unobservable Behaviour: Part I', *Review of Economic Studies*, **66**, 3–21.

Monsen, R.J. and A. Downs (1963), 'A Theory of Large Managerial Firms', *Journal of Political Economy*, **73**, 221–36.

Nalebuff, B.J. and J. Stiglitz (1983), 'Information, Competition, and Markets', *American Economic Review*, **73**, 278–83.

Ng, Y. (1974), 'Utility and Profit Maximisation by an Owner-Manager', *Journal of Industrial Economics*, **23**, 97–108.

Osborne, D. (1964), 'On the Goals of the Firm', *Quarterly Journal of Economics*, **78**, 592–603.

Penrose, E. (1959), *The Theory of the Growth of the Firm*, Oxford, Wiley.

Piccolo, S., M. D'Amato and R. Martina (2008), 'Product Market Competition and Organizational Slack Under Profit-Target Contracts', *International Journal of Industrial Organization*, **26**, 1389–406.

Raith, M. (2003), 'Competition, Risk, and Managerial Incentives', *American Economic Review*, **93**, 1425–36.

Riordan, M. and O. Williamson (1986), 'Asset Specificity and Economic Organization', *International Journal of Industrial Organization*, **3**, 365–78.

Robertson, D.H. (1928), *The Control of Industry*, London, Nisbet & Co.

Rogerson, W. (1985a), 'Repeated Moral Hazard', *Econometrica*, **53**, 69–76.

Rogerson, W. (1985b), 'The First-Order Approach to Principal-Agent Problems', *Econometrica*, **53**, 1357–68.

Rosen, S. (1982), 'Authority, Control, and the Distribution of Earnings', *Bell Journal of Economics*, **13**, 311–23.

Ross, S. (1973), 'The Economic Theory of Agency: The Principal's Problem', *American Economic Review*, **63**, 134–9.

Salanie, B. (1997), *The Economics of Contracts: A Primer*, Cambridge, MA, MIT Press.

Sappington, D. (1991), 'Incentives in Principal-Agent Relationships', *Journal of Economic Perspectives*, **5**, 45–66.

Scharfstein, D. (1988a), 'Product-Market Competition and Managerial Slack', *RAND Journal of Economics*, **19**, 147–55.

Scharfstein, D. (1988b), 'The Disciplinary Role of Takeovers', *Review of Economic Studies*, **55**, 185–99.

Schmidt, K.M. (1997), 'Managerial Incentives and Product Market Competition', *Review of Economic Studies*, **64**, 191–213.

Senbongi, S. and J.E. Harrington (1995), 'Managerial reputation and the competitiveness of an industry', *International Journal of Industrial Organization Organization*, **13**, 95–110.

Shavell, S. (1979), 'Risk Sharing and Incentives in the Principal and Agent Relationship', *Bell Journal of Economics*, **10**, 55–73.

Shepherd, W. (1962), 'On Sales Maximizing and Oligopoly Behaviour', *Economica*, **29**, 420–4.

Simon, H. (1961), *Administrative Behavior*, New York, Macmillan.

Simon, H. (1964), 'On the Concept of Organizational Goal', *Administrative Science Quarterly*, **9**, 1–22.

Slater, M. (1980), 'The Managerial Limitation to the Growth of Firms', *Economic Journal*, **90**, 520–8.

Smirnov, V. and A. Wait (2016), 'Technology, Team Production and Incentives', *Economics Letters*, **141**, 91–4.

Smith, A. (1776, 1976), *An Inquiry into the Nature and Causes of the Wealth of Nations*, Oxford, Clarendon Press.

Solow, R. (1971), 'Some Implications of Alternative Criteria for the Firm', in R. Marris and A. Wood (eds), *The Corporate Economy*, London, Macmillan.

Tirole, J. (1986), 'Hierarchies and Bureaucracies: On the Role of Collusion in Organizations', *Journal of Law, Economics and Organization*, **2**, 181–214.

Tirole, J. (1988), *The Theory of Industrial Organization*, Cambridge, MA, MIT Press.

Tirole, J. (2009), 'Cognition and Incomplete Contracts', *American Economic Review*, **99**, 265–94.

Whinston, M. (2003), 'On the Transaction Cost Determinants of Vertical Integration', *Journal of Law, Economics and Organization*, **19**, 1–23.

Williamson, J. (1966), 'Profit, Growth and Sales Maximisation', *Economica*, **33**, 1–16.

Williamson, O. (1964), *The Economics of Dicretionary Behavior: Managerial Objectives in a Theory of the Firm*, Englewood Cliffs, NJ, Prentice-Hall.

Williamson, O. (1967), 'Hierarchical Control and Optimum Firm Size', *Journal of Political Economy*, **75**, 123–38.

Williamson, O. (1971a), 'The Vertical Integration of Production: Market Failure Considerations', *American Economic Review*, **61**, 112–23.

Williamson, O. (1971b), 'Managerial Discretion, Organisation Form, and the Multi-Division Hypothesis', in R. Marris and A. Wood (eds), *The Corporate Economy*, London, Macmillan.

Williamson, O. (1975), *Markets and Hierarchies: Analysis and Antitrust Implications*, New York, Free Press.

Williamson, O. (1979), 'Transaction-Cost Economics: The Governance of Contractual Relations', *Journal of Law and Economics*, **22**, 233–61.

Williamson, O. (1985), *The Economic Institutions of Capitalism*, New York, Free Press.

Williamson, O. (1986), *Economic Organization: Firms, Markets, and Policy Control*, New York, Harvester Wheatsheaf.

Winter, E. (2009), 'Incentive Reversal', *American Economic Journal: Microeconomics*, **1**, 133–47.

Yarrow, G. (1973), 'Managerial Utility Maximization under Uncertainty', *Economica*, **40**, 155–73.

Yarrow, G. (1976), 'On the Predictions of the Managerial Theory of the Firm', *Journal of Industrial Economics*, **24**, 267–79.

2 Strategic delegation in oligopoly

This section provides a detailed survey of the bulk of models constituting the building blocks of the ensuing literature. Here, you will find models wherein managers are hired by firms to control a single activity, either a quantity or a price strategy, on the basis of delegation contracts specifying managerial incentives defined as combinations of profits and sales (i.e. output levels or revenues), profit and market shares, or comparative profit performance. Here, delegation is unaffected by informational issues and does not take place because owners are unable to run their firms themselves. Rather, it is adopted under full information for purely strategic reasons, i.e. to possibly acquire an advantage over rivals who don't separate control from ownership or to avoid playing the underdog role if they do. Delegation is a market-oriented decision which has little to do with any problems connected with the internal organization of the firm.

All of the alternative approaches to strategic delegation have two essential aspects in common.

- Managerial contracts are assumed to be observable in order for them to constitute credible commitments when it comes to shaping market competition. This hypothesis is essential in that the rivals of a managerial firm, irrespective of whether they are managerial themselves or not, must form rational expectations about the behaviour of all players in order for their best reply functions to identify optimal strategies. In other words, if delegation contracts were unobservable, the assumption of common knowledge would be violated and the usual chain of implications whereby 'a player knows that other players know...' would break up.
- In markets where some firms delegate control of their market variables to managers while others do not, those which go managerial replicate the performance of the Stackelberg leader and force the pure profit-seeking or entrepreneurial rivals to accept the follower's role, without invoking sequential play. This is also a pervasive feature of the extensions of these baseline models in many directions which are exposed in the next chapters. Hence, one could say that what follows tells the story of managerial firms' obsession for acquiring a dominant position, in itself a convincing synthetic portrayal of their attitude. At the same time, it tells that they may well be unable to grasp

the prize they are looking for, because their incentives enhance the degree of competition (at least under Cournot competition) and therefore hinder profits. The flavour of the resulting picture reminds us of the essence of the Bertrand model, where firms striving for monopoly power end up reproducing perfect competition.

The rush for Stackelberg leadership in managerial oligopoly models overlaps with a parallel literature dealing with an analogous but different vindication of the Stackelberg model, revisited as a problem of endogenous role choice. To complete the background for the extensions appearing in the next chapters, this one also provides a connection between delegation and endogenous timing. Then, a benchmark model revisiting entry and the rise of strategic entry barriers is also outlined, to prepare the ground for this topic to pop up again throughout the book.

Finally, a brief overview of the empirical evidence about executive compensation is accompanied by a look at the parallel stream of experimental research on strategic delegation.

2.1   Sales expansion

The point of departure of the literature has apparently a twofold nature, since in Vickers (1985) managerial contracts combine profits and output while in Fershtman (1985), Fershtman and Judd (1987) and Sklivas (1987) they combine profits and revenues. In fact, at a closer look, one soon discovers that the two approaches are the same, because both of them rely on managerial incentives based on *sales*. In a sense, we could interpret this bulk of contributions as a description of the behaviour of *sales managers*.

2.1.1   *Cournot competition*

The seminal paper by Vickers (1985) relied on a simple Cournot oligopoly model in which $n \geq 2$ fully symmetric firms face a linear demand for a homogeneous good, $p = a - Q$, with $Q = \sum_{i=1}^{n}$, and operate with the same constant returns to scale technology summarized by the individual cost function $C_i = cq_i$. The model parameters respect $a > c > 0$, and, in order to simplify notation, I will often use $A = a - c$ in the remainder, whenever possible. Firm i's profit function is $\pi_i = (p - c)q_i$.

Each firm's stockholders consider the possibility of hiring a manager interested in output expansion, in such a way that the delegation contract requires the manager of firm i to maximize the function

$$M_i = \pi_i + \theta_i q_i \tag{2.1}$$

with $\theta_i \geq 0$. The case in which $\theta = 0$ portrays a situation in which the manager must stick to a pure profit-seeking behaviour or the firms remains an entrepreneurial unit. Obviously, the two situations are observationally equivalent.

The game has a three-stage structure. In the first stage, owners decide whether to delegate or not control to managers. In the second, the optimal contracts are designed by those owners who have decided to separate ownership from control, by choosing the delegation variables θ_i. The third stage describes market competition in output levels given the organizational structure of all firms resulting from the previous two stages. Hence, the first stage takes place in discrete strategies, while the second and the third are defined over continuous strategy spaces. In each stage, players move simultaneously and non-cooperatively, and the solution concept is subgame perfection attained by backward induction, with perfect information between any two stages. In particular, the details of the contract (i.e. the values of all θ_i) are fully observable before the market subgame takes place (more on this aspect below).

Before characterizing the subgame perfect equilibrium strategy profile, it is worth noting that, under the contract based on the output level, the managerial objective function could be rewritten as

$$\widehat{\pi}_i = \left(\widehat{A}_i - q_i - Q_{-i} \right) q_i \tag{2.2}$$

where $Q_{-i} = \sum_{j \neq i} q_j$ is the collective output of firm i's rivals, and $\widehat{A}_i = A - \theta_i$ can be interpreted in two different ways, whereby, alternatively, the delegation of control to a manager is observationally equivalent to carrying out either

- some R&D effort for process innovation (i.e. cost reduction), so that $\widehat{A}_i = a - \widehat{c}_i = a - (c - \theta_i)$; or
- some advertising effort, so that $\widehat{A}_i = \widehat{a}_i - c = (a + \theta_i) - c$.

Be that as it may, delegation entails an expansion of market size (or the reservation price) as seen from the standpoint of a manager, with relevant consequences that will be entirely spelled out in the ensuing analysis. The first is that, for a generic vector of θ_i (some of which might well be nil, in line of principle), the downstream market game replicates one essential feature of Cournot competition with asymmetric marginal costs, namely, that a firm being endowed with a technology more efficient than the rivals' (i) will expand its output and force the less efficient opponent to shrink their own to such an extent that the same firm (ii) may be able to acquire monopoly power.

At the Cournot–Nash equilibrium, the optimal output writes indeed as in the Cournot oligopoly game with asymmetric marginal costs:

$$q_i^{CN} = \frac{a - (n+1)\widehat{c}_i + \sum_{j \neq i} \widehat{c}_j}{n + 1} \tag{2.3}$$

Proceeding backwards to the second stage, the generic reaction function in the space of delegation contracts is

$$\theta_i^* = \frac{(n-1)\left(A - \sum_{j \neq i} \theta_j \right)}{2n} \tag{2.4}$$

which immediately reveals that $\theta_i^* = 0$ if and only if the sector is monopolized. At the symmetric Nash equilibrium of the second stage,

$$\theta^N = \frac{(n-1)A}{n^2+1} \tag{2.5}$$

so that per firm equilibrium output and profits are

$$q^{CN} = \frac{nA}{n^2+1}; \quad \pi^{CN} = \frac{nA^2}{(n^2+1)^2} \tag{2.6}$$

Now note that $\theta^N = 0$ if $n = 1$. This obviously means that a monopolist has no incentive to hire a manager in the absence of any competitor. This fact stresses once more the purely strategic nature of this form of managerialization. However, this is no longer true if the demand side is characterized by a network externality, whereby a consumer's utility increases in the number of consumers buying the same good or using the same service. In such a case, delegation based on output or sales becomes convenient to the owner, as shown by Pal (2014). Moreover, in such a case delegation based on sales is Pareto-efficient, as the firm and consumers are better off as compared to the pure profit-seeking case.[1]

At this point, we may restrict our attention to the duopoly case by setting $n = 2$, in order to show that delegation is a compelling strategy. If $\theta_j = 0$, firm i's stockholders choose $\theta^* = A/4$, whereby the outcome of this asymmetric game replicates the Cournot–Stackelberg equilibrium:

$$q_i(D, ND) = \frac{A}{2}; \quad q_j(ND, D) = \frac{A}{4}$$
$$\pi_i(D, ND) = \frac{A^2}{8}; \quad \pi_j(ND, D) = \frac{A^2}{16} \tag{2.7}$$

where D and ND denote the presence or absence of delegation, respectively. This asymmetric setup explains in more explicit terms the issue I was mentioning above. That is, that delegation mimics a cost reduction or an advertising effort to the advantage of the firm being managerialized, to the extent that the latter becomes a dominant firm by performing as a Stackelberg leader *without invoking sequential moves*, i.e. without requiring perfect information. This is the reason why delegation is a way of reviving the Stackelberg model while at the same time getting rid of some of its uneasy features.[2] To appreciate this property of the present game, it suffices to take a look at the map of best replies in the output space, depicted in Figure 2.1.[3] If firm i hires a manager while firm j does not, it is intuitively optimal for the owners of firm i to choose the unique value of θ_i which causes their firm's reaction function to cross the rival's on the vertical of the horizontal intercept of the original best reply of firm i, thereby replicating the performance of the Stackelberg leader without the usual tangency condition this would require, should the firm remain entrepreneurial.

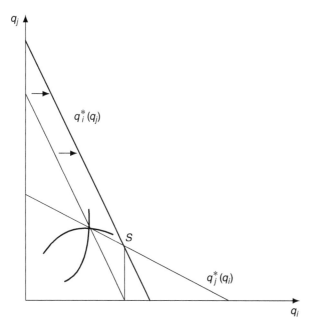

Figure 2.1 Unilateral delegation in output levels, Cournot competition.

Before continuing the illustration of the model, I would like you to appreciate a particular aspect of the delegation problem that lies behind the curtains of Figure 2.1, i.e. the need for managerial contracts to be *observable*. This is because, at the market stage, common knowledge enabling a firm (irrespective of the subject in charge of the output decision) to pick a strategy also involves the position of the opponent's best reply function. If this were not the case, then the commitment mechanism implicit in delegation would not work properly – actually, one should in fact expect to observe systematic mistakes. The debate about this feature of strategic delegation games, as well as the possibility that unobservable contracts constitute credible commitments, dates back to Coughlan and Wernerfelt (1989), Fershtman *et al.* (1991) and Katz (1991, 2006). We will see more about the observability of contracts (or lack thereof) in Chapter 5, as this matter is also relevant when it comes to vertical relations and the divisional structure of a firm. To fully grasp the essence of the matter, one needs just to note that *observability* can be dubbed as *transparency* about managerial rewards (see, e.g., Fershtman and Kalai (1997); Bagnoli and Watts (2015)). This is also connected with *risk neutrality*; owners and managers are assumed to be risk neutral, and this, accompanied by the observability of contracts and common knowledge about the fact that the delegation contract 'clears out' the agency problem, turns strategic delegation into a credible commitment. Should contracts be unobservable, their impact on the map of best replies in the market stage would be nil, and delegation would not be a credible commitment device.

Back to the Vickers (1985) model, the residual case is that in which both firms remain strict profit-seeking units controlled by their stockholders, attaining the familiar Cournot–Nash profits $\pi(ND, ND) = A^2/9$. Putting things together, one can represent the relevant reduced form at the first stage of the game as in Matrix 2.1.

		j	
		D	ND
i	D	$\dfrac{2A^2}{25}; \dfrac{2A^2}{25}$	$\dfrac{A^2}{8}; \dfrac{A^2}{16}$
	ND	$\dfrac{A^2}{16}; \dfrac{A^2}{8}$	$\dfrac{A^2}{9}; \dfrac{A^2}{9}$

Matrix 2.1

Examining Matrix 2.1, we see that

$$\pi(D, D) > \pi(ND, D); \quad \pi(D, ND) > \pi(ND, ND) \tag{2.8}$$

whereby (D, D) emerges as the unique pure strategy equilibrium at the intersection of strictly dominant strategies. Moreover, $\pi(ND, ND) > \pi(D, D)$. Hence, the game is a prisoners' dilemma, as the Nash equilibrium is Pareto-inefficient for firms because delegation by both firms intensifies market competition and therefore is detrimental to profits. Obviously, the opposite considerations apply when it comes to consumer surplus and welfare.

If the delegation contract involves a linear combination of profits and revenues, as in Fershtman (1985), Fershtman and Judd (1987) and Sklivas (1987), the managerial objective function becomes

$$\Omega_i = \alpha_i \pi_i + (1 - \alpha_i)\, pq_i \tag{2.9}$$

where no restriction is imposed on α_i (that is, these variables can be negative, see below). The owners of firm i set α_i to maximize profits at the second stage, provided they have chosen to hire a manager at the first. It turns out that the outcomes of this game, generated by unilateral as well as bilateral delegation, fully replicate those of Vickers (1985) in terms of both output and profit levels. The reason for this result can be quickly grasped on the basis of a proof which can be found in Lambertini and Trombetta (2002, Appendix A, p. 371).

It suffices to rewrite (2.1) and (2.9) as

$$\begin{aligned} M_i &= pq_i - (c - \theta_i)\, q_i \\ \Omega_i &= pq_i - \alpha_i c q_i \end{aligned} \tag{2.10}$$

to see that $M_i = \Omega_i$ iff $\theta_i = (1 - \alpha_i)c$, and then check that this holds when either one or both firms are managerial. As a preliminary step, observe that the reaction function of the managerial firm is

$$q_i = \frac{a - q_j - \alpha_i c}{2} \tag{2.11}$$

From (2.11), we see that the output of the managerial firm increases as α_i decreases, i.e. as the weight attached to profits decreases, so the managerial incentive has the same flavour as in Vickers (1985), as it induces an output expansion as long as the manager behaves *as if* his firm were more efficient than the rival. When both firms are managerial, solving the Cournot–Nash equilibrium at the market stage yields:

$$q_i^{CN}(\alpha_i, \alpha_j) = \frac{a - c(2\alpha_i - \alpha_j)}{3} \tag{2.12}$$

and the relevant profit function at the second stage is

$$\pi_i(\alpha_i, \alpha_j) = \frac{[a - c(2\alpha_i - \alpha_j)][a - c(3 - \alpha_i - \alpha_j)]}{9} \tag{2.13}$$

so that the Nash equilibrium in delegation levels is attained at

$$\alpha^N = \frac{6c - a}{5c} \tag{2.14}$$

which is always lower than 1 but becomes negative for all $a > 6c$, with

$$\theta^N = (1 - \alpha^N) c \tag{2.15}$$

as can be immediately ascertained by setting $n = 2$ in (2.5), whereby $\theta^N = (a - c)/5$. Profits therefore coincide under the two contracts. A similar exercise can be worked out if a single firm hires a manager while the other remains purely entrepreneurial.

The foregoing analysis boils down to the following.

Proposition 2.1 *Delegation contracts based on a linear combination of profits and either output levels or revenues are equivalent. Moreover:*

- *one-sided delegation reproduces the Stackelberg outcome under simultaneous play;*
- *the subgame perfect equilibrium among quantity-setters involves all firms delegating control to managers and is Pareto-inefficient for firms, being the outcome of a prisoners' dilemma.*

As you may have noticed, a possible interpretation of the duopoly model where delegation relies on output or revenues is that if one firm becomes managerial and the other does not, the industry replicates the outcome generated by sequential play between pure profit-seeking units. However, incentive compatibility at the first stage involves both firms operating the separation between ownership and control. So, the final message seems to be orthogonal with the initial intuitive interpretation. In fact, if one were to insist on finding analogies, one could then say that two-sided delegation is a sensible and elegant way out of the conundrum posed by the so-called Stackelberg warfare dating back to Dowrick (1986).

However, there is a simple way of reviving the Stackelberg outcome. The foregoing illustration of the cornerstones of strategic delegation in a Cournot industry assumes that the stockholders' cost of hiring a manager is a linear function of the managerial objective function, either M_i or Ω_i, but does not account for the reservation wage a manager may obtain outside these firms. This aspect is considered in Basu (1995), using the same approach illustrated in Chapter 1. The main difference between the approach used so far and Basu's (1995) is that the latter admits asymmetry in firms' marginal costs, c_i and c_j, and managerial reservation utilities as well, u_i and u_j. That is, quite realistically, heterogeneous firms have access to a heterogeneous population of managers.

Suppose Ω_i is the relevant objective function. Firm i offers a manager a contract stating that his salary will be $w_i = A_i + B_i\Omega_i$, where A_i and B_i are positive constants. Clearly, the output which maximizes Ω_i also maximizes the wage w_i. The consequence of hiring a manager is that the owner acquires some additional time off, whose utility can be quantified by x_i. Hence, the cost of hiring a manager at equilibrium is $\Delta_i = w_i - x_i = A_i + B_i\Omega_i - x_i$, which in turn reveals that, once owners make the manager indifferent between accepting the contract or not, the profits accruing to a managerial firm are diminished by a given amount Δ_i, and the relevant reduced form game played by owners at the first stage takes the form depicted in Matrix 2.2.[4]

		D	ND
i	D	$\pi_i(D, D) - \Delta_i$; $\pi_j(D, D) - \Delta_j$	$\pi_i(D, ND) - \Delta_i$; $\pi_j(ND, D)$
	ND	$\pi_i(ND, D)$; $\pi_j(D, ND) - \Delta_j$	$\pi_i(ND, ND)$; $\pi_j(ND, ND)$

$$j$$

Matrix 2.2

It takes a small amount of algebra to verify that (D, D) is an equilibrium if and only if

$$\pi_i(D, D) - \Delta_i \geq \pi_i(ND, D) \qquad (2.16)$$

If Δ_i does not satisfy this inequality, and instead

$$\pi_i(D, D) - \Delta_i < \pi_i(ND, D) \qquad (2.17)$$
$$\pi_i(D, ND) - \Delta_i \geq \pi_i(ND, ND) \qquad (2.18)$$

jointly hold, then the game described in Matrix 2.2 has two asymmetric pure-strategy equilibria along the secondary diagonal, (D, ND) and (ND, D), with one-sided delegation. Therefore, the punch line of the framework envisaged by Basu (1995) can be spelled out as follows.

Proposition 2.2 *Under Cournot competition, one-sided delegation replicating the Stackelberg outcome may arise at equilibrium provided that firms have asymmetric technologies and hire managers from a population of asymmetric individuals.*

As we are about to see in the remainder of this section, some of these conclusions are deeply sensitive to the market variable being used. To delve in the details of this matter, we have to go through the analysis of delegation under price-setting behaviour, which has been investigated in Fershtman and Judd (1987) and Sklivas (1987).

2.1.2 Bertrand competition

To describe the effects of delegation under price competition, we have to introduce product differentiation so as to avoid the perfectly competitive outcome (with marginal cost pricing) which would necessarily prevail under the assumption of product homogeneity, irrespective of the internal organization of both firms. Both Fershtman and Judd (1987) and Sklivas (1987) used the following demand function:

$$q_i = a - b p_i + \gamma p_j \tag{2.19}$$

where parameter $\gamma \in (0, b]$ measures the degree of product substitutability, and is therefore an inverse measure of product differentiation. However, it is more appropriate to use the formulation introduced by Spence (1976) and Singh and Vives (1984):[5]

$$q_i = \frac{a}{1 + \sigma} - \frac{p_i}{1 - \sigma^2} + \frac{\sigma p_j}{1 - \sigma^2} \tag{2.20}$$

in which parameter $\sigma \in (0, 1]$ has the same interpretation as γ in (2.19). Firms share the same technology with constant returns to scale. For the sake of simplicity, and in view of the coincidence between the models based on output or revenues, I will assume delegation takes place *à la* Vickers (1985).

The Bertrand–Nash equilibrium with entrepreneurial firms can be quickly worked out to find that the equilibrium price is

$$p^{\text{BN}}(ND, ND) = \frac{a(1 - \sigma) + c}{2 - \sigma} \tag{2.21}$$

and the resulting profits are

$$\pi^{\text{BN}}(ND, ND) = \frac{(a - c)^2 (1 - \sigma)}{(2 - \sigma)^2 (1 + \sigma)} \tag{2.22}$$

falling, respectively, to marginal cost and zero as $\sigma = 1$, i.e. under product homogeneity.

The asymmetric case in which firm i hires a manager through a Vickers-type contract $M_i = \pi_i + \theta_i q_i$, while firm j is run by its owner, delivers a first relevant message. Observe the first order condition (FOC) of the managerial firm at the market stage:

$$\frac{\partial M_i}{\partial p_i} = \frac{a(1-\sigma)+c-2p_i+\sigma p_j - \theta_i}{1-\sigma^2} = 0 \qquad (2.23)$$

while the opponent's is

$$\frac{\partial \pi_j}{\partial p_j} = \frac{a(1-\sigma)+c-2p_j+\sigma p_i}{1-\sigma^2} = 0 \qquad (2.24)$$

Solving (2.23), one obtains the best reply of the single manager involved in this particular subgame:

$$p_i^* = \frac{a(1-\sigma)+c-2p_i+\sigma p_j - \theta_i}{2} \qquad (2.25)$$

from which it clearly emerges that any $\theta_i > 0$ would have a pro-competitive effect, while, conversely, any $\theta_i < 0$ would have a quasi-collusive flavour. In the latter case, the effect of delegation is an upward shift in the managerial firm's best

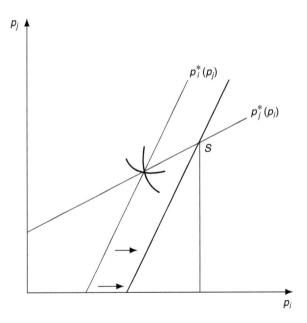

Figure 2.2 Unilateral delegation in output levels, Bertrand competition.

reply, as represented in Figure 2.2. Since prices are strategic complements for all $\sigma \in (0, 1]$, reaction functions are positively sloped in the price space, and the perfectly collusive outcome (the point whose coordinates coincide with the monopoly price) lies to the north-east of the Bertrand–Nash equilibrium at the intersection of best replies. Hence, if the contract offered to a manager implies an output restriction, the resulting price will necessarily rise as compared to the standard level attained where both firms remain in the hands of their respective owners.

Plugging the expression of optimal prices into the profit functions and differentiating with respect to θ_i the profits of the managerial firm, the subgame perfect contract is easily characterized:

$$\theta^N (D, ND) = \frac{(a-c)(\sigma - 1)\sigma^2 (2+\sigma)}{4(2-\sigma^2)} < 0 \tag{2.26}$$

which shows that profits are indeed overcompensated in order to drive a price increase, as opposed to what we have observed under quantity competition. In fact, the same underlying logic applies under price competition, as one-sided delegation replicates the Bertrand–Stackelberg equilibrium, with equilibrium profits

$$\pi^{BN} (D, ND) = \frac{(a-c)^2 (1-\sigma)(2+\sigma)^2}{8(2-\sigma^2)(1+\sigma)}$$

$$\pi^{BN} (ND, D) = \frac{(a-c)^2 (1-\sigma)[4+\sigma(2-\sigma)]^2}{16(2-\sigma^2)^2 (1+\sigma)} \tag{2.27}$$

which are non-negative for all $\sigma \in (0, 1]$. If $\sigma = 1$, both firms' prices fall to marginal cost.

When both firms delegate, the Nash equilibrium prices at the market stage are

$$p_i^{BN} = \frac{a[2-\sigma(1+\sigma)]+c(2+\sigma)-2\theta_i - \sigma\theta_j}{4-\sigma^2} \tag{2.28}$$

and the equilibrium contracts at the second stage are identified by solving the system of FOCs at the second stage, which generate the best replies:

$$\theta_i^* = \frac{\sigma^2 [\sigma\theta_j - (a-c)(2-\sigma(1+\sigma))]}{4(2-\sigma^2)} \tag{2.29}$$

This expression shows that the weights attached to outputs are strategic complements, because

$$\frac{\partial \theta_i^*}{\partial \theta_j} = \frac{\sigma^3}{4(2-\sigma^2)} > 0 \tag{2.30}$$

everywhere. So, any unilateral restriction along this dimension by either owner brings about a restriction by the other, and both jointly contribute to push prices upwards.

The Nash equilibrium at the contract stage is identified by the symmetric pair

$$\theta^N(D, D) = \frac{(a-c)(\sigma-1)\sigma^2}{4-\sigma(2+\sigma)} < 0 \tag{2.31}$$

for all $\sigma \in (0, 1)$. This confirms the overcompensation of profits under price competition. Moreover,

$$\left|\theta^N(D, D)\right| - \left|\theta^N(D, ND)\right| = \frac{(a-c)(1-\sigma)\sigma^5}{4(2-\sigma^2)[4-\sigma(2+\sigma)]} > 0 \tag{2.32}$$

for all $\sigma \in (0, 1)$. This fact reveals the following.

Lemma 2.1 *Profit overcompensation appearing under Bertrand behaviour is enhanced by two-sided delegation.*

That is, the anti-competitive flavour of strategic delegation is inflated when all firms decide to separate control from ownership, as one may expect from (2.30).
The resulting symmetric profits are

$$\pi^{BN}(D, D) = \frac{(a-c)^2(1-\sigma)(2-\sigma^2)}{(1+\sigma)[4-\sigma(2+\sigma)]^2} \tag{2.33}$$

which, again, are nil iff $\sigma = 1$, as under product homogeneity the equilibrium price equals marginal production cost.
The first stage of the game is represented in Matrix 2.3, which is structurally equivalent to Matrix 2.1 but delivers a qualitatively different message, because

$$\begin{aligned} \pi^{BN}(D, D) &> \pi^{BN}(ND, D) \\ \pi^{BN}(D, ND) &> \pi^{BN}(ND, ND) \\ \pi^{BN}(D, D) &> \pi^{BN}(ND, ND) \end{aligned} \tag{2.34}$$

for all $\sigma \in (0, 1)$. Obviously, at $\sigma = 1$,

$$\pi^{BN}(D, D) = \pi^{BN}(ND, D) = \pi^{BN}(D, ND) = \pi^{BN}(ND, ND) = 0 \tag{2.35}$$

as marginal cost prevails under perfect product substitutability.

		j	
		D	ND
i	D	$\pi^{BN}(D, D)$; $\pi^{BN}(D, D)$	$\pi^{BN}(D, ND)$; $\pi^{BN}(ND, D)$
	ND	$\pi^{BN}(ND, D)$; $\pi^{BN}(D, ND)$	$\pi^{BN}(ND, ND)$; $\pi^{BN}(ND, ND)$

Matrix 2.3

The above list of inequalities entails the following.

Proposition 2.3 *Under Bertrand competition in differentiated products and delegation contracts based on a linear combination of profits and output levels or revenues, the game has a unique subgame perfect equilibrium* (D, D) *with two-sided delegation, which is Pareto-efficient for firms.*

The above proposition deserves a couple of comments. The first is that, in view of the anti-competitive flavour of delegation contracts under price-setting behaviour, the separation between ownership and control should attract the attention of the antitrust authority, as it delivers profits above those the same firms would attain in the absence of delegation, with some degree of partial collusion in prices. This is an aspect on which more will emerge in the remainder. The second is that, in order for the foregoing analysis to be robust, owners must have access to a population of managers who, in principle, have a taste for output expansion but, in practice, accept delegation contracts pointing at output restrictions. How come? A possible and perhaps sensible answer consists in noting that the overcompensation of profits underpinning both $\theta^N(D, D)$ and $\theta^N(D, ND)$ is observationally equivalent to a contract establishing that a considerable part of managerial remuneration consists of stock options, whereby managers' incentives become aligned with stockholders'.

This setting has been extended by Lambertini (2000a) to allow firms to choose whether to be price or quantity setters, whether to move as quickly as possible or to delay as much as possible and whether to delegate or not control to managers. This extension requires the analysis of the mixed (price–quantity) market subgame and puts together Vickers (1985), Fershtman (1985), Fershtman and Judd (1987) and Sklivas (1987) with Singh and Vives (1984) and Hamilton and Slutsky (1990). This analysis illustrates that a Stackelberg leader always decides to remain entrepreneurial, as delegation is a net substitute of the first mover advantage. Its complement is that delegation is observed along the subgame perfect equilibrium strategy profile only if firms move simultaneously. At the subgame perfect equilibrium, firms move simultaneously (by delaying), and then choose to be Cournot agents and then delegate control to managers. Hence, observationally the outcome coincides with the Cournot model with delegation, but the interesting additional detail is that the Nash equilibrium is not generated by early moves and delegation explicitly works as an insurance against the risk of playing the follower's role.

As stressed in the introduction, the use of any given magnitude in the construction of managerial incentives depends on two aspects which must ideally match: the inclination of the specific manager a firm might interview during the recruiting process and what a firm expects from the manager whom it will finally decide to hire. Offering a contract in which incentives are based on output or revenues means that the firm is looking for a very aggressive manager. Fine, as we know, if competitors are not managerialized, but not necessarily a good choice if (i) they are managerial too and (ii) if their managers have received other instructions. Let's see what happens under different managerial mandates.

2.2   Market shares

Suppose market shares are used to shape managerial incentives. One might say that these are closely related to output or revenues. True, to some extent, but not so much when it comes to the performance of firms in a fully managerialized industry using this type of contract (which, by the way, are often used in the telecommunications and automotive industries, for example).

If an incentive scheme based on a linear combination of profits and market share is adopted, as in Jansen *et al.* (2007, 2009) and Ritz (2008), the managerial objective function is

$$M_i = \pi_i + \frac{\theta_i q_i}{q_i + q_j} \tag{2.36}$$

and generates the following FOC:

$$\frac{\partial M_i}{\partial q_i} = A - 2q_i - q_j - \frac{\theta_i}{q_i + q_j}\left(1 - \frac{q_i}{q_i + q_j}\right) = 0 \tag{2.37}$$

so that the resulting reaction function $q_i^*(q_j)$ is concave in q_j. If firm j has remained a purely entrepreneurial unit, its reaction function in the output space is the classical downward sloping linear best reply of a Cournot agent. The concavity of $q_i^*(q_j)$ turns out to be required in order for the managerial best reply to intersect the opponent's in correspondence with the Stackelberg leader output $q_i = A/2$ once firm i's owner has written a contract fixing the optimal delegation weight at $\theta^N(D, ND) = 2(5\sqrt{2} - 1)A^2/49$. This asymmetric situation, illustrated in Figure 2.3, replicates the Cournot–Stackelberg outcome in all respects (quantities, profits and welfare), except the shape of one of the best reply functions.

Under two-sided delegation, (2.37) can be conveniently rewritten as

$$\frac{\partial M_i\left(\theta_i, \theta_j\right)}{\partial q_i\left(\theta_i, \theta_j\right)} = A - 2q_i\left(\theta_i, \theta_j\right) - q_j\left(\theta_i, \theta_j\right)$$

$$- \frac{\theta_i}{q_i\left(\theta_i, \theta_j\right) + q_j\left(\theta_i, \theta_j\right)}\left[1 - \frac{q_i\left(\theta_i, \theta_j\right)}{q_i\left(\theta_i, \theta_j\right) + q_j\left(\theta_i, \theta_j\right)}\right] = 0 \tag{2.38}$$

where the effect of delegation contracts on outputs is in evidence. Since the above expressions are cubic in $q_i(\theta_i, \theta_j)$ and $q_j(\theta_i, \theta_j)$, one has to adopt an indirect approach to characterize the subgame perfect equilibrium strategies. What follows is equivalent – although not identical – to the procedure used in Jansen *et al.* (2007, 2009) and Ritz (2008). Write the relevant FOC at the second stage as

$$\frac{\partial \pi_i\left(\theta_i, \theta_j\right)}{\partial \theta_i} = \left[A - q_j\left(\theta_i, \theta_j\right)\right]\frac{\partial q_i\left(\theta_i, \theta_j\right)}{\partial \theta_i}$$

$$- q_i\left(\theta_i, \theta_j\right)\left[2\frac{\partial q_i\left(\theta_i, \theta_j\right)}{\partial \theta_i} + \frac{\partial q_j\left(\theta_i, \theta_j\right)}{\partial \theta_i}\right] = 0 \tag{2.39}$$

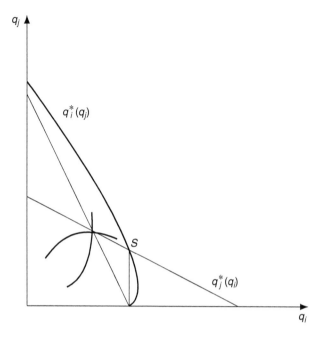

Figure 2.3 Unilateral delegation in market shares, Cournot competition.

and then differentiate both sides of the system (2.38) to obtain

$$\frac{\partial^2 M_i\left(\theta_i,\theta_j\right)}{\partial q_i\left(\theta_i,\theta_j\right)\partial\theta_i}=f_{ii}\left[\frac{\partial q_i\left(\theta_i,\theta_j\right)}{\partial\theta_i},\frac{\partial q_j\left(\theta_i,\theta_j\right)}{\partial\theta_i}\right]=0 \qquad (2.40)$$

$$\frac{\partial^2 M_i\left(\theta_i,\theta_j\right)}{\partial q_i\left(\theta_i,\theta_j\right)\partial\theta_j}=f_{ij}\left[\frac{\partial q_i\left(\theta_i,\theta_j\right)}{\partial\theta_j},\frac{\partial q_j\left(\theta_i,\theta_j\right)}{\partial\theta_j}\right]=0 \qquad (2.41)$$

$$\frac{\partial^2 M_j\left(\theta_i,\theta_j\right)}{\partial q_j\left(\theta_i,\theta_j\right)\partial\theta_i}=f_{ji}\left[\frac{\partial q_i\left(\theta_i,\theta_j\right)}{\partial\theta_i},\frac{\partial q_j\left(\theta_i,\theta_j\right)}{\partial\theta_i}\right]=0 \qquad (2.42)$$

$$\frac{\partial^2 M_j\left(\theta_i,\theta_j\right)}{\partial q_j\left(\theta_i,\theta_j\right)\partial\theta_j}=f_{jj}\left[\frac{\partial q_i\left(\theta_i,\theta_j\right)}{\partial\theta_j},\frac{\partial q_j\left(\theta_i,\theta_j\right)}{\partial\theta_j}\right]=0 \qquad (2.43)$$

The system (2.40)–(2.43) can be solved to obtain the partial derivatives

$$\frac{\partial q_i\left(\theta_i,\theta_j\right)}{\partial\theta_i},\frac{\partial q_j\left(\theta_i,\theta_j\right)}{\partial\theta_i},\frac{\partial q_i\left(\theta_i,\theta_j\right)}{\partial\theta_j},\frac{\partial q_j\left(\theta_i,\theta_j\right)}{\partial\theta_j} \qquad (2.44)$$

which can be plugged back into (2.38), delivering the symmetric pair of subgame perfect delegation weights

$$\theta^{N}(D, D) = \frac{2\left(5\sqrt{2}-1\right)A^2}{49} \tag{2.45}$$

in correspondence with which optimal output and profits are

$$q^{CN}(D, D) = \frac{\left(4+\sqrt{2}\right)A}{14}; \quad \pi^{CN}(D, D) = \frac{\left(10-\sqrt{2}\right)A^2}{98} \tag{2.46}$$

Hence, the 2×2 discrete game at the first stage looks as in Matrix 2.4, which has the structure of a prisoners' dilemma with a unique and Pareto-inefficient Nash equilibrium in pure strategies at (D, D), since

$$\frac{\left(10-\sqrt{2}\right)A^2}{98} > \frac{A^2}{16}$$

$$\frac{A^2}{8} > \frac{A^2}{9} \tag{2.47}$$

$$\frac{\left(10-\sqrt{2}\right)A^2}{98} < \frac{A^2}{9}$$

		j	
		D	ND
i	D	$\dfrac{\left(10-\sqrt{2}\right)A^2}{98}; \dfrac{\left(10-\sqrt{2}\right)A^2}{98}$	$\dfrac{A^2}{8}; \dfrac{A^2}{16}$
	ND	$\dfrac{A^2}{16}; \dfrac{A^2}{8}$	$\dfrac{A^2}{9}; \dfrac{A^2}{9}$

Matrix 2.4

It is worth stressing that this type of delegation contract has not been exhaustively discussed in detail under the assumption of Bertrand behaviour, with the exception of a brief sketch appearing in Jansen *et al.* (2007, p. 536) and a slightly extended rejoinder by Kopel and Lambertini (2013), where it was shown that under two-sided delegation the equilibrium profits are higher than under sales or output-based delegation with price-setting behaviour.

2.3 Comparative performance

Here, we suppose that a firms' owner contemplates the perspective on delegating control to managers whose incentives are designed in terms of comparative (profit) performance, as in Salas Fumas (1992), Lundgren (1996), Aggarwal and Samwick (1999) and Miller and Pazgal (2001).

Inverse and direct market demand functions can be appropriately specified as in Singh and Vives (1984),

$$p_i = a - q_i - \sigma q_j \tag{2.48}$$

$$q_i = \frac{a}{1+\sigma} - \frac{p_i}{1-\sigma^2} + \frac{\sigma p_j}{1-\sigma^2} \tag{2.49}$$

depending on whether Cournot or Bertrand competition is considered, and the cost function is $C_i = cq_i$. Hence, the profit function of firm i is $\pi_i = (p_i - c)q_i$, and the manager of firm i maximizes

$$M_i = \pi_i + \theta_i \pi_j \tag{2.50}$$

2.3.1 Cournot competition

Assume firms are quantity setters. Considering that the profit function of firm j writes

$$\pi_j = \left(A - q_j - \sigma q_i\right) q_j \tag{2.51}$$

this contract instructs the manager of firm i to maximize

$$\widetilde{M}_i = \pi_i - \theta_i \sigma q_i q_j \tag{2.52}$$

whereby

$$\frac{\partial M_i}{\partial q_i} = \frac{\partial \pi_i}{\partial q_i} + \theta_i \cdot \frac{\partial \pi_j}{\partial q_i} = 0 \tag{2.53}$$

is equivalent to

$$\frac{\partial \widetilde{M}_i}{\partial q_i} = \frac{\partial \pi_i}{\partial q_i} + \theta_i \sigma q_j = 0 \tag{2.54}$$

In either case, the contract requires the manager to account for the externality exerted on the rival in such a way that any $\theta_i > 0$ (respectively, $\theta_i < 0$) has an anti-competitive (respectively, pro-competitive) effect. That is, a contract based on a linear combination of the profits of all firms acting in the industry might turn the industry itself into an explicit cartel without invoking the theory of repeated games to envisage the possibility of implicit collusion. To avoid this outcome, the delegation variable *must take negative values at equilibrium*. As we shall see in the remainder, this detail is of paramount importance when firms behave *à la* Bertrand.

Looking at the best reply function of firm i, which is the solution of the FOC taken on (2.50),

$$q_i^* (q_j) = \frac{A - \sigma q_j (1 + \theta_i)}{2} \tag{2.55}$$

one immediately notices that here delegation modifies its slope,

$$\frac{\partial q_i^*(q_j)}{\partial q_j} = -\frac{\sigma(1+\theta_i)}{2} \tag{2.56}$$

while leaving the intercept along the axis of q_i unaffected. Hence, comparative performance pops up into the strategic interplay in the quantity space by imposing a rotation of the reaction function.

If the rival remains entrepreneurial (with $\theta_j = 0$), we may expect the present model to replicate the Cournot–Stackelberg outcome. It is indeed so, as in correspondence with the optimal unilateral contract, identified by

$$\theta^N(D, ND) = -\frac{\sigma(2-\sigma)}{4 - \sigma(2+\sigma)} < 0 \tag{2.57}$$

a firms' equilibrium profits are

$$\pi(D, ND) = \frac{A^2(2-\sigma)^2}{8(2-\sigma^2)}; \quad \pi(ND, D) = \frac{A^2[4 - \sigma(2+\sigma)]^2}{16(2-\sigma^2)^2} \tag{2.58}$$

which are the Cournot–Stackelberg profits in the presence of product differentiation. It is worth observing that if the latter is totally absent ($\sigma = 1$), then $\theta^N(D, ND) = -1$ and consequently $\partial q_i^*(q_j)/\partial q_j = 0.$[6] This proves the following.

Remark 2.1 *If the product is homogeneous, in the Cournot setting unilateral delegation based on comparative performance enables the managerial firm to solve the market stage through a dominant strategy.*

This means that, if unilateral delegation is adopted, then (i) 'pure' comparative performance evaluation appears in the managerial contract and (ii) this makes the managerial firm's best reply function in the output space flat with respect to the rival's production decisions, thanks to the optimal delegation contract. The dominant strategy mentioned in the remark is the monopoly output, as firm i's reaction function is flat at $A/2$, representing the best reply to any quantity chosen by the profit-seeking opponent. This situation is depicted in Figure 2.4.

Putting together the outcomes of unilateral delegation across the three alternative types of managerial incentives, there emerges an interesting result highlighted by Berr (2011).

Proposition 2.4 *Unilateral delegation reproduces the Stackelberg outcome, irrespective of the structure of managerial incentives.*

This fact has an intuitive interpretation, which consists of observing that, if delegation is unilaterally adopted, then the best thing to do from the ownership's standpoint is to write the contract in such a way to induce the manager to replicate

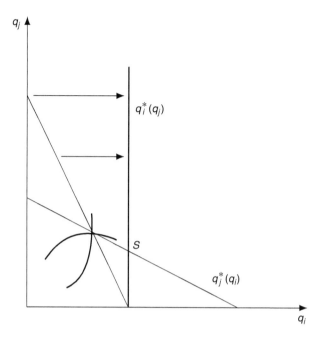

Figure 2.4 Unilateral delegation based on comparative performance, Cournot behaviour and product homogeneity.

the strategy of a Stackelberg leader, had the same firm the first mover advantage. This possibility is not conditional upon the specific magnitude accompanying profits in the definition of the managerial objective, and extends to the Bertrand case as well (although Berr's analysis is confined to Cournot behaviour).

If delegation is bilateral, the optimal contract is identified by

$$\theta^{N}(D, D) = -\frac{\sigma}{2+\sigma} < 0 \tag{2.59}$$

and per firm equilibrium output and profits amount to

$$q^{CN}(D, D) = \frac{A(2+\sigma)}{4(1+\sigma)}$$
$$\pi^{CN}(D, D) = \frac{A^2(4-\sigma^2)}{16(1+\sigma)} \tag{2.60}$$

Recalling from Singh and Vives (1984) that the Cournot–Nash profits of the game without delegation are $\pi^{CN}(ND, ND) = A^2/(2+\sigma)^2$, one may reconstruct the first stage of the game as in Matrix 2.5.

		j	
		D	ND
i	D	$\dfrac{A^2\left(4-\sigma^2\right)}{16\left(1+\sigma\right)}$; $\dfrac{A^2\left(4-\sigma^2\right)}{16\left(1+\sigma\right)}$	$\dfrac{A^2\left(2-\sigma\right)^2}{8\left(2-\sigma^2\right)}$; $\dfrac{A^2\left[4-\sigma\left(2+\sigma\right)\right]^2}{16\left(2-\sigma^2\right)^2}$
	ND	$\dfrac{A^2\left[4-\sigma\left(2+\sigma\right)\right]^2}{16\left(2-\sigma^2\right)^2}$; $\dfrac{A^2\left(2-\sigma\right)^2}{8\left(2-\sigma^2\right)}$	$\dfrac{A^2}{\left(2+\sigma\right)^2}$; $\dfrac{A^2}{\left(2+\sigma\right)^2}$

Matrix 2.5

The examination of Matrix 2.5 reveals, as usual, that (D, D) is the unique equilibrium at the intersection of dominant strategies, and the first stage has the nature of a prisoners' dilemma, since $\pi^{CN}(D, D) < \pi^{CN}(ND, ND)$ for all $\sigma \in (0, 1]$.

2.3.2   Bertrand competition and the mixed case

Here firms choose prices. For brevity (as the outcome of unilateral delegation is intuitive by now), we may focus on the case in which both firms are managerial. The FOC taken on (2.50) with respect to p_i produces the reaction function

$$p_i^*\left(p_j\right) = \frac{a+c-\sigma\left(a+c\theta_i\right)+\sigma\left(1+\theta_i\right)p_j}{2} \tag{2.61}$$

with θ_i affecting both the intercept and the slope of $p_i^*(p_j)$. Solving for optimal prices, we may proceed by backward induction to the second stage, where non-cooperative profit maximization is attained at

$$\theta^N\left(D, D\right) = \frac{\sigma}{2-\sigma} > 0 \tag{2.62}$$

This indicates that, if the market stage takes place in the price space, then the optimal contract is anti-competitive. In itself, no news, as also the other delegation schemes show the same feature. Here, however, there's more to it, because outputs and profits are exactly the same as those identified at the subgame perfect equilibrium of the Cournot model:

$$q^{BN}\left(D, D\right) = q^{CN}\left(D, D\right) = \frac{A\left(2+\sigma\right)}{4\left(1+\sigma\right)}$$
$$\pi^{BN}\left(D, D\right) = \pi^{CN}\left(D, D\right) = \frac{A^2\left(4-\sigma^2\right)}{16\left(1+\sigma\right)} \tag{2.63}$$

Hence, the adoption of managerial incentives based on comparative performance nullifies the gap usually characterizing Bertrand vs Cournot. As a result, the reduced form at the first stage is obviously not a prisoner's dilemma, with all-out delegation emerging as the unique and efficient equilibrium outcome.

The same applies to the mixed setting in which firm i chooses output while firm j chooses price. This amounts to saying the following.

Proposition 2.5 *If managerial incentives are based upon comparative performance, the choice between price and quantity becomes immaterial.*

One crucial detail of this version of the delegation model deserves some additional attention. Since the competition mode is irrelevant, the equilibrium price is unique,

$$p^N = \frac{a\,(2-\sigma)+c\,(2+\sigma)}{4} \qquad (2.64)$$

and *never falls to marginal cost*. In particular, it is not equal to c for $\sigma = 1$, when the product is homogeneous. Analogously, from (2.63) we see that profits are not nil if $\sigma = 1$. This implies that *this type of contract prevents the industry from reproducing the perfectly competitive outcome when substitutability is perfect*, which is instead the case if incentives are based on output levels or revenues as in Vickers (1985), Fershtman (1985), Fershtman and Judd (1987) and Sklivas (1987), as one can easily verify by looking at (2.28) and (2.33). There, the anti-competitive flavour of delegation under price competition fades away as product differentiation decreases. Here, all outcomes being the same irrespective of the strategic variables chosen to generate them, the collapse of the market stage produces profits which can never be annihilated even under extreme conditions. Hence, comparative performance evaluation makes Bertrand firms decidedly more collusive than any other form of managerial incentives. Indeed, (2.62) implies that under price competition this model is observationally equivalent to cross-ownership[7] and should attract the attention of anti-trust agencies.

2.4 All eggs in one basket

On the basis of the conclusions drawn from the foregoing exposition of the three delegation schemes, what if owners ask themselves how to delegate, i.e. which incentive scheme should they adopt in writing managerial contracts? This issue has been tackled in Jansen *et al.* (2009), which I will summarize in this section, where the game possesses a four-stage structure, the first stage being for the choice of the specific type of managerial incentive.

2.4.1 Output level vs comparative performance

Here we consider the case in which firm i's owner behaves *à la* Vickers, whereas firm j's owner adopts a comparative performance contract as in Miller and Pazgal (hereafter MP). Hence, at the market stage the managerial objective functions are

$$M_i = \pi_i + \theta_i q_i; \quad M_j = \pi_j + \theta_j \pi_i \qquad (2.65)$$

The relevant FOCs are

$$\frac{\partial M_i}{\partial q_i} = A + \theta_i - 2q_i - q_j = 0 \tag{2.66}$$

$$\frac{\partial M_j}{\partial q_j} = A - (1 + \theta_j) q_i - 2q_j = 0 \tag{2.67}$$

which deliver the following unique Nash equilibrium in output levels:

$$q_i^N = \frac{A + 2\theta_i}{3 - \theta_j}; \quad q_j^N = \frac{A(1 - \theta_j) - \theta_i(1 + \theta_j)}{3 - \theta_j} \tag{2.68}$$

Hence, the relevant profits at the first stage are

$$\pi_i = \frac{(A + 2\theta_i)\left[A - \theta_i(1 - \theta_j)\right]}{(3 - \theta_j)^2}$$

$$\pi_j = \frac{\left[A(1 - \theta_j) - \theta_i(1 + \theta_j)\right]\left[A - \theta_i(1 - \theta_j)\right]}{(3 - \theta_j)^2} \tag{2.69}$$

Here, owners play simultaneously and non-cooperatively in the space of delegation variables, θ_i and θ_j. The resulting FOCs are[8]

$$\frac{\partial \pi_i}{\partial \theta_i} = \frac{A(1 + \theta_j) - 4\theta_i(1 - \theta_j)}{(3 - \theta_j)^2} = 0 \tag{2.70}$$

$$\frac{\partial \pi_j}{\partial \theta_j} = \frac{(A + 2\theta_i)\left[(A)(1 + \theta_j) - \theta_i(1 - 3\theta_j)\right]}{(3 - \theta_j)^2} = 0 \tag{2.71}$$

Now, solving (2.70) with respect to θ_i gives

$$\theta_i^N = -\frac{A(1 + \theta_j)}{4(\theta_j - 1)} \tag{2.72}$$

which can be plugged into (2.71), which simplifies as follows:

$$\frac{\partial \pi_j}{\partial \theta_j} = \frac{A^2(1 + \theta_j)}{8(\theta_j - 3)(\theta_j - 1)^2} = 0 \tag{2.73}$$

The above equation admits the unique solution $\theta_j^N = -1$. Hence, $\theta_i^N = 0$. This amounts to saying that the Vickers-type firm, in fact, does not delegate. The interpretation of the equilibrium at the delegation stage relies on the map of reaction functions at the market stage, as illustrated in Figure 2.4. To begin with, the pair (θ_i^N, θ_j^N) entails that equilibrium outputs in (2.68) are $q_i^N = A/4$ and $q_j^N = A/2$, which correspond to the familiar Cournot–Stackelberg output levels, with the MP firm as the leader. By choosing $\theta_j^N = -1$, the owner of the MP firm makes his manager's best reply in the output space flat. By doing so, the intersection between reaction functions indeed coincides with the tangency point between firm j's best reply and firm i's highest isoprofit curve. Therefore, Nash and Stackelberg equilibrium points coincide and this forces the Vickers-type firm not to delegate.

We are now in a position to examine the first stage in which owners decide whether to delegate or not, and, in the former case, what kind of incentive is given to managers. The first stage is illustrated in Matrix 2.6. The set of discrete strategies is $\{V, MP, ND\}$, with V standing for sales incentive *à la* Vickers, MP for comparative performance incentive *à la* Miller and Pazgal and ND for no delegation.

			j				
		V		MP		ND	
i	V	$\dfrac{2A^2}{25}$;	$\dfrac{2A^2}{25}$	$\dfrac{A^2}{16}$;	$\dfrac{A^2}{8}$	$\dfrac{A^2}{8}$;	$\dfrac{A^2}{16}$
	MP	$\dfrac{A^2}{8}$;	$\dfrac{A^2}{16}$	$\dfrac{3A^2}{32}$;	$\dfrac{3A^2}{32}$	$\dfrac{A^2}{8}$;	$\dfrac{A^2}{16}$
	ND	$\dfrac{A^2}{16}$;	$\dfrac{A^2}{8}$	$\dfrac{A^2}{16}$;	$\dfrac{A^2}{8}$	$\dfrac{A^2}{9}$;	$\dfrac{A^2}{9}$

Matrix 2.6

Since strategy MP is weakly dominant, the first stage has a unique pure-strategy Nash equilibrium at (MP, MP).

2.4.2 *Market share vs comparative performance*

Let's have a look at the case in which firm i's delegation contract incorporates an incentive based on market share as in Jansen *et al.* (2007) and Ritz (2008), while firm j's owner still adopts a comparative performance contract. Hence, at the market stage the managerial objective functions are

$$M_i = \pi_i + \frac{\theta_i q_i}{q_i + q_j}; \quad M_j = \pi_j + \theta_j \pi_i \tag{2.74}$$

The relevant FOCs are

$$\frac{\partial M_i}{\partial q_i} = A - 2q_i - q_j - \frac{\theta_i}{q_i + q_j}\left(1 - \frac{q_i}{q_i + q_j}\right) = 0 \tag{2.75}$$

$$\frac{\partial M_j}{\partial q_j} = A - \left(1 + \theta_j\right)q_i - 2q_j = 0 \tag{2.76}$$

Since output levels in (2.75)–(2.76) are affected by the choice of managerial incentives, the above system of FOCs at the market stage can be conveniently rewritten as follows:

$$\frac{\partial M_i\left(\theta_i,\theta_j\right)}{\partial q_i\left(\theta_i,\theta_j\right)} = A - 2q_i\left(\theta_i,\theta_j\right) - q_j\left(\theta_i,\theta_j\right)$$

$$- \frac{\theta_i}{q_i\left(\theta_i,\theta_j\right)+q_j\left(\theta_i,\theta_j\right)}\left[1 - \frac{q_i\left(\theta_i,\theta_j\right)}{q_i\left(\theta_i,\theta_j\right)+q_j\left(\theta_i,\theta_j\right)}\right] = 0 \tag{2.77}$$

$$\frac{\partial M_j\left(\theta_i,\theta_j\right)}{\partial q_j\left(\theta_i,\theta_j\right)} = A - \left(1+\theta_j\right)q_i\left(\theta_i,\theta_j\right) - 2q_j\left(\theta_i,\theta_j\right) = 0 \tag{2.78}$$

Going back to the second stage, the relevant FOCs are

$$\frac{\partial \pi_i\left(\theta_i,\theta_j\right)}{\partial \theta_i} = \left[A - q_j\left(\theta_i,\theta_j\right)\right]\frac{\partial q_i\left(\theta_i,\theta_j\right)}{\partial \theta_i}$$

$$- q_i\left(\theta_i,\theta_j\right)\left[2\frac{\partial q_i\left(\theta_i,\theta_j\right)}{\partial \theta_i} + \frac{\partial q_j\left(\theta_i,\theta_j\right)}{\partial \theta_i}\right] = 0 \tag{2.79}$$

$$\frac{\partial \pi_j\left(\theta_i,\theta_j\right)}{\partial \theta_j} = \left[A - 2q_j\left(\theta_i,\theta_j\right) - q_i\left(\theta_i,\theta_j\right)\right]\frac{\partial q_j\left(\theta_i,\theta_j\right)}{\partial \theta_j}$$

$$- q_j\left(\theta_i,\theta_j\right)\frac{\partial q_i\left(\theta_i,\theta_j\right)}{\partial \theta_j} = 0 \tag{2.80}$$

Since the system (2.75)–(2.76) does not lend itself to a straightforward solution as (2.76) is cubic, we follow a procedure which is equivalent although not identical to that used in Jansen *et al.* (2007) in order to identify the four partial derivatives of outputs with respect to managerial incentives, $\partial q_j(\theta_i,\theta_j)/\partial\theta_i$ appearing in the system (2.77)–(2.80).

To this end, we take the partial derivatives of the left- and right-hand sides of (2.77)–(2.78) with respect to θ_i and θ_j, so as to obtain the following system of four equations:

$$\frac{\partial^2 M_i\left(\theta_i,\theta_j\right)}{\partial q_i\left(\theta_i,\theta_j\right)\partial\theta_i} = f_{ii}\left[\frac{\partial q_i\left(\theta_i,\theta_j\right)}{\partial\theta_i}, \frac{\partial q_j\left(\theta_i,\theta_j\right)}{\partial\theta_i}\right] = 0 \tag{2.81}$$

$$\frac{\partial^2 M_i\left(\theta_i,\theta_j\right)}{\partial q_i\left(\theta_i,\theta_j\right)\partial\theta_j} = f_{ij}\left[\frac{\partial q_i\left(\theta_i,\theta_j\right)}{\partial\theta_j}, \frac{\partial q_j\left(\theta_i,\theta_j\right)}{\partial\theta_j}\right] = 0 \tag{2.82}$$

$$\frac{\partial^2 M_j\left(\theta_i,\theta_j\right)}{\partial q_j\left(\theta_i,\theta_j\right)\partial\theta_i} = f_{ji}\left[\frac{\partial q_i\left(\theta_i,\theta_j\right)}{\partial\theta_i}, \frac{\partial q_j\left(\theta_i,\theta_j\right)}{\partial\theta_i}\right] = 0 \tag{2.83}$$

$$\frac{\partial^2 M_j\left(\theta_i,\theta_j\right)}{\partial q_j\left(\theta_i,\theta_j\right)\partial\theta_j} = f_{jj}\left[\frac{\partial q_i\left(\theta_i,\theta_j\right)}{\partial\theta_j}, \frac{\partial q_j\left(\theta_i,\theta_j\right)}{\partial\theta_j}\right] = 0 \tag{2.84}$$

where each $f_{ij}[\cdot]$ is an expression containing two of the relevant partial derivatives we are looking for, in such a way that system (2.81)–(2.84) can be solved with respect to the four partial derivatives of outputs, to yield

$$\frac{\partial q_i\left(\theta_i,\theta_j\right)}{\partial\theta_i}=-\frac{2q_j\left(q_i+q_j\right)}{\Phi} \tag{2.85}$$

$$\frac{\partial q_i\left(\theta_i,\theta_j\right)}{\partial\theta_j}=-\frac{q_i\left[\left(q_i+q_j\right)^3+\theta_i\left(q_j-q_i\right)\right]}{\Phi} \tag{2.86}$$

$$\frac{\partial q_j\left(\theta_i,\theta_j\right)}{\partial\theta_j}=\frac{2q_i\left[q_i\left(q_i^2+3q_j\left(q_i+q_j\right)\right)+q_j\left(q_j^2+\theta_i\right)\right]}{\Phi} \tag{2.87}$$

$$\frac{\partial q_j\left(\theta_i,\theta_j\right)}{\partial\theta_i}=\frac{q_j\left(q_i+q_j\right)\left(1+\theta_j\right)}{\Phi} \tag{2.88}$$

where

$$\Phi\equiv\left(\theta_j-3\right)\left[q_i\left(q_i\left(q_i+3q_j\right)+3q_j^2\right)+q_j\left(\theta_i+q_j^2\right)\right]-\theta_i\left(1+\theta_j\right)q_i \tag{2.89}$$

Expressions (2.85)–(2.88) can be used to rewrite (2.79)–(2.80) as follows:

$$\frac{\partial\pi_i\left(\theta_i,\theta_j\right)}{\partial\theta_i}=-\frac{q_j\left(q_i+q_j\right)\left[2A-q_i\left(\theta_j-3\right)-2q_j\right]}{\Phi}=0 \tag{2.90}$$

$$\frac{\partial\pi_j\left(\theta_i,\theta_j\right)}{\partial\theta_j}=-\frac{q_i\left(q_i+q_j\right)^3\left[2A-2q_i-3q_j\right]+q_iq_j\left[2A-3\left(q_i+q_j\right)\right]\theta_i}{\Phi}=0 \tag{2.91}$$

FOCs (2.90)–(2.91), together with (2.75)–(2.76), form a system of four equations in four unknowns, $\{q_i,q_j,\theta_i,\theta_j\}$. The system delivers the unique solution

$$q_i^N=\frac{A}{4};\quad q_j^N=\frac{A}{2};\quad \theta_i^N=0;\quad \theta_j^N=-1 \tag{2.92}$$

The intuition behind the subgame perfect equilibrium strategy profile (2.92) is the same as the one provided in the previous section, where firm i is of the Vickers type: delegating via the comparative performance incentive entails that the owners of firm j design the contract in such a way that their manager has a flat best response (i.e. a dominant strategy) at the market stage. As a consequence, the firm relying on a managerial incentive linear in its own output level decides not to hire a manager (or, equivalently, forces her/him to behave as a pure profit maximizer). The resulting picture again coincides with Figure 2.4.

At the first stage, the owners' choice is again between delegating or not and the nature of the specific incentive administered to managers. This is illustrated in Matrix 2.7, where the set of discrete strategies is now $\{MS, MP, ND\}$, with MS

standing for market share incentive, MP for comparative performance incentive and ND for no delegation.

		|		MP	ND
		MS	j		
i	MS	$\dfrac{\left(10-\sqrt{2}\right)A^2}{98}$;	$\dfrac{\left(10-\sqrt{2}\right)A^2}{98}$	$\dfrac{A^2}{16}$; $\dfrac{A^2}{8}$	$\dfrac{A^2}{8}$; $\dfrac{A^2}{16}$
	MP	$\dfrac{A^2}{8}$;	$\dfrac{A^2}{16}$	$\dfrac{3A^2}{32}$; $\dfrac{3A^2}{32}$	$\dfrac{A^2}{8}$; $\dfrac{A^2}{16}$
	ND	$\dfrac{A^2}{16}$;	$\dfrac{A^2}{8}$	$\dfrac{A^2}{16}$; $\dfrac{A^2}{8}$	$\dfrac{A^2}{9}$; $\dfrac{A^2}{9}$

Matrix 2.7

Since $(10-\sqrt{2})/98 \simeq 0.088$, strategy MP is again weakly dominant, so that the first stage has a unique pure-strategy Nash equilibrium at (MP, MP).

2.4.3   Output level vs market share

This case can be quickly dealt with as, from Jansen *et al.* (2007) and Ritz (2008), we know that if contracts contemplate the following reward schemes for managers,

$$M_i = \pi_i + \theta_i q_i \frac{\theta_i q_i}{q_i + q_j}; \quad M_j = \pi_j + \frac{\theta_j q_j}{q_i + q_j} \tag{2.93}$$

then the relevant reduced form at the first stage appears as in Matrix 2.8.

		V	j	MS		ND
i	V	$\dfrac{2A^2}{25}$; $\dfrac{2A^2}{25}$		$\dfrac{(13\sqrt{17}-53)A^2}{8}$;	$\dfrac{(21-5\sqrt{17})A^2}{4}$	$\dfrac{A^2}{8}$; $\dfrac{A^2}{16}$
	MS	$\dfrac{(21-5\sqrt{17})A^2}{4}$;	$\dfrac{(13\sqrt{17}-53)A^2}{8}$	$\dfrac{(10-\sqrt{2})A^2}{98}$;	$\dfrac{(10-\sqrt{2})A^2}{98}$	$\dfrac{A^2}{8}$; $\dfrac{A^2}{16}$
	ND	$\dfrac{A^2}{16}$; $\dfrac{A^2}{8}$		$\dfrac{A^2}{16}$; $\dfrac{A^2}{8}$		$\dfrac{A^2}{9}$; $\dfrac{A^2}{9}$

Matrix 2.8

Since

$$\frac{\left(21-5\sqrt{17}\right)A^2}{4} > \frac{2A^2}{25} \tag{2.94}$$

and

$$\frac{\left(10-\sqrt{2}\right)A^2}{98} > \frac{\left(13\sqrt{17}-53\right)A^2}{8} \tag{2.95}$$

strategy MS strictly dominates strategy V, and owners simultaneously and non-cooperatively choose to delegate via contracts based on a combination of profits and market shares.

Summing up, the one-to-one confrontations between alternative incentive schemes deliver the impression that delegation based upon simple output expansion is a losing strategy. To find out exactly which delegation strategy is the winning one, we have to reconstruct the full picture of the landscape seen by owners from the top of the tree.

2.4.4 The reduced form

The above says that comparative performance incentives overcome both sales and market share incentives, and market share incentives are selected against sales incentives. Moreover, it also establishes that remaining purely entrepreneurial cannot be part of a subgame perfect equilibrium strategy profile. Hence, the first stage takes the form represented in Matrix 2.9.

		j		
		MS	MP	V
i	MS	$\frac{(10-\sqrt{2})A^2}{98}$; $\frac{(10-\sqrt{2})A^2}{98}$	$\frac{A^2}{16}$; $\frac{A^2}{8}$	$\frac{(21-5\sqrt{17})A^2}{4}$; $\frac{(13\sqrt{17}-53)A^2}{8}$
	MP	$\frac{A^2}{8}$; $\frac{A^2}{16}$	$\frac{3A^2}{32}$; $\frac{3A^2}{32}$	$\frac{A^2}{8}$; $\frac{A^2}{16}$
	V	$\frac{(13\sqrt{17}-53)A^2}{8}$; $\frac{(21-5\sqrt{17})A^2}{4}$	$\frac{A^2}{16}$; $\frac{A^2}{8}$	$\frac{2A^2}{25}$; $\frac{2A^2}{25}$

Matrix 2.9

Since strategy MP is strictly dominant, the game in Matrix 2.9 has a unique Nash equilibrium, (MP, MP). Moreover, since

$$\frac{3A^2}{32} > \frac{\left(10 - \sqrt{2}\right)A^2}{98} > \frac{2A^2}{25} \tag{2.96}$$

the equilibrium where managerial incentives are based upon comparative performance evaluation is Pareto-efficient for firms. Obviously, the socially efficient outcome is that where firms choose a Vickers-type delegation contract based on sales. This is a straightforward – and intuitive – consequence of the fact that adopting incentives based on output expansion leads to a higher industry output and therefore to a lower equilibrium price and a higher consumer surplus. This can be summarized as follows.

Proposition 2.6 *If owners can select the type of incentives administered to managers from the set* $\{MS, MP, V\}$*, they choose contracts based on comparative performance. This outcome is Pareto-efficient for stockholders and Pareto-inefficient from a social standpoint.*

2.5 Endogenous timing

By now we are well aware that strategic delegation reformulates a problem that goes back to the Stackelberg outcome without requiring firms to play sequentially. Taking a look at the credibility of sequential play from a different angle, several authors have modelled the endogenous timing problem in terms of the choice of roles in duopoly games with profit-seeking firms (see Gal-Or, 1985; Dowrick, 1986; Boyer and Moreaux, 1987a,b; and Robson, 1990, *inter alia*).

The identification of Stackelberg-solvable games is in d'Aspremont and Gérard-Varet (1980), where it was shown that a game can be solved sequentially if and only if Stackelberg (or sequential play) equilibria Pareto-dominate Nash (or simultaneous play) equilibria. This concept was pushed even further by Hamilton and Slutsky (1990), where the emergence of Stackelberg (respectively, Nash) equilibria occurs in the presence of increasing (respectively, decreasing) best reply functions, or equivalently strategic complementarity (respectively, substitutability) between choice variables, in the sense of Bulow *et al.* (1985).

Shall we expect managerial firms to replicate the choice of timing that would characterize pure profit-seeking firms, under both Cournot and Bertrand competition? The answer is not a priori obvious, as delegation *modifies* the nature and intensity of market competition and, as a result, the choice of timing could change significantly. Moreover, the decisions shaping the choice of roles may or may not be in the hands of managers, owners being possibly determined to keep such instruments for themselves.

All of these issues were addressed by Lambertini (2000b) using the same demand setup as in Singh and Vives (1984) and strategic delegation as in Vickers (1985). Two symmetric firms compete in a market for differentiated products, supplying one good each. The inverse demand function faced by firm i is

$$p_i = a - q_i - \sigma q_j \tag{2.97}$$

where $j \neq i$ denotes i's rival, and $|\sigma| \leq 1$. When σ is negative, the two goods are complements, while in the positive range of the same parameter they are substitutes. In the remainder of the paper, I shall confine to the latter case, since once one avails of the results pertaining to substitute goods, a simple reversion gives those pertaining to the case of complements. Inverting system (2.97), the direct demand function for firm i is easily obtained and coincides with (2.20). Firms are endowed with identical technologies, characterized by a constant marginal production cost, and hence individual profits are $\pi_i = (p_i - c)q_i$.

Firms (irrespective of the subjects in charge of taking this decision) can choose whether to move at the same time or scatter their respective decisions. If they decide to move simultaneously, no matter whether early or late, a Nash equilibrium in prices or quantities (or mixed) is obtained. If, conversely, they move sequentially, then a Stackelberg equilibrium is observed. This is what Hamilton and Slutsky (1990) defined as an *extended game with observable delay*. In order to illustrate this concept, consider the simplest extended game where firms can set a single strategic variable (e.g. price or quantity) and must choose between moving first or second. I shall adopt here a symbology which largely replicates that in Hamilton and Slutsky (1990, p. 32). Define $\Gamma^1 = (N, \Sigma^1, \Omega^1)$ as the extended game with observable delay. The set of players (or firms) is $\mathcal{N} = \{A, B\}$, and α and β are the compact and convex intervals of $\mathbb{R}^1$ representing the actions available to A and B in the basic game. Ω^1 is the payoff function. Payoffs depend on the actions undertaken in the basic (market) game, according to the following functions: $a : \alpha \times \beta \rightarrow \mathbb{R}^1$ and $b : \alpha \times \beta \rightarrow \mathbb{R}^1$. The set of times at which firms can choose to move is $T = \{F, S\}$, i.e. *first* or *second*. The set of strategies for player A is $\Sigma_A^1 = \{F, S\} \times \Phi_A$, where Φ_A is the set of functions that map $\{(F, F), (F, S), (S, S), (S, F) \times \beta\}$ into α. Likewise, the set of strategies for player B is $\Sigma_B^1 = \{F, S\} \times \Phi_B$, where Φ_B is the set of functions that map $\{(F, F), (F, S), (S, S), (S, F) \times \alpha\}$ into β. Let $r = (N, \ell, f)$ define the role (Nash competitor, leader and follower, respectively) that firm i plays as a result of the combined choice of timing taken by the two firms. If both firms choose to move at the same time, they obtain the payoffs associated with the simultaneous Nash equilibrium, (π_A^N, π_B^N), otherwise they get the payoffs associated with the Stackelberg equilibrium; e.g. (π_A^ℓ, π_B^f) if A moves first and B moves second or *vice versa*. The reduced form of the timing game can be described as the 2×2 Matrix 2.10 (cf. Hamilton and Slutsky, 1990, p. 33).

		B	
		F	S
A	F	π_A^N, π_B^N	π_A^ℓ, π_B^f
	S	π_A^f, π_B^ℓ	π_A^N, π_B^N

Matrix 2.10

If firms' owners delegate control to managers, the hiring contract is stipulated *à la* Vickers (1985), so that, in the case of separation between ownership and control, firm i's manager is remunerated on the basis of the objective function $M_i = \pi_i + \theta_i q_i$. For reasons that will emerge in the remainder, in Lambertini (2000b), θ_i is not assumed to be strictly positive.

What follows illustrates two different versions of a three-stage game in which the first stage is for the design of delegation contracts (if any), the second is for the choice of roles and the third is for market competition. At the second stage, owners or managers can be the relevant players, depending on the preferences of the owners as to what exactly they want to leave in the hands of managers.

Let's consider first the case in which managers are delegated the choice of timing in addition to output decisions.

2.5.1 Managers choose timing

Since delegation replicates the effect of an expansion in market size $a - c$, it doesn't take any explicit algebra to understand that it is trivial to verify that the managerial payoffs $M_i^r(J)$, with $r = \ell, f$ and $J = B, C$, are ranked in the same sequence followed by profits in the corresponding game without managers; all of this under both types of market interaction:

$$M_i^\ell(C) > M_i^N(C) > M_i^f(C) \tag{2.98}$$

$$M_i^f(B) > M_i^\ell(B) > M_i^N(B) \tag{2.99}$$

for all $\sigma \in (0, 1]$.[9] Consequently, from the standpoint of managers:

- $F \succ S$ under Cournot competition:

$$\ell(C) \succ n(C) \succ f(C) \tag{2.100}$$

where the symbol $\succ$ means 'preferred to', while no dominant strategy emerges under Bertrand competition:

$$f(B) \succ \ell(B) \succ n(B) \tag{2.101}$$

Thus, (2.98)–(2.101) prove the following.

Proposition 2.7 *Suppose $\sigma \in (0, 1]$. If managers are delegated both the output and the timing decision, the extended game with observable delay has: (i) a unique subgame perfect equilibrium in pure strategies with firms moving simultaneously, under Cournot competition; (ii) two asymmetric pure-strategy subgame perfect equilibria with firms moving sequentially, under Bertrand competition.*

The opposite holds if $\sigma \in [-1, 0)$, and of course when two equilibria exist in pure strategies then randomization (i.e. the mixed-strategy Nash equilibrium of Matrix 2.10) becomes also relevant. If one firm chooses quantity while the rival chooses price, Matrix 2.10 has a unique equilibrium in pure strategies, with the quantity-setting firm playing the leader's role. In view of these considerations, how can we expect owners to behave in determining the respective timing of their as well as the optimal delegation contracts?

2.5.2   Owners choose timing

In the Cournot setting, the optimal symmetric incentive scheme maximizing profits is

$$\theta^N(C) = \frac{\sigma^2(2 - \sigma)}{\sigma^2(\sigma - 4) + 8} \tag{2.102}$$

if the Cournot–Nash equilibrium is played at the market stage. If instead managers play sequentially, the relevant partial derivatives of profits are

$$\frac{\partial \pi_i^f}{\partial \theta_i} = \frac{2\sigma^2(2 - \sigma) - \sigma^4 - 16\theta_i([1 - \sigma^2(1 - 3\sigma^2)] - 2\sigma^3\theta_j}{8(2 - \sigma)^2} \tag{2.103}$$

and

$$\frac{\partial \pi_j^\ell}{\partial \theta_j} = \frac{\theta_j}{\sigma^2 - 2} \tag{2.104}$$

Note that the right-hand side of (2.104) is nil in correspondence with $\theta_j^\ell(C) = 0$, which amounts to saying that the owner of firm i, anticipating the acquisition of the leading position in the market stage, decides not to delegate (or to provide the manager with a strict profit incentive) because any other value of θ_j would simply be detrimental to profits: *Stackelberg leadership cannot be augmented by delegation*, if it is already acquired by proper timing. Conversely, the rival uses delegation 'properly', writing a contract containing

$$\theta_j^f(C) = \frac{\sigma^2 (2 (2 - \sigma) - \sigma^2)}{16 (1 - \sigma^2) + 3\sigma^4} > 0 \tag{2.105}$$

for all $\sigma \in (0, 1]$.

$\theta^N(C), \theta_i^f(C)$ and $\theta_j^\ell(C) = 0$ imply the following chain of inequalities on profits evaluated at the first stage:

$$\pi_i^f(C) > \pi_i^n(C) > \pi_i^\ell(C) \quad \forall \quad \sigma \in (0, 1] \tag{2.106}$$

Sequence (2.106) implies that S is the dominant strategy, even if firms are quantity-setters. So, owners would like their respective managers to try and become followers instead of leaders by 'waiting', strategic complementarity at the market stage notwithstanding. Of course, given the full symmetry of incentives, this involves the selection of simultaneous play; as such, in terms of timing the equilibrium looks equivalent to the one envisaged in Hamilton and Slutsky (1990) – not in terms of profits, obviously, given that here we are in presence of delegation. This is confirmed by the examination of Matrix 2.11, on the basis of (2.106).

		j	
		F	S
i	F	$\pi_i^N(C), \pi_j^N(C)$	$\pi_i^\ell(C), \pi_j^f(C)$
	S	$\pi_i^f(C), \pi_j^\ell(C)$	$\pi_i^N(C), \pi_j^N(C)$

Matrix 2.11

Summing up, the game where both decisions are entrusted to managers yields the following.

Lemma 2.2 *Suppose $\sigma \in (0, 1]$. Under Cournot behaviour, simultaneous play is univocally selected at the intersection of dominant strategies, with owners asking managers to delay as much as possible.*

What happens under price competition? In this case, the relevant contracts contain

$$\theta^N(B) = \frac{\sigma^2(\sigma - 1)}{2(2-\sigma) - \sigma^2} < 0, \tag{2.107}$$

$$\theta_i^f(B) = \frac{\sigma^2(\sigma - 1)\left[2(2+\sigma) - \sigma^2\right]}{16(1-\sigma^2) + 3\sigma^4} < 0 \tag{2.108}$$

for all $\sigma \in (0, 1]$, and $\theta_j^\ell(B) = 0$. Once again, if leadership is acquired through timing, then delegation becomes irrelevant (or very tight, which is equivalent). Profits follow the sequence

$$\pi_i^l(B) \geq \pi_i^f(B) \geq \pi_i^n(B) \tag{2.109}$$

for all $\sigma \in (0, 1]$. Here, leading is preferred to following, contrary to what we are accustomed to seeing in pricing games without managers. However, (2.109) implies the same equilibrium pattern of timing as under profit-seeking behaviour.

Lemma 2.3 *Suppose $\sigma \in (0, 1]$. Under Bertrand behaviour, two asymmetric pure-strategy equilibria exist, (F, S) and (S, F), reproducing the Stackelberg outcome between managerial firms.*

Clearly, there exists a positive probability of playing simultaneously, as can be ascertained by inspecting the mixed strategy equilibrium.

All of the above analysis boils down to the following.

Proposition 2.8 *Suppose $\sigma \in (0, 1]$. If managers control market variables only, the equilibrium of the extended game with observable delay replicates the same subgame perfect equilibria arising if both decisions were delegated to managers.*

Intuitively, the same applies if one firm is a quantity-setter while the other is a price-setter. Again intuitively, all of the foregoing claims are reversed if goods are complements in demand, i.e. for all $\sigma \in [-1, 0)$.

One particular aspect deserves attention here, namely, the fact that $\theta_j^\ell(J)$ is nil in both setups. This puts into further evidence the net substitutability between managerialization and Stackelberg leadership, which is the *fil rouge* of the literature discussing the primary motive for hiring a manager with a mandate to control the relevant market variable on behalf of the firm's owners. If the first mover advantage can be attained via a pre-play stage establishing the distribution of roles in the ensuing market competition, then the presence of a manager becomes redundant for the leader.

To conclude the treatment of basic delegation schemes, it is appropriate to briefly account for the temporal dimension of contracts. In the real world, managers are hired for long periods, the duration being indeterminate in several cases. In particular – and we'll come back to this aspect in Chapter 6 – the time span is usually finite and specified in the contract in US Corporations, while often it is not in firms based in Western Europe (especially in the EU). So, the twofold question arises as to whether time plays a role in shaping the structure or duration of managerial contracts, and whether these features have a connection with the type of market competition. Examining the duopoly case, Bárcena-Ruiz and Espinosa (1996) explicitly addressed this issue using delegation incentives loosely based on Vickers (1985), Fershtman and Judd (1987) and Sklivas (1987). Their analysis shows that, if market variables are strategic substitutes (respectively, complements), then managerial incentives are also strategic substitutes (respectively, complements). Moreover, replicating a structural feature of one-shot games, adopting a long-term contract reproduces Stackelberg leadership in the space of incentive schemes; conversely (and intuitively) the adoption of a short-term contract turns the firm into a Stackelberg follower. Consequently, if final goods are substitutes in demand and therefore instantaneous best replies in quantities (respectively, prices) are downward (respectively, upward) sloping, the subgame perfect equilibrium arising under price competition prescribes one firm signing a long-term contract and the other firm signing a short-term one. Instead, under quantity-setting behaviour, it is optimal for both firms to sign long-term incentive contracts, this choice being dictated by dominant strategies.[10]

2.6 Entry barriers

Ever since the seminal papers by Spence (1977) and Dixit (1979, 1980)[11] – which, if I may say so, constituted the Trojan horse for the adoption of game theory in industrial economics and therefore offered a fundamental contribution to the construction of the modern theory of industrial organization – the strategic use of entry barriers by incumbent firms to neutralize entry threats has been a *leitmotiv* of oligopoly models. The theory of strategic delegation makes no exception, the earliest analysis of the impact of managerialization on entry having been carried out by Vickers (1985, p.143) himself.

The setting envisages a monopolist (the incumbent, firm I) facing potential entry by an outsider (the entrant, firm E). Of course, as long as E stands alone on the market and no externalities operate, it has no interest in hiring a manager. However, things change as soon as entry threat looms at the horizon. Suppose that: (i) firms are quantity-setters selling a homogeneous good with the usual linear demand function and a symmetric technology with the same constant marginal cost; (ii) the entrant has to bear a fixed entry cost $F > 0$,; and (iii) the incumbent hires a manager at the time of entry with a contract based on output expansion, having already abated the fixed entry cost in a distant past.

If so, the incumbent behaves as a Cournot–Stackelberg leader even though firms set output levels simultaneously, and profits are

$$\pi_I^{CN} = \frac{A^2}{8}; \quad \pi_E^{CN} = \frac{A^2}{16} - F \qquad (2.110)$$

where $\pi_E^{CN} > 0$ for all $F \in (0, A^2/16)$. In this range, entry occurs and the former monopolist must be happy to enjoy a dominant position. Otherwise, for all

$F \geq A^2/16$, firm E stays out and the incumbent remains a monopolist. Note that in absence of managerialization, the fixed cost would constitute a natural barrier to entry under simultaneous play as along as $F \geq A^2/9$. Resorting to managerialization, the incumbent curbs its own profit by 50%, but the Stackelberg leader's position is still preferable to accepting entry *à la* Nash.

This simple argument proves the following.

Proposition 2.9 *Strategic delegation based on output or sales expansion can be used by an incumbent firm to build up a strategic barrier to entry in absence of a natural one.*

One could object that asymmetric delegation is not subgame perfect, as we already know. Right, but going managerial is not necessarily a safe conduct for the entrant, as in that case its profits would become $\pi_E^{CN} = 2A^2/25 - F$. For all $F \geq 2A^2/25$, hiring a manager still does not guarantee a successful entry.

This subject matter has subsequently been extended in several directions by von der Fehr (1992), Sen (1993) and Mukherjee and Tsai (2014). von der Fehr (1992) considered the possibility that entry threats induce slack because owners may prefer lower profits as high profit levels make entry more attractive (and conversely). Sen (1993) extended the initial idea in Vickers (1985) to show that if a Nash bargaining process between managers determines the output decisions, then the owner of the incumbent firm will find it optimal to reward her/his manager exclusively on the basis of profits, without using any incentive defined in terms of output or sales, while the entrant will combine both elements. Mukherjee and Tsai (2014) evaluated the social efficiency of the entry process, showing that delegation may cancel out the well known *business stealing effect* generated by entry (Mankiw and Whinston (1986)) if the entrant is more efficient than the incumbent.

We will come back to entry deterring strategies based upon strategic delegation in Chapters 5 and 6, which deal with innovation and multidivisional or multi-product firms, respectively. There, the strategic use of contracts will take a flavour which dates back to Gilbert and Newbery (1982), who opened the long-standing debate on the persistence of monopoly, and Aghion and Bolton (1987), who were the first to outline a role for such instruments in games studying strategic barriers to entry.

2.7 Empirical and experimental evidence

Empirical research on managerialization and the consequent adoption on the part of firms of objectives differing from pure profit maximization started well before the appearance of the debate on strategic delegation. For instance, Amihud and Kamin (1979) tested the bottom line of Baumol's (1958) analysis, showing that their data support the hypothesis that revenue maximization is indeed prevalent among oligopolistic firms controlled by managers. And of course, the subsequent literature inaugurated by Fershtman (1985) and Vickers (1985) quickly triggered a parallel flow of empirical analysis, whose cornerstone is the paper by Aggarwal and Samwick (1999), where the theoretical model based on comparative performance evaluation common to Salas Fumas (1992), Lundgren (1996) and Miller and Pazgal (2001) was contextually tested empirically. To appreciate Aggarwal and Samwick's (1999) findings, one has to keep in mind that the theoretical model predicts the emergence of an identical equilibrium irrespective of market variables being used. This, literally, means that comparative performance is observed under Cournot behaviour, but not under Bertrand behaviour. That is, the intensity of incentives based on relative performance should be expected to be inversely related to the intensity of market competition, all else equal. According to the analysis performed by Aggarwal and Samwick (1999) using a large data set on executive compensation, this prediction appears to be confirmed.

Their conclusions add up to a previous empirical debate delivering diverging evidence on the same matter, as in Jensen and Murphy (1990), relative performance evaluation seems not to be an important factor in shaping managerial incentives. Gibbons and Murphy (1990) and Antle and Smith (1986) found that increases in CEO's rewards are positively related to firm performance but negatively related to industry performance. The opposite conclusion is supported by Barro and Barro (1990), Joh (1999) and Janakiraman et al. (1992), according to whom managerial compensation is indeed positively related to industry performance. In this regard, a remark is in order, which – as far as I know – has not been put forward thus far: this discordance among empirically oriented works, all being apparently focusing on performance – be that comparative or not – indirectly tells us something relevant also about other forms of strategic delegation based on output, sales or market shares, which, without referring directly to absolute or comparative profits, do exert relevant bearing on profits, in particular when the industry is heterogeneous as to the diffusion of delegation or in terms of productive efficiency. Hence, a promising avenue for extending the empirical investigation on these matters would be to look at the relationship between absolute and relative profit performance of firms, managerial compensation and the appearance of these elements in managerial contracts.

More on empirical research will be mentioned, where appropriate, in the next chapters, dealing with specific applications of the baseline theoretical models discussed here.

A more direct connection with strategic delegation models, mentioning the idea that delegation is designed to gain a competitive advantage over rivals, can be found in the empirical research carried out by Irwin (1991), Kedia (2006) and Karuna (2007). In particular, Kedia (2006) offered a clearcut empirical support to the predictions stemming from the theoretical models illustrated in this chapter, as data appear to prove that managers are rewarded on the basis of a combination of profits and sales, with the weight attached to sales being higher.

Another route is that of carrying out controlled experiments in labs, which, by the way, has the non-negligible advantage of allowing one to set up the experiment in such a way that the twin properties whereby delegation contracts must be observable and agency problems connected with asymmetric information and moral hazard are absent will be 'plugged into the experiment', so to speak. This avenue of research is already being pursued since Schotter *et al.* (2000), Fershtman and Gneezy (2001) and Huck *et al.* (2004). While Schotter *et al.* (2000) found that delegation increases inefficiency, Fershtman and Gneezy (2001) set up an experiment based upon the ultimatum game, in which the behaviour of participants shows that: (i) if the proposer 'hires' a delegate, her/his share increases; (ii) if the responder is unaware of delegation by the proposer, the latter's share shrinks. Huck *et al.* (2004) set up the experiment to closely mimic a Cournot industry in which delegation relies on a sales bonus, and surprisingly found that such a contract is rarely observed in the experiment even if the opponent is a pure profit seeker, in sharp contrast with the theoretical prediction. Bartling and Fischbacher (2012) built up an experiment on delegation having in mind that the matter is one of responsibility for crucial decisions, turning delegation in a useful tool shifting the blame for a poor performance. The latest developments on this ground are in Hamman *et al.* (2016) and Barreda-Tarrazona *et al.* (2016). Hamman *et al.* (2016) empirically tested the possibility that delegation might not be related to efficiency gains but rather to hire agents willing to take decisions or actions which principals or owners would be reluctant to implement, in such a way to dilute responsibility and accountability for morally questionable behaviour along the vertical structure of the organization. In Barreda-Tarrazona *et al.* (2016), the Cournot duopoly with delegation was replicated in the lab, showing that contracts based on comparative performance are chosen more often than others relying on output expansion or revenues, as the theoretical results in Jansen *et al.* (2009) suggest.

Further reading

A recent and comprehensive overview of the debate on strategic delegation and managerial firms covering the extant material in both industrial organization and management science is in Sengul *et al.* (2012). The latest survey is in Kopel and Pezzino (2017). Additional insights concerning unobservable contracts are in Koçkesen *et al.* (2000), Koçkesen and Ok (2004) and Koçkesen (2007). For more on delegation and the choice of roles, see Lambertini (2000a). Additional insights on the possibility of observing unilateral delegation at equilibrium can be found in Kopel and Löffler (2012). Szymanski (1994) extended the delegation process to include wage bargaining between managers and unions. Further empirical evidence is in Gupta and Govindarajan (1984, 1985), Morck *et al.* (1988), Thomas *et al.* (1991), Yermack (1995, 1996), Loderer and Martin (1997), Vroom and Gimeno (2007) and Beiner *et al.* (2011). Experiments on relevant aspects of the internal organization of firms date back at least to Burton and Obel (1988), focusing on opportunistic behavior in the M-form enterprise. A recent survey of experiments on oligopoly games is in Potters and Suetens (2013).

Notes

1 For more on the role of delegation and its optimal design in presence of network externalities, see Hoernig (2012) and Chirco and Scrimitore (2013).

2 Moving sequentially requires a firm to accept the follower's role, behaving as a sort of underdog. As shown in Hamilton and Slutsky (1990), with downward sloping reaction functions this is not part of the subgame perfect equilibrium of an extended game with observable delay in which firms non-cooperatively determine upstream their respective roles.

3 Here – the good being homogeneous – quantity competition yields downward sloping reaction functions, corresponding to the case of strategic substitutes. The opposite holds under price competition, with prices being strategic complements whenever goods are demand substitutes (Bulow *et al.*, 1985).

4 All of this makes sense if Δ_i is positive, as assumed in Basu (1995). Indeed, this is reasonable as it amounts to requiring that the gross gain accruing to stockholders from delegation, x_i, is strictly lower than the cost of hiring a manager, w_i.

5 For more on the most appropriate parameterization of direct demand systems accounting for product differentiation, see Kopel *et al.* (2017).

6 As we know from Chapter 1, under uncertainty or asymmetric information, this type of contract is convenient if managers are risk averse, their behaviour is unobservable or uncertainty across firms is highly correlated (Lazear and Rosen, 1981; Nalebuff and Stiglitz, 1983).

7 On cross-ownership and its effects on competition (or collusion), see Reynolds and Snapp (1986), Malueg (1992), Reitman (1994) and Gilo *et al.* (2006).

8 Second-order conditions are met, and examining the Hessian matrix at the first stage it is easily checked that the equilibrium is stable.

9 If goods are complements in demand, one needs just to replace C with B in (2.98) and B with C in (2.99). Clearly, the same applies to (2.100) and (2.101).

10 This of course holds true if delegation is purely strategic and does not give rise to an agency problem. If instead it is so, then Fudenberg *et al.* (1990) showed that long run commitments are not necessary if any public information can be used and agent and principal can renegotiate the terms of their contract under common knowledge about their respective preference structures and the technology in use inside the firm.

11 For more, see Bernheim (1984) and Mankiw and Whinston (1986). About the welfare consequence of the entry process, see von Weizsäcker (1980) and Suzumura and Kiyono (1987).

References

Aggarwal, R.K. and A.A. Samwick (1999), 'Executive Compensation, Strategic Competition, and Relative Performance Evaluation: Theory and Evidence', *Journal of Finance*, **54**, 1999–2043.

Aghion, P. and P. Bolton (1987), 'Long-Term Contracts as a Barrier to Entry', *American Economic Review*, **77**, 388–401.

Amihud, Y. and J. Kamin (1979), 'Revenue vs Profit Maximization: Differences in Behavior by the Type of Control and by Market power', *Southern Economic Journal*, **45**, 838–46.

Antle, R. and A. Smith (1986), 'An Empirical Investigation of the Relative Performance Evaluation of Corporate Executives', *Journal of Accounting Research*, **24**, 1–39.

Bagnoli, M. and S.G. Watts (2015), 'Delegating Disclosure and Production Choices', *The Accounting Review*, **90**, 835–57.

Bárcena-Ruiz, J.C. and M.P. Espinosa (1996), 'Long-Term or Short-Term Managerial Incentive Contracts', *Journal of Economics and Management Strategy*, **5**, 343–59.

Barreda-Tarrazona, I., N. Georgantzís, C. Manasakis, E. Mitrokostas and E. Petrakis (2016), 'Endogenous Managerial Compensation Contracts in Experimental Quantity-Setting Duopolies', *Economic Modelling*, **54**, 205–17.

Barro, J.R., and R.J. Barro (1990), 'Pay, Performance, and Turnover of Bank CEOs', *Journal of Labor Economics*, **8**, 448–81.

Bartling, B. and U. Fischbacher (2012), 'Shifting the Blame: On Delegation and Responsibility', *Review of Economic Studies*, **79**, 67–87.

Basu, K. (1995), 'Stackelberg Equilibrium in Oligopoly: An Explanation Based on Managerial Incentives', *Economics Letters*, **49**, 459–64.

Baumol, W. (1958), 'On the Theory of Oligopoly', *Economica*, **25**, 187–98.

Beiner, S., M. Schmid and G. Wanzenried (2011), 'Product Market Competition, Managerial Incentives and Firm Valuation', *European Financial Management*, **17**, 331–66.

Bernheim, D. (1984), 'Strategic Entry Deterrence of Sequential Entry into an Industry', *RAND Journal of Economics*, **15**, 1–11.

Berr, F. (2011), 'Stackelberg Equilibria in Managerial Delegation Games', *European Journal of Operational Research*, **212**, 251–62.

Boyer, M. and Moreaux, M. (1987a), 'Being a Leader or a Follower: Reflections on the Distribution of Roles in Duopoly', *International Journal of Industrial Organization*, **5**, 175–92.

Boyer, M. and Moreaux, M. (1987b), 'On Stackelberg Equilibria with Differentiated Products: The Critical Role of the Strategy Space', *Journal of Industrial Economics*, **36**, 217–30.

Bulow, J., J. Geanakoplos and P. Klemperer (1985), 'Multimarket Oligopoly: Strategic Substitutes and Complements', *Journal of Political Economy*, **93**, 488–511.

Burton, R.M. and B. Obel (1988), 'Opportunism, Incentives and the M-Form Hypothesis. A Laboratory Study', *Journal of Economic Behaviour and Organization*, **10**, 99–119.

Chirco, A. and M. Scrimitore (2013), 'Choosing Price or Quantity? The Role of Delegation and Network Externalities', *Economics Letters*, **121**, 482–6.

Coughlan, A. and B. Wernerfelt (1989), 'On Credible Delegation by Oligopolists: A Discussion of Distribution Channel Management', *Management Science*, **35**, 226–39.

d'Aspremont, C. and L.-A. Gérard-Varet (1980), 'Stackelberg-Solvable Games and Pre-Play Communication', *Journal of Economic Theory*, **23**, 201–17.

Dixit, A. (1979), 'A Model of Duopoly Suggesting a Theory of Entry Barriers', *Bell Journal of Economics*, **10**, 20–32.

Dixit, A. (1980), 'The Role of Investment in Entry Deterrence', *Economic Journal*, **90**, 95–106.

Dowrick, S. (1986), 'von Stackelberg and Cournot Duopoly: Choosing Roles', *RAND Journal of Economics*, **17**, 251–60.

Fershtman, C. (1985), 'Managerial Incentives as a Strategic Variable in a Duopolistic Environment', *International Journal of Industrial Organization*, **3**, 245–53.

Fershtman, C. and U. Gneezy (2001), 'Strategic Delegation: An Experiment', *RAND Journal of Economics*, **32**, 352–68.

Fershtman, C. and K. Judd (1987), 'Equilibrium Incentives in Oligopoly', *American Economic Review*, **77**, 927–40.

Fershtman, C. and E. Kalai (1997), 'Unobserved Delegation', *International Economic Review*, **38**, 763–74.

Fershtman, C., K. Judd and E. Kalai (1991), 'Observable Contracts: Strategic Delegation and Cooperation', *International Economic Review*, **32**, 551–9.

Fudenberg, D., B. Holmström and P. Milgrom (1990), 'Short-Term Contracts and Long-Term Agency Relationships', *Journal of Economic Theory*, **51**, 1990, 1–31.

Gal-Or, E. (1985), 'First Mover and Second Mover Advantages', *International Economic Review*, **26**, 649–53.

Gibbons, R. and K.J. Murphy (1990), 'Relative Performance Evaluation for Chief Executive Officers', *Industrial and Labor Relations Review*, **43** (Special Issue), 30S–51S.

Gilbert, R. and D. Newbery (1982), 'Preemptive Patenting and the Persistence of Monopoly', *American Economic Review*, **72**, 514–26.

Gilo, D., Y. Moshe and Y. Spiegel (2006), 'Partial Cross Ownership and Tacit Collusion', *RAND Journal of Economics*, **37**, 81–99.

Gupta, A. and V. Govindarajan (1984), 'Business Unit Strategy, Managerial Characteristics, and Business Unit Effectiveness at Strategy Implementation', *Academy of Management Journal*, **27**, 25–41.

Gupta, A. and V. Govindarajan (1985), 'Linking Control Systems to Business Unit Strategy: Impact on Performance', *Accounting Organizations and Society*, **10**, 51–66.

Hamilton, J. and S. Slutsky (1990), 'Endogenous Timing in Duopoly Games: Stackelberg or Cournot Equilibria', *Games and Economic Behavior*, **2**, 29–46.

Hamman, J.R., G. Loewenstein and R.A. Weber (2016), 'Self-Interest through Delegation: An Additional Rationale for the Principal-Agent Relationship', *American Economic Review*, **100**, 1826–46.

Hoernig, S. (2012), 'Strategic Delegation under Price Competition and Network Effects', *Economics Letters*, **117**, 487–9.

Huck, S., W. Müller and H.-T. Normann (2004), 'Strategic Delegation in Experimental Markets', *International Journal of Industrial Organization*, **22**, 561–74.

Irwin, D.A. (1991), 'Mercantilism as Strategic Trade Policy: The Anglo-Dutch Rivalry for the East India Trade, *Journal of Political Economy*, **99**, 1296–314.

Janakiraman, S., R. Lambert and D. Larcker (1992), 'An Empirical Investigation of the Relative Performance Evaluation Hypothesis', *Journal of Accounting Research*, **30**, 53–69.

Jansen, T., A. van Lier and A. van Witteloostuijn (2007), 'A Note on Strategic Delegation: The Market Share Case', *International Journal of Industrial Organization*, **25**, 531–9.

Jansen, T., A. van Lier and A. van Witteloostuijn (2009), 'On the Impact of Managerial Bonus Systems on Firm Profit and Market Competition: The Cases of Pure Profit, Sales, Market Share and Relative Profits Compared', *Managerial and Decision Economics*, **30**, 141–53.

Jensen, M.C. and K.J. Murphy (1990), 'Performance Pay and Top-Management Incentives', *Journal of Political Economy*, **98**, 225–64.

Joh, S. (1999), 'Strategic Managerial Incentive Compensation in Japan: Relative Performance Evaluation and Product Market Collusion', *Review of Economics and Statistics*, **81**, 303–13.

Karuna, C. (2007), 'Industry Product Market Competition and Managerial Incentives', *Journal of Accounting and Economics*, **43**, 275–97.

Katz, M. (1991), 'Game-Playing Agents: Unobservable Contracts as Precommitments', *RAND Journal of Economics*, **22**, 307–28.

Katz, M. (2006), 'Observable Contracts as Commitments: Interdependent Contracts and Moral Hazard', *Journal of Economics and Management Strategy*, **15**, 685–706.

Kedia, S. (2006), 'Estimating Product Market Competition: Methodology and Application', *Journal of Banking and Finance*, **30**, 875–94.

Koçkesen, L. (2007), 'Unobservable Contracts as Precommitments', *Economic Theory*, **31**, 539–52.

Koçkesen, L. and E.A. Ok (2004), 'Strategic Delegation by Unobservable Incentive Contracts', *Review of Economic Studies*, **71**, 397–424.

Koçkesen, L., E.A. Ok, and R. Sethi (2000), 'The Strategic Advantage of Negatively Interdependent Preferences', *Journal of Economic Theory*, **92**, 274–99.

Kopel, M. and C. Löffler (2012), 'Organizational Governance, Leadership, and the Influence of Competition', *Journal of Institutional and Theoretical Economics*, **168**, 362–92.

Kopel, M. and L. Lambertini (2013), 'On Price Competition with Market Share Delegation Contracts', *Managerial and Decision Economics*, **34**, 40–3.

Kopel. M. and M. Pezzino (2017), 'Strategic Delegation in Oligopoly', in L. Corchòn and M. Marini (eds), *Handbook of Game Theory and Industrial Organization*, Cheltenham, Edward Elgar, forthcoming.

Kopel, M., A. Ressi and L. Lambertini (2017), 'Capturing Direct and Cross Price Effects in a Differentiated Products Duopoly Model', *Manchester School*, forthcoming.

Lambertini, L. (2000a), 'Strategic Delegation and the Shape of Market Competition', *Scottish Journal of Political Economy*, **47**, 550–70.

Lambertini, L. (2000b), 'Extended Games Played by Managerial Firms', *Japanese Economic Review*, **51**, 274–83.

Lambertini, L. and M. Trombetta (2002), 'Delegation and Firms' Ability to Collude', *Journal of Economic Behavior and Organization*, **47**, 359–73.

Lazear, E. and S. Rosen (1981), 'Rank-Order Tournaments as Optimal Labor Contracts', *Journal of Political Economy*, **89**, 841–64.

Loderer, C. and K. Martin (1997), 'Executive Stock Ownership and Performance - Tracking Faint Traces', *Journal of Financial Economics*, **45**, 223–55.

Lundgren, C. (1996), 'Using Relative Profit Incentives to Prevent Collusion', *Review of Industrial Organization*, **11**, 533–50.

Malueg, D. (1992), 'Collusive Behavior and Partial Ownership of Rivals', *International Journal of Industrial Organization*, **10**, 27–34.

Mankiw, A.G. and M.D. Whinston (1986), 'Free Entry and Social Inefficiency', *RAND Journal of Economics*, **17**, 48–58.

Miller, N.H. and A.I. Pazgal (2001), 'The Equivalence of Price and Quantity Competition with Delegation', *RAND Journal of Economics*, **32**, 284–301.

Morck, R., A. Shleifer and R. Vishny (1988), 'Management Ownership and Market Valuation - An Empirical Analysis', *Journal of Financial Economics*, **20**, 293–316.

Mukherjee, A. and Y. Tsai (2014), 'Managerial Delegation, Cost Asymmetry and Social Efficiency of Entry', *Economic Record*, **90**, 90–7.

Nalebuff, B. and J. Stiglitz (1983), 'Prizes and Incentives: Towards a General Theory of Compensation and Competition', *Bell Journal of Economics*, **14**, 131–47.

Pal, R. (2014), 'Managerial Delegation in Monopoly and Social Welfare', *International Journal of Economic Theory*, **10**, 403–10.

Potters, J. and S. Suetens (2013), 'Oligopoly Experiments in the Current Millennium', *Journal of Economic Surveys*, **27**, 439–60.

Reitman, D. (1994), 'Partial Ownership Arrangements and the Potential for Collusion', *Journal of Industrial Economics*, **42**, 313–22.

Reynolds, R. and B. Snapp (1986), 'The Competitive Effects of Partial Equity Interests and Joint Ventures', *International Journal of Industrial Organization*, **4**, 141–53.

Ritz, R.A. (2008), 'Strategic Incentives for Market Share', *International Journal of Industrial Organization*, **26**, 586–97.

Robson, A.J. (1990), 'Duopoly with Endogenous Strategic Timing: Stackelberg Regained', *International Economic Review*, **31**, 263–74.

Salas Fumas, V. (1992), 'Relative Performance Evaluation of Management: The Effects on Industrial Competition and Risk Sharing', *International Journal of Industrial Organization*, **10**, 473–89.

Schotter, A., W. Zheng and B. Snyder (2000), 'Bargaining Through Agents: An Experimental Study of Delegation and Commitment', *Games and Economic Behavior*, **30**, 248–92.

Sen, A. (1993), 'Entry and Managerial Incentives', *International Journal of Industrial Organization*, **11**, 123–37.

Sengul, M., J. Gimeno and J. Dial (2012), 'Strategic Delegation: A Review, Theoretical Integration, and Research Agenda', *Journal of Management*, **38**, 375–414.

Singh, N. and X. Vives (1984), 'Price and Quantity Competition in a Differentiated Duopoly', *RAND Journal of Economics*, **15**, 546-54.

Spence, A.M. (1976), 'Product Differentiation and Welfare', *American Economic Review*, **66**, 407–14.

Spence, A.M. (1977), 'Entry, Capacity, Investment and Oligopolistic Pricing', *Bell Journal of Economics*, **8**, 534–44.

Sklivas, S.D. (1987), 'The Strategic Choice of Managerial Incentives', *RAND Journal of Economics*, **18**, 452–8.

Suzumura, K. and K. Kiyono (1987), 'Entry Barriers and Economic Welfare', *Review of Economic Studies*, **54**, 157–67.

Szymanski, S. (1994), 'Strategic Delegation with Endogenous Costs: A Duopoly with Wage Bargaining', *International Journal of Industrial Organization*, **12**, 105–16.

Thomas, A., R. Litschert and K. Ramaswamy (1991), 'The Performance Impact of Strategy-Manager Coalignment: An Empirical Examination', *Strategic Management Journal*, **12**, 509–22.

Vickers, J. (1985), 'Delegation and the Theory of the Firm', *Economic Journal*, **95** (Conference Papers), 138–47.

von der Fehr, N.-H.M. (1992), 'How Entry Threats Induce Slack', *International Journal of Industrial Organization*, **10**, 231–49.

von Weizsäcker, C.C. (1980), 'A Welfare Analysis of Barriers to Entry', *Bell Journal of Economics*, **11**, 399–420.

Vroom, G. and J. Gimeno (2007), 'Ownership Form, Managerial Incentives, and the Intensity of Rivalry', *Academy of Management Journal*, **50**, 901–22.

Yermack, D. (1995), 'Do Corporations Award CEO Stock Options Effectively?', *Journal of Financial Economics*, **39**, 237–69.

Yermack, D. (1996), 'Higher Market Valuation of Companies with a Small Board of Directors', *Journal of Financial Economics*, **40**, 185–211.

3 Mixed oligopolies

The title might sound misleading, as the material in Chapter 2 covers cases of 'mixed' oligopolies with managerial firms competing with entrepreneurial ones. Indeed, the subject of this chapter is the characterization of the role of managers in industries where private and public firms coexist.

The features of the mixed markets theme attracted the interest of industrial economists in a phase during which IO developed a discussion about the possibility of using public firms to regulate oligopolistic industries, taking a typical second-best angle (Merrill and Schneider, 1966; Hagen, 1979; Harris and Wiens, 1980; Beato and Mas-Colell, 1984; and Rees, 1984). The last developments of this literature date back to Cremer *et al.* (1989) and De Fraja and Delbono (1989) in which – not surprisingly, in some sense – the idea that a public firm might behave as an endogenous regulatory tool by taking the Stackelberg leadership was extensively discussed. All of this was flanked by a lively debate about privatization (Vickers and Yarrow, 1988; Bös, 1991).

To facilitate the illustration of the models summarized in the remainder of the chapter, I will briefly expose here the benchmark oligopoly setting in which a single public firm interacts with $n - 1$ private ones in a Cournot industry where a homogeneous good is supplied by all firms using an identical technology involving total costs $C_i = cq_i$ for all $i = 1, 2, 3, \ldots n$, and market demand is $p = a - Q$, $Q = \sum_{i=1}^{n} q_i$. Identify as firm 1 the public unit, which is supposed to maximize social welfare

$$SW = \Pi + CS \tag{3.1}$$

where $\Pi = \sum_{i=1}^{n} \pi_i$ is industry profit and $CS = Q^2/2$ is consumer surplus. All other firms are standard Cournot players maximizing individual profits non-cooperatively. There are no managers around, and firms move simultaneously.

It takes an elementary textbook exercise to verify that, at the resulting Nash equilibrium,

$$q_1^N = a - c; \; q_j^N = 0 \quad \forall \; j = 2, 3, \ldots n \tag{3.2}$$

so that the public firm becomes a monopolist by flooding the market with the perfectly competitive outcome. Consequently, the equilibrium price falls to marginal cost c.

It is worth stressing that the aforementioned literature relies instead on the assumption of increasing marginal costs, which creates the possibility of attaining leadership a sensible and practicable one for the public firm, although its presence may not be welfare-improving and the price stays above marginal cost when the public firm acquires the Stackelberg leadership (as illustrated in De Fraja and Delbono, 1989).

It is fairly natural for a background like this to generate some question marks as to whether there may be a role for managers when private and public firms coexist, since a quick glance at the baseline model suggests that a public firm might just flood the market to destroy the profit margin, thereby maximizing welfare. As we shall see, this is not the case, in general. Yet, what follows tells that inserting the additional element of strategic delegation into a picture that seemed already completed when the literature on delegation started flourishing revives our conception of mixed markets in non-trivial ways.

3.1 Strategic delegation and asymmetric information

Barros (1994, 1995) took a look at this problem by combining the strategic nature of delegation borrowed from Vickers (1985), Fershtman and Judd (1987) and Sklivas (1987) with an informational asymmetry between principals and agents coming straight from agency theory. By doing so, she shows that, under such circumstances, the presence of a public firm can improve allocative efficiency, although productive efficiency measured by average or marginal costs may actually decrease. Here I will follow Barros (1995).

The industry is a duopoly, with a demand function for a homogeneous good produced through a technology operating at constant returns to scale, as above.

Obviously, the public firm is interested in maximizing social welfare, while owners of the private firm want to maximize profits. However, both hire managers and delegate to them their respective output decisions. The utility function of manager i closely replicates that appearing in the Holmström (1982) model illustrated in Chapter 1:

$$U_i = M_i - \frac{b\alpha_i^2}{2} \tag{3.3}$$

In (3.3), $M_i = \theta_i \pi_i + (1 - \theta_i) p q_i$ is managerial remuneration, defined as in Fershtman and Judd (1987), while α_i is the *action* or *effort* produced by the manager and involving a convex cost; b is a positive parameter. The managerial input enters a linear technology delivering the final output, $q_i = \alpha_i + \varepsilon_i$, where ε_i is a random variable affecting managerial productivity; it is identically and independently distributed across firms, and has mean $\bar{\varepsilon}$ and variance ς^2. Manager i observes ε_i but not ε_j, while principals cannot observe actions and shocks, just outputs and consequently profits, consumer surplus and welfare. The resulting two-stage game is solved by backward induction, under simultaneous play in both stages.

The seemingly odd feature of the model, due to the assumption of managers being assigned a mix of profits and revenues, may indeed generate an explicit and twofold question in the reader's mind, as to (i) why the public sector should hire a manager at all and (ii) supposing it does, why managerial remuneration should coincide with that usually adopted by private firms. The answers will come in due course. For the moment, it suffices to observe that the choice of optimal output by manager i is independent of the ultimate goal (welfare or profits) of the firm hiring her/him. This manager has to solve

$$\max_{q_i} E(U_i) = \left[a - q_i - E(q_j(\varepsilon_j))\right] - \theta_i c q_i - \frac{b(q_i - \varepsilon_i)^2}{2} \tag{3.4}$$

in which E denotes the expected value (in this case, of the manager's utility and the rival's strategy), and expected utility has been written in terms of output levels. Skipping the details of the second stage, we can concentrate ourselves on the first stage, where the public firm chooses θ_{SW} to maximize $E(SW)$, while the private firm chooses θ_π to maximize expected profits, as usual. The meaning of subscripts is intuitive. This yields

$$\theta_{SW} = 1 - \frac{(a - c + b\bar{\varepsilon})\left[1 + b\left(5 + 4b + b^2\right)\right]}{c\left[1 + b\left(12 + 16b + 7b^2 + b^3\right)\right]}$$

$$\theta_\pi = 1 - \frac{(a - c + b\bar{\varepsilon})\,b\,(2 + b)}{c\left[1 + b\left(12 + 16b + 7b^2 + b^3\right)\right]} \tag{3.5}$$

and both are lower than one, with $1 > \theta_\pi > \theta_{SW}$. The resulting expected output levels at Nash equilibrium of the the second stage are then $E(q_{SW}^N) > E(q_\pi^N) > 0$. This implies the following.

Proposition 3.1 *Since* $1 > \theta_\pi > \theta_{SW}$, *both firms exploit the aggressiveness of managers to expand output.*

The private firm does so aiming at the acquisition of a dominant position (as usual); the public one adopts a similar stance to enhance consumer surplus and welfare. An interesting by-product of this mechanism, which is nothing but a struggle for market share although this is not made explicit in the public firm's intents, is that $E(\pi_{SW}^N) > E(\pi_\pi^N)$, i.e. the public firm's profits are higher than the private firm's, at equilibrium.

In the traditional approach, managers are absent, so the government chooses q_{SW} to maximize $E(SW)$ while the owners of the private firm choose q_π to maximize $E(\pi_\pi)$. Define the resulting expected output level of the industry as $E(\widehat{Q})$. Comparing it with the expected output $E(Q^N)$ attained in the previous case, we have $E(\widehat{Q}) > E(Q^N)$. This fact notwithstanding, $E(SW^N) > E(\widehat{SW})$.

Proposition 3.2 *The expected social welfare level arising when both firms hire managers is higher than the corresponding expected social welfare generated in absence of managers.*

This apparently counterintuitive result depends on the fact that managers dislike costly efforts, as we know from (3.3), or, equivalently, that managerial efforts add up to cq_i in the total cost function. Therefore, it is surely true that the passage from $E(\widehat{Q})$ to $E(Q^N)$ implies a loss in terms of allocative efficiency, which in itself would make us expect a welfare reduction as soon as firms become managerial. However, there is a countervailing factor connected with productive efficiency, since

$$E(\widehat{q}_{SW}) > E(q_{SW}^N)$$
$$E(\widehat{q}_\pi) < E(q_\pi^N)$$

(3.6)

and the balance between these two effects speaks in favour of the fully managerialized industry, as far as expected welfare is concerned. This also implies that the public sector should not privatize its firm, as this would hinder the expected value of social welfare.

To conclude the exposition of Barros (1995), a last remark is in order. To be completely honest, one has to stress that the welfare increase induced by productive efficiency materializes through an increase in producer surplus (profits), more than offsetting the loss in consumer surplus certainly brought about by $E(Q^N) < E(\widehat{Q})$. In a general equilibrium perspective, this would call for an income redistribution policy, in the form of a corporate income tax to be redistributed to consumers. This perspective is neither explicitly mentioned nor modelled in Barros (1995), but would represent an obvious answer to any objections raised about the source of the welfare increment engendered by managerialization.

3.2 Strategic delegation without agency issues

What Barros (1994, 1995) shows is that managers can be useful tools in the hand of the public sector in presence of a proper agency relationship under asymmetric information. Can we say the same under full information, ruling out moral hazard and agency problems? The first to provide a positive answer to this question was White (2001) who adopted the Cournot setup illustrated at the outcome of the chapter, with a slight modification consisting of assuming X-inefficiency *à la* Leibenstein (1966) in the public firm, whose marginal cost is $c_{SW} \in (c, a)$, while the remaining $n - 1$ Cournot profit-seeking firms share the same marginal cost c.

Using this variation on the initial theme, White (2001) showed that, at the subgame perfect equilibrium, social welfare is higher when all firms are managerial – again using incentives *à la* Fershtman and Judd (1987) – with the public firm's output level falling as c_{SW} increases.[1] Yet, if the separation between ownership and control is modelled, making the game a three-stage one, the public firm chooses not to go managerial and does not produce at all, its very presence being sufficient to regulate the rest of the industry made up by $n - 1$ managerial firms.

White (2001) also proved that, in such a case, it is socially efficient not to privatize or shut down the public enterprise.

White's (2001) conclusions could well have put an end to the literature discussing the role of public firms as regulatory instruments in mixed oligopolies back in 2001. Yet, things didn't go this way, the point being that quantity may not be used as a strategic variable, in presence of a single public firm – at least, not by all firms alike. To become aware of this fact and its bearings on the organizational structure of firms as well as the welfare performance of the mixed industry, we had to wait for Bárcena-Ruiz (2009) and, especially, Chirco *et al.* (2014).

In the remainder, I will expose a synthesis of the results attained in the latter contribution, encompassing the model by Bárcena-Ruiz (2009) as a special case and combining the approach of White (2001) with the idea – exposed in Chapter 2 – that the choice of the market variable and the design of internal organization may indeed be connected, as in Lambertini (2000a,b).

Chirco *et al.* (2014) focused on a mixed duopoly in which the representative consumer has a taste for variety as in Singh and Vives (1984), so that the inverse demand function for product i is

$$p_i = a - q_i - \sigma q_j \tag{3.7}$$

with $i, j = 12, i \neq j$ and $\sigma \in (0, 1)$. The case of perfect substitutes is ruled out as, trivially, it replicates the results in White (2001).

Firm 1 is public and maximizes social welfare:

$$SW = \pi_1 + \pi_2 + U(q_1, q_2) - p_1 q_1 - p_2 q_2 \tag{3.8}$$

where

$$U(q_1, q_2) = a(q_1 + q_2) - \frac{\left(q_1^2 + q_2^2 + 2q_1 q_2\right)}{2} \tag{3.9}$$

is the representative consumer's utility function. Firm 2 is a profit-maximizing firm. With the same constant marginal cost c for both firms, the profit function of i is $\pi_i = (p_i - c)q_i$. Given the linearity of cost functions, social welfare simply writes $SW = U(q_1, q_2) - c(q_1 + q_2)$. If a firm hires a manager, the remuneration of the latter is based on Fershtman and Judd's (1987) function $M_i = \theta_i \pi_i + (1 - \theta_i) p_i q_i$.

To this regard, a few words are necessary to sweep away any legitimate doubt as to why a public firm interested in social welfare should decide to compensate a manager with a mix of profits and revenues. As shown in White (2002) and Benassi *et al.* (2014), the specification of the managerial objective selected by a firm (in particular, but not exclusively, a public enterprise) may well be irrelevant because what matters is finely tuning the contractual variable (θ_i, in the present case) at the delegation stage. Note that this has been neatly pointed out by Berr (2011) in the domain of games played by private firms, as stressed in Chapter 2.

Chirco *et al.* (2014) stipulated that the choice of output or price levels are delegated to managers while the choice of the strategic variable to be delegated, together with the optimal design of managerial contracts, remains in the hands of the ownership (or the public sector, as far as the public firm is concerned). Then, a four-stage game is envisaged,[2] in which (i) the first stage models the choice between quantity and price as the relevant market variable; (ii) the second is for the choice between delegating or not; (iii) the third stage investigates the optimal extent of delegation; (iv) the fourth describes market competition. Every stage takes place under non-cooperative and simultaneous play, with complete, symmetric and imperfect information, while information is perfect between any two adjacent stages.

This gives rise to sixteen market subgames, for all possible combinations among price, quantity and the presence or absence of managers. Four of these subgames are clearly known from previous literature and are those in which managers are not hired and the owner of the private firm competes with the public sector controlling its own firm, both using either a price or a quantity strategy. This case is not reported in Chirco *et al.* (2014), since it is the topic of Matsumura and Ogawa (2012), who demonstrated that both firms choose to be price-setters.

If only one firm delegates control to a manager while the other does not, the choice of market variable is summarized in.

Proposition 3.3 *If only the public firm hires a manager, then it finds it optimal to be a price-setter, while the private firm is indifferent between p and q. If only the private firm hires a manager, then it also chooses to be a price-setter and again the rival (this time, public) is indifferent between p and q.*

The intuition for this result (in particular, for the indifference of the rival) dates back to Klemperer and Meyer (1986): under full information, once a firm expects the other to set a price or a quantity, it becomes aware of choosing as a monopolist along a residual demand curve, and therefore it *must* be indifferent between p and q.

The remaining and intriguing case is that in which both entities are managerial, as here we have

$$SW_{pp}(D, D) > SW_{qp}(D, D) > SW_{qq}(D, D) > SW_{pq}(D, D) \qquad (3.10)$$

for the public firm, and

$$\pi_{pq}(D, D) > \pi_{pp}(D, D) > \pi_{qp}(D, D) > \pi_{qq}(D, D) \qquad (3.11)$$

for the private one. In (3.10)–(3.11), the subscript consistently reveals the market variable set by the public and the private firm, in such a way that if the public (respectively, private) firm is a price (respectively, quantity) setter, the resulting welfare and profit levels are $SW_{pq}(D, D)$ and $\pi_{pq}(D, D)$.

The sequences of inequalities appearing in (3.10)–(3.11) reveal that the private firm has a strict incentive to deviate from any symmetric outcome, while the public firm has an analogous incentive to deviate from asymmetric outcomes. This implies the following.

Proposition 3.4 *If both firms are managerial, the choice between price and quantity has no pure-strategy equilibrium.*

This result is somewhat puzzling, as one should come to terms with the need to characterize the mixed strategy equilibrium, being aware at the same time of the difficulties of interpreting it, as in fact mixed strategies must collapse into pure ones when the time comes, at which both firms are required to write a contract (if any) and then act on the market. Another thing to note (not underlined in the paper) is that the above proposition entails that there exists no subgame perfect equilibrium profile in pure strategies either, because mixed ones are called for in one of the stages.

The solution to this conundrum comes from the analysis of the delegation choices, for any given combination of market variables initially selected by owners. This exercise offers the following set of insights:

- if both firms are quantity-setters, then the private firm hires a manager while the public one does not;
- if both firms are price-setters, then both of them hire a manager, this being the result obtained by Bárcena-Ruiz (2009);
- if the public firm is a quantity-setter and the private firm is a price-setter, then again both of them separate control from ownership;
- if the public firm is a price-setter and the private firm is a quantity-setter, then the private firm hires a manager while the public one does not.

Now, putting things together, all of this implies what appears in the following.

Proposition 3.5 *At the subgame perfect equilibrium of the four-stage game, both firms choose to be price-setters and to become managerial.*

The intuitive proof relies on the examination of Matrix 3.1, which portrays the first stage of the game.

$$j$$

		q	p
1	q	$SW_{qq}(ND, D)$; $\pi_{qq}(ND, D)$	$SW_{qp}(D, D)$; $\pi_{qp}(D, D)$
	p	$SW_{pq}(ND, D)$; $\pi_{pq}(ND, D)$	$SW_{pp}(D, D)$; $\pi_{pp}(D, D)$

Matrix 3.1

Since $SW_{pq}(ND, D) > SW_{qq}(ND, D)$ and $SW_{pp}(D, D) > SW_{qp}(D, D)$, the public firm prefers to be a price-setter. Likewise, $\pi_{pq}(ND, D) > \pi_{qq}(ND, D)$ and

$\pi_{pp}(D, D) > \pi_{qp}(D, D)$. Hence, (p, p) is indeed the unique equilibrium at the intersection of strictly dominant strategies. This, implicitly, also serves the purpose of dealing with the issue raised above concerning the lack of a pure-strategy equilibrium when both firms are managerial.

In a nutshell, the analysis carried out by Chirco *et al.* (2014) generates the result obtained by Bárcena-Ruiz (2009) as the subgame perfect equilibrium of a full-fledged game in which firms strategically choose both the market variable and their own internal structure. While it appears natural that a public firm chooses to be a price player, because price competition has an inherently competitive nature and serves the purpose of increasing welfare, what is not a priori obvious here is that strategic interaction at the first stage induces the private firm to become a price player as well.

3.3 Delegation and tax policy

A completely different approach to managerialization in mixed markets was proposed by Anant *et al.* (1995) and Basu *et al.* (1997). These authors modelled a monopolistic industry where a private firm confronts itself with a policy maker using an ad valorem taxation policy to generate a revenue. The scope of the model is twofold, as it shows that (i) delegation may be adopted on both sides (in particular, by the private firm, its monopolistic power notwithstanding) and (ii) the bilateral delegation scenario is more inefficient than that where no managers are hired.

Here, the firm is a price-setter, and the market demand function is $q = a - p$. Production takes place at constant returns to scale, with an average and marginal cost $c \in (0, a)$. The instrument manoeuvred by the government is an *ad valorem tax* rate τ. In the baseline game, there is no delegation and the firm maximizes profits

$$\pi = (p - c)\left[a - p(1 + \tau)\right] \tag{3.12}$$

with respect to p, while the policy maker maximizes the tax revenue

$$R = \tau p\left[a - p(1 + \tau)\right] \tag{3.13}$$

The Nash equilibrium of this game is unique, at

$$p^{N} = \frac{c + \sqrt{c(8a + c)}}{4} > c \tag{3.14}$$

$$\tau^{N} = \frac{1}{4}\left(\sqrt{\frac{c(8a + c)}{c}} - 3\right) > 0 \tag{3.15}$$

and the associated equilibrium output is

$$q^{N} = \frac{4a - c - \sqrt{c(8a + c)}}{4} > 0 \tag{3.16}$$

for all $c \in (0, a)$. The equilibrium policy is indeed a tax and the firm is viable, as its output is everywhere positive (and the profit is positive, too).

Now suppose the firm's owner and the policy maker hire managers, with incentives based on Fershtman and Judd (1987) and Sklivas (1987). The manager of the firm must choose price in order to maximize a combination of profits and revenues:

$$M_\pi = \theta_\pi \pi + (1 - \theta_\pi) p \left[a - p (1 + \tau) \right] \tag{3.17}$$

while the manager hired by the public sector is a bureaucrat instructed to choose τ so as to maximize a combination of tax revenues and the firm's revenues,

$$M_R = \theta_R R + (1 - \theta_R) p \left[a - p (1 + \tau) \right]$$

perhaps due to lobbying pressure. The resulting game has the usual two-stage structure, with p and τ being set downstream, after the optimal contractual design has been worked out upstream. In both stages players behave non-cooperatively and simultaneously, under full information. The explicit analytical solution remains out of reach as first- and second-order conditions are cumbersome. However, the qualitative analysis in Anant *et al.* (1995) and Basu *et al.* (1997) shows that, at the subgame perfect equilibrium, $\theta_\pi^N > 1$ because owners strive to protect their profits, and $\theta_R^N > 1$ as well because the policy maker wants to force its bureaucrat to expand tax revenues. The outcome of increasing pressure on both sides is that the equilibrium output under bilateral delegation drops below the level (3.16) emerging without delegation. This implies the main conclusion, according to which bilateral managerialization aggravates the inefficiency traditionally associated with monopoly power.

Further reading

Exhaustive surveys on mixed oligopolies and privatization can be found in De Fraja and Delbono (1990) and De Fraja (2009), and in Vickers and Yarrow (1991), respectively. For a general overview of the discussion about public enterprises in their heydays, see Bös (1986) and Parris *et al.* (1987). Mixed markets may involve firms maximizing several other objectives, arbitrarily different from profits and welfare (see Matsumura, 1998; Wang *et al.*, 2009). An interesting and detailed analysis of strategic delegation in consumer cooperatives can be found in Kopel and Marini (2014). Even without using managers, the presence of a public firm may prevent the rise of implicit collusion, as shown in Delbono and Lambertini (2016). The impact of managerial remuneration based upon comparative performance *à la* Salas Fumas (1992) and Miller and Pazgal (2001) in a mixed duopoly is in Nakamura (2015). Delegation and privatization in a mixed duopoly with intraindustry trade is the subject matter of Chang (2007). The interplay between endogenous timing and managerialization in a mixed duopoly is in Nakamura and Inoue (2009), where the Bertrand game with simultaneous moves illustrated in Bárcena-Ruiz (2009) and Chirco *et al.* (2014) obtains as the subgame perfect equilibrium of an extended game with observable delay *à la* Hamilton and Slutsky (1990).

Notes

1 Conversely, should c_{sw} be equal or lower than c, then all of the output would be produced by the public firm, driving price to c_{sw}, as in the early literature on this subject.
2 Chirco *et al.* (2014, p. 525) say '... we shall solve by backward induction the following three stage game', and then add that three mutually exclusive cases may arise at the second: only the public (respectively, private) firm delegates, or both do. Obviously, this amounts to saying that the structure is a four-stage one, which becomes evident in their Section 4.2 (Chirco *et al.*, 2014, pp. 540–1).

References

Anant, T.C.A., K. Basu and B. Mukherji (1995), 'A Model of Monopoly with Strategic Government Intervention', *Journal of Public Economics*, **57**, 25–43.

Bárcena-Ruiz, J.C. (2009), 'The Decision to Hire Managers in Mixed Markets under Bertrand Competition', *Japanese Economic Review*, **60**, 376–88.

Barros, F. (1994), 'Delegation and Efficiency in a Mixed Oligopoly', *Annales d'Économie et de Statistique*, **33**, 51–72.

Barros, F. (1995), 'Incentive Schemes as Strategic Variables: An Application to a Mixed Duopoly', *International Journal of Industrial Organization*, **13**, 373–86.

Basu, K., A. Ghosh and T. Ray (1997), 'The Babu and the Boxwallah: Managerial Incentives and Government Intervention in a Developing Economy', *Review of Development Economics*, **1**, 71–80.

Beato, P. and A. Mas-Colell (1984), 'The Marginal Cost Pricing as a Regulation Mechanism in Mixed Markets', in M. Marchand, P. Pestieau and H. Tulkens (eds), *The Performance of Public Enterprises*, Amsterdam, North-Holland.

Benassi, C., A. Chirco and M. Scrimitore (2014), 'Optimal Manipulation Rules in a Mixed Duopoly', *Journal of Economics*, **112**, 61–84.

Berr, F. (2011), 'Stackelberg Equilibria in Managerial Delegation Games', *European Journal of Operational Research*, **212**, 251–62.

Bös, D. (1986), *Public Enterprise Economics*, Amsterdam, North-Holland.

Bös, D. (1991), *Privatization: A Theoretical Treatment*, Oxford, Clarendon Press.

Chang, W. (2007), 'Optimal Trade, Industrial, and Privatization Policies in a Mixed Duopoly with Strategic Managerial Incentives', *Journal of International Trade and Economic Development*, **16**, 31–52.

Chirco, A., C. Colombo and M. Scrimitore (2014), 'Organizational Structure and the Choice of Price versus Quantity in a Mixed Duopoly', *Japanese Economic Review*, **65**, 521–42.

Cremer, H., M. Marchand and J.-F. Thisse (1989), 'The Public Firm as an Instrument for Regulating an Oligopolistic Market', *Oxford Economic Papers*, **41**, 283–301.

De Fraja, G. (2009), 'Mixed Oligopoly: Old and New', Working Paper no. 09/20, Department of Economics, University of Leicester.

De Fraja, G. and F. Delbono (1989), 'Alternative Strategies of a Public Enterprise in Oligopoly', *Oxford Economic Papers*, **41**, 302–11.

De Fraja, G. and F. Delbono (1990), 'Game Theoretic Models of Mixed Oligopoly', *Journal of Economic Surveys*, **4**, 1–17.

Delbono, F. and L. Lambertini (2016), 'Nationalization as a Credible Threat against Collusion', *Journal of Industry, Competition and Trade*, **16**, 127–36.

Fershtman, C. and K. Judd (1987), 'Equilibrium Incentives in Oligopoly', *American Economic Review*, **77**, 927–40.

Hagen, K.P. (1979), 'Optimal Pricing in Public Firms in an Imperfect Market Economy', *Scandinavian Journal of Economics*, **81**, 475–93.

Hamilton, J. and S. Slutsky (1990), 'Endogenous Timing in Duopoly Games: Stackelberg or Cournot Equilibria', *Games and Economic Behavior*, **2**, 29–46.

Harris, R.G. and E.G. Wiens (1980), 'Government Enterprise: An Instrument for the Internal Regulation of Industry', *Canadian Journal of Economics*, **13**, 125–32.

Holmström, B. (1982), 'Moral Hazard in Teams', *Bell Journal of Economics*, **13**, 324–40.

Klemperer, P. and M. Meyer (1986), 'Price Competition vs Quantity Competition: The Role of Uncertainty', *RAND Journal of Economics*, **17**, 618–38.

Kopel, M. and M. Marini (2014), 'Strategic Delegation in Consumer Cooperatives under Mixed Oligopoly', *Journal of Economics*, **113**, 275–96.

Lambertini, L. (2000a), 'Strategic Delegation and the Shape of Market Competition', *Scottish Journal of Political Economy*, **47**, 550–70.

Lambertini, L. (2000b), 'Extended Games Played by Managerial Firms', *Japanese Economic Review*, **51**, 274–83.

Leibenstein, H. (1966), 'Allocative Efficiency versus X-Efficiency', *American Economic Review*, **56**, 392–415.

Matsumura, T. (1998), 'Partial Privatization in Mixed Duopoly', *Journal of Public Economics*, **70**, 473–83.

Matsumura, T. and A. Ogawa (2012), 'Price versus Quantity in a Mixed Duopoly', *Economics Letters*, **116**, 174–77.

Merrill, W.C. and N. Schneider (1966), 'Government Firms in Oligopoly Industries: A Short-Run Analysis', *Quarterly Journal of Economics*, **80**, 400–12.

Miller, N.H. and A.I. Pazgal (2001), 'The Equivalence of Price and Quantity Competition with Delegation', *RAND Journal of Economics*, **32**, 284–301.

Nakamura, Y. (2015), 'Price versus Quantity in a Mixed Duopoly: The Case of Relative Profit Maximization', *Economic Modelling*, **44**, 37–43.

Nakamura, Y. and T. Inoue (2009), 'Endogenous Timing in a Mixed Duopoly: Price Competition with Managerial Delegation', *Managerial and Decision Economics*, **30**, 325–33.

Parris, H., P. Pestieau and P. Saynor (1987), *Public Enterprise in Western Europe*, London, Croom Helm.

Rees, R. (1984), 'The Public Enterprise Game', *Economic Journal* (Conference Papers), **94**, 109–23.

Salas Fumas, V. (1992), 'Relative Performance Evaluation of Management: The Effects on Industrial Competition and Risk Sharing', *International Journal of Industrial Organization*, **10**, 473–89.

Singh, N. and X. Vives (1984), 'Price and Quantity Competition in a Differentiated Duopoly', *RAND Journal of Economics*, **15**, 546–54.

Sklivas, S.D. (1987), 'The Strategic Choice of Managerial Incentives', *RAND Journal of Economics*, **18**, 452–8.

Vickers, J. (1985), 'Delegation and the Theory of the Firm', *Economic Journal*, **95** (Conference Papers), 138–47.

Vickers, J. and G.K. Yarrow (1988), *Privatization: An Economic Analysis*, Cambridge, MA, MIT Press.

Vickers, J. and G.K. Yarrow (1991), 'Economic Perspectives on Privatization', *Journal of Economic Perspectives*, **5**, 111–32.

Wang, L.F.S., Y.-C.Wang and L. Zhao (2009), 'Managerial Delegation and Partial Privatization in General Equilibrium with Sector-Specific Unemployment', *International Review of Economics*, **56**, 393–9.

White, M.D. (2001), 'Managerial Incentives and the Decision to Hire Managers in Markets with Public and Private Firms', *European Journal of Political Economy*, **17**, 877–96.

White M.D. (2002), 'Political Manipulation of a Public Firm's Objective Function', *Journal of Economic Behavior and Organization*, **49**, 487–99.

4 Collusive behaviour and horizontal mergers

Cartel behaviour and mergers (or acquisitions), together with several other forms of anti-competitive behaviour, such as the abuse of dominant position, are the core objects of the attention of anti-trust laws and agencies since the adoption of the Sherman Act in the USA, in 1890.[1]

The rise of implicit collusion in repeated games has received a large amount of attention in oligopoly theory, entering textbooks very early in the development of the theory of Industrial Organization (see, e.g., Friedman, 1977; and Tirole, 1988). The main body of this subset of the IO literature deals with implicit cartel behaviour, either in prices or in quantities, among firms interested in increasing profits as compared to those generated by the Nash equilibrium of the one-shot game. Its main focus has been the effect of cartel size and product differentiation on the stability of implicit collusion, and the relative stability of cartels setting prices or quantities, at least since Deneckere (1983) and Majerus (1988).

Simultaneously, IO has also consistently investigated horizontal merger incentives under Cournot and Bertrand competition alike, again measuring incentives through profits generated by entrepreneurial firms. In both cases, the underlying idea is that these strategies lessen the degree of competition and therefore are keen to generate systematic welfare damages.

All of this leaves managers out of the picture, while casual observation as well as anti-trust cases demonstrate that managers and their incentives do play a relevant role in shaping both types of behaviour. So, the twofold question arises as to whether, and how, collusion and mergers may be influenced by the presence of managers interested in the maximization of objective functions combining profits with some other magnitude possibly negatively related to profits themselves.

4.1 Stock-based compensation and collusion

The first author to illustrate the possibility of replicating collusive outcomes through the adoption of managerial incentives based on stock (in particular, stock options) was Reitman (1993), who relied on a modified version of the model used by Fershtman and Judd (1987) and Sklivas (1987). The idea is that, since stock prices reflect future discounted profit flows, managers holding stock or stock options will be rewarded by any increase in their firms' profitability. That is, in

Reitman (1993) future matters but the quasi-collusive outcome is not generated by a repeated game.

Suppose that the delegation contract establishes that the reward to a manager is the difference between the stock price and a strike price, provided the latter is positive. This happens when profits are themselves above a given strike level $\overline{\pi}_i$, chosen by the owner together with α_i. Accordingly, the objective function of manager i is

$$M_i = \alpha_i (\pi_i - \overline{\pi}_i) + (1 - \alpha_i) p q_i \tag{4.1}$$

which coincides with Fershtman and Judd (1987) if $\overline{\pi}_i = 0$. The presence of stock options and the strike level of profits makes the managerial objective function not quasi-concave, with a discontinuity appearing in the reaction function at the market stage, as represented in Figure 4.1. Such a discontinuity pops up in correspondence with the rival's quantity at which the manager of firm i switches from (4.1) to pure sales maximization, because the increase in the rival's output has eroded the value of the stock option to such an extent that the manager of firm i finds it convenient to forgo the stock option altogether and just expand sales revenues as much as possible. The map of best replies at the market stage is presented in Figure 4.1, where the relevant functions are drawn as thick lines. This situation is one in which the equilibrium is identified by point E, where both firms' managers have their respective options *in the money*.

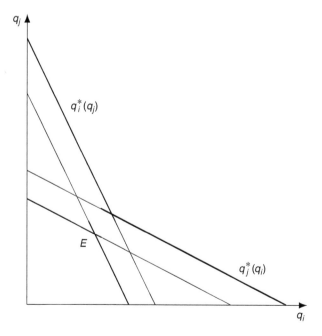

Figure 4.1 Stock options and quasi-collusion.

The intuition behind the restraint posed by the presence of stock options upon the typical aggressiveness of managers we are used to observing in strategic delegation models lies in the fact that, indeed, a manager's options are in the money as long as the rival does not expand output too much. As a result, best replies become discontinuous and the output restriction prevails, to such an extent that industry production may indeed fall down to the pure monopoly output. Hence, the use of stock options in delegation contracts allows owners to generate the equivalent of a collusive outcome which would alternatively require either an explicit or an implicit agreement. The sustainability of an equilibrium of this nature hinges upon the threat of switching to sales maximization, but no repeated game structure is explicitly invoked in this model, although Reitman (1993, pp. 520–1) alluded to it without developing this argument.

The connection between the stock option ingredient in managerial compensation and the sustainability of implicit collusion in supergames is made explicit in Spagnolo (2000). The layout of his model is as follows. Firms are managerial and delegation contracts are linked to stock prices, i.e. managerial compensation is based on stock or stock options. Managers are allowed to sell shares or options as soon as they receive them. Time is discrete and the horizon is infinite, with $t = 0, 1, 2, 3 \ldots \infty$. All agents share the same intertemporal preferences measured by the discount factor $\delta \in [0, 1]$. At any time t, the market evaluates a share of firm i on the basis of the current and future discounted profit flow of the same firm, so that – before dividends are paid to stockholders – the market price of a single share of firm i is

$$p_{it}^s = \frac{\pi_{it} + \sum_{\tau=t+1}^{\infty} \delta^\tau \pi_{i\tau}}{v_i} \tag{4.2}$$

where v_i is the number of shares issued by firm i.

The supergame follows the rules of Friedman (1971), collusion being sustained by grim trigger strategies. Suppose for a moment that firms are entrepreneurial units. Hence, letting π_i^C and π_i^D identify the highest collusive profits attainable given time preferences and the deviation profits, respectively, the discount factor δ must satisfy the following inequality:

$$\frac{\pi_i^C}{1-\delta} \geq \pi_i^D + \frac{\delta \pi_i^N}{1-\delta} \tag{4.3}$$

with the second term of the right-hand side of the above condition measuring the discounted profit flow associated with the reversion to the everlasting Nash punishment after any deviation from the collusive path. Solving (4.3) with respect to δ, the stability of implicit collusion requires

$$\delta \geq \frac{\pi_i^D - \pi_i^C}{\pi_i^D - \pi_i^N} \equiv \delta_g \in (0, 1) \tag{4.4}$$

in which the subscript g mnemonics for the use of grim trigger strategies.[2]

Here I will illustrate in some detail a single case presented by Spagnolo (2000, pp. 27–8). Assume the incentive contract offered to the manager of firm i establishes that managerial compensation is a function $M_i = f(p_{it}^s)$, which is monotone and strictly increasing in p_{it}^s. The compensation is paid to the manager in period t prior to the distribution of dividends to stockholders. Accordingly, if one can disregard the impact of managerial compensation on stock prices – which makes sense if compensation is low enough – condition (4.3) for the manager of firm i writes

$$\frac{1}{1-\delta} f\left(\frac{\pi_i^C}{v_i(1-\delta)}\right) \geq f\left(\frac{1}{v_i}\left(\pi_i^D + \frac{\delta\pi_i^N}{1-\delta}\right)\right) + \frac{\delta}{1-\delta} f\left(\frac{\pi_i^N}{v_i(1-\delta)}\right)$$

(4.5)

where managerial payoffs replace the pure profits appearing in (4.3), in each phase of the supergame. In particular, it is worth noting that the deviation payoff

$$f\left(\frac{1}{v_i}\left(\pi_i^D + \frac{\delta\pi_i^N}{1-\delta}\right)\right)$$

(4.6)

incorporates the future impact of profits during the Nash punishment, whereby every single manager anticipates that a deviation from the cartel path triggering the Nash reversion will be discounted into the compensation package in the very same deviation period. Therefore, condition (4.5) and the characteristics of (4.6) jointly lead to the following implication.

Proposition 4.1 *Stock-based managerial compensation makes any given level of collusion easier to sustain than under pure profit-maximizing behaviour. Or, equivalently, it expands the set of sustainable collusive paths for any given level of time discounting.*

The intuition is that managerial incentives based on the stock price, which in turn depends on the future profit path, make managers more sensitive to the future performance of their firms (as also stressed by Holmström and Tirole, 1993), and therefore more keen on colluding than they would be if these intertemporal considerations did not enter explicitly in their remuneration schemes.

Qualitatively the same conclusion applies if the managerial compensation package (i) is 'large' enough to exert a non-negligible impact on the market price of a firm's stock (Spagnolo, 2000, pp. 28–30) or (ii) is based on stock options. In the latter case, the manager is granted the right to buy a time-invariant number of options n_i in each period, at a predetermined price p_i, also time invariant. This happens in every period, prior to the distribution of dividends. The relevant managerial payoffs in the three phases of the supergame unravelling under grim trigger strategies become

$$\max\left\{n_i\left(\frac{\pi_i^C}{v_i(1-\delta)} - p_i, 0\right)\right\}$$

(4.7)

along the collusive path,

$$\max\left\{ n_i \left[\frac{1}{\nu_i} \left(\pi_i^D + \frac{\delta \pi_i^N}{1-\delta} \right) - p_i, 0 \right] \right\} \tag{4.8}$$

in the deviation period and

$$\max\left\{ n_i \left(\frac{\delta \pi_i^N}{\nu_i (1-\delta)} - p_i, 0 \right) \right\} \tag{4.9}$$

along the reversion to the Nash equilibrium of the constituent game. Then, it suffices to rewrite the above proposition changing the *incipit* from 'stock-based' to 'stock option-based', leaving the remainder as well as the intuition unmodified.

Spagnolo (2005) extended the analysis to price competition, with a few variations. In particular, he introduced into the model a relevant additional feature, whereby firms are averse to profits' variance. Then, the adoption of long-term profit-sharing contracts for managers and the latter have a preference for income-smoothing, managerialization makes it possible to sustain any given level of collusion at lower discount factors. Additionally, (i) the critical level of the discount factor above which collusion is sustainable is decreasing in the aversion to profit variance and (ii) the effect of income smoothing may neutralize the counter-cyclical behaviour of prices under stochastic demand highlighted by Rotemberg and Saloner (1986).

4.2 Output-based compensation and collusion

The Vickers (1985) model is an obvious candidate to be used for the analysis of the stability of implicit collusion among managerial firms. This is the topic of Lambertini and Trombetta (2002), where the original homogeneous Cournot layout is considered, and three alternative scenarios are investigated under the assumption that only two firms are present. If managers have been hired:

- implicit collusion in output levels may arise at the market stage (i.e. between managers), while owners are assumed to set delegation contracts in a strictly non-cooperative way;
- Cournot–Nash behaviour prevails at the market stage, while owners try to collude at the contract stage;
- both owners and managers try to stabilize collusion in their respective strategy spaces.

The supergame follows Friedman's (1971) grim trigger strategies, and firms are supposed to maximize the joint payoff if they collude. As a first step, we may write the stability condition (4.3) for the Cournot supergame played by two profit-seeking firms:

$$\frac{\pi^M}{2(1-\delta)} \geq \pi^D + \frac{\delta\pi^{CN}}{1-\delta} \tag{4.10}$$

where $\pi^M = (a-c)^2/4$ is the pure monopoly profit, $\pi^{CN} = (a-c)^2/9$ is the Cournot–Nash equilibrium profit and $\pi^D = 9(a-c)^2/64$ is the unilateral deviation profit. As a result, inequality (4.10) establishes that implicit collusion along the frontier of industry profits is perpetually sustainable for all $\delta \geq \delta_{mg} = 9/17$, where subscript mg indicates that this is the critical threshold of the discount factor which is relevant for the stability of collusion between managers using grim trigger strategies.

Now imagine what happens in the infinite repetition of the market subgame if both firms are managerial, with each manager being given an incentive $M_i = \pi_i + \theta_i q_i$, and owners non-cooperatively set variables θ_i at the outset of the supergame and never modify them thereafter. For instance they could write the delegation contracts having in mind that their managers will play the Cournot–Nash equilibrium forever. As long as the contracts are identical, i.e. $\theta_i = \theta_j = \theta$, the exact level of θ and the conjecture driving the owners' decision are both immaterial as to the stability of collusion in output levels, because, as we know from Chapter 2, this form of delegation is equivalent to a change (in particular, an increase) in market size $a - c$. Therefore, as long as contracts are symmetrically fixed at time zero, the separation between ownership and control has no effect whatsoever on the stability of implicit collusion in output levels in the market supergame. That is, as follows.

Proposition 4.2 *Under symmetric and time-invariant delegation contracts based on output levels, the impact of delegation on collusion is nought.*

Assessing the second perspective is a bit less straightforward. The behaviour of managers in any period t is summarized by the individual reaction function

$$\frac{\partial M_i}{\partial q_i} = \widehat{A}_i - 2q_i - q_j = 0 \tag{4.11}$$

in which $\widehat{A}_i = A + \theta_i = a - c + \theta_i$. Hence, the individual equilibrium output is

$$q_i^{CN}(m,m) = \frac{A + 2\theta_i - \theta_j}{3} \tag{4.12}$$

for any pair (θ_i, θ_j). As a result, the profit function of firm i is

$$\pi_i = \frac{\left(A + 2\theta_i - \theta_j\right)\left(A - \theta_i - \theta_j\right)}{9} \tag{4.13}$$

and the joint profit maximization requires $\theta_i + \theta_j = -A/2$. Since any asymmetric pair of contracts would generate the need of ex post side payments, Lambertini and Trombetta (2002, p. 365) restrict themselves to considering the symmetric strategy

$\theta^C = -A/4$, which generates full monopoly profits to be split evenly between owners.

The optimal unilateral deviation from θ^C being $\theta^D = 5A/16$, deviation profits are $\pi^D = 25A^2/128 > 9A^2/64$; deviation profits in the collusive ownership between the owners are higher than those appearing in the corresponding phase of the supergame between managers, which suggests that delegation may hinder the stability of collusion if the supergame takes place at the delegation stage. However, the Nash equilibrium profits $\pi^{CN} = 2A^2/25$ are lower than those we are accustomed to from textbook exercises with profit-maximizing firms. Hence, here delegation is more appealing but the Nash reversion is harsher, and therefore one has to use (4.4) to appreciate the balance between these two opposite effects. Doing so, one finds that the stability of collusion between owners requires

$$\delta \geq \frac{25}{41} \equiv \delta_{og} \tag{4.14}$$

where subscript og indicates that this is the critical threshold of the discount factor which is relevant for the stability of collusion between owners using grim trigger strategies. The comparison between δ_{mg} and δ_{og} proves the following.

Proposition 4.3 *Since $\delta_{og} > \delta_{mg}$, collusion at the contract stage with managers behaving non-cooperatively is more demanding than collusion at the market stage without managers or with managers being hired through a time-invariant delegation contract.*

Propositions 4.2–4.3 have a straightforward implication.

Corollary 4.1 *For all $\delta \in [\delta_{og} = 25/41, 1]$, firms can stabilize collusion along the frontier of monopoly profits forever.*

This happens because if at least one subset of the players involved (either owners or managers) meet the requirement posed by δ_{mg} or δ_{og} then firms locate themselves on the profit frontier of the industry using either the appropriate contracts or the appropriate output decisions. Obviously, if $\delta \in [\delta_{mg} = 9/17, 1]$, then both categories of players can collude, one form of collusion being redundant.

Now we can make one step back to revisit the 2×2 matrix summarizing the first stage of the game in Vickers (1985), to look at it from the standpoint of repeated games. Matrix 4.1 coincides with Matrix 2.1 in chapter 2.

		m	e
i	m	$\dfrac{2A^2}{25}; \dfrac{2A^2}{25}$	$\dfrac{A^2}{8}; \dfrac{A^2}{16}$
	e	$\dfrac{A^2}{16}; \dfrac{A^2}{8}$	$\dfrac{A^2}{9}; \dfrac{A^2}{9}$

j

Matrix 4.1

This being a prisoners' dilemma, the supergame structure we are examining can be used to let owners solve the dilemma in such a way that delegation never takes place and firms remain entrepreneurial units forever. This is possible iff

$$\delta \geq \frac{\pi\,(m, e) - \pi\,(e, e)}{\pi\,(m, e) - \pi\,(m, m)} \equiv \delta_{eg} = \frac{25}{81} \tag{4.15}$$

with subscript eg indicates that this is the critical threshold of the discount factor above which firms may remain entrepreneurial under grim trigger strategies. This result yields the following.

Proposition 4.4 *For all* $\delta \in [\delta_{eg} = 25/81, 1]$, *owners can avoid delegation to managers forever.*

This poses another problem to owners, though. Its nature may be easily appreciated by assessing what happens if firms don't become managerial: in this case, owners remain in control and, in order to collude and get 50% of the pure monopoly profits, they have to satisfy the condition $\delta > 9/17 = \delta_{mg}$, i.e. the same condition that managers should meet were they running these firms. In other words, contracts must not be used as a collusive instrument and δ_{og} has become irrelevant. Hence, solving the prisoners' dilemma necessarily means good news for owners, as it softens the requirement for collusive stability.

Summing up, the analysis carried out by Lambertini and Trombetta boils down to the following.

Theorem 1 *Spanning the admissible range of time discounting, four relevant intervals of the discount factor δ emerge.*

1. *For all* $\delta \in [0, \delta_{eg})$, *no category is able to collude and owners cannot avoid delegating control to managers. Hence, the subgame perfect equilibrium replicates the one-shot game in Vickers (1985), with per-period individual profits* $\pi\,(m, m) = 2A^2/25$.
2. *For all* $\delta \in [\delta_{eg}, \delta_{mg})$, *no category is able to collude, but owners can avoid delegating control to managers. Hence, the subgame perfect equilibrium is the Cournot–Nash equilibrium between entrepreneurial firms, with per-period individual profits* $\pi\,(e, e) = A^2/9$.
3. *For all* $\delta \in [\delta_{mg}, \delta_{og})$, *managers can collude while owners are able to do so if and only if they do not hire managers. Hence, the separation between ownership and control does not take place and the outcome is a cartel, with per-period individual profits* $\pi\,(e, e) = A^2/8$.
4. *For all* $\delta \in [\delta_{og}, 1]$, *both categories are able to collude and owners can avoid delegating control to managers. Hence, the outcome is a cartel, with per-period individual profits* $\pi\,(m, m) = \pi\,(e, e) = A^2/8$.

The last claim in the above theorem can be further spelled out as follows. Since owners can (i) avoid delegation and (ii) collude themselves in output levels, as well as (iii) delegate control to managers who are able to collude in outputs or just (iv) collude at the contract stage, then one could label Theorem 4.1.4 as the 'Nirvana' of strategic delegation in supergames.

Theorem 4.1 has an implication concerning the delegation decision, which appears to be non-monotone with respect to time preferences: delegation is necessarily observed for all $\delta \in [0, \delta_{eg})$, and then, it is not adopted for all $\delta \in [\delta_{eg}, \delta_{og})$, to possibly appear again for all $\delta \in [\delta_{og}, 1]$.

4.2.1   Extension: partial collusion with grim trigger strategies or optimal punishment

To conclude the discussion about the impact of delegation on implicitly collusive behavior, I would like to draw your attention once again to the fact that, under fully symmetric delegation, the critical threshold $\delta_{mg} = 9/17$ is observationally equivalent to that characterizing the supergame between entrepreneurial firms under the same demand and cost conditions. Shall we take the associated interpretation that delegation has no impact on the sustainability of collusion at face value? Does it extend to any possible collusive target?

The second – and more explicit – question is indeed a crucial one, as there exist infinitely many profit levels between the fully non-cooperative one and the monopoly performance. More explicitly, is it necessarily the case that if time preferences fall short of the fully collusive requirement then firms will play the Nash equilibrium of the constituent game forever? The answer is no, as we already know from the analysis carried out by Spagnolo (2000, 2005), and the same partially collusive perspective can also be investigated in the cornerstone model of Vickers (1985), invoking once again its basic feature whereby the managerial objective function is equivalent to the profit function of a similar firm endowed with a more efficient technology.

Suppose, once again, that owners write delegation contracts symmetrically at the outset of the supergame. If $\theta_i = \theta_j = \theta > 0$, the Cournot–Nash equilibrium output is $q^{CN}(e, e) = (A + \theta)/3$, while the fully collusive output is $q^C(e, e) = (A + \theta)/4$.

The following exercise can be executed using the Nash reversion as in Friedman (1971) as well as the optimal one-shot stick-and-carrot punishment as in Abreu (1986, 1988).

Consider first the case of grim trigger strategies. The infinite replication of the latter strategy is sustainable iff $\delta \geq \delta_{mg}$. If this is not the case, then managers could pick the lowest

$$q^C \in \left(\frac{A + \theta}{4}, \frac{A + \theta}{3} \right) \tag{4.16}$$

which is compatible with $\delta \in (0, \delta_{mg})$. Of course, in the extreme (and unrealistic) circumstance in which $\delta = 0$, managers play the Cournot–Nash strategy in every period.

The partially collusive payoff is

$$M^C = \left(A - 2q^C + \theta\right) q^C \tag{4.17}$$

while a unilateral deviation from q^C yields

$$M^D\left(q^C\right) = \frac{\left(A - q^C + \theta\right)^2}{4} \tag{4.18}$$

Given θ, the Nash equilibrium payoff is $M^N = (A + \theta)^2/9$. Therefore, the stability condition is

$$\frac{M^C}{1 - \delta} \geq M^D\left(q^C\right) + \frac{\delta M^N}{1 - \delta} \Leftrightarrow \tag{4.19}$$

$$\frac{\left(A - 2q^C + \theta\right) q^C}{1 - \delta} \geq \frac{\left(A - q^C + \theta\right)^2}{4} + \frac{\delta\left(A + \theta\right)^2}{9\left(1 - \delta\right)}$$

which is satisfied by any

$$q^C \in \left[\frac{(9 - 5\delta)(A + \theta)}{3(9 - \delta)}, \frac{A + \theta}{3}\right) \tag{4.20}$$

The expression defining the lower bound of the interval in (4.20) is monotonically decreasing in δ and equals $q^C(e, e) = (A + \theta)/4$ at $\delta = 9/17$, while it equals $q^{CN}(e, e) = (A + \theta)/3$ at $\delta = 0$. However, its partial derivative with respect to θ is evidently positive, which entails that a Vickers-type delegation contract indeed hinders collusion stability in the output space for all positive values of θ.

This conclusion can be easily extended to the case of optimal punishments. From Abreu (1986), we know that a one-shot optimal (i.e. most efficient) stick-and-carrot punishment strategy does exist in the Cournot model with entrepreneurial firms. The analogy between this and the delegation based on output levels implies that it also exists if the supergame is played by Cournot managerial firms. The solution is more involved because (i) the collusive path must not be abandoned and (ii) the optimal penal code must be adopted, if need be. That is, since the optimal punishment differs from the Nash strategy prevailing in the constituent game (which, in itself, is obviously part of a subgame perfect equilibrium strategy profile), an additional condition must be satisfied in order for the act of adopting the punishment to be incentive compatible.

The stability of the collusive path requires

$$M^D\left(q^C\right) - M^C \leq \delta\left(M^C - M^{op}\right) \tag{4.21}$$

where M^{op} is the punishment payoff generated by the symmetric adoption of the unknown optimal punishment q^{op}:

$$M^{op} = \left(A - 2q^{op} + \theta\right) q^{op} \tag{4.22}$$

and the meaning of the superscript op is intuitive.

In turn, the incentive compatibility constraint which must be satisfied for firms to be willing to implement the punishment if any deviation from the collusive path takes place is

$$M^D(q^{op}) - M^{op} \leq \delta\left(M^C - M^{op}\right) \qquad (4.23)$$

where the payoff accruing to the manager deviating from the optimal penal code is

$$M^D(q^{op}) = \frac{(A - q^{op} + \theta)^2}{4} \qquad (4.24)$$

Constraints (4.21) and (4.23) define a simultaneous system of two inequalities in two unknown variables: the maximum level of collusion (i.e. the minimum output level q^C) sustainable given δ and the minimum intensity of the punishment q^{op} incorporating the deterrence against deviations from the collusive path. Solving such a system, we obtain

$$q^C \in \left[\frac{(9 - 8\delta)(A + \theta)}{27}, \frac{A + \theta}{3}\right) \qquad (4.25)$$

and

$$q^{op} \geq \frac{(9 + 8\delta)(A + \theta)}{27} \qquad (4.26)$$

As under grim trigger strategies, also here the lower bound of the interval in (4.25) is monotonically decreasing in δ, with

$$\frac{(9 - 8\delta)(A + \theta)}{27} = \frac{A + \theta}{4} \qquad (4.27)$$

at $\delta = 9/32$ and the interval assuming measure zero if $\delta = 0$. And again, the most collusive output level is strictly increasing in the extent of delegation, as is also the lower bound of the optimal stick-and-carrot punishment q^{op} in (4.26).

Overall, the foregoing analysis demonstrates the following.

Proposition 4.5 *The presence of delegation relying on output expansion destabilizes implicit partial collusion in outputs, for any given level of time preferences.*

This outcome – which, it is worth noting, is in sharp contrast with what happens if managerial rewards rely on stock options – is fully in line with our intuitive understanding of Vickers' (1985) model, where delegation has a pro-competitive flavour from the very outset. Moreover, the analysis of partial collusion clarifies that the coincidence between critical discount factors for full collusion with and without delegation is a very specific result with no general validity.

As we have seen, changing the shape of managerial incentives has evident effects on the stability of implicit collusion, in one direction or the other. Hence, the actual design of managerial rewards in real-world firms and its impact on these firms' performance should attract the attention of researchers and anti-trust authorities alike. Some elements in this direction have emerged here and there also in the empirical literature (see, e.g., Baker *et al.*, 1988; Jensen and Murphy, 1990; Scholes, 1991; Kaplan, 1994a,b), but still not enough to provide a detailed picture of the relationship between managerial remuneration and collusive activities that might exist out there in markets.

4.3 Horizontal mergers

The early debate on horizontal mergers has relied on the Cournot model with a homogeneous good, starting with Salant *et al.* (1983), where it was shown that for a horizontal merger to be efficient for firms, it should involve at least 80% of the firms in the industry. This result, based on the assumption of constant returns to scale, triggered a lively discussion about the role of more realistic cost functions allowing for an *efficiency effect* to arise, as the entity resulting from the merger could and possibly should embody some cost advantages over the sum of the merging units, thereby justifying the merger from a social standpoint (see Perry and Porter, 1985, and Farrell and Shapiro, 1990, *inter alia*).

Not surprisingly, the theory of strategic delegation has a say in this respect, modelling the firms' incentives towards horizontal mergers with divisionalization (Wickelgren, 2005; Ziss, 1995, 2007) and without it (Fauli-Oller and Motta, 1996; González-Maestre and López-Cuñat, 2001; Ziss, 2001). As divisionalization is the subject matter of the next chapter, here I will illustrate the impact of managerialization in the simplest setting where firms are single-product and single-division units.

That is, the purpose of this section is to take the setup analysed by Fauli-Oller and Motta (1996), González-Maestre and López-Cuñat (2001) and Ziss (2001) as a basis for revisiting the discussion on horizontal mergers in a homogeneous Cournot oligopoly under constant returns to scale, and reconstruct the basic result attained in these three papers. The managerial incentive is defined as in Vickers (1985), Fershtman and Judd (1987) and Sklivas (1987).

Consider a market for a homogeneous good, whose inverse market demand function is $p = a - Q$, with $Q = \sum_{i=1}^{n} q_i$. The market is supplied by n fully symmetric Cournot firms endowed with the same technology represented by the cost function $C_i = cq_i$. The issue at stake is the evaluation of the profit incentive towards a merger involving $2 \leq m \leq n - 1$ out of the initial n firms, whereby the number of firms drops to $n - m + 1$ if the merger takes place. The incentive is calculated on the basis of the relevant Nash equilibrium profits in two polar cases, namely (i) the fully entrepreneurial and (ii) the fully managerial oligopoly.

The first case coincides with Salant *et al.* (1983); the merger is profitable iff

$$\pi^{\text{CN}}(ND, m) > m\pi^{\text{CN}}(ND, n) \Leftrightarrow \tag{4.28}$$

$$\frac{A^2}{(n - m + 2)^2} > \frac{mA^2}{(n + 1)^2}$$

with $A \equiv a - c$, as usual. $\pi^{CN}(ND, m)$ is the profit accruing to the entrepreneurial firm created by merging horizontally m previously independent firms, and $\pi^{CN}(ND, n)$ is the individual Cournot profit with n entrepreneurial firms.

The second scenario relies on the Cournot–Nash equilibrium played by a population of managerial firms and characterized in Vickers (1985), Fershtman and Judd (1987) and Sklivas (1987). Here, the merger is profitable iff

$$\pi^{CN}(D, m) > m\pi^{CN}(D, n) \Leftrightarrow \qquad (4.29)$$
$$\frac{(n - m + 1) A^2}{\left[(n - m + 1)^2 + 1\right]^2} > \frac{mn A^2}{\left(n^2 + 1\right)^2}$$

Both (4.28) and (4.29) reveal that m must be large enough for the m firms to be willing to merge. However, the following result is easily established through numerical calculations.

Proposition 4.6 *The minimum size m at which the merger becomes profitable is lower if firms are all managerial.*

One can grasp this fact on qualitative grounds by looking at Figure 4.2, where

$$\Delta(ND, m) \equiv \pi^{CN}(ND, m) - m\pi^{CN}(ND, n) \qquad (4.30)$$

and

$$\Delta(D, m) \equiv \pi^{CN}(D, m) - m\pi^{CN}(D, n) \qquad (4.31)$$

are drawn together.

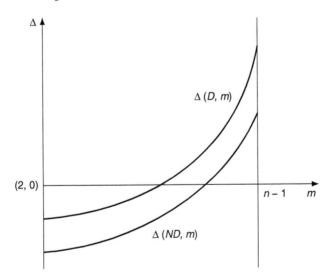

Figure 4.2 Merger incentives with and without delegation.

Note that it is also quickly checked that, in the special case $\{n = 3, m = 2\}$, $\Delta(D, m) > 0$, which implies a relevant corollary to the above proposition.

Corollary 4.2 *A bilateral merger out of an initial managerial triopoly is profitable.*

Why focus on this? Indeed, the specific case of triopoly deserves some space of its own, since it has attracted a large amount of attention and can be easily used for expositional as well as didactic purposes. Last but not least, it is empirically relevant, as many important industries around the globe do have a triopolistic structure, the paramount example being the aircraft industry, where Boeing McDonnel Douglas, Airbus and Lockheed Martin hold most of the global demands in their hands. More precisely, long-range civil transport is a duopoly as it is in the hands of BMD and Airbus, since Lockheed Martin is working on the military side only.

We may leave the merger to monopoly aside. As we know from Salant *et al.* (1983), i.e. from (4.28), if two of these firms have in mind the possibility of merging horizontally, they quickly learn that there is no profit incentive to carry out such a merger because the resulting duopolistic profits are lower than the sum of their triopolistic profits. So, we (and the anti-trust authorities) shouldn't be afraid of the wolf because there's no wolf around, only lambs. This result has been often termed as the 'puzzle' of the bilateral merger in a Cournot industry. More honestly, we shouldn't call it a puzzle, as it is just an example of a naive answer to a sound question, produced by too simplistic a modelization. Indeed, if the technology takes some slightly more sophisticated form, as in Perry and Porter (1985) and in Farrell and Shapiro (1990), the picture changes considerably and mergers involving small numbers become a relevant issue, as casual observation and common sense systematically suggest.[3]

If only one firm – say, firm 1 – has separated ownership from control, the relevant profits at the pre-merger equilibrium are

$$\pi_1^{CNt}(D, ND) = \frac{A^2}{12}; \quad \pi_i^{CNt}(ND, D) = \frac{A^2}{36}, \quad i = 2, 3 \tag{4.32}$$

with $\pi_1^{CNt}(D, ND) = 3\pi_i^{CNt}(ND, D)$, where apex t stands for *triopoly*. A merger involving two firms out of three may take place either between the two entrepreneurial units or between one of them and the managerial entity. In the latter case, it can be reasonably assumed that the firm resulting from the merger will be managerial. In both scenarios, the industry becomes a heterogeneous duopoly in which a managerial firm and an entrepreneurial one coexist, with Stackelberg-like profits

$$\pi_1^{CNd}(D, ND) = \frac{A^2}{8}; \quad \pi_2^{CNd}(ND, D) = \frac{A^2}{16} \tag{4.33}$$

where apex d stands for *duopoly*. It is immediately apparent that the merger between the two pure profit seekers is profitable, since

$$\pi_2^{CNd}(ND, D) - 2\pi_i^{CNt}(ND, D) = \frac{A^2}{144} > 0 \tag{4.34}$$

The same applies in the second case, since

$$\pi_1^{CNd}(D, ND) - \pi_1^{CNt}(D, ND) - \pi_i^{CNt}(ND, D) = \frac{A^2}{72} > 0 \tag{4.35}$$

The alternative scenario, where two firms are managerial enterprises, gives rise to the following ex ante profit performance:

$$\pi_i^{CNt}(D, ND) = \frac{3A^2}{64}; \quad \pi_3^{CNt}(D, D) = \frac{A^2}{64}, \quad i = 1, 2 \tag{4.36}$$

again with $\pi_i^{CNt}(D, ND) = 3\pi_3^{CNt}(ND, D)$. If the bilateral merger transforms the industry into a duopoly, profits are as in (4.33). If the two managerial firms merge, we have

$$\pi_1^{CNd}(D, ND) - 2\pi_i^{CNt}(D, ND) = \frac{A^2}{32} > 0 \tag{4.37}$$

If instead the merger involves a managerial firm and the entrepreneurial firm, the resulting duopoly is entirely managerialized, and the relevant per-firm profits are

$$\pi^{CNd}(D, D) = \frac{2A^2}{25} \tag{4.38}$$

This merger is profitable since

$$\pi^{CNd}(D, D) - \pi_1^{CNt}(D, ND) - \pi_i^{CNt}(ND, D) = \frac{7A^2}{400} > 0 \tag{4.39}$$

In both settings, the outsider always gains from the merger, while consumers lose and welfare decreases, as usual in the extant literature. The take home message of this exercise is as follows.

Proposition 4.7 *Under constant returns and product homogeneity, a merger involving two firms in a Cournot triopoly is profitable iff at least one of the three firms has delegated control to a manager using an incentive based on output or revenues.*

This amounts to saying that the bottom line of the early analysis carried out by Salant *et al.* (1983) is not robust to a simple extension allowing for the presence of a Vickers-type managerial entity even in the simplest setup in which marginal and average costs are the same and no efficiency effect takes place; therefore, this matter should be taken into account by the anti-trust agency as a merger proposal might well reach it, and, on welfare grounds, should be rejected. For the sake of intellectual honesty, I should stress that here I have assumed a heterogeneous composition of the industry, with managerial and entrepreneurial firms coexisting at least before (and possibly after) any bilateral merger is carried out. Strictly speaking, this cannot be part of a subgame perfect equilibrium outcome, as we know from Vickers (1985). However, casual observation reveals that real-world industries often possess such a mixed firm population, although possibly with heterogeneous technologies, as in Basu (1995). Hence, one could take the above triopoly example as implying that Proposition 4.7 should *a fortiori* apply should one account for such asymmetries in the model.

Faulì-Oller and Motta (1996) also showed that managers rewarded *à la* Fershtman and Judd (1987), if in charge of merger decisions, may actually carry out unprofitable takeovers, because the aggressiveness implicit in a delegation contract based on sales expansion makes the acquisition easier but shrinks the overall profits of the conglomerate firm ex post. That is, the inclination to work out a merger and the profitability of the latter are the two sides of the same coin, the mint being the separation of ownership from control.

We shall deal again with mergers among managerial firms in Chapter 5, whose topic is divisionalization. There, these two themes will overlap in the analysis carried out by Wickelgren (2005) and Ziss (1995, 2007).

Further reading

For more on the theory of implicit collusion in supergames, see Fudenberg and Maskin (1986) and Fudenberg and Tirole (1991), among many others. For additional insights on the impact of managerialization on collusion arising in one-shot two-stage games where managerial incentives are based on comparative profits, see Polo and Tedeschi (1992) and Aggarwal and Samwick (1999). An interesting modelization of cartels among managerial firms as a problem of coalition formation is in Olaizola (2007). Further elements on managerial rewards are in Murphy (1985) and Hall and Liebman (1998). For the analysis of the viability of horizontal mergers in a managerialized oligopoly where resource expenditures are decided upon through contests, see Kräkel and Sliwka (2006) who showed that the presence of contests increasing the scope for merging is higher than under pure Cournot competition. Dragone (2007) described the interplay between collusion, delegation and trade. A similar subject was taken up by Heywood and McGinty (2011). The effects of asymmetric production costs on mergers among managerial firms are illustrated in Straume (2006) and Nakamura (2011).

Notes

1 It is worth stressing that the legislative process leading to the Sherman Act was triggered by the intent to preserve competition at a time (the period following the end of the Civil War) when the first great wave of mergers and acquisition gave rise to a number of large corporations threatening the survival of small and medium sized firms all over the USA.

Thence came the competition-oriented attitude of US anti-trust norms, with little proper room for consumer surplus and social welfare, which instead exists in EU law. Different from both is the Anti-monopoly Law in Japan, which admits strategies ultimately leading to the economic development of the country. For a detailed discussion of a number of aspects of anti-trust laws and their evolution, as well as the related academic debate, see, e.g., Martin (1993, 2002).
2 The Nash reversion is known not to be efficient. In Spagnolo (1998) it is shown that the results are qualitatively the same if one uses optimal stick and carrot strategies as in Abreu (1986, 1988).
3 If price competition takes place, then any merger is profitable irrespective of its size, as shown by Deneckere and Davidson (1985) using the Singh and Vives (1984) model with imperfect product substitutability.

References

Abreu, D. (1986), 'Extremal Equilibria of Oligopolistic Supergames', *Journal of Economic Theory*, **39**, 191–225.

Abreu, D. (1988), 'On the Theory of Infinitely Repeated Games with Discounting', *Econometrica*, **56**, 383–96.

Aggarwal, R.K. and A.A. Samwick (1999), 'Executive Compensation, Strategic Competition, and Relative Performance Evaluation: Theory and Evidence', *Journal of Finance*, **54**, 1999–2043.

Baker, G.P., M.C. Jensen and K.J. Murphy (1988), 'Compensation and Incentives: Practice versus Theory', *Journal of Finance*, **43**, 593–616.

Basu, K. (1995), 'Stackelberg Equilibrium in Oligopoly: An Explanation Based on Managerial Incentives', *Economics Letters*, **49**, 459–64.

Deneckere, R. (1983), 'Duopoly Supergames with Product Differentiation', *Economics Letters*, **11**, 37–42.

Deneckere, R. and C. Davidson (1985), 'Incentives to Form Coalitions with Bertrand Competition', *Rand Journal of Economics*, **16**, 473–86.

Dragone, D. (2007), 'Should One Sell Domestic Firms to Foreign Ones? A Tale of Delegation, Acquisition and Collusion', in L. Lambertini (ed.), *Firms' Objectives and Internal Organisation in a Global Economy: Positive and Normative Analysis*, Basingstoke, Palgrave Macmillan.

Farrell, J. and C. Shapiro (1990), 'Horizontal Mergers: An Equilibrium Analysis', *American Economic Review*, **80**, 107–26.

Faulì-Oller, R. and M. Motta (1996), 'Managerial Incentives for Takeover', *Journal of Economics and Management Strategy*, **5**, 497–514.

Fershtman, C. and K. Judd (1987), 'Equilibrium Incentives in Oligopoly', *American Economic Review*, **77**, 927–40.

Friedman, J.W. (1971), 'A Noncooperative Equilibrium for Supergames', *Review of Economic Studies*, **38**, 1–12.

Friedman, J.W. (1977), *Oligopoly and the Theory of Games*, Amsterdam, North-Holland.

Fudenberg, D. and F. Maskin (1986), 'The Folk Theorem in Repeated Games with Discounting or with Incomplete Information', *Econometrica*, **54**, 533–54.

Fudenberg, D. and J. Tirole (1991), *Game Theory*, Cambridge, MA, MIT Press.

González-Maestre, M. and J. López-Cuñat (2001), 'Delegation and Mergers in Oligopoly', *International Journal of Industrial Organization*, **19**, 1263–79.

Hall, B.J. and J.B. Liebman (1998), 'Are CEOs Really Paid Like Bureaucrats?', *Quarterly Journal of Economics*, **113**, 653–91.

Heywood, J. and M. McGinty (2011), 'Cross-Border Mergers in a Mixed Oligopoly', *Economic Modelling*, **28**, 382–89.

Holmström, B. and J. Tirole (1993), 'Market Liquidity and Performance Monitoring', *Journal of Political Economy*, **101**, 678–709.

Jensen, M.C. and K.J. Murphy (1990), 'Performance Pay and Top-Management Incentives', *Journal of Political Economy*, **98**, 225–64.

Kaplan, S.N. (1994a), 'Top Executive Rewards and Firm Performance: A Comparison of Japan and the United States', *Journal of Political Economy*, **102**, 510–46.

Kaplan, S.N. (1994b), 'Top Executives, Turnover, and Firm Performance in Germany', *Journal of Law, Economics and Organization*, **10**, 142–59.

Kräkel, M. and D. Sliwka (2006), 'Strategic Delegation and Mergers in Oligopolistic Contests', *Journal of Economics and Business*, **58**, 119–36.

Lambertini, L. and M. Trombetta (2002), 'Delegation and Firms' Ability to Collude', *Journal of Economic Behavior and Organization*, **47**, 359–73.

Majerus, D.W. (1988), 'Price vs Quantity Competition in Oligopoly Supergames', *Economics Letters*, **27**, 293–97.

Martin, S. (1993), *Advanced Industrial Economics*, Oxford, Blackwell.

Martin, S. (2002), *Advanced Industrial Economics. Second Edition*, Oxford, Blackwell.

Murphy, K.J. (1985), 'Corporate Performance and Managerial Remuneration: An Empirical Analysis', *Journal of Accounting and Economics*, **7**, 11–42.

Nakamura, Y. (2011), 'Bargaining over Managerial Delegation Contracts and Merger Incentives with Asymmetric Costs', *Manchester School*, **79**, 718–39.

Olaizola, N. (2007), 'Cartel Formation and Managerial Incentives', *Spanish Economic Review*, **9**, 219–36.

Perry, M. and R. Porter (1985), 'Oligopoly and the Incentive for Horizontal Merger', *American Economic Review*, **75**, 219–27.

Polo, M. and P. Tedeschi (1992), 'Managerial Contracts, Collusion and Mergers', *Ricerche Economiche*, **46**, 281–302.

Reitman, D. (1993), 'Stock Options, and the Strategic Use of Managerial Incentives', *American Economic Review*, **83**, 513–24.

Rotemberg, J. and G. Saloner (1986), 'A Supergame-Theoretic Model of Price Wars during Booms', *American Economic Review*, **76**, 390–407.

Salant, S.W., S. Switzer and R.J. Reynolds (1983), 'Losses from Horizontal Merger: The Effects of an Exogenous Change in Industry Structure on Cournot-Nash Equilibrium', *Quarterly Journal of Economics*, **98**, 185–213.

Scholes, M. (1991), 'Stock and Compensation', *Journal of Finance*, **46**, 803–23.

Singh, N. and X. Vives (1984), 'Price and Quantity Competition in a Differentiated Duopoly', *RAND Journal of Economics*, **15**, 546–54.

Sklivas, S.D. (1987), 'The Strategic Choice of Managerial Incentives', *RAND Journal of Economics*, **18**, 452–8.

Spagnolo, G. (1998), 'Shareholder-Value Maximization and Tacit Collusion', Working Paper in Economics and Finance no. 235, Stockholm School of Economics.

Spagnolo, G. (2000), 'Stock-Related Compensation and Product-Market Competition', *Rand Journal of Economics*, **31**, 22–42.

Spagnolo, G. (2005), 'Managerial Incentives and Collusive Behavior', *European Economic Review*, **49**, 1501–23.

Straume, O.R. (2006), 'Managerial Delegation and Merger Incentives with Asymmetric Costs', *Journal of Institutional and Theoretical Economics*, **162**, 450–69.

Tirole, J. (1988), *The Theory of Industrial Organization*, Cambridge, MA, MIT Press.

Vickers, J. (1985), 'Delegation and the Theory of the Firm', *Economic Journal*, **95** (Conference Papers), 138–47.

Wickelgren, A.L. (2005), 'Managerial Incentives and the Price Effects of Mergers', *Journal of Industrial Economics*, **53**, 327–53.

Ziss, S. (1995), 'Vertical Separation and Horizontal Mergers', *Journal of Industrial Economics*, **43**, 63–75.

Ziss, S. (2001), 'Horizontal Merger and Delegation', *International Journal of Industrial Organization*, **19**, 471–92.

Ziss, S. (2007), 'Hierarchies, Intra-Firm Competition and Mergers', *International Journal of Industrial Organization*, **25**, 237–60.

5 Divisionalization and vertical relations

In this chapter, we enter a territory in which IO meets the early theory about the internal organization of large firms belonging to the tradition of the New Institutional Economics, i.e. the description of corporations in terms of M-form and U-form and, in general, divisionalization, dating back to Hirshleifer (1957), Chandler (1969), Williamson (1975), Klein *et al.* (1978) and Caves (1980), and contract theory (e.g. Aghion and Bolton, 1987), and enriches both with ingredients belonging to the debate on market preemption and strategic entry barriers.

Typically, one can think that large firms are more likely to become multidivisional than medium or small ones – this is part of the early view of this aspect, and is largely no longer true, though it may have been in the (by now distant) past. Globalization has called for a step in this direction also on the part of firms whose size (in terms of employment, production or turnover) might not suggest a multidivisional structure. Indeed, towards the end of this chapter I will mention a few examples telling the opposite. However, it is still true that big corporations or industrial groups provide evident examples of this sort. Japanese *Keiretsu* such as Mitsubishi and Matsushima are two obvious ones, as much as others in the EU and USA. All of these firms have a complex vertical and horizontal structure, and are not only multidivisional but also multiproduct entities. The Airbus Group (formerly, until 2013, EADS), operates the aerospace, aircraft and defence industries and has divisions located all over the EU territory and 170 locations around the world. As an example, wings for the civil transport Airbus range are produced in UK (near Bristol) while the quality control is based in the Federal Republic of Germany (in Bremen). Mitsubishi is involved in shipbuilding, consumer electronics, merchant banking and the car industry, amongst other things. GE (General Electric), incorporated in New York and headquartered in Boston, Mass., operates through power, aircraft, health care, pharmaceutical and several other sectors.

These introductory notes point out that a firm going multidivisional has to deal with two dimensions defining its organization: a vertical one and a horizontal one. Of course, in the real world, these two dimensions interact with each other in a significant and complex way, but, as is often the case in economic theory, more often than not each of these two aspects has been treated in isolation. Not surprisingly, this theme has triggered empirical research in parallel with the construction of the theoretical framework (see, e.g., Lafontaine, 1992), finding strong evidence confirming the models' predictions (see Slade, 1998; and, for a thorough account of the empirical debate, Lafontaine and Slade, 2007).

I will set out with the strategic delegation view on vertical relations. Here, the analysis complements a well established literature on vertical relations and the strategic management of supply chains where exclusive dealing and foreclosure mix up with manoeuvring vertical restraints so as to raise rivals' costs (see, e.g., Mathewson and Winter, 1984; Aghion and Bolton, 1987; Salop and Scheffman, 1987; Rey and Stiglitz, 1988; Salinger, 1988; Ordover *et al.*, 1990; Gal-Or, 1991; Kühn, 1997). As Bernheim and Whinston (1998) note, the spectrum of vertical agreements lead to very different outcomes for very different reasons; in particular, exclusionary contracts may turn out to be anti-competitive or efficient depending on the specific context. What the interpretation of vertical relations as a strategic delegation problem adds to this picture is the idea that observable contracts are credible commitment devices to be used to condition the ensuing market competition in order to obtain an advantage over rivals, rather than keeping (or throwing) them out of business.

The second part of the chapter is for the horizontal dimension of divisionalization. Here, again, the early interpretation of such a strategy is that it aims at building up entry barriers (Schwartz and Thompson, 1986; Veendorp, 1991). Divisionalization protects the value of incumbency by deterring entry in industries where divisionalization is cheaper to the incumbent than to potential entrants (Schwartz and Thompson, 1986). Moreover, this strategy is convenient insofar as it produces a credible crowding out effect through output expansion, profitably using internal competition among divisions against potential entrants. Veendorp (1991) adds a crucial element to this argument, stressing that the effectiveness of entry barriers built up through divisionalization are enhanced by centralized investment decisions concerning long-run variables such as installed capacity or R&D projects, which contribute to raise rivals' costs – a feature connecting this part of the debate to the aforementioned parallel strand concerned with the vertical separation vs integration choices. Going back to the aforementioned examples, in particular that of Japanese corporations, it must be noted that being multidivisional might well be a consequence of mergers with or acquisitions of previously independent firms, whereby divisionalization actually appears as an entry strategy (and sometimes, also a very aggressive one) circumventing the need for costly highly uncertain and time-consuming investment projects to be carried out in-house to penetrate new markets. So, the case for entry barriers could be just one side of the coin.

The perspective currently offered by the theory of multidivisional firms retains the entry-deterring motive but enriches it with the commitment motive, whereby firms going multidivisional may profit from the mix-and-match of intra-firm competition (among managers of different units inside the same enterprise) and market competition (with other firms – which may or may not have the same internal organization – operating in the same industry).

5.1 Vertical separation: supply chain management

The building blocks of the extant discussion about vertical integration vs separation in connection with strategic delegation can be found in Bonanno and Vickers (1988), where – quite intuitively – there emerges a direct connection between the vertical structure of firms and the effects of delegation on market behaviour as well as the intensity of competition. Here, the owners' motive for vertical delegation through observable contracts is indeed that of inducing retailers to adopt a more or less aggressive behaviour in the market stage, depending on the specific market variable being chosen. Their model illustrates that the misalignment between manufacturers' and retailers' incentives, which is usually taken to be the source of the need for vertical integration, can actually be manipulated to the advantage of the former via appropriate delegation contracts aimed at conditioning market behaviour, as represented by the firms' best reply functions in the space of prices or output levels.

The basic structure of the model is the same as above. Let the industry consist of four firms: two upstream units, 1 and 2, and two downstream ones, A and B. It is assumed that there exists a vertical relation between 1 and A and 2 and B, thereby excluding the case of vertical foreclosure examined in the parallel and alternative stream of literature on the same matter.

Suppose the final good sold to consumers is differentiated *à la* Singh and Vives (1984) to facilitate the analysis of price competition, with inverse demand functions $p_{1A} = a - q_{1A} - \sigma q_{2B}$ and $p_{2B} = a - q_{2B} - \sigma q_{1A}$, $\sigma \in (0, 1]$. This entails that the case of independent goods ($\sigma = 0$) is ruled out, for obvious reasons. Additionally, assuming σ to be positive, i.e. that goods are (imperfect) demand substitutes, ensures that quantities are strategic substitutes and prices are strategic complements, in the jargon of Bulow *et al.* (1985). In the Bertrand case, the direct demand function is

$$q_{iJ} = \frac{a}{1+\sigma} - \frac{p_{iJ}}{1-\sigma^2} + \frac{\sigma p_{jK}}{1-\sigma^2} \qquad (5.1)$$

with $i, j = 1, 2$, $J, K = A, B$, $i \neq j$ and $J \neq K$.

Both manufacturers share the same production technology characterized by a common and constant marginal cost which, for the sake of simplicity, can be set equal to zero. Hence, the profit function of the vertically integrated firm would be $\pi_{iVI} = p_{iJ}q_{iJ}$, $i = 1, 2$, $J = A, B$, where subscript iVI indicates that the firm is vertically integrated (or owner i retains control of the retailer).

Since firms are vertically separated, manufacturer i transfers each unit of the good (or, in the alternative but equivalent interpretation of the model, sells a unit of the input) to its retailer J at a wholesale price w_i, so that retailer j's profit function is $\pi_{iJ} = (p_{iJ} - w_i)q_{iJ}$. As a result, the industry outcome will depend on whether $w_i \gtrless 0$ (note that it must be lower than a). Needless to say, if $w_i = 0$ along both vertical supply chains, the outcome will coincide with that generated by vertically integrated firms. The wholesale price combines with a fixed franchise fee $F > 0$ to form a classical two-part tariff $TPT_i = w_i q_{iJ} + F$ along the marketing channel or supply chain consisting of firms i and J, with manufacturer i in a position to manipulate w_i to alter the intensity of downstream competition and use F to extract surplus from retailer J's pockets.

What happens under either Cournot or Bertrand competition can be easily deduced from the structure of incentives as identified by the wholesale prices, without delving into the details of calculations. Keeping in mind that marginal production cost is nil, consider first quantity-setting behaviour. One may just observe that any $w_i < 0$ has the same effect on the intercept of retailer J's reaction function as a positive value of the Vickers (1985) delegation variable θ_i (cf. Chapter 2): that is, if the wholesale price is lower than marginal production cost, the best reply in the output space shifts outward, keeping its slope unchanged. Conversely, if competition takes place in the price space, an analogous outward shift is obtained for all $w_i > 0$. This reasoning delivers Figures 5.1 and 5.2, which, except for a change in labels and wording, replicate Figures 2.1 and 2.2.

Here the Stackelberg equilibrium points are not represented, as the interesting element of the supply chain version of the delegation game is the manipulation of downstream competition through managerial incentives. In particular, looking at Figure 5.2, one can easily notice that the strategic use of managerial incentives under price competition shift the resulting downstream equilibrium outwards, i.e. in the direction of collusive pricing.

These properties illustrate a fundamental feature of the vertical relation between manufacturer and retailer, which can be spelled out as follows.

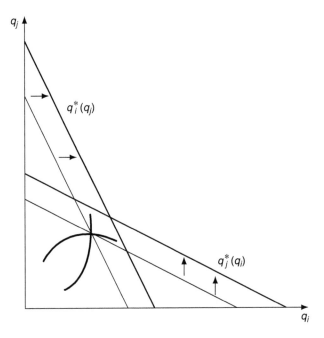

Figure 5.1 Delegation in supply chains, Cournot competition.

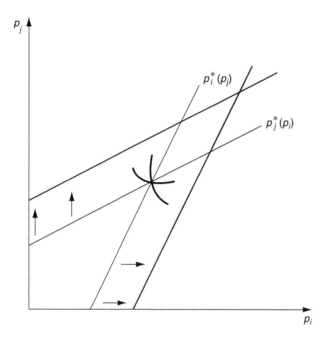

Figure 5.2 Delegation in supply chains, Bertrand competition.

Proposition 5.1 *If strategic variables are strategic substitutes (respectively, complements), manufacturers (owners) tune wholesale prices so as to induce a more (respectively, less) aggressive behaviour on the part of their respective retailers.*

The intuition about this fact is easily outlined. Under Cournot competition, an owner wants her/his retailer to be aggressive by expanding its output, and this requires the wholesale price to be lower than marginal cost in order for the retailer to be willing to produce more. Conversely, when it comes to price-setting strategies, the owner chooses a wholesale price higher than marginal cost to provoke an increase in *every price* that her/his retailer is then induced to select along the best reply for any price set by the rival. This latter mechanism is inherently characterized by a collusive flavour, in itself clearly revealing of a less aggressive attitude.

The latter observation implies that vertical separation is in the collective interest of manufacturers/owners, as the resulting equilibrium will be located to the northeast of the equilibrium emerging under two-sided vertical integration, with prices approaching the fully collusive outcome.[1]

The picture emerging from Bonanno and Vickers (1988) is one of fully symmetric *vertical separation though delegation*. This is not, however, a univocal conclusion. That asymmetric managerial incentives adopted within otherwise fully symmetric firms may arise at equilibrium is known since Hermalin (1994), in a model where managers exert stochastic cost-reducing efforts (more on this in chapter 6). The same result emerges again in Balasubramanian and Bhardwaj (2004) and Chou (2014). In the latter, in particular, contract asymmetry is driven by the presence of price competition in the market subgame: since prices are strategic complements, the asymmetry in delegation contracts reflects the Stackelberg solvability of the market stage, as implied by d'Aspremont and Gérard-Varet (1980) and Hamilton and Slutsky (1990) (cf. the discussion on this topic in Chapter 2).

A couple of other extensions are worth mentioning, concerning the possibility for unobservable contracts to impact on downstream strategic interaction. The first is in Corts and Neher (2003), where vertical separation takes place in an environment in which contracts are unobservable, as in Coughlan and Wernerfelt (1989) and Katz (1991, 2006). These authors showed that unobservable or renegotiable contracts may indeed affect the ensuing market competition and induce favourable reactions on the part of a firm's rivals. This happens provided that (i) there are multiple agent firms, and (ii) the ownership of such agent firms is decentralized. When these conditions are jointly satisfied, delegation may act as a commitment device, unobservability and renegotiation notwithstanding. Secondly, Pagnozzi and Piccolo (2012) argued that if contracts are unobservable but retailers formulate the same beliefs about the design of contracts offered by symmetric manufacturers, then vertical separation may have a strategic effect, unobservability notwithstanding. We will come back to relevant applications of the Bonanno and Vickers (1988) model in Chapters 7 and 8, concerning the impact of the vertical structure of the industry on (i) product differentiation and (ii) international trade and the environment.

The second contribution has a direct connection with Bonanno and Vickers (1988). It is the model proposed by Vroom (2006), where the setup is the same, although in the original paper the wording slightly differs from the one I have chosen above. There are two Cournot firms, 1 and 2, supplying a market for a homogeneous good, whose demand function is $p = a - Q$. Marginal production cost is symmetric, constant and equal to $c \in (0, a)$. Firms have a two-division vertical structure, with a production division and a marketing division. Agents in charge of running production divisions are given pure profit incentives, while those managing the marketing divisions are hired via contracts based on comparative profit evaluation, as in Salas Fumas (1992), Lundgren (1996) and Miller and Pazgal (2001). Hence, equivalently, one can think that production divisions are run by owners themselves.

The game takes place in four stages. In stage 1, owners decide whether to centralize ($\mathcal{C}$) or decentralize ($\mathcal{D}$) their respective firms. In stage 2, owners determine the marketing managers' incentives. In stage 3, if firms are decentralized, the transfer prices are set through a negotiation process taking place between the production and the marketing managers of each firm. Stage 4 describes competition in output levels. Managerial contracts are observable, and each stage is characterized by complete, symmetric and imperfect information, i.e. moves are simultaneous. Information is perfect across stages.

The symbology is the same as in the initial setup. The (marketing) manager of the downstream division $J = A, B$ receives an incentive specified as follows:[2]

$$M_J = \pi_J + \theta_i \left(\pi_j + \pi_K \right) \tag{5.2}$$

where $\pi_J = (p - w_i)q_{iJ}$ are the profits generated by the downstream division J, $\pi_j = w_j q_{jK}$ are the profits of the production division j and $\pi_K = (p - w_j)q_{jK}$ are those generated by the marketing division K. The contractual variable θ_i has the usual interpretation. In plain words, (5.2) says that the manager of a downstream division is paid on the basis of her/his own performance *vis à vis* that of the whole vertical channel of the rival firm. Of course, if $\theta_i = 0$, we are back into Bonanno and Vickers (1988), with strategic delegation operating through transfer prices.

The transfer price w_i is determined by the following equation:

$$w_i = \phi w_i^* + (1 - \phi)c \tag{5.3}$$

where w_i^* identifies the transfer price maximizing the production division's profits. Hence, w_i^* coincides with the solution of the model in Bonanno and Vickers (1988) for the homogeneous Cournot case, and we know by now that this should involve $w_i^* < 0$ (this is surely true if $\theta_i = 0$). The weight represented by parameter $\phi \in [0, 1]$ measures the relative bargaining power of the agents in charge of the two divisions. If $\phi = 1$, the transfer price is marginal cost; otherwise if $\phi = 0$, it takes the value preferred by the production manager. In the latter case, the vertical supply chain behaves as if it were centralized even if it is not. Hence, ϕ can be thought of as measuring the degree of centralization. Vroom (2006) left thus the bargaining problem out of the endogenous process taking place throughout the game, and treated it as a parametric problem. It is worth noting that transfer prices might be chosen by other subjects, such as the CEO (cf. Alles and Datar, 1998), and that leaving the negotiation of transfer prices to agents along the vertical channel might produce inefficient outcomes which could be coped with using two-part tariffs (cf. Kaplan and Atkinson, 1998).

In a sense, the advantage of letting bargaining power be an exogenous parametric feature of the model means that the subgame perfect solution of the four-stage game by the usual backward induction procedure yields an equilibrium which is bound to be itself parametric in ϕ.

The equilibrium outcome, and therefore the equilibrium structure of both firms in the industry, is determined by the inequality among the profits appearing in Matrix 5.1, where each profit is defined as the sum of both divisions' profits.

		j	
		C	D
i	C	$\pi(C,C); \pi(C,C)$	$\pi(C,D); \pi(D,C)$
	D	$\pi(D,C); \pi(C,D)$	$\pi(D,D); \pi(D,D)$

Matrix 5.1

As one could anticipate from the parametric nature of the bargaining process at the third stage, the results critically hinge upon ϕ. In particular, there exist two critical levels of ϕ, which can be labelled as $\widehat{\phi}$ and $\widetilde{\phi}$, with $\widetilde{\phi} < \widehat{\phi}$ and $\widetilde{\phi}, \widehat{\phi} \in (0, 1)$. $\widehat{\phi}$ determines the equilibrium vertical structure of firms, and both $\widetilde{\phi}$ and $\widehat{\phi}$ contribute to characterizing the sequence of profits appearing in Matrix 5.1 and their ranking relative to the standard Cournot–Nash profits. All of this can be summarized as follows (cf. Vroom, 2006, Proposition 1, p. 1699).

- For all $\phi \in (0, \widehat{\phi})$, $(\mathcal{D}, \mathcal{D})$ is the unique Nash equilibrium of the first stage, at the intersection of dominant strategies, and owners choose $\theta^N(\mathcal{D}, \mathcal{D}) < 0$ at the second stage.
- For all $\phi \in (\widehat{\phi}, 1)$, both outcomes along the secondary diagonal, $(\mathcal{D}, \mathcal{C})$ and $(\mathcal{C}, \mathcal{D})$, are pure-strategy Nash equilibria of the first stage, and the owner of the decentralized firm sets $\theta^N(\mathcal{D}, \mathcal{C}) < 0$ while that of the centralized one sets $\theta^N(\mathcal{C}, \mathcal{D}) > 0$ at the second stage. In this parameter range, $\pi(\mathcal{D}, \mathcal{C}) > \pi(\mathcal{C}, \mathcal{D})$.
- For all $\phi \in (0, \widetilde{\phi})$, equilibrium profits $\pi(\mathcal{D}, \mathcal{D})$ are lower than Cournot–Nash profits.
- For all $\phi \in (\widetilde{\phi}, 1)$, equilibrium profits are higher than Cournot–Nash profits, irrespective of the firms' vertical structure.

A few additional comments are in order. First of all, the fully decentralized equilibrium $(\mathcal{D}, \mathcal{D})$ is not the outcome of a prisoners' dilemma as $\pi(\mathcal{D}, \mathcal{D}) > \pi(\mathcal{C}, \mathcal{C})$. Secondly, when $(\mathcal{D}, \mathcal{D})$ is the unique equilibrium, the nature of managerial incentives is the same as in Miller and Pazgal (2001). Thirdly, the multiplicity of equilibria arising for any $\phi \in (\widehat{\phi}, 1)$ makes the analysis of the mixed-strategy equilibrium also relevant, as in probabilistic terms any pure-strategy outcome of Matrix 5.1 can indeed materialize, due to the coordination problem faced by owners.

To conclude this illustration, it is important to explicitly note that this model reproduces a result already highlighted in Jansen (2003), namely, that asymmetric vertical arrangements can arise at equilibrium, even if firms are ex ante fully symmetric (and share the same symmetric strategy set). The coexistence of firms with different vertical structures has been identified by Jansen (2003) in a Cournot model where n upstream firms consider the possibility of vertically integrating themselves *forward* with as many downstream units, whose total number is very large (i.e. larger than n). The necessary condition for asymmetry to arise is that the take-it-or-leave-it offer to a downstream firm involves a sunk cost (which does not appear in Vroom's model), combined with the requirement that at least two firms supply close substitutes (a condition of which product homogeneity used by Vroom (2006) is indeed a special case).[3]

The possibility of generating a range of theoretical models delivering asymmetric vertical structures across the population of firms is highly appealing, because casual observation regularly confirms that enterprises with different divisional arrangements operate in the same industry. This fact is accounted for by Moner-Colonques *et al.* (2004), where two manufacturers are *assumed* to be asymmetric in terms of their product ranges: one is a single-product firm, while the other supplies two differentiated varieties.[4] Let m stand for *manufacturer*, index $i = 1, 2$ identify the product variety and index $J = A, B$ identify the firm. Then, the demand function for variety i is

$$p_i = a_i - Q_i - \sigma Q_j \tag{5.4}$$

where $\sigma \in (0, 1]$, as in Singh and Vives (1984). Manufacturer m_A is multiproduct, while firm m_B is producing only variety 2. As a consequence, $Q_1 = q_{1A}$, while $Q_2 = q_{2A} + q_{2B}$. Both manufacturers use the same technology characterized by constant returns to scale, with average and marginal cost c. Demand (5.4) implies a specific choke price $a_i > c$ for each variety, and the ratio a_1/a_2 will play a role in shaping several aspects of the firms' equilibrium behaviour.

Upstream firms m_J have to decide whether to delegate marketing to retailers, or run sales departments themselves, in house. In the case of manufacturer A, if it decides to delegate, then it also has to choose whether to delegate the sales of both varieties (possibly to two independent retailers) or just one. Hence, the model allows for *no delegation* (which is observationally equivalent to vertical integration), *partial delegation* and *full delegation*. Note that the two situations equally labelled as partial delegation are not equivalent to each other, because variety 1 is exclusive to manufacturer A while variety 2 is also supplied by manufacturer B.

The game features three stages: in the first, manufacturers decide whether to delegate sales to retailers or not; in the second, delegation contracts (if any) are appropriately designed by manufacturers in the form of a two-part tariff including the wholesale price w_{iJ} and a fixed fee F_{iJ} fully extracting the profits gained by the retailer J of variety i (the retailer r_{iJ} is identified by a subscript combining the index associated with the manufacturer whom it is in a vertical relation with and the product whose sales r_{iJ} is taking care of); in the third, the relevant players choose output strategies. Moves are simultaneous throughout the game, which is solved by backward induction.

Without delving into the details of calculations,[5] here I would like to draw your attention to a relevant result which lends itself to an intuitive explanation.

Lemma 5.1 *Delegation to retailers may or may not expand the sales of the multi-product manufacturer, while it always expands those of the single-product one, as compared to the no delegation scenario.*

This depends on the fact that, while the single-product upstream firm, m_B, sets a wholesale price $w_{2B} < c$ over the entire parameter space, while the multiproduct rival's wholesale prices depend on the level of a_1/a_2. This fact can be represented graphically, as in Figure 5.3, where the curves

$$f_I = s; \quad f_{II} = \frac{2\left(1+\sigma^2\right) - \sigma^4}{\sigma\left(5 - 2\sigma^2\right)}; \quad f_{III} = \frac{1+\sigma^2}{2\sigma} \tag{5.5}$$

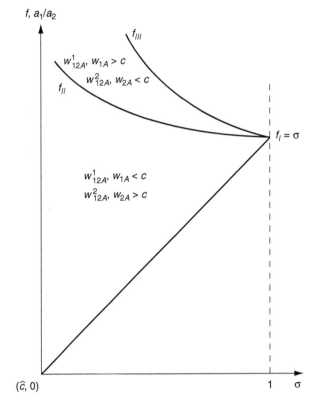

Figure 5.3 The multiproduct manufacturer's wholesale prices.

are drawn to identify the regions where the wholesale prices w_{12A}^1, w_{12A}^2, w_{1A} and w_{2A} are above or below marginal production cost; w_{12A}^i is the wholesale price chosen by m_A for variety i when delegating sales of both varieties, while w_{iA} is the wholesale price m_A sets when delegating sales of variety i only. In both cases, manufacturer m_B is delegating sales of its only variety.

In the parameter region identified by $a_1/a_2 \in (f_{II}, f_{III})$, w_{12A}^1 and w_{1A} are both above marginal cost c. In the region where $a_1/a_2 \in (f_I, f_{II})$, the same happens to w_{12A}^2 and w_{2A}. In a nutshell, m_A *never sets all wholesale prices simultaneously below marginal cost*. That is to say, the multiproduct manufacturer never finds it optimal to make all of her/his retailers simultaneously more aggressive then she/he would be if retaining the control of sales in house. The reason for seemingly weird behaviour on the part of m_A is to be found in the fact that this manufacturer has to cope with the simultaneous presence of inter-firm (or intra-brand) competition (as usual in oligopoly games) and intra-firm (or inter-brand) competition as m_A is a multiproduct entity. The combination of these factors affects the retailers' ability to extract surplus from consumers' pockets in the downstream stage and therefore also the dimension of the fixed fee appearing in the two-part tariff. Intuitively, for a given $\sigma \in (0, 1)$, m_A

finds it convenient to raise the wholesale price for its exclusive variety 1 when the ratio a_1/a_2 (that is, when a_1) is sufficiently high, in order to reproduce the equivalent of Stackelberg leadership against the single product competitor. Conversely, if a_1/a_2 is low enough, then it is convenient for m_A to reduce the same price in order to use variety 1 to flood the market via a more aggressive behaviour of the retailer.

Then, Moner-Colonques *et al.* (2004, pp. 413–16) addressed the question whether, under full delegation by m_A, a single retailer or two separate ones should be used. The balance between inter-firm and intra-firm competition establishes that, under full delegation, the multiproduct supplier prefers to delegate the sales of each variety to a separate seller. However – and this is the core of their contribution – there emerges that full delegation is not necessarily part of the subgame perfect equilibrium profile, since the following holds.

Proposition 5.2 *At the first stage of the game, m_A does not choose full delegation if the degree of substitutability is sufficiently high.*

To understand this result, we may consider that σ can be thought of as an inverse measure of profitability. In general, mark-ups are inversely related to σ (or directly related to product differentiation), irrespective of the specific setup. Any decrease in product differentiation diminishes the multiproduct manufacturers' ability to control intra-firm and inter-brand competition with the only available instruments, i.e. wholesale prices. Indeed, if substitutability is almost perfect (i.e. σ is very close to 1), m_A decides not to delegate at all, preferring vertical integration to any other options.

An objection which may be raised to the framework investigated by Moner-Colonques *et al.* (2004) is that the asymmetry between product ranges they assume may not be part of the subgame perfect equilibrium of a full-fledged game contemplating the possibility for firms to endogenously choose their respective number of products. That is, shall we expect m_B to supply one variety only?[6] Or, shouldn't a manufacturer replicate the product proliferation strategy adopted by competitors? These authors briefly considered competition between multiproduct suppliers and concluded that they would select the fully integrated industry structure (i.e. no delegation at all) at equilibrium (Moner-Colonques *et al.*, 2004, pp. 418–19). However, the above question remains open. This leads us to the subject matter of the next section, which illustrates a parallel strand of literature describing the behaviour of multidivisional (and possibly multiproduct) firms.

5.2 Multidivisional firms

This section contains a survey of a few models belonging to the current revisitation of the debate about the choice between U-form and M-form dating back to Williamson (1975), with the strategic nature of modern oligopoly theory taking the centre stage.

The bulk of the recent revival of the theoretical debate about multidivisional firms and strategic delegation actually consists of a relatively large number of papers studying the firms' incentives to create multiple divisions competing independently, with each agent in charge of running a division aiming at maximizing her/his division's profits, with no allowance for a proper characterization of managerial contracts. So, almost paradoxically, we might think of it as a discussion about multidivisional firms 'without managers', quite at odds with the real world cases mentioned at the outset of the chapter.

In a nutshell, the initial formulation of the sub-literature we are about to look at revisits the pervasive idea of recreating the conditions for a firm to acquire Stackelberg leadership without invoking sequential play, a *leitmotiv* of the discussion on strategic delegation since Vickers (1985). This, as we will see, combines with the theme of the social efficiency of the entry process and its limit properties, as in Mankiw and Whinston (1986), among others.[7]

This stream of research was initiated by Corchón (1991), extending the ideas of Schwartz and Thompson (1986) and Veendorp (1991) to oligopoly games. In his model, under Cournot competition and product homogeneity, firms have an incentive to divisionalize themselves as a commitment to expand output (which is an epiphany of the Stackelberg leadership motive). Then, Polasky (1992) showed that, if divisionalization is costless and demand is linear, the persistent incentive to increase the number of divisions jeopardizes the existence of a pure-strategy equilibrium with a finite number of divisions per firm. This is due to the fact that the owners' obsession about having at least a division more than all of their opponents prevents the attainment of a finite equilibrium through a persistent escalation. This mechanism intensifies market competition so much that it leads the oligopolistic industry towards the perfectly competitive outcome, as the number of divisions and the industry output increases, bringing the equilibrium price down to marginal cost. Baye *et al.* (1996a,b) amended this problem by showing that if the presence of a sunk cost per division is allowed for, then the equilibrium in pure strategies does exist. They also proved, still relying on product homogeneity, that divisionalization is socially efficient if the number of firms is very low (typically, in the duopoly or triopoly case).

To grasp the essence of the early debate of *divisionalization without managers*, we can rely on a synthesis contained in Ziss (1998), where the model is expanded to generalize and extend previous results – simultaneously testing their robustness – in the presence of some degree of product differentiation. His model is an accurate summary of pure profit incentives towards divisionalization and therefore deserves to be exposed in some detail. The industry is populated by $n \geq 2$ quantity-setting firms, operating at the same constant marginal cost c. Define as $d_i \geq 1$ the number of divisions within firm i. Creating each single division involves a sunk cost $F > 0$. The output of division j belonging to firm i is q_{ij}, so that the total output of firm i is $Q_i = \sum_{j=1}^{d_i} q_{ij}$ and total industry output is $\mathbf{Q} = \sum_{i=1}^{n} Q_i$.

All divisions inside the same firm sell a homogeneous good, which is differentiated *à la* Singh and Vives (1984) from the output sold by the rest of the firms in the industry,[8] in such a way that the inverse demand function for firm i is

$$p_i = a - Q_i - \sigma \mathbf{Q}_{-i} \tag{5.6}$$

where $\mathbf{Q}_{-i} = \mathbf{Q} - Q_i = \sum_{j \neq i} Q_j$ and $\sigma \in (0, 1]$. If divisions are run by owners (or managers are given pure profit incentives) the maximand of the jth division of firm i is the following profit function

$$\pi_{ij} = (a - Q_i - \sigma \mathbf{Q}_{-i}) q_{ij} \tag{5.7}$$

while firm i's profits are

$$\Pi_i = \sum_{j=1}^{d_i} \pi_{ij} - d_i F \tag{5.8}$$

Note that the definition of Π_i reveals the rise of intra-firm competition among divisions, adding up to the usual inter-firm competition we are accustomed with from the standard oligopoly models assuming single-division firms. This means that through (5.6) two effects jointly operate: the first is an externality among a firm's own division, and the second is the usual pre-emption effect among firms, which in this case is softened by product differentiation.

The game unravels through two stages, each being characterized by complete, symmetric and imperfect information. At the first stage, owners non-cooperatively set the number of divisions; at the second, Cournot–Nash competition takes place.

Proceeding by backward induction, we have d_i FOCs taken with respect to each quantity q_{ij}, which can be manipulated to yield the optimal output of the generic division of firm i:

$$q_{ij}^{CN} = \frac{a - c}{1 + \sigma \sum_{j \neq i} \varpi_j + d_i \left[1 + \sigma (1 - \sigma) \sum_{j \neq i} \varpi_j \right]} \tag{5.9}$$

Then the total output of firm i is

$$Q_i^{CN} = \sum_{j=1}^{d_i} q_{ij}^{CN} = \frac{(a - c) \varpi_i}{1 + \sum_{j \neq i} \varpi_j} \tag{5.10}$$

and finally the total industry output at the Cournot–Nash equilibrium is

$$\mathbf{Q}^{CN} = \frac{(a - c) \sum_{j \neq i} \varpi_j}{1 + \sigma \sum_{j \neq i} \varpi_j} \tag{5.11}$$

all of them defined for a generic number of divisions across the population of firms. In (5.9)–(5.11),

$$\varpi_i \equiv \frac{d_i}{1 + d_i (1 - \sigma)} \tag{5.12}$$

We are left with the choice concerning the extent of divisionalization, which is taken to maximize the firm's overall profits Π_i. Let's consider first the limit case in which divisionalization is costless. If $F = 0$, the number of divisions maximizing Π_i is determined by the following best reply function:

$$d_i^* = \frac{1 + \sigma \sum_{j \neq i} \varpi_j}{1 + \sigma(1 - \sigma) \sum_{j \neq i} \varpi_j} \tag{5.13}$$

where d_j appear in the summation $\sum_{j \neq i} \varpi_j$, as from (5.12). It can be easily shown that $\partial d_i^* / \partial d_j > 0$ for all $j \neq i$. This property, using the jargon of Bulow *et al.* (1985) implies the following.

Lemma 5.2 *If divisionalization is costless, the profit incentive to divisionalize firms determines the emergence of strategic complementarity at the first stage of the game.*

This lemma captures the very nature of the game as initially formulated in Corchón (1991) and Polasky (1992). In the extreme case in which product varieties are perfect substitutes ($\sigma = 1$), we have $\varpi_j = d_j$ and therefore, imposing symmetry, (5.13) becomes $d(n - 2) + 1 = 0$, which has no meaningful solution as $d(n - 2) + 1 > 0$ for all $n \geq 2$ and $d \geq 1.^9$

Provided $\sigma \in (0, 1)$, the only admissible symmetric solution at the intersection of best replies (5.13) is $d^N(n, \sigma)$, with the following properties (treating n as a continuous variable):

$$\frac{\partial d^N(n, \sigma)}{\partial n} > 0 \tag{5.14}$$

and

$$\lim_{n \to \infty} d^N(n, \sigma) = \frac{1}{1 - \sigma} \tag{5.15}$$

everywhere. The partial derivative in (5.14) and the limit in (5.15) jointly demonstrate the following.

Proposition 5.3 *In presence of imperfect substitutes and costless divisionalization, the optimal number of divisions per firm is monotonically increasing in the number of firms, reaching an upper bound at $\overline{d}^N(n, \sigma) = 1/(1 - \sigma)$, itself decreasing in the degree of product differentiation.*

This amounts to saying that product differentiation plays a major role in (i) moderating the escalation, (ii) establishing a finite equilibrium extent of divisionalization and (iii) ruling out the competitive outcome. Additionally, note that the upper bound $\overline{d}^N(n, \sigma)$ shoots up to infinity as σ tends to one – bringing us back to the original conundrum generated by product homogeneity – while it obviously becomes equal to one if goods do not interact, which happens when $\sigma = 0$.

If instead setting up a division involves a sunk cost, the characterization of the equilibrium at the first stage is obviously cumbersome, requiring numerical simulations, some of which appear in Ziss (1998, p. 138). There emerges the following.

Proposition 5.4 *If divisionalization is costly, its equilibrium extent is concave and single peaked in n for any given level of product substitutability* $\sigma \in (0, 1]$. *Optimal divisionalization is decreasing in* σ.

The non-monotone effect of n on divisionalization means that entry has an ambiguous effect when sunk costs enter the picture. In other words, the usual externality associated with the entry process dominates (respectively, is dominated by) the output effect if the industry is sufficiently concentrated (respectively, fragmented).

If one had to summarize this literature is a short sentence, this could well be that *the incentive to divisionalize, which in itself is a very aggressive move, may reproduce perfect competition with just two firms in the market, if the cost of divisionalization is either altogether absent or very small.* Bárcena-Ruiz and Espinosa (1999), Corchón and González-Maestre (2000) and González-Maestre (2000, 2001) extended this debate in several directions.

Corchón and González-Maestre (2000) assumed product homogeneity as in the early literature, and set out to generalize the results contained in Corchón (1991) and Polasky (1992) to the case of concave demand functions. Then, they showed that either perfect competition or a *natural oligopoly* (in the sense of Shaked and Sutton, 1983), may arise as the cost of divisionalization shrinks to zero, depending on the way frictions affecting the industry vanish. In particular, such frictions are generated by a fixed fee each firm has to pay, and an upper bound imposed on the number of divisions each firm may create. The same result was reproduced by González-Maestre (2001) in a spatial differentiation model based on Salop's (1979) circular city, under price-setting behaviour.

The remaining papers I am about to illustrate significantly depart from the above strand of literature by allowing for the presence of managers having a role in shaping the behaviour as well as the internal structure of firms.

5.2.1 Multidivisionalization with managers

By now, we are acquainted with multidivisional firms controlled by owners who control divisions and use them as an aggressive tools. Looking at the matter from a different angle, Ziss (1999), Bárcena-Ruiz and Espinosa (1999) and González-Maestre (2000) extended the setup to allow for the presence of managers taking output decisions, being hired on the basis of incentives defined as a combination of profits and revenues as in Fershtman and Judd (1987).

More precisely, Ziss (1999) used a managerial remuneration based on a linear combination of revenues and costs, which included the wholesale price adopted by a single upstream firm supplying a population of downstream managerial ones, which have to decide whether to become multidivisional or not, and then design delegation contracts. The model is stochastic, with uncertainty affecting marginal production costs. Once managers are hired, they observe the shock and then choose output levels simultaneously. Using this model, Ziss (1999) proved that that the synergy between divisionalization and managerial incentives produces a high-powered rent-shifting effect, a rationale for divisionalization emerging if contracts are not state-contingent.

Bárcena-Ruiz and Espinosa (1999) were the first (and, to the best of my knowledge, the only) authors to explicitly model the choice between U-form and M-form under duopolistic interaction and both Cournot and Bertrand competition. In particular, they addressed the following question: should firms provide managers with corporate or divisional incentives? To answer, they constructed a three-stage game in which (i) the first stage describes the owners' choice between U-form and M-form; (ii) the second hosts the design of optimal delegation contracts; and (iii) the third is for either quantity or price competition among managers, who can be more than two if at least one firm has taken the M-form structure at the first stage. Moves are simultaneous in every stage and information is perfect across stages.

Unlike Ziss (1998), here each firm $J = A, B$ sells two differentiated varieties of the same good $i = 1, 2$, where again differentiation is modelled as in Singh and Vives (1984). Note that indices are the same as in the model of Bonanno and Vickers (1988), but their meaning is different. The inverse demand function for product variety i is

$$p_i = a - q_{iA} - q_{iB} - \sigma \left(q_{jA} + q_{jB} \right) \tag{5.16}$$

with $\sigma \in [-1, 1]$, so that the case of complements in demand is also considered. Inverting the demand system (5.16) yields the direct demand function for variety i to be used under Bertrand behaviour. Firms operate with the same constant marginal cost $c \in [0, a)$.

If the owner of firm J adopts the U-form, a single manager is hired with a contract containing an incentive based on a combination of the profits and sales generated by both varieties, as in Fershtman and Judd (1987):

$$M_J^U = \theta_J \Pi_J + (1 - \theta_J) R_J \tag{5.17}$$

where $\Pi_J = \pi_{1J} + \pi_{1J}$ and $R_J = R_{1J} + R_{2J} = p_1 q_{1J} + p_2 q_{2J}$. The interpretation of the superscript U is straightforward. If instead the M-form is adopted, a manager is hired to run each division, thereby generating intra-firm competition intermingled with the usual inter-firm competition associated with the managerial taste for output expansion. In this case, the manager in charge of the ith division of firm J receives the following incentive:

$$M_{iJ}^M = \theta_{iJ} \pi_{iJ} + (1 - \theta_{iJ}) R_{iJ} \tag{5.18}$$

Note that $M_{1J}^M + M_{2J}^M = M_J^U$ if and only if θ_{1J} and θ_{2J} add up to θ_J. Needless to say, there is no reason to expect this to hold at equilibrium.

The backward induction procedure solving the market stage and the delegation stage is familiar and can be omitted. It is worth noting that three possible subgames may arise at the third stage, depending upon the decisions taken by owners at the first stage: both firms may have adopted the same form, either M or U, or one is of the M-form type while the other is a U-form enterprise. This gives rise to the 2×2 game in discrete strategies appearing in Matrix 5.2, describing the problem faced by owners at the first stage, where they have to non-cooperatively choose the organizational structure of their respective firms, trying to maximize total profits.

		B	
		M-form	U-form
A	M-form	Π_A (M, M); Π_B (M, M)	Π_A (M, U); Π_B (U, M)
	U-form	Π_A (U, M); Π_B (M, U)	Π_A (U, U); Π_B (U, U)

Matrix 5.2

With firms setting quantities, the relevant inequalities are

$$\Pi_J (U, U) > \Pi_J (M, U)$$
$$\Pi_J (U, M) > \Pi_J (M, M) \qquad (5.19)$$
$$\Pi_J (U, U) > \Pi_J (M, M)$$

for all $\sigma \in (0, 1]$, while the opposite applies for $\sigma \in [-1, 0)$. This yields the following.

Proposition 5.5 *Under Cournot competition, (U, U) (respectively, (M, M)) is the unique equilibrium at the intersection of dominant strategies for all $\sigma \in (0, 1]$ (respectively, $\sigma \in [-1, 0)$). The equilibrium is Pareto-efficient for firms, for all $\sigma \in [-1, 1]$.*

The above proposition says that if goods are demand *substitutes* (respectively, complements), then firms provide their managers with *corporate* (respectively, divisional) incentives, and the equilibrium is not the outcome of a prisoners' dilemma. The same conclusion holds under price-setting behaviour, inequalities between profit pairs being unchanged in the Bertrand setting. In both cases, the organizational form yielding a lower output and a higher price per-firm is selected at equilibrium, and the owners' behaviour at the first stage seems to capture the tendency to avoid intra-firm competition. This, in turn, is reasonable in view of the fact that here firms only deploy sales divisions, any other type of strategic activities (like R&D or advertising) being absent. Typically, this is to be neither expected nor observed in large corporations where divisionalization goes hand-in-hand with the firm's growth in expanding markets, especially in view of the globalization process characterizing the world economy, irrespective of the nature of the goods being supplied. Indeed, one or more managers of different ranks are usually running single divisions in firms like Coca-Cola, Airbus Group, Toyota,

Honda or Matsushita, to mention only a few big names operating in very different industries, but the same applies in smaller entities such as Ducati and Ferrari.[10] These observations suggest that – the merits of the contribution by Bárcena-Ruiz and Espinosa (1999) notwithstanding – it would be highly desirable to extend the research on the choice between U-form and M-form to account for the presence of divisions taking care of different phases of a firm's spectrum of activities.

Bárcena-Ruiz and Espinosa (1999) also considered the case in which managerial incentives and market variables are simultaneously chosen. This entails that the game has only two stages, with managers and owners playing under imperfect information at the second stage. At the subgame perfect equilibrium of this game, we observe the following.

Proposition 5.6 *Under both Cournot and Bertrand competition, if contracts and market variables are chosen in the same stage then owners select (U, U) as the unique equilibrium at the intersection of dominant strategies for all $\sigma \in [-1, 1]$.*

This happens because, by doing so, owners force managers to maximize profits. However, this scenario is, admittedly, a bit unrealistic, as managerial contracts (i) involve long-run decisions and, as logic as well as casual observation suggest, (ii) are set prior to market strategies. Indeed, this is possibly the only case in which simultaneity between contractual design and price or quantity choices is explicitly accounted for.

In González-Maestre (2000), the game has also three stages, but their nature differs from those appearing in the game investigated by Bárcena-Ruiz and Espinosa (1999), since González-Maestre (2000) firms are taken to be of the M-form type. In the first, owners choose the number of divisions. In the second, they optimally set contracts and hire managers, one for each division; this, in principle, creates a strong intra-firm competition among divisions which may not arise in Bárcena-Ruiz and Espinosa (1999). In the third, the latter compete *à la* Cournot. All phases are characterized by simultaneous play.

Here firms supply a homogeneous good, whose market demand function can be non-linear (provided that profits remain strictly concave at least with respect to output levels). As we shall see, the curvature of market demand, measured by the ratio $\mathfrak{D} = (Q \cdot \partial^2 Q/\partial p)/\partial Q/\partial p$, plays an important role in shaping the main results of the model.

Creating a division involves a fixed cost $F > 0$, while marginal production costs are constant and equal to c across divisions and firms. The managerial contract involves a reward based upon $M_{ij} = (1 - \theta_{ij})\pi_{ij} + \theta_{ij}pq$, where π_{ij} is the profit generated by division j of firm i. At the second stage, the owners of firm i choose the vector of θ_{ij} to maximize gross profits $\widehat{\Pi}_i = \sum_{j=1}^{d_i} \pi_{ij}$. At the first, they choose d_i to maximize net profits $\widehat{\Pi}_i = \sum_{j=1}^{d_i} \pi_{ij} - d_i F$.

Omitting the details of the solutions of the second and third stage, we may concentrate on the first, where the relevant partial derivative for firm i is

$$\frac{\partial \Pi_i}{\partial d_i} = (p - c)\left[(1 - d_i)\frac{\partial Q_i}{\partial d_i} - d_i\left(\frac{\partial Q}{\partial \mathcal{D}} - \frac{\partial Q_i}{\partial \mathcal{D}}\right)\right] - \frac{d_i \theta_i^{N}}{c} \cdot \frac{\partial Q}{\partial \mathcal{D}} - F \quad (5.20)$$

where $\mathcal{D}$ is the overall number of divisions in the industry and $\theta_i^N < 0$ is the symmetric Nash equilibrium expression of θ_{ij}, for all $j = 1, 2, \ldots d_i$.[11] In (5.20), the expression in square brackets, multiplied by the mark-up, summarizes the balance between two effects (or the lack thereof): the first is the distortion generated by divisionalization, which is negative for all $d_i > 1$, and the second is the strategic effect of divisionalization, which is positive if $\partial \mathbf{Q}_{-i}/\partial \mathcal{D} = \partial \mathbf{Q}/\partial \mathcal{D} - \partial Q/\partial \mathcal{D} < 0$. These two effects always appear in the above literature about 'divisionalization without managers' and yield either a finite equilibrium (if $F > 0$) or an escalation (if $F = 0$). Here, a third one pops up because managers do appear explicitly and control quantities. This is captured by the third term in (5.20), which González-Maestre (2000, p. 327) labeled as *interaction effect* as it captures the interplay between divisionalization and strategic delegation. This is always negative because both $\theta_i^N < 0$ and $\partial \mathbf{Q}/\partial \mathcal{D} < 0$, and may cause firms to refrain from divisionalization, if $\partial \Pi_i/\partial d_i < 0$, in which case $d^N = 1$. The main message conveyed by González-Maestre's (2000) analysis is the following.

Proposition 5.7 *If the industry is a duopoly (for any $\mathfrak{D}$), or $-\mathfrak{D} > n$, then at the subgame perfect equilibrium all firms consist of a single division. If instead the industry is at least a triopoly and $\mathfrak{D} > 0$, or $-\mathfrak{D} < n$, then at the subgame perfect equilibrium firms are multidivisional and, if the fixed cost becomes negligible, the market outcome will replicate perfect competition in the limit via excess divisionalization.*

Hence, González-Maestre (2000) reproduced the essential conclusions drawn from the early models, in the presence of managerialization modelled as in the classical contributions reviewed in Chapter 2, showing that in some cases managerialization can be held responsible for the lack of divisionalization.

It is worth noting that the first claim appearing in the above proposition can be rephrased as follows: in a duopoly where managerial firms compete in output levels, the game and its subgame perfect equilibrium are observationally equivalent to those appearing in Vickers (1985), Fershtman and Judd (1987) and Sklivas (1987), where the possibility for firms to become multidivisional is not even considered, and this holds true irrespective of the properties of the demand function. This is no longer true if more than two firms are present. This means that the present model explicitly illustrates that relying on duopoly models 'because two is representative of any integer larger than one' may not be a sound idea. The problem is that the use of duopoly is way too common and out there in the enormous IO literature outside the boundaries of the issues dealt with in this book there exist many other examples of the same nature, of which we are not currently aware.

Last but not least, there comes the model by Faulí-Oller and Giralt (1995), which I have intentionally left aside thus far because it is the only contribution featuring technological externalities within a firm, in the form of economies of scope in the supply of an enterprise's product range. The demand side is the same as in Bárcena-Ruiz and Espinosa (1999), the relevant inverse demand function for Cournot competition coinciding with (5.16), but these authors confined themselves to the analysis of demand substitutes, i.e. $\sigma \in (0, 1]$.

As far as production technology is concerned, the cost function of firm $J = A, B$ is now

$$C_J = c\,(q_{1J} + q_{2J}) + (b + \varepsilon)\left(q_{1J}^2 + q_{2J}^2\right) - 2\varepsilon q_{1J} q_{2J} \tag{5.21}$$

Both firms are divisionalized, with one division taking care of producing a single variety, so that (5.21) can be decomposed to yield the cost function to division $i = 1, 2$ of firm J:

$$C_{iJ} = cq_{iJ} + (b + \varepsilon)\,q_{iJ}^2 - \varepsilon q_{1J} q_{2J}, \tag{5.22}$$

with $c \in [0, a)$, $b, \varepsilon \geq 0$ and $\varepsilon \neq \sigma$. Parameter ε measures the degree of positive technological spillover between product varieties, giving rise to scope economies in production. The requirement $\varepsilon \neq \sigma$ is a delicate assumption, whose role will become clear in the remainder of the exposition.

Here the matter of choosing the internal organization of the firm is not an issue. Both firms adopt the M-form and assign the control of their two divisions to two managers, provided with incentives based on

$$M_{iJ} = \pi_{iJ} + \theta_J \pi_{jJ} \tag{5.23}$$

where $i, j = 1, 2$ and $j \neq i$. This means that delegation contracts are designed as in Salas Fumas (1992) and Miller and Pazgal (2001) and require the managers working inside the same firm to compete against each other (respectively, cooperate with each other) for any $\theta_J < 0$ (respectively, $\theta_J > 0$). If $\theta_J = 0$, each manager behaves as if she/he were the owner of a division, decisions being fully decentralized. If instead $\theta_J = 1$, then managers are forced to cooperate to maximize their firm's profits – as if it were manoeuvred by its owner in person. The latter case is that of full centralization of production decisions. The game has a simple two-stage structure: the first for delegation contracts and the second for Cournot–Nash competition.

The usual backward induction procedure reveals that the condition

$$\theta_J < \frac{1 + 2b + \varepsilon}{\varepsilon - \sigma} \tag{5.24}$$

must hold in order for the equilibrium price to ensure a positive mark-up. In turn, the expression on the right-hand side of (5.24) also requires $\varepsilon \neq \sigma$, otherwise it would be impossible for θ_J to satisfy the above inequality. Assuming (5.24) and $\varepsilon \neq \sigma$ are both satisfied, at the Nash equilibrium of the first stage the following emerges.

Proposition 5.8 *Due to the presence of scope economies in production, owners find it optimal to induce their managers to cooperate by choosing $\theta^N > 1$ for all $\varepsilon > \sigma$.*

Indeed, the optimal delegation contract features

$$\theta^N = \frac{1+b+\varepsilon - \sqrt{b\left[b+2\left(1+\sigma\right)\right]}}{\varepsilon - \sigma} \tag{5.25}$$

which is larger than one if the externality parameter outweighs product substitutability. If this is the case, then the presence of considerable economies of scope
more than offsetting the intensity of market competition measured by σ is a strong
incentive for owners to push their managers to over-internalize the spillover effect.
Conversely, if $\varepsilon < \sigma$, then $\theta^N < 1$. Note that also the expression of θ^N is admissible if and only if $\varepsilon \neq \sigma$. This problem isn't simply a technical detail, as both key
parameters, ε and σ, are exogenous to the firms. In particular, σ is in the representative consumer's mind, and therefore might well happen to coincide with ε
by chance. Of course this will not happen if $\varepsilon > 1$, which is very demanding and
much less than general.

Be that as it may, the take-home message of the model deployed by Faulí-Oller
and Giralt (1995) is that firms will ask their managers to cooperate in the direction of profit maximization whenever the degree of technological spillovers across
divisions in the same firm dominates the intensity of market competition, and conversely. Their approach to multidivisional firms takes divisionalization for granted
and combines the taste for variety (or product differentiation) with a more detailed
description of production technology to single out a convincing link between
these two features and the appropriate attitude that should characterize managerial
behaviour, as implied by their optimal hiring contracts.

To conclude this section, I would like to stress the relevance of two details
appearing in Faulí-Oller and Giralt (1995). The first is the presence of economies
of scope. This element, which came to the fore in the early 1980s as one of the
key factors in the theory of contestable markets (Baumol *et al.*, 1982), quite rarely
appears in oligopoly models, its high degree of realism and empirical relevance
notwithstanding. Indeed, casual observation reveals that economies of scope are
pervasive in several industries. In the car industry, the same engine and chassis are
used for different models (think of the VW-Audi Group, using the same engines
and chassis across models and brands – VW, Audi and Skoda). The same happens
for essential components (e.g. CPUs for PCs and laptops, or transistors for hi-fi
amplifiers) in consumer electronics. Plenty of additional examples could be easily
mentioned.

An interesting story connected with the subject matter of this chapter is that
of Avid Hi-Fi Ltd, based in Alconbury, Cambridgeshire, since 1995. For a long
time, their product line included only several high-quality turntable models, rig-
orously belt-driven. Now it also includes phono stages, equally top-notch items.
Production relies on precision-cut metallic parts being assembled to deliver the
final product, all of this assisted by an engineering equipment including computer-
numerical-control (CNC) machining, which has allowed Avid to produce original-
equipment-manufacturer (OEM) parts for sports cars such as Lightning Car
Company's all-electric GTS model presented at the London Motor Show 2009,

among others. This piece of anecdotal evidence connects economies of scope to the second element I still have to mention explicitly, which is the extent of product substitutability (or differentiation). Usually, as in Faulí-Oller and Giralt (1995), the case of independent products (using the above symbology, $\sigma = 0$) is overlooked as this is a case in which strategic interaction is absent. Correct observation, but not necessarily a wise choice, as the Avid case illustrates too well: on the one hand, we can take for granted that substitutability between turntables and cars is nil; on the other, this example says that the absence of strategic interaction can make room for OEM production via scope economies.[12]

An analogous picture, although with a reverse time line, comes out of the story of yet another UK firm operating in the hi-fi industry. SME (Scale Model Equipment) Ltd, founded in 1946 and based in Steyning, West Sussex. SME started is activity producing scale models and detail parts for the model engineering trade, then (from 1960) also aircraft instruments and business machines. The hi-fi production came out as a spin-off generated by a request from its founder, Alastair Robertson-Aikman, for a quality pick-up arm for his personal use. After the prototype was approved, it entered large scale production, badged as SME 3009, to quickly become one of the preferred tonearms of audio enthusiasts worldwide.[13]

And there is more. The case of independent products is relevant for the interpretation of the phenomenon known as *umbrella branding*, whereby firms may supply product ranges including completely different products having in common only a brand and the loyalty effect it generates in the consumer's mind, which is the driver of this type of strategy. This marketing behaviour is behind head-to-head competition, which is enhanced by the presence of switching costs (Klemperer, 1992). Several tobacco brands have been used this way, and analogous cases exist in the automotive industry (e.g. Ferrari).

5.2.2 *Divisionalization and mergers*

The economic analysis of multidivisional firms has something relevant to say about horizontal mergers as well, as anticipated in Chapter 4. Indeed, a multidivisional enterprise may be the outcome of a merger between two or more formerly independent firms of which the merged entity can decide to maintain each division in existence. In fact, casual observation suggests so, the automotive industry again providing plenty of examples. Two notable ones involve Chrysler, which first merged with Daimler Benz in 1998 to create Daimler Chrysler and then, after separating from Daimler, merged with FIAT in 2009 to create FCA. What follows can be read as a theory of horizontal mergers explaining the formation of multidivisional corporations.

The first theoretical contribution in this area is in Ziss (1995). The layout is analogous to Bonanno and Vickers (1988), with a two-division (manufacturer–retailer) vertical structure characterizing two supply chains operating in the same industry, and retailing contracts specified in the form of a standard two-part tariff. Using this model, Ziss (1995) examined two alternative horizontal mergers taking place between either upstream firms (manufacturers) or downstream firms (retailers). He showed that (i) the upstream merger has anti-competitive effects, if not intra-brand competition exists, while, conversely (ii) the downstream merger has no anti-competitive effects irrespective of whether intra-brand competition is present or not.[14]

More recently, Wickelgren (2005) explained the formation of a multiproduct/ multidivisional firm through a merger in the presence of managerial incentives shaped in a form which combines Miller and Pazgal (2001) and Holmström (1982). That is, managerial efforts to improve products are non-negotiable and each manager is provided with an incentive based on a linear combination of the profits generated by all products supplied by the firm.

To fix ideas, the linear-quadratic example in Wickelgren (2005) can be quickly summarized. Suppose the firm generated by the merger is selling two products, each supplied by a different division controlled by a manager. Let the demand function of product i be

$$q_i = a - p_i + \varepsilon_i - \beta \varepsilon_j + v \left(p_j - \varepsilon_j - p_i + \varepsilon_i \right) \tag{5.26}$$

where $\varepsilon_i > 0$ is the non-contractible effort of the manager responsible for producing and selling good i and $\beta \in [0, 1]$ is the spillover occurring between the two managers' activities. If $v = 0$, goods are independent of each other (this case corresponds to $\sigma = 0$ in the previous models); if $v \to \infty$, goods are perfect substitutes (as with $\sigma = 1$). Unit production cost is constant and equal to c for both goods.

The manager in charge of division/product i has a net utility defined as

$$u_i = M_i - k\varepsilon_i^2 \tag{5.27}$$

where parameter $k > 0$ determines the steepness of the cost of managerial effort, and

$$M_i = \theta_i \pi_i + (1 - \theta_i) \pi_j \tag{5.28}$$

is a reward based on a linear combination of the profits generated by both goods.

The game has a two-stage structure. In the first period, each manager chooses θ_i to maximize u_i; in the second, each manager chooses price p_i and effort ε_i, again to maximize u_i. Hence, if $\theta_i = \theta_j = 1/2$, managers are motivated by a pure profit-sharing incentive, which of course has a straightforward effect on market prices and efforts at the second stage. Moreover, this procedure establishes an endogenous interaction between strategic variables and the two key parameters, namely, the steepness of the effort cost, k, and the degree of substitutability, measured by v, in such a way that the following are true.

- The equilibrium symmetric weight $\theta^* \geq 1/2$ if and only if

$$\beta \in \left[0, \frac{1+v}{1+3v} \right] \tag{5.29}$$

That is, very high spillovers prevent the attainment of perfect profit-sharing. Put differently, the spillover must be low enough in order for an increase in θ_i to induce an increase in ε_i (which is costly) and therefore in sales. When the positive externality received by the other manager is very high, the manager of division i prefers to lay back and slack off a bit.

- If k is large and β is low, then

$$\frac{\partial \theta^*}{\partial k}, \frac{\partial \theta^*}{\partial v} < 0; \quad \frac{\partial \theta^*}{\partial \beta} > 0 \tag{5.30}$$

i.e. profit sharing at equilibrium is decreasing in the cost of effort and product substitutability and increasing in the knowledge spillover. Since the opposite inequalities apply if k is low and β is large, then it appears that θ^N is non-monotone in the whole set of model parameters; in particular, it is U-shaped with respect to the spillover level.

Now it suffices to observe that, intuitively, perfect profit-sharing ($\theta^* = 1/2$) means higher prices: in practice, it eliminates intra-firm competition inducing a cooperative behaviour on the part of managers. Any pronounced increase in θ^*, conversely, intensifies intra-firm competition and may lead to a non-negligible decrease in the symmetric equilibrium prices as compared to the pre-merger duopolistic configuration. If so, then the merger turns out to be socially efficient by virtue of the increase in consumer surplus. In view of the presence of a problem whose nature is the same as that of moral hazard in teams (Holmström, 1982), then one may say that moral hazard can be a source of socially efficient industry structures or market allocations.

The alternative approach to the same theme, proposed by Ziss (2007), shares a few elements with Ziss (1998) and combines them with the hierarchical structure in Bonanno and Vickers (1988). Here firms have a corporate centre, followed by production divisions and local units (or outlets) facing customers. Consider first what happens in the absence of any mergers. The corporate centre delegates production divisions the tasks of designing the incentives for sales managers and assessing the sales performance of local outlets. The game consists of two stages: in the first, production units design managerial incentives and in the second, local outlets compete either in quantities or in prices. If a merger takes place between any two firms, the corporate centre must choose whether to intervene in order to modify the degree of intra-firm competition or not.

The product range consists of n differentiated varieties. The demand function of each product i is

$$p = a - q_i - \sigma Q_{-i} \tag{5.31}$$

with $\sigma \in [0, 1]$ and $Q_{-i} = \sum_{j \neq i} q_j$. Before the merger, each variety is supplied by an independent firm, whose outlet manager receives an incentive defined as in

Fershtman and Judd (1987):

$$M_i = \theta_i \pi_i + (1 - \theta_i) \, p_i q_i \tag{5.32}$$

i.e. a combination of the profits and revenues generated by local unit i. Hence, the pre-merger subgame perfect equilibrium also replicates the original outcome in Vickers (1985), except for the presence of product differentiation.

Now imagine the merger involves product (or firms) 1 and 2. These become part of the new entity, whose corporate centre must decide upon variables λ_i and $\varkappa_i$, $i = 1, 2$, both discrete and belonging to the binary set $\{0, 1\}$ and appearing in

$$LU_i = M_i + \lambda_i M_j; \quad PU_i = \pi_i + \varkappa_i \pi_j, \ \ i, j = 1, 2, \ i \neq j \tag{5.33}$$

where LU_i (PU_i) is the objective function of local (production) unit i. Hence, the values taken by λ_i and $\varkappa_i$ indicate whether the centre has decided to merge or not the pairs of its downstream divisions. This yields four alternative scenarios:

- no merger: $\lambda_i = \varkappa_i = 0$;
- local unit merger: $\lambda_i = 1$, $\varkappa_i = 0$;
- production unit merger: $\lambda_i = 0$, $\varkappa_i = 1$;
- full merger: $\lambda_i = \varkappa_i = 1$.

The subgame perfect equilibrium of the post-merger game is obtained as follows. Each local unit has to choose its quantity or price strategy to maximize LU_i, while each production unit has to choose θ_i to maximize PU_i. Then, proceeding backwards, the corporate centre sets the values of λ_i and $\varkappa_i$ to maximize corporate profits. The qualitative predictions delivered by the solution of the game can be outlined as follows.

Proposition 5.9 *Under Cournot competition and sufficiently high industry concentration, a profitable merger entails $\lambda_i = \varkappa_i = 1$. In general, such a merger diminishes welfare.*

The intuition is as follows. Any partial merger at the same level allows the units operating at that level to fully internalize the externality between themselves and better absorb the burden of managerial incentives of the corresponding divisions belonging to outsiders not taking part in the merger. Hence, a double-layer merger allows the corporate centre to enhance the complementarity between mergers at each level and create a credible commitment toward output restriction (once again, the *leitmotiv* of Stackelberg leadership pops up). The output restriction, in turn, is responsible for the welfare loss which makes the merger socially inefficient. Note that 'sufficiently high' requires $n \leq 7$. This reveals that modelling the vertical structure of firms puts into question the classical result in Salant *et al.* (1983), whereby about 80% of the firms in the industry should merge in order for the merger to be profitable (cf. Chapter 4). This is no longer true if the internal structure of firms is described in some more detail.

Proposition 5.10 *Under Bertrand competition, a merger is always profitable and entails* $\lambda_i = \varkappa_i = 1$. *Such a merger diminishes welfare.*

This result is even more intuitive. Price competition being harsher than output competition (if varieties are substitutes in demand), then we already know from Deneckere and Davidson (1985) that any merger is profitable and welfare-reducing in the traditional oligopoly model without divisionalization and managers. *A fortiori* this must apply here, where three layers of responsibility appear along the hierarchical structure of firms.

Further reading

For comprehensive surveys on vertical relations and supply chain coordination, see Irmen (1998) and Iyer (1998). A summary of the discussion on delegation in supply chains is in Caillaud and Rey (1994). An updated account of more recent material is in Etro (2011). For more on the theory of vertical relations and transfer pricing, see McGuire and Staelin (1983), Moorthy (1988), Whinston (1990), Holmström and Tirole (1991), Shaffer (1991), O'Brien and Shaffer (1993), Caillaud *et al.* (1995), Gérard and Long (1996), Villas-Boas (1998), Häckner (2003), Fumagalli and Motta (2006) and Calzolari and Denicolò (2013), among many others. Other aspects of strategic delegation among vertically related firms are investigated in Park (2002) and Ho and Sung (2014). Additional empirical research is in Norton (1988) and Corts (2001).

Notes

1 In a related paper where, however, delegation is not explicitly modelled, Milliou and Petrakis (2007) characterized incentives to carry out horizontal mergers between upstream firms in a vertically related industry in which vertical contracts are endogenously designed. In particular, they showed that the presence of two-part tariffs altogether wipes out any incentive to merge for manufacturers, which exists instead if wholesale pricing is used.
2 Strong empirical evidence illustrates that sales managers are indeed rewarded in proportion to their outlets' sales, even when these outlets are company owned (Hadfield, 1990, 1991; Lafontaine, 1992).
3 In the Bertrand version of the same model, Gal-Or (1990) demonstrated that only symmetric configurations may obtain at equilibrium.
4 The theory of multiproduct firms, either in monopoly or in oligopoly, has a long tradition in IO, too vast to be summarized here. In general, a recurrent theme is the obvious interplay between preemption and product proliferation, and their welfare consequences. Among many others, see Brander and Eaton (1984), Judd (1985), Wernerfelt (1986), Bonanno and Haworth (1998) and Lambertini (2003). See also the end of the next section.
5 The total number of market subgame is eight: two with two sellers (in one of these, one of the seller is a multiproduct player), and six with three single-product sellers.
6 Indeed, this may be justified thinking of a past history of this industry, during which m_A has acquired a patent on variety 1, with m_B being unsuccessful in trying to 'invent around the patent'.
7 This is also connected with the idea of preempting rivals using multiple retailers, which dates back to the early days of the modern theory of vertical restraints (Mathewson and Winter, 1984; Rey and Tirole, 1986; Rey and Stiglitz, 1988, 1995).

8 This assumption is particularly meaningful: the firms do not worry about supplying product ranges, as in this class of models their dreams are exclusively haunted by the need to expand output. The allowance made to the realistic possibility that products may be imperfect substitutes across firms is, however, full of consequences.
9 This excess divisionalization closely resembles the excess product proliferation characterizing equilibria in games among multiproduct firms. See, e.g., Brander and Eaton (1984) and Klemperer and Padilla (1997).
10 Note that, according to official data for 2013, Honda sold almost 16.8 million bikes worldwide, while Ducati produced less that 45,000. See http://www.autoevolution.com.
11 Note that this implies that the weight attached to profits in the managerial incentive M_i is actually higher than one.
12 For additional material, see the firm's website, www.avidhifi.com.
13 For more on the history of SME, see the website http://www.sme-audio.com.
14 In a related paper, Lin (1990) examined the scenario where upstream firms decide to share a common retailer, which is observationally equivalent to a downstream merger. Lin (1990) showed that, in the absence of intra-brand competition, this type of downstream merger fosters competition if prices are used as strategic variables.

References

Aghion, P. and P. Bolton (1987), 'Long-Term Contracts as a Barrier to Entry', *American Economic Review*, **77**, 388–401.
Alles, M. and S. Datar (1998), 'Strategic Transfer Pricing', *Management Science*, **44**, 451–61.
Balasubramanian, S. and P. Bhardwaj (2004), 'When not All Conflict Is Bad: Manufacturing-Marketing Conflict and Strategic Incentive Design', *Management Science*, **50**, 489–503.
Bárcena-Ruiz, J.C. and M.P. Espinosa (1999), 'Should Multiproduct Firms Provide Divisional or Corporate Incentives?', *International Journal of Industrial Organization*, **17**, 751–64.
Baumol, W., J. Panzar and R. Willig (1982), *Contestable Markets and the Theory of Industry Structure*, New York, Harcourt Brace Jovanovich.
Baye, M.R., K.J. Crocker and J. Ju (1996a), 'Divisionalization, Franchising, and Divestiture Incentives in Oligopoly', *American Economic Review*, **86**, 223–36.
Baye, M.R., K.J. Crocker and J. Ju (1996b), 'Divisionalization and Franchising Incentives with Integral Competing Units', *Economics Letters*, **50**, 429–35.
Bernheim, B.D. and M.D. Whinston (1998), 'Exclusive Dealing', *Journal of Political Economy*, **106**, 64–103.
Bonanno, G. and B. Haworth (1998), 'Intensity of Competition and the Choice between Product and Process Innovation', *International Journal of Industrial Organization*, **16**, 495–510.
Bonanno, G. and J. Vickers (1988), 'Vertical Separation', *Journal of Industrial Economics*, **36**, 257–65.
Brander, J. and J. Eaton (1984), 'Product Line Rivalry', *American Economic Review*, **74**, 323–34.
Bulow, J., J. Geanakoplos and P. Klemperer (1985), 'Multimarket Oligopoly: Strategic Substitutes and Complements', *Journal of Political Economy*, **93**, 488–511.
Caillaud, B. and P. Rey (1994), 'Strategic Aspects of Vertical Delegation', *European Economic Review*, **39**, 421–31.
Caillaud, B., B. Jullien and P. Picard (1995), 'Competing Vertical Structures: Precommitment and Renegotiation', *Econometrica*, **63**, 621–46.

Calzolari, G. and V. Denicolò (2013), 'Competition with Exclusive Contracts and Market-Share Discounts', *American Economic Review*, **103**, 2384–411.

Caves, R.E. (1980), 'Industrial Organization, Corporate Strategy and Structure', *Journal of Economic Literature*, **18**, 64–92.

Chandler, A.D. Jr. (1969), *Strategy and Structure: The History of the American Industrial Enterprise*, Cambridge, MA, MIT Press.

Chou, C.-H. (2014), 'Strategic Delegation and Vertical Integration', *Managerial and Decision Economics*, **35**, 580–6.

Corchón, L. (1991), 'Oligopolistic Competition among Groups', *Economics Letters*, **36**, 1–3.

Corchón, L. and M. González-Maestre (2000), 'On the Competitive Effects of Divisional-ization', *Mathematical Social Sciences*, **39**, 71–9.

Corts, K. (2001), 'The Strategic Effects of Vertical Market Structure: Common Agency and Divisionalization in the U.S. Motion Picture Industry', *Journal of Economics and Management Strategy*, **10**, 509–28.

Corts, K. and D. Neher (2003), 'Credible Delegation', *European Economic Review*, **47**, 395–407.

Coughlan, A.T. and B. Wernerfelt (1989), 'On Credible Delegation by Oligopolists: A Discussion of Distribution Channel Management', *Management Science*, **35**, 226–39.

d'Aspremont, C. and L.-A. Gérard-Varet (1980), 'Stackelberg-Solvable Games and Pre-Play Communication', *Journal of Economic Theory*, **23**, 201–17.

Deneckere, R. and C. Davidson (1985), 'Incentives to Form Coalitions with Bertrand Competition', *Rand Journal of Economics*, **16**, 473–86.

Etro, F. (2011), 'Endogenous Market Structures and Contract Theory: Delegation, Principal-Agent Contracts, Screening, Franchising and Tying', *European Economic Review*, **55**, 463–79.

Faulí-Oller, R. and M. Giralt (1995), 'Competition and Cooperation within a Multidivi-sional Firm', *Journal of Industrial Economics*, **43**, 77–99.

Fershtman, C. and K. Judd (1987), 'Equilibrium Incentives in Oligopoly', *American Economic Review*, **77**, 927–40.

Fumagalli, C. and M. Motta (2006), 'Exclusive Dealing and Entry, when Buyers Compete', *American Economic Review*, **96**, 785–95.

Gal-Or, E. (1990), 'Excessive Retailing at the Bertrand Equilibria', *Canadian Journal of Economics*, **23**, 294–304.

Gal-Or, E. (1991), 'Duopolistic Vertical Restraints', *European Economic Review*, **35**, 1237–53.

Gérard, G. and N. Long (1996), 'Vertical Integration, Foreclosure, and Profits in the Pres-ence of Double Marginalization', *Journal of Economics and Management Strategy*, **5**, 409–32.

González-Maestre, M. (2000), 'Divisionalization and Delegation in Oligopoly', *Journal of Economics & Management Strategy*, **9**, 321–38.

González-Maestre, M. (2001), 'Divisionalization with Spatial Differentiation', *Interna-tional Journal of Industrial Organization*, **19**, 1297–313.

Häckner, J. (2003), 'Vertical Integration and Competition Policy', *Journal of Regulatory Economics*, **24**, 213–22.

Hadfield, G. (1990), 'Problematic Relations: Franchising and the Law of Incomplete Contracts', *Stanford Law Review*, **42**, 927–92.

Hadfield, G. (1991), 'Credible Spatial Preemption through Franchising', *RAND Journal of Economics*, **22**, 531–43.

Hamilton, J. and S. Slutsky (1990), 'Endogenous Timing in Duopoly Games: Stackelberg or Cournot Equilibria', *Games and Economic Behavior*, **2**, 29–46.

Hermalin, B. (1994), 'Heterogeneity in Organizational Form: Why Otherwise Identical Firms Choose Different Incentives for Their Managers', *RAND Journal of Economics*, **25**, 518–37.

Hirshleifer, J. (1957), 'Economics of the Divisionalized Firm', *Journal of Business*, **30**, 96–108.

Ho, S.J. and H.-C. Sung (2014), 'Strategic Delegation in a Multiproduct Mixed Industry', *Managerial and Decision Economics*, **35**, 278–87.

Holmström, B. (1982), 'Moral Hazard in Teams', *Bell Journal of Economics*, **13**, 324–40.

Holmström, B. and J. Tirole (1991), 'Transfer Pricing and Organizational Form', *Journal of Law, Economics and Organization*, **7**, 201–28.

Irmen, A. (1998), 'Precommitment in Competing Vertical Chains', *Journal of Economic Surveys*, **12**, 333-59.

Iyer, G. (1998), 'Coordinating Channels under Price and Nonprice Competition', *Marketing Science*, **17**, 338–55.

Jansen, J. (2003), 'Coexistence of Strategic Vertical Separation and Integration', *International Journal of Industrial Organization*, **21**, 699–716.

Judd, K. (1985), 'Credible Spatial Preemption', *RAND Journal of Economics*, **16**, 153–66.

Kaplan, R.S. and A.A. Atkinson (1998), *Advanced Management Accounting*, Upper Saddle River, NJ, Prentice-Hall.

Katz, M. (1991), 'Game-Playing Agents: Unobservable Contracts as Precommitments', *RAND Journal of Economics*, **22**, 307–28.

Katz, M. (2006), 'Observable Contracts as Commitments: Interdependent Contracts and Moral Hazard', *Journal of Economics and Management Strategy*, **15**, 685–706.

Klein, B., R. Crawford and A. Alchian (1978), 'Vertical Integration, Appropriable Rents, and the Competitive Contracting Process', *Journal of Law and Economics*, **21**, 297–326.

Klemperer, P. (1992), 'Equilibrium Product Lines: Competing Head-to-Head May Be Less Competitive', *American Economic Review*, **82**, 740–55.

Klemperer, P. and A.J. Padilla (1997), 'Do Firms' Product Lines Include Too Many Vatieties?', *RAND Journal of Economics*, **28**, 472–88.

Kühn, K.-U. (1997), 'Nonlinear Pricing in Vertically Related Duopolies', *RAND Journal of Economics*, **28**, 37–62.

Lafontaine, F. (1992), 'Agency Theory and Franchising: Some Empirical Results', *RAND Journal of Economics*, **23**, 263–83.

Lafontaine, F. and M. Slade (2007), 'Vertical Integration and Firm Boundaries: The Evidence', *Journal of Economic Literature*, **45**, 629–85.

Lambertini, L. (2003), 'The Monopolist's Optimal R&D Portfolio', *Oxford Economic Papers*, **55**, 561–78.

Lin, Y.L. (1990), 'The Dampening-of-Competition Effect of Exclusive Dealing', *Journal of Industrial Economics*, **39**, 209–23.

Lundgren, C. (1996), 'Using Relative Profit Incentives to Prevent Collusion', *Review of Industrial Organization*, **11**, 533–50.

McGuire, T. and R. Staelin (1983), 'An Industry Equilibrium Analysis of Downstream Vertical Integration', *Marketing Science*, **2**, 161–92.

Mankiw, N.G. and M.D. Whinston (1986), 'Free Entry and Social Inefficiency', *Rand Journal of Economics*, **17**, 48–58.

Mathewson, G. and R. Winter (1984), 'An Economic Theory of Vertical Restraints', *RAND Journal of Economics*, **15**, 27–38.

Miller, N. and A. Pazgal (2001), 'The Equivalence of Price and Quantity Competition with Delegation', *RAND Journal of Economics*, **32**, 284–301.

Milliou, C. and E. Petrakis (2007), 'Upstream Horizontal Mergers, Vertical Contracts, and Bargaining', *International Journal of Industrial Organization*, **25**, 963–87.

Moner-Colonques, R., J.J. Sempere-Monerris and A. Urbano (2004), 'Strategic Delegation with Multiproduct Firms', *Journal of Economics and Management Strategy*, **13**, 405–27.

Moorthy, K. (1988), 'Strategic Decentralization in Channels', *Marketing Science*, **7**, 335–55.

Norton, S.W. (1988), 'An Empirical Look at Franchising as an Organizational Form', *Journal of Business*, **61**, 197–218.

O'Brien, D. and G. Shaffer (1993), 'On the Dampening-of-Competition Effect of Exclusive Dealing', *Journal of Industrial Economics*, **41**, 215–21.

Ordover, J.A., G. Saloner and S. Salop (1990), 'Equilibrium Market Foreclosure', *American Economic Review*, **80**, 127–42.

Pagnozzi, M. and S. Piccolo (2012), 'Vertical Separation With Private Contracts', *Economic Journal*, **122**, 173–207.

Park, E.-S. (2002), 'Vertical Externality and Strategic Delegation', *Managerial and Decision Economics*, **23**, 137–41.

Polasky, S. (1992), 'Divide and Conquer: On the Profitability of Forming Independent Rival Divisions', *Economics Letters*, **40**, 365–71.

Rey, P. and J. Stiglitz (1988), 'Vertical Restraints and Producers' Competition', *European Economic Review*, **32**, 561–8.

Rey, P. and J. Stiglitz (1995), 'The Role of Exclusive Territories in Producers' Competition', *RAND Journal of Economics*, **26**, 431–51.

Rey, P. and J. Tirole (1986), 'The Logic of Vertical Restraints', *American Economic Review*, **76**, 923–39.

Salant, S.W., S. Switzer and R.J. Reynolds (1983), 'Losses from Horizontal Merger: The Effects of an Exogenous Change in Industry Structure on Cournot-Nash Equilibrium', *Quarterly Journal of Economics*, **98**, 185–213.

Salas Fumas, V. (1992), 'Relative Performance Evaluation of Management: The Effects on Industrial Competition and Risk Sharing', *International Journal of Industrial Organization*, **10**, 473–89.

Salinger, M.A. (1988), 'Vertical Mergers and Market Foreclosure', *Quarterly Journal of Economics*, **77**, 345–56.

Salop, S. (1979), 'Monopolistic Competition with Outside Goods', *Bell Journal of Economics*, **10**, 141–56.

Salop, S. and D. Scheffman (1987), 'Cost-Raising Strategies', *Journal of Industrial Economics*, **36**, 19–34.

Schwartz, M. and E.A. Thompson (1986), 'Divisionalization and Entry Deterrence', *Quarterly Journal of Economics*, **101**, 307–21.

Shaffer, G. (1991), 'Capturing Strategic Rent: Full-Line Forcing, Brand Discounts, Aggregate Rebates, and Maximum Resale Price Maintenance', *Journal of Industrial Economics*, **39**, 557–75.

Shaked, A. and J. Sutton (1983), 'Natural Oligopolies', *Econometrica*, **51**, 1469–83.

Singh, N. and X. Vives (1984), 'Price and Quantity Competition in a Differentiated Duopoly', *RAND Journal of Economics*, **15**, 546–54.

Sklivas, S.D. (1987), 'The Strategic Choice of Managerial Incentives', *RAND Journal of Economics*, **18**, 452–8.

Slade, M. (1998), 'Strategic Motives for Vertical Separation: Evidence from Retail Gasoline Markets', *Journal of Law, Economics and Organization*, **14**, 84–113.

Veendorp, E.C.H. (1991), 'Entry Deterrence, Divisionalization, and Investment Decisions', *Quarterly Journal of Economics*, **106**, 297–307.

Vickers, J. (1985), 'Delegation and the Theory of the Firm', *Economic Journal*, **95** (Conference Papers), 138–47.

Villas-Boas, J.M. (1998), 'Product Line Design for a Distribution Channel', *Marketing Science*, **17**, 156–69.

Vroom, G. (2006), 'Organizational Design and the Intensity of Rivalry', *Management Science*, **52**, 1689–702.

Wernerfelt, B. (1986), 'Product Line Rivalry: A Note', *American Economic Review*, **76**, 842–4.

Whinston, M. (1990), 'Tying, Foreclosure and Exclusion', *American Economic Review*, **80**, 837–59.

Wickelgren, A.L. (2005), 'Managerial Incentives and the Price Effects of Mergers', *Journal of Industrial Economics*, **53**, 327–53.

Williamson, O. (1975), *Markets and Hierarchies: Analysis and Antitrust Implications*, New York, Free Press.

Ziss, S. (1995), 'Vertical Separation and Horizontal Mergers', *Journal of Industrial Economics*, **43**, 63–75.

Ziss, S. (1998), 'Divisionalization and Product Differentiation', *Economics Letters*, **59**, 133–8.

Ziss, S. (1999), 'Divisionalization and Strategic Managerial Incentives in Oligopoly under Uncertainty', *International Journal of Industrial Organization*, **17**, 1163–87.

Ziss, S. (2007), 'Hierarchies, Intra-Firm Competition and Mergers', *International Journal of Industrial Organization*, **25**, 237–60.

6 Innovation and technical progress

This chapter accounts for the role of strategic delegation in shaping firms' innovation incentives. As such, the material we are about to review nests into a large literature which has taken a prominent position in the modern IO literature.[1]

The fundamental research question taken up here can be formulated as follows. As we know from reading the previous chapters, industries where at least some of the firms are managerialized are more competitive than those made up of pure profit-seeking firms, if managers are rewarded on the basis of a combination of profits and some output-related magnitudes, and this type of delegation acts as a substitute of marginal cost reductions. Accordingly, what direction shall we expect managerial firms to take when some forms of costly R&D enter the picture? Or shall we expect managerial firms to produce higher or lower R&D efforts and technical progress, as compared to pure profit-seeking units?

Anecdotal as well as empirical evidence points out that we should expect managerial firms to outperform their entrepreneurial counterparts in producing technical progress in every direction – more specifically, in terms of both process and product innovations. Available data sustain this claim (see Galbraith and Merrill, 1991; Czarnitzki and Kraft, 2004; and Cunat and Guadalupe, 2006), and so does also the observation of famous recent cases. Hutton (2002) forcefully stressed that firms where managers are driven to adopt a short-run profit-maximizing perspective are consequently less prone to reinvesting profits in long-run risky R&D projects instead of leaving the same profits to the distribution of dividends, as compared to firms in which managers are in a position to adopt wide ranging views on the basis of looser bridles granted by the incentives defined in their contracts. A relevant example is provided by the race for the new large civil transport jet airliner which led to the introduction of the Airbus A380 when its rival, at the time nicknamed Boeing 7e7, was still paperwork.[2]

As we are about to see throughout the chapter, this is indeed the take-home message consistently delivered – with at least one relevant exception related to licensing – by the theoretical literature taking up this issue, in a variety of models considering: (i) the relationship between the intensity of competition and the industry R&D performance; (ii) exogenously given R&D expenses; (iii) managerial firms coexisting with entrepreneurial ones and endogenously choose R&D efforts for either process or product innovation; (iv) endogenous technological spillovers; (v) technology licensing; (vi) outsourcing. This seemingly long list of variations notwithstanding, a large space still exists for further investigations in several other directions.

Before treating R&D incentives in the domain of strategic delegation, I will illustrate them in the context of agency relationships using the theoretical background offered by models embedding moral hazard in strategic market competition, which we encountered at the end of Chapter 1.

6.1 Preliminaries: the principal-agent relationship with R&D

On the basis of the Cournot model with strategic delegation and full information – irrespective of the specific incentive scheme adopted by owners – one might be induced to think that symmetric firms will systematically adopt symmetric managerial contracts. This, however, ceases to be true if moral hazard matters, i.e. if managers' actions are not observable. In such a case, Cournot competition coupled with R&D for process innovation may indeed drive owners (principals) to design asymmetric incentives for their managers. This is the situation envisaged in Hermalin (1994), on the basis of Hart (1983) and Hermalin (1992), *inter alia*.

A population of n Cournot firms operate in a market for a homogeneous good, with demand $p = a - Q$. Principals hire managers, who are assigned the task of carrying out cost-reducing efforts $x_i \in [0, 1]$. As a result, firm i's marginal cost is either c_L with probability $\mathfrak{p}x_i \in [0, 1]$ or c_H with probability $1 - \mathfrak{p}x_i$, and clearly $c_H > c_L$. To ensure viability of all firms, $a > (n+1)c_H - nc_L$. The managerial contract stipulated in firm i is unobservable for players in any firm j, so that an owner cannot write a contract conditional on the contract adopted by rival firms. Consequently, here it is also true that delegation cannot be an instrument to achieve Stackelberg leadership (see, e.g., Fershtman *et al.*, 1991), and downstream competition involves pure expected profit maximization, owners being risk neutral. The utility function of a generic manager i is $U_i = f(M_i) - g(x_i)$, where $f(M_i)$ is increasing in remuneration M_i and the cost of effort $g(x_i)$ is increasing and convex in x_i.

The generic profit function of firm i is

$$\pi_i(c_i|\ell) = \frac{[a + \ell c_L + (n - \ell - 1)c_H - nc_i]^2}{(n+1)^2} \tag{6.1}$$

if its marginal cost is c_i, $i = H, L$ and ℓ of its rivals have marginal cost c_L. The above expression can be used to construct the expected profit whose maximization with respect to x_i yields the best reply of manager i to the efforts produced by the managers of the rivals, for a generic partition of the sets ℓ and $n - \ell - 1$.

Principals do not observe effort levels and must condition managerial remuneration on observed marginal costs, with $M_i = M_L$ iff $c_i = c_L$ and $M_i = M_H$ iff $c_i = c_H$, $M_L > M_H$. Suppose the desired effort level, common to all firms, is $\bar{x}$.

This is implementable if it is (i) incentive compatible, i.e. iff

$$p\bar{x}u(M_L) + (1 - p\bar{x})u(M_H) - g(\bar{x}) \geq$$
$$pxu(M_L) + (1 - px)u(M_H) - g(x) \, \forall x \neq \bar{x} \quad\quad (6.2)$$

and (ii) if it is individually rational, i.e. iff

$$p\bar{x}u(M_L) + (1 - p\bar{x})u(M_H) - g(\bar{x}) \geq U_0 \quad\quad (6.3)$$

where U_0 is the reservation utility.

Solving this agency problem, Hermalin (1994) found out that the hidden action problem may cause asymmetric delegation contracts to arise at equilibrium, the reason being that since the expected marginal cost of any rival firm is decreasing in its manager's effort, the firm we are looking at perceives the advantage generated by any marginal cost reduction as decreasing in the efforts of the managers of the rivals (Hermalin, 1994, Lemma 5, p. 523). Since the distribution of marginal costs affects equilibrium outputs and profits in the same way, and Cournot competition implies decreasing best replies at the market stage, then high efforts (cost reductions) implemented by managers in a subset of the firms in the industry imply an expansion of their outputs, which calls for an output restriction by the remaining subset of firms, inducing asymmetry in delegation contracts (Hermalin, 1994, Proposition 2, p. 524). This amounts to saying that the presence of moral hazard triggers a mechanism which creates an interplay between the nature of market competition and the design of agency relationships.

This message appeared reinforced in Chalioti (2015). The underlying idea is the same, although modelled in a different way, with novel conclusions. The market is a Cournot duopoly, and firm i's marginal cost is

$$c_i = \bar{c} - k_i$$
$$k_i = x_i + \beta x_j + \varepsilon_i \quad\quad (6.4)$$

where k_i is the *effective* R&D effort, ε_i is a specific shock hitting firm i's managerial effort x_i and $\beta \in [0, 1]$ is a parameter measuring technological spillovers, as in d'Aspremont and Jacquemin (1988). As we are about to see, the crucial assumption is that spillovers are publicly observable.

Each principal must solve the equivalent of the problem identified by (6.1)–(6.3), while each agent is risk averse, with preferences described by the utility function

$$U_i = -e^{-\mathfrak{r}[M_i - g(x_i)]} \qu\quad (6.5)$$

where $\mathfrak{r}$ is the Arrow–Pratt index of risk aversion.

Downstream Cournot–Nash equilibrium output is

$$q_i^{CN} = \frac{a - \bar{c} + (2 - \beta)x_i - (1 - 2\beta)x_j}{3} \qu\quad (6.6)$$

i.e. the certainty-equivalent output we also find in d'Aspremont and Jacquemin (1988), while the optimal R&D effort is

$$x^N = \frac{1}{1+\beta}\left[\frac{9(1+\tau\mathrm{var}\,(\varepsilon)g''(x))g'(x)}{2(2-\beta)} - a + \bar{c}\right] \tag{6.7}$$

in which var (ε) is the variance of the shock and $g'(x)$ and $g''(x)$, both positive, are the first and second derivatives of the cost of effort.

The manager receives

$$M_i = \alpha + \gamma_{ii}k_i + \gamma_{ij}k_j \tag{6.8}$$

i.e. rewards are based on observable variables represented by effective R&D efforts. The contractual variables $(\alpha, \gamma_{ii}, \gamma_{ij})$, at equilibrium, write as follows:

$$\gamma_{ii}^N = \frac{g'(x)}{1-\beta^2}; \quad \gamma_{ij}^N = -\frac{\beta g'(x)}{1-\beta^2} = -\beta\gamma_{ii}^N \tag{6.9}$$

showing that the agency contract filters spillover effects: the owner doesn't like the idea of rewarding the manager for something that has been received for free via the technological spillover; accordingly, the incentive scheme produces a reward insensitive to the rival manager's effort. This boils down to saying that slacking off is punished explicitly, and the optimal contract in (6.9) can be interpreted as an intriguing reformulation of the comparative performance contract in Miller and Pazgal (2001) and others.

6.2 The persistence of monopoly

Henceforth, we turn our attention to the bearings of delegation on technical progress under full information. While it is indeed useful to open up a perspective on a relevant question mark concerning the R&D performance of managerial versus entrepreneurial firms, regarding which I will tell you more in the remainder, to the best of my knowledge, the material contained in this section has not been explicitly laid out anywhere else.

A *fil rouge* of the economics of innovation is the Schumpeter (1942) vs Arrow (1962) debate about the relationship between the intensity of competition or the structure of the industry on one side and the intensity of R&D efforts or the pace of technical progress on the other. The literature generated by these two pioneering contributions is very large and still growing. While, according to the Schumpeterian view, monopoly is the industry structure from which we should expect the most intense R&D activity and consequently the fastest technical progress, since competition hinders profits and therefore the *competitive* or *efficiency effect* should play in favour of a pure monopolist,[3] the Arrovian position holds that the opposite should be true, because of the so-called *replacement effect*, according to which the best a monopolistic firm can hope for is to replace itself through innovation, and therefore it might well rest on its laurels, while perfectly competitive firms know that the final price to the winner of an innovation race is monopoly power granted by patent laws all over the planet, and therefore they should end up investing, in the aggregate, a lot more than a monopolist.

A strand of this discussion, initiated by Gilbert and Newbery (1982) and Reinganum (1983), has focused on the issue of the persistence of monopoly. The simplest way of illustrating the problem they consider is the following. Suppose for the moment firms are pure profit seekers. The basic model is largely the same as the entry model we encountered in Section 2.6, but without fixed costs. Players are an incumbent, I, currently enjoying monopoly power, and an entrant, E. A third subject, the innovator, has no production facilities and therefore is auctioning an infinitely lived patent on an innovation, to be awarded to the highest bidder between I and E. Winning the auction is the only way for the entrant to actually enter the industry.

The basic assumptions are that (i) the innovation is non-drastic, i.e. it does not throw the loser out of business, and (ii) the time span of patent protection is infinite. Hence, if E acquires the innovation, the industry becomes a duopoly. Let w and l denote the winner and the loser, respectively. Then, note that the three relevant profits are $\pi_I(w)$, $\pi_I(l)$ and $\pi_E(w)$, identifying the incumbent firm's profits when it wins (thereby remaining a monopolist) or loses (thereby remaining on the market as a duopolist) and the entrant's profits. If E looses the auction, its profits are by definition equal to zero. Assuming both firms share the same discount rate $\rho > 0$, the incumbent's highest bid is

$$B_I = \frac{\pi_I(w) - \pi_I(l)}{\rho} \tag{6.10}$$

while the entrant's highest bid is

$$B_I = \frac{\pi_E(w) - 0}{\rho} \tag{6.11}$$

Hence, the incumbent wins the auction, acquires the patent on the innovation and monopoly persists iff

$$\pi_I(w) - \pi_I(l) > \pi_E(w) \Leftrightarrow \pi_I(w) > \pi_I(l) + \pi_E(w) \tag{6.12}$$

Note that the second version of the inequality appearing in (6.12) reads as follows: monopoly persists if and only if the monopolist holding the latest technology earns more profits than those of duopolists endowed with a mixture of old and new technologies. Since, *coeteris paribus*, a monopolist is always able to replicate the performance of any population of oligopolists, the same *a fortiori* holds in a situation like the present one, in which the *coeteris paribus* condition does not apply, the winning monopolist being endowed with a technology matched only by the most efficient duopolist. Accordingly, monopoly shall persist – which delivers a confirmation of the Schumpeterian hypothesis.

Now we can turn our attention to the case in which firms can operate a separation between ownership and control by hiring managers. Three things should be stressed. The first is that the owners of a monopolistic firm, uncertainty being absent, have no incentives to hire a manager. The second is that both firms should be expected to managerialize themselves if E wins the auction and transforms the industry into a duopoly. The third is that the highest bids of both I and E are still measured by the difference between the profits generated by winning or losing the auction. One of the three key profits, $\pi_I(w)$, is unmodified, while $\pi_I(l)$ and $\pi_E(w)$ are diminished by the presence of managers, independently of the exact shape of incentives appearing in their contracts; think, for instance, of the contract based on output expansion as in Vickers (1985). Hence, the left-hand side of the second version of the inequality in (6.12) remains the same, while the sum of duopoly profits on the right-hand side goes down as soon as managers are given control of market variables. This appears to imply that not only monopoly persists (as expected on the basis of the intuitive argument outlined above), but also the following.

Proposition 6.1 *The widespread adoption of strategic delegation in an industry hinders the innovative capacity of the latter as compared to the same industry fully composed of entrepreneurial firms.*

Should we buy this result at face value, the chapter would finish here. Let me say that this is an intentionally provocative appetizer to stimulate your attention to what follows, where exactly the opposite conclusion is often reached.

6.3 Delegation vs process innovation: a toy model

As we know from Chapter 2, the Vickers (1985) model implies that delegation based on output levels – or revenues, as in Fershtman (1985), Fershtman and Judd (1987) and Sklivas (1987) – generates an output expansion which should alternatively be the outcome of a costly R&D effort for marginal cost abatement. Hence, one could argue that the sensible choice is not between delegating or not but rather between delegating and investing in process innovation. This is the topic dealt with in Lambertini and Primavera (2001), in a simple model in which the R&D effort is assumed to be an exogenous sunk cost.

The basic layout is the same as in Vickers (1985). Consider a Cournot duopoly where firms, labelled as i and j, supply a homogeneous good. Market demand is

$$p = a - q_i - q_j \tag{6.13}$$

Both firms initially share the same technology, with an identical marginal cost $c \in (0, a)$, which may be 'reduced' through either strategic delegation or costly R&D activities.

In the first case, the profit function of firm i is $\pi_i = (p - c)q_i$ and the manager has to maximize $M_i = \pi_i + \theta_i q_i$. In the second, marginal cost becomes $\widehat{c} \in (0, c)$ and profits are $\pi_i = (p - \widehat{c})q_i - k$, where $k > 0$ is the R&D cost, but the firm remains a pure profit seeker. At the first stage of the game, owners have to choose (simultaneously and non-cooperatively) between delegation and cost-reducing R&D. The resulting 2 × 2 structure appears in Matrix 6.1.

<table>
<tr><td></td><td></td><td colspan="2" align="center">j</td></tr>
<tr><td></td><td></td><td align="center">k</td><td align="center">θ</td></tr>
<tr><td>i</td><td>k</td><td>$\pi(k,k);\ \pi(k,k)$</td><td>$\pi(k,\theta);\ \pi(\theta,k)$</td></tr>
<tr><td></td><td>θ</td><td>$\pi(\theta,k);\ \pi(k,\theta)$</td><td>$\pi(\theta,\theta);\ \pi(\theta,\theta)$</td></tr>
</table>

Matrix 6.1

The relevant payoffs filling up the cells in Matrix 6.1 are easily computed:

$$\pi(k,k)=\frac{(a-\widehat{c})^2}{9}-k\ ;\ \pi(\theta,\theta)=\frac{2(a-c)^2}{25} \tag{6.14}$$

$$\pi(\theta,k)=\frac{(a-2c+\widehat{c})^2}{8}-k\ ;\ \pi(k,\theta)=\frac{(a+2c-3\widehat{c})^2}{16}-k \tag{6.15}$$

Since $c \in (\widehat{c},a)$, the equilibrium outcome of the first stage can be fully characterized by studying the curves identified by

$$k_k:\pi(k,k)-\pi(\theta,k)=0 \tag{6.16}$$

$$k_\theta:\pi(\theta,\theta)-\pi(k,\theta)=0 \tag{6.17}$$

and

$$k_{\text{pd}}:\pi(\theta,\theta)-\pi(k,k)=0 \tag{6.18}$$

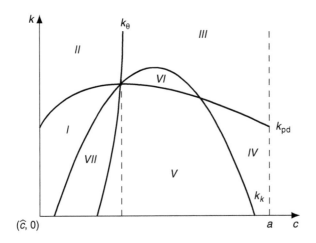

Figure 6.1 Delegation vs process innovation.

in the space (c, k). Note that subscript pd stands for *prisoners' dilemma*, since it results from the comparison of profits along the main diagonal. This exercise is done in Figure 6.1.

Accordingly, one can formulate the following.

Proposition 6.2 *Suppose delegation and process innovation are mutually exclusive alternatives. The examination of owners' profit incentives in the parameter space (c, k) reveals that:*

i. *in region I, both owners delegate and the unique equilibrium (θ, θ) is the outcome of a prisoners' dilemma;*

ii. *in region II, both owners delegate and the unique equilibrium (θ, θ) is Pareto-efficient;*

iii. *in regions III and IV, the upstream stage is a chicken game with two asymmetric equilibria in pure strategies, (θ, k) and (k, θ), along the secondary diagonal;*

iv. *in region V, the upstream stage has a unique Nash equilibrium at (k, k), which is also Pareto-efficient;*

v. *in region VI, the upstream stage has a unique Nash equilibrium at (k, k), which is the outcome of a prisoners' dilemma;*

vi. *in region VII, the upstream stage is a coordination game generating two symmetric equilibria in pure strategies along the main diagonal, with (k, k) Pareto-dominating (θ, θ).*

The above proposition deserves a few comments. To begin with, for costly R&D activities to be selected by both firms at equilibrium, the size of the R&D expenditure must be low enough, quite intuitively. In fact, the observation of Figure 6.1 suggests the sensible idea that the size of regions wherein R&D is chosen by at least one firm increases (respectively, decreases) monotonically in the effectiveness of R&D activity (respectively, the cost of the R&D project). Additionally, the present game generates an overall picture in which bilateral delegation does not appear to be as compelling as in the original setup in Vickers (1985) and related contributions. The reason has to be found in the fact that when the possibility of attaining an actual marginal cost reduction is envisaged, it can indeed be pursued in place of an alternative *mimicking* the same result. That is, it is no longer granted that a mirage seen from the standpoint of a manager with a preference for output expansion performs at least as well as *real* technical progress.[4]

Lambertini and Primavera (2001) also considered the scenario in which a firm may decide to separate control from ownership and undertake a costly R&D project. Given that the latter does not involve shaping an endogenous effort (or taking a first-order condition on a continuous variable), what matters is just the impact of process innovation on profits, and therefore we can interpret this perspective as one in which owners may choose to delegate and carry out the project generating a process innovation. From the standpoint of owners, the upstream stage becomes the one appearing in Matrix 6.2.

		k	j θ	$k\theta$
i	k	$\pi(k,k);\ \pi(k,k)$	$\pi(k,\theta);\ \pi(\theta,k)$	$\pi(k,k\theta);\ \pi(k\theta,k)$
	θ	$\pi(\theta,k);\ \pi(k,\theta)$	$\pi(\theta,\theta);\ \pi(\theta,\theta)$	$\pi(\theta,k\theta);\ \pi(k\theta,\theta)$
	$k\theta$	$\pi(k\theta,k);\ \pi(k,k\theta)$	$\pi(k\theta,\theta);\ \pi(\theta,k\theta)$	$\pi(k\theta,k\theta);\ \pi(k\theta,k\theta)$

Matrix 6.2

In view of the parametric nature of the R&D choices, the explicit expressions of payoffs appearing in Matrix 6.2 can be easily reconstructed and therefore I will omit listing them all to concentrate on the characterization of firms' equilibrium behaviour. This is captured by Figure 6.2, again drawn in the space (c, k).

The curves appearing in Figure 6.2 are

$$\bar{k} : \pi(\theta,\theta) - \pi(k\theta,\theta) = 0 \tag{6.19}$$
$$\widehat{k} : \pi(\theta,k\theta) - \pi(k\theta,k\theta) \tag{6.20}$$

and

$$k'_{pd} : \pi(\theta,\theta) - \pi(k\theta,k\theta) = 0 \tag{6.21}$$

These curves suffice to understand what is going on when delegation and cost-reducing R&D may coexist because strategy $k\theta$ strictly dominates strategy k. The intuition behind this fact is that delegation is a dominant strategy for any given marginal cost, irrespective of whether this is inherited from an undescribed past

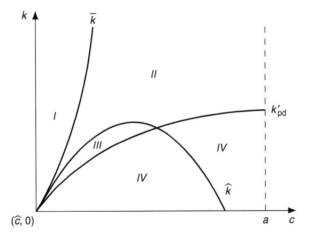

Figure 6.2 Delegation and process innovation.

or is the outcome of an upstream R&D activity. Hence, once a firm has decided to invest any amount of resources in process innovation, then necessarily owners find it convenient to put the control of production in the hands of managers.

The observation of Figure 6.2 yields the following.

Proposition 6.3 *Suppose delegation and process innovation can be adopted in isolation or jointly. The examination of owners' profit incentives in the parameter space* (c, k) *reveals that:*

    i. *in region* I, *both owners delegate and the unique equilibrium* (θ, θ) *is Pareto-efficient;*

    ii. *in regions* II *and* V, *the upstream stage is a chicken game with two asymmetric equilibria in pure strategies,* $(\theta, k\theta)$ *and* $(k\theta, \theta)$, *along the secondary diagonal;*

    iii. *in region* III, *the upstream stage has a unique Nash equilibrium at* $(k\theta, k\theta)$, *which is the outcome of a prisoners' dilemma;*

    iv. *in region* IV, *the upstream stage has a unique Nash equilibrium at* $(k\theta, k\theta)$, *which is also Pareto-efficient.*

Perhaps the most relevant message coming from the second version of the game is that it rules out the possibility for process R&D to take place in purely entrepreneurial firms at the subgame perfect equilibrium. Put differently, the realistic possibility of going managerial and activating R&D projects entails that both firms will always hire managers at equilibrium and possibly sustain output expansion via R&D efforts, if the investment cost is low enough. This suggests that delegation based on output or revenue-based contracts and R&D incentives might well go hand in hand, allowing managerial firms to outperform entrepreneurial ones also along the dimension of process (and possibly also product) innovation. This theme is further developed in the next section.

6.4 Delegation vs process innovation: endogenous R&D

Here, to offer a plausible formalization of ideas emerging from Hutton's (2002) discussion of investment incentives of managerial *vis à vis* entrepreneurial firms, I rely on Lambertini (2004). The industry is the same quantity-setting duopoly as above, with market demand (6.13) and production costs $C_i = c_i q_i$ for each firm. The profit function of firm i becomes $\pi_i = (p - c_i)q_i - \Gamma_i(k_i)$, where $\Gamma_i(k_i)$ is the R&D cost associated with the effort k_i that firm i puts into innovative activities. These efforts can be aimed either at process or product innovation. It is assumed that firm i is managerial while firm j is entrepreneurial.

6.4.1 Process innovation

If R&D takes the form of cost-reducing activities, marginal cost $c_i \in (0, a)$ can be decreased according to the following technology, which is commonly used after d'Aspremont and Jacquemin (1988):[5]

$$c_i = \bar{c} - k_i - \beta k_j \qquad (6.22)$$

In (6.22), k_i is the R&D effort of firm i, while parameter $\beta \in [0, 1]$ measures the spillover that firm i receives from the rival. The cost of R&D activity is $\Gamma_i(k_i) = bk_i^2$, $b > 0$, to indicate that R&D is characterized by decreasing returns. The resulting profit function is $\pi_i = (p - c_i)q_i - bk_i^2$.

The managerial remuneration is modelled *à la* Vickers (1985), whereby the incentive to firm i's manager is a linear combination of profits and output:

$$M_i = \pi_i + \theta_i q_i = (a - q_i - q_j)q_i - (c_i - \theta_i)q_i - bk_i^2 \qquad (6.23)$$

Additionally, for reasons that will become clearer in a moment, delegation is assumed to be costly, as in Basu (1995), where the fixed cost of hiring a manager is Δ, so that the firm's net profits are $\pi_i - \Delta$. As we know from Chapter 2, the upstream stage where owners non-cooperatively choose between hiring a manager or not, can be illustrated by the 2×2 Matrix 6.3, where strategies D and ND have the usual meaning. This apparently coincides with Matrix 2.2, but here profits also account for the R&D costs.

j

		D	*ND*
i	*D*	$\pi_i(D, D) - \Delta; \pi_j(D, D) - \Delta$	$\pi_i(D, ND) - \Delta; \pi_j(ND, D)$
	ND	$\pi_i(ND, D); \pi_j(D, ND) - \Delta$	$\pi_i(ND, ND); \pi_j(ND, ND)$

Matrix 6.3

In Vickers (1985), it is shown that $\pi_i(D, D) > \pi_i(ND, D)$, $\pi_i(D, ND) > \pi_i(ND, ND)$ and $\pi_i(ND, ND) > \pi_i(D, D)$ in a Cournot model with perfect substitute goods, like the one used here. That is, given that the delegation of control to managers is costless (i.e. $\Delta = 0$), then it is a strictly dominant strategy, and the resulting equilibrium outcome whereby both firms are managerial is compelling, although Pareto-inefficient from the shareholders' standpoint. On the contrary, if $\Delta > 0$ and – as in Basu (1995) – the following inequalities hold:

$$\begin{aligned} \pi_i(ND, D) &> \pi_i(D, D) - \Delta \\ \pi_i(D, ND) - \Delta &> \pi_i(ND, ND) \end{aligned} \qquad (6.24)$$

and then Matrix 6.3 takes the form of a chicken game yielding two pure-strategy Nash equilibria, (D, ND) and (ND, D) on the secondary diagonal (cf. Basu, 1995, p. 463).

The analysis focuses upon the asymmetric case where conditions (6.24) do apply and $\theta_i > 0$ while $\theta_j = 0$, $i, j = 1, 2$, $i \neq j$. This justifies the idea that one firm is managerial while the other is entrepreneurial. In such an asymmetric setup, there emerges that provided the rival firm is entrepreneurial, then hiring an aggressive manager yields superior productive efficiency, a larger market share and higher profits for the managerial firm, which under certain conditions may even become a monopolist. Therefore, (i) delegation is indeed a dominant strategy and (ii) adopting a strict profit-maximizing behaviour turns out to be myopic and counterproductive. Clearly, avoiding the separation between ownership and control is out of equilibrium, so that in the long run one should expect to observe that all surviving firms are managerial, but the analysis of the *ad interim* performance of industries populated by both types of firms at the same time remains of interest.

Under (6.24), the three-stage game unravels as follows. In the first stage, firm i's shareholders choose θ_i to maximize profits; in the second (respectively, third) stage, the manager of firm i and the shareholders of firm j choose non-cooperatively and simultaneously their respective R&D efforts (respectively, output levels). As usual, the solution concept is the subgame perfect equilibrium by backward induction, under complete, symmetric and imperfect information in each stage. Information is instead perfect across stages.

The objective functions at the market stage are[6]

$$M_i = (a - q_i - q_j - c_i)q_i + \theta_i q_i - bk_i^2$$
$$\pi_j = (p - c_j)q_j - bk_j^2 \tag{6.25}$$

Taking FOCs with respect to output levels and solving, one obtains

$$q_i^{CN} = \frac{a - 2c_i + c_j + 2\theta_i}{3}; \quad q_j^{CN} = \frac{a - 2c_j + c_i - \theta_i}{3}, \tag{6.26}$$

which can be plugged into M_i and π_j together with (6.22) to write the relevant objective functions at the second stage, where R&D efforts are determined:

$$M_i = \frac{1}{9}[(a - \bar{c})^2 + (2k_i - k_j)^2 - k_i^2(9b + 4\beta - \beta^2) - 4k_j^2\beta(1 - \beta) +$$
$$+ 4\theta_i^2 + 2(a - \bar{c})(k_i(2 - \beta) - k_j(2\beta - 1) + 2\theta_i) +$$
$$+ 2k_ik_j\beta(5 - 2\beta) + 4\theta_i(k_i(2 - \beta) - k_j(2\beta - 1))] \tag{6.27}$$

$$\pi_j = \frac{[a - \bar{c} + k_i(2\beta - 1) + k_j(2 - \beta) - \theta_i]^2}{9} - bk_j^2. \tag{6.28}$$

From (6.27)–(6.28), one can derive the following FOCs with respect to R&D efforts, as follows:

$$\frac{\partial M_i}{\partial k_i} = \frac{2}{9}[(a - \bar{c})(2 - \beta) + k_i(4(1 - \beta) - 9b + \beta^2) +$$
$$- k_j(2(1 - \beta^2) - 5\beta) + 2\theta_i(2 - \beta)] = 0 \tag{6.29}$$

$$\frac{\partial \pi_j}{\partial k_j} = 2\left[\frac{(2 - \beta)(a - \bar{c} + k_i(2\beta - 1) + k_j(2 - \beta) - \theta_i)}{9} - bk_j\right] = 0. \tag{6.30}$$

The solution of the system (6.29)–(6.30) delivers the equilibrium expressions of R&D efforts, for a generic value of θ_i:

$$k_i^* = \frac{(2-\beta)[(a-\bar{c})(2-3b-\beta(3-\beta))-\theta_i(6b+\beta-2)]}{[9b-(2-\beta)(1+\beta)][2-3b-\beta(3-\beta)]} \qquad (6.31)$$

$$k_j^* = \frac{(2-\beta)[(a-\bar{c})(2-3b-\beta(3-\beta))+\theta_i(3b-\beta(2-\beta))]}{[9b-(2-\beta)(1+\beta)][2-3b-\beta(3-\beta)]} \qquad (6.32)$$

which clearly coincide with the optimal R&D efforts in d'Aspremont and Jacquemin (1988) iff $\theta_i = 0$. Substituting (6.31)–(6.32) into π_i and solving $\partial \pi_i / \partial \theta_i = 0$, the optimal extent of delegation is determined:

$$\theta_i^* = \Psi \cdot \frac{[27b^2-6b(2-\beta)(1+\beta)+(2-\beta)^2(1+\beta(3\beta-2))]}{[27b^2+4+3b(2-\beta)(4\beta-5)-\beta^2(15-\beta(13-3\beta))]} \qquad (6.33)$$

where

$$\Psi \equiv \frac{(a-\bar{c})(2-3b-\beta(3-\beta))}{2(2-\beta-6b)} \qquad (6.34)$$

If the ratio b/β is sufficiently high, θ_i^* is positive. For instance, if one takes $b=1$, then $\theta_i^* > 0$ for all $\beta \in [0,1]$. It is worth noting that b/β is the ratio between the parameter determining the steepness of the R&D cost function and that measuring the size of the free lunch one can enjoy in the dining hall of technical knowledge through spillover. That is, it could be taken as a rough measure of the ratio between what a firm has to pay and what it gets for free from the rival.

Having characterized the subgame perfect equilibrium, one obtains the following list of the equilibrium expressions of outputs, R&D efforts and profits of the two firms:

$$q_i^* = \frac{9b(a-\bar{c})[3b-(2-\beta)(1-\beta)]}{2[27b^2+4+3b(2-\beta)(4\beta-5)-\beta^2(15-\beta(13-3\beta))]} \qquad (6.35)$$

$$q_j^* = \frac{3b(a-\bar{c})[3b-4+\beta(8-3\beta)][9b-(2-\beta)(1+\beta)]}{2(6b+\beta-2)[27b^2+4+3b(2-\beta)(4\beta-5)-\beta^2(15-\beta(13-3\beta))]} \qquad (6.36)$$

$$k_i^* = \frac{3(a-\bar{c})(2-\beta)[3b-(2-\beta)(1-\beta)]}{2[3b(2-\beta)(5-4\beta)-27b^2+(2-\beta)^2(\beta(3\beta-1)-1)]} \qquad (6.37)$$

$$k_j^* = \frac{(a-\bar{c})(2-\beta)[9b-(2-\beta)(1+\beta)][(2-\beta)(2-3\beta)-3b]}{2(6b+\beta-2)[3b(2-\beta)(5-4\beta)-27b^2+(2-\beta)^2(\beta(3\beta-1)-1)]} \qquad (6.38)$$

$$\pi_i^* = \frac{9b(a-\bar{c})^2[3b-(2-\beta)(1-\beta)]^2}{4(6b+\beta-2)[27b^2+4+3b(2-\beta)(4\beta-5)-\beta^2(15-\beta(13-3\beta))]} \qquad (6.39)$$

$$\pi_j^* = \frac{b(a-\bar{c})[3b-4+\beta(8-3\beta)]^2[9b-(2-\beta)^2][9b-(2-\beta)(1+\beta)]^2}{4(6b+\beta-2)[27b^2+4+3b(2-\beta)(4\beta-5)-\beta^2(15-\beta(13-3\beta))]}$$

$$(6.40)$$

The corresponding equilibrium expressions of marginal costs and market price are omitted for brevity. Notice that, when comparing equilibrium outputs, R&D efforts and profits, the measure of market size, $a-\bar{c}$, is obviously irrelevant, such comparison depending upon $\{b,\beta\}$ only. The first relevant result is as follows.

Lemma 6.1 $k_i^*, q_i^* > 0$ *for all* $\beta \in [0,1]$; $k_j^*, q_j^* > 0$ *for all* $\beta \in (0.131,1]$, *and conversely for all* $\beta \in [0,0.131)$.

That is, while the managerial firm is viable for all admissible spillover levels, the entrepreneurial firm needs a sufficiently high spillover from the rival, in order to be active. Moreover, we have the following.

Lemma 6.2 $k_i^* > \max\{0,k_j^*\}$ *and* $q_i^* > \max\{0,q_j^*\}$ *for all* $\beta \in [0,1]$.

These results can be interpreted as follows. The present model is one where two asymmetric firms compete in output levels. In particular, the asymmetry relates to their respective marginal costs, due to the fact that R&D incentives are different, since firm i has hired a manager while firm j has not. As the manager has a taste for output expansion, she/he has also a higher propensity to invest in process R&D, because an increase in productive efficiency will bring about an increase in output. Therefore, a managerial firm competing against an entrepreneurial firm will invest more than the rival in R&D activities. This ultimately implies that, as in any asymmetric Cournot market, there exists a range of the cost differential $c_j - c_i$ above which the relatively less efficient firm, in this case the entrepreneurial one, is thrown out of business. Hence, $\pi_j^* = 0$ for all $\beta \in [0,0.131)$. Note that this conclusion has a remarkable Schumpeterian flavour: R&D incentives reflect the relative size (as measured by market shares) and the profit performance of firms.

Hence, Lemmas 6.1–6.2 entail the following.

Proposition 6.4 *For all* $\beta \in [0,0.131)$, *the managerial firm is a monopolist.*

Finally, comparing (6.39) and (6.40), we obtain the following.

Proposition 6.5 $\pi_i^* > \pi_j^*$ *for all* $\beta \in (0.131,1]$.

The above Proposition of course replicates the result we have known since the seminal paper by Vickers (1985). However, in the present model, a novel result adds to the picture. More precisely, it is worth stressing that if firms endogenously control their reciprocal spillovers, then it is possible for the managerial firm to monopolize the market by keeping the spillover outgoing to the rival low enough to lead the entrepreneurial firm to shut down. This would require, of course, rearranging the model by making spillovers β_i and β_j firm specific. However, even in the case of exogenously given external effects, it is quite sensible to presume that the effective spillover that each firm receives from the rival is smaller than 10% (see, e.g., Jaffe, 1986). In such a case, the empirical relevance of Proposition 6.4 would be non-negligible.

6.4.2   Product innovation

Now, to formalize the same problem in terms of product innovation, consider the following perspective. The market is served by two single-product firms selling imperfect substitutes with the same technology operating at a constant marginal cost $c \in (0, a)$, which here remains exogenously given. Firm i is managerial, while firm j is entrepreneurial. However, in the present setting either firm i or firm j may consider the opportunity of introducing a second variety, which is an imperfect substitute to the existing ones, at a cost equal to $k > 0$, summarizing the R&D expenditure for product innovation.[7] Hence, the R&D cost is $\Gamma_i(k) = k$ for the firm that does invest and $\Gamma_j(k) = 0$ for the firm that does not. The manager of firm i controls the output level(s) of the same firm, while stockholders decide upon the introduction of a new variety on the basis of a profit comparison.

At the outset, market demand for variety i is written as in Spence (1976) and Singh and Vives (1984):

$$p_i = a - q_i - \sigma q_j \tag{6.41}$$

with $\sigma \in [0, 1]$. The objective functions are

$$M_i(1, 1) = p_i q_i - (c_i - \theta_i)q_i$$
$$\pi_j(1, 1) = (p_j - c_j)q_j \tag{6.42}$$

so that the equilibrium profits are[8]

$$\pi_i^*(1, 1) = \frac{(a - c)^2(2 - \sigma)^2}{8(2 - \sigma^2)}$$
$$\pi_j^*(1, 1) = \frac{(a - c)^2[4 - \sigma(2 + \sigma)]^2}{16(2 - \sigma^2)^2} \tag{6.43}$$

The question is: which one of the two firms has the highest incentive to invest to introduce an additional variety? The remainder of the section illustrates the two alternative perspectives, both envisaging a firm becoming multiproduct while the other remains a single-product one.

To begin with, suppose the third product is supplied by the managerial firm. If so, the inverse demand functions write as follows:

$$p_{i1} = a - q_{i1} - \sigma(q_{i2} + q_j)$$
$$p_{i2} = a - q_{i2} - \sigma(q_{i1} + q_j) \tag{6.44}$$
$$p_j = a - q_j - \sigma(q_{i1} + q_{i2})$$

and the corresponding objective functions are

$$M_i(2, 1) = p_{i1}q_{i1} + p_{i2}q_{i2} - (c - \theta_i)(q_{i1} + q_{i2}) - k$$
$$\pi_j(1, 2) = (p_j - c)q_j \tag{6.45}$$

Omitting FOCs for brevity, we can look at the equilibrium profits for the two firms, which are, respectively,

$$\pi_i^*(2, 1) = \frac{(a - c)^2(2 - \sigma)^2}{8[1 + \sigma(1 - \sigma)]} - k$$
$$\pi_j^*(1, 2) = \frac{(a - c)^2(2 - \sigma^2)^2}{16[1 + \sigma(1 - \sigma)]} \tag{6.46}$$

with

$$\pi_i^*(2, 1) > 0 \text{ for all } k \in (0, \widehat{k}), \quad \widehat{k} \equiv \frac{(a - c)^2(2 - \sigma)^2}{8[1 + \sigma(1 - \sigma)]} \tag{6.47}$$

However, from the standpoint of the owners of the managerial firm, product innovation is profitable if and only if $\pi_i^*(2, 1) > \pi_i^*(1, 1)$, which holds for all $k \in (0, \widetilde{k})$, where

$$\widetilde{k} \equiv \frac{(a - c)^2(2 - \sigma)(2 - 3\sigma + \sigma^2)}{8(2 + 2\sigma - 3\sigma^2 - \sigma^3 + \sigma^4)} \tag{6.48}$$

where obviously $\widetilde{k} < \widehat{k}$ for all admissible values of σ, entailing that there exists a range of the innovation cost wherein innovation is feasible but not profitable.

The outcome of this game can be summarized as follows.

Lemma 6.3 *Suppose R&D activities are carried out by the managerial firm, while the entrepreneurial firm remains a single-product unit. Product innovation is feasible for all $k \in (0, \widehat{k})$, while it is profitable for all $k \in (0, \widetilde{k})$, with $\widehat{k} \geq \widetilde{k}$ for all $\sigma \in [0, 1]$.*

Now we can move on to investigate the case where product innovation is possibly carried out by the entrepreneurial firm j. The system of inverse demand functions becomes

$$p_i = a - q_i - \sigma(q_{j1} + q_{j2})$$
$$p_{j1} = a - q_{j1} - \sigma(q_i + q_{j2})$$
$$p_{j2} = a - q_{j2} - \sigma(q_i + q_{j1}) \tag{6.49}$$

so that the objective functions are

$$M_i(1, 2) = p_i q_i - (c - \theta_i)q_i$$
$$\pi_j(2, 1) = (p_{j1} - c)q_{j1} + (p_{j2} - c)q_{j2} - k \tag{6.50}$$

Solving the game by backward induction and simplifying the profit functions, one obtains the following expressions:

$$\pi_i^*(1, 2) = \frac{(a - c)^2}{4[1 + \sigma(2 - \sigma^2)]}$$

$$\pi_j^*(2, 1) = \frac{(a - c)^2[2 + \sigma(1 - 2\sigma)]^2}{8(1 + \sigma)[1 + \sigma(1 - \sigma)]^2} - k \tag{6.51}$$

with

$$\pi_j^*(2, 1) > 0 \text{ for all } k \in (0, \overline{k}), \ \overline{k} \equiv \frac{(a - c)^2[2 + \sigma(1 - 2\sigma)]^2}{8(1 + \sigma)[1 + \sigma(1 - \sigma)]^2} \tag{6.52}$$

Product innovation is convenient for the stockholders of firm j if and only if $\pi_j^*(2, 1) > \pi_j^*(1, 1)$, which holds for all $k \in (0, \underline{k})$, with

$$\underline{k} \equiv \frac{(a-c)^2(1-\sigma)[16(1+\sigma) - 4\sigma^2(9-7\sigma) + \sigma^4(27 + 16\sigma - 7\sigma^2 - 4\sigma^3 + \sigma^4)]}{16(1 + \sigma)(2 - \sigma^2)^2[1 + \sigma(1 - \sigma)]^2} \tag{6.53}$$

and $\underline{k} < \overline{k}$ for all $\sigma \in [0, 1)$, entailing that there exists a range of the innovation cost wherein innovation is feasible but not profitable.

The following lemma summarizes the result of this game.

Lemma 6.4 *Suppose R&D activities are carried out by the entrepreneurial firm, while the managerial firm remains a single-product unit. Product innovation is feasible for all $k \in (0, \overline{k})$, while it is profitable for all $k \in (0, \underline{k})$, with $\overline{k} \geq \underline{k}$ for all $\sigma \in [0, 1]$.*

Then, comparing expressions (6.48) and (6.53), one can easily verify that $\widetilde{k} > \underline{k}$ for all admissible values of product substitutability, except $\sigma = 1$; in the case of product homogeneity, $\widetilde{k} = \underline{k} = 0$, but this intuitively entails that neither firm would expand its product range under full substitutability. Hence, given any generic degree of product differentiation, the above lemmas produce the following implication.

Proposition 6.6 *Suppose $\sigma \in [0, 1)$. If so, then for all $k \in (\underline{k}, \widetilde{k})$, the managerial firm finds it profitable to expand its product range, while the entrepreneurial firm cannot do so.*

That is, the range of values of the R&D cost wherein product innovation is profitable to the entrepreneurial firm is a proper subset of the set of values of k such that the managerial firm wants to innovate. Put differently, if an independent lab auctioned off the patent on the new product variety, then the highest bid would be offered by the managerial firm. As for the model laid out in the previous section, also here the main conclusion lends itself to a Schumpeterian interpretation, quite similar in spirit to the well known argument associated with the persistence of monopoly (as in Gilbert and Newbery, 1982, and Shaked and Sutton, 1990, *inter alia*).

Summing up, the scenario in which R&D competition takes place between a managerial firm and an entrepreneurial one, although seemingly at odds with the economic incentives that – according to the baseline models – should lead to a separation between ownership and control within all firms alike, yields interesting insights which are in line with well known real-world cases. In particular, this model seems to explain the dynamics of R&D behaviour on the opposite shores of the Atlantic, with firms behaving as short termers in the US *vis à vis* their more forward looking counterparts in Western Europe, at least before the outbreak of the subprime crisis in 2007. While the former set of firms has traditionally provided their managers with (large) incentives designed for them to align to profit maximization as much as possible, Western European corporations have often adopted a looser hold on managers, who may consequently reinvest profits into long-term development plans. The outcome of the simple theoretical model above seems to be in line with casual observation, i.e. it predicts that delegation to managers interested in output expansion will translate into larger R&D efforts aimed at either increasing productive efficiency or expanding product variety, as compared to the performance of a strictly profit-seeking firm. In the case of process R&D, this may ultimately yield monopoly power for the managerial firm, if technological spillovers in the industry are low enough. More on the consequences of unilateral managerialization on innovation in Section 6.6 below.

6.5 Process innovation in a managerialized industry

Back to a fully symmetric industry, this section considers the case in which the duopolistic industry is made up by managerial firms which compete in a three-stage game where: (i) in the first stage, owners design the managerial incentives; (ii) in the second, managers compete in R&D efforts for process innovation with a technology admitting spillovers, i.e. marginal cost results from (6.22) as in d'Aspremont and Jacquemin (1988); (iii) in the third, managers compete *à la* Cournot on the market place with a homogeneous good whose demand function is (6.13). Information is complete, symmetric and imperfect (i.e. moves are simultaneous) in each stage and perfect between stages. Here, the delegation costs envisaged by Basu (1995) are ruled out and therefore bilateral managerialization is taken for granted and left unmodelled.

The benchmark of this discussion is the papers by Zhang and Zhang (1997), Kräkel (2004) and Kopel and Riegler (2006, 2008), where managerial incentives are based on a linear combination of profits and revenues as in Fershtman (1985), Fershtman and Judd (1987) and Sklivas (1987):

$$M_i = \theta_i \pi_i + (1 - \theta_i) p q_i \tag{6.54}$$

and $\pi_i = (p - c_i)q_i - bk_i^2$. The procedure to characterize the Cournot–Nash equilibrium behaviour of managers at the downstream stage is described in detail in

Chapter 2, so here we may simply note that the effect of the R&D effort of firm i on the optimal output levels of both firms is captured by the following partial derivatives:

$$\frac{\partial q_i^{CN}(\alpha_i, \alpha_j)}{\partial k_i} = \frac{2\theta_i - \beta\theta_j}{3}; \quad \frac{\partial q_j^{CN}(\alpha_i, \alpha_j)}{\partial k_i} = \frac{2\beta\theta_j - \theta_i}{3} \tag{6.55}$$

These derivatives show that any increase in firm i's R&D effort certainly increases its equilibrium output, while the effect on the rival's equilibrium output depends on the intensity of technological spillovers, or information leakage in the R&D stage. If β is large (typically, under the symmetry condition $\theta_j = \theta_i$ which can be expected to hold at the subgame perfect equilibrium, if $\beta \in (1/2, 1]$), then an increase in firm i's R&D effort induces an analogous increase in the rival's optimal output, while the opposite applies if β is small. Hence, if the diffusion of technical progress *in fieri* is considerable, the output expansion effect it generates adds up to the analogous impulse intrinsically associated with managerialization, intensifying market competition.

At the second stage, the problem of the manager of firm i is

$$\max_{k_i} M_i = \theta_i \pi_i(\mathbf{q}^{CN}(\theta, \mathbf{k})) + (1 - \theta_i)p(\mathbf{q}^{CN}(\theta, \mathbf{k}))(q_i^{CN}(\theta, \mathbf{k})) \tag{6.56}$$

where θ, $\mathbf{k}$ and $\mathbf{q}$ are the vectors of delegation variables, R&D efforts and outputs. The FOC emerging from (6.56) can be omitted as it is overlong and scarcely illustrative. However, it is interesting to examine the equilibrium solution of the system of necessary conditions, using the symmetry $\theta_j = \theta_i = \theta$ which surely holds at the subgame perfect equilibrium. Doing so, one writes the Nash equilibrium R&D effort as follows:

$$k^N = \frac{(2 - \beta)(a - \theta c_0)}{9b - \theta(2 + \beta)(1 + \beta)} \tag{6.57}$$

This is positive for all $b > \theta(2 + \beta)(1 + \beta)/9 \equiv \bar{b} > 0$, and

$$\frac{\partial k^N}{\partial \theta} = -\frac{(2 - \beta)[9bc_0 - a(2 + \beta)(1 + \beta)]}{[9b - \theta(2 + \beta)(1 + \beta)]^2} \gtrless 0 \tag{6.58}$$

for all

$$b \lessgtr \frac{a(2 + \beta)(1 + \beta)}{9c_0} \equiv \hat{b} \tag{6.59}$$

Now note that

$$\bar{b} - \hat{b} = \frac{(2 + \beta)(1 + \beta)}{9} \left(\theta - \frac{a}{c_0}\right) > 0 \tag{6.60}$$

for all $\theta > a/c_0 > 1$, and conversely. Therefore, (6.60) implies the following.

Proposition 6.7 *Consider symmetric delegation contracts* $\theta_j = \theta_i = \theta$. *For all* $\theta \in$ $(0, a/c_0)$, $\bar{b} < \hat{b}$. *Hence, for any* $b > \bar{b}$ *ensuring* $k^N > 0$, $\partial k^N/\partial\theta$ *is surely negative. For all* $\theta > a/c_0$, $\bar{b} > \hat{b}$. *Hence, for any* $b \in (\bar{b}, \hat{b})$, $k^N > 0$ *and* $\partial k^N/\partial\theta > 0$, *while for any* $b > \hat{b}$, $k^N > 0$ *and* $\partial k^N/\partial\theta < 0$.

In plain words, this result tells that if the extent of delegation is below a well defined critical threshold, managerialization hinders a firm's innovation incentives. One can appreciate that this may indeed be the case by taking a look at

$$\left.\frac{\partial\pi_i}{\partial\theta_i}\right|_{\theta_j=\theta_i=a/c_0} = \frac{3a(a-c_0)[6bc_0 - a(2-\beta)][9bc_0 - a(2+\beta)(1+\beta)]}{c_0^3}$$

(6.61)

which changes sign twice in correspondence with

$$\hat{b} = \frac{a(2+\beta)(1+\beta)}{9c_0} ; \tilde{b} = \frac{a(2-\beta)}{6c_0}$$

(6.62)

with $\tilde{b} > \hat{b}$ for all $\beta \in [0, 1/2)$ and conversely in the remainder of the admissible range of spillover levels.

The remainder of the analysis in Zhang and Zhang (1997) has a few flaws which have been spotted by Kopel and Riegler (2006). Unfortunately, given the cumbersome nature of the FOCs at the contract stage (which are quartic equations in θ_i), the counterarguments put forward by Kopel and Riegler (2006) rely mostly on numerical calculations providing counterexamples. However, the upside of this discussion makes it evident that the analysis of the interplay between delegation and innovation incentives needs a closer look which should desirably take into account the other known forms of managerial contracts, namely, those based on either market shares as in Jansen *et al.* (2007, 2009) and Ritz (2008), or stock options (Spagnolo, 2000) and comparative performance (Salas Fumas, 1992; Aggarwal and Samwick, 1999; Miller and Pazgal, 2001).

In three related papers, Overvest and Veldman (2008), Veldman *et al.* (2014) and Veldman and Gaalman (2015) kept focusing on Cournot competition but took an alternative and novel route to model managerial incentive as a combination of profits and the in-house R&D effort, so that the delegation contract establishes that the manager of firm i has to maximize:

$$M_i = \pi_i + \theta_i k_i,$$

(6.63)

the building blocks of the model remaining the same as above. Using this setup, Overvest and Veldman (2008) and Veldman *et al.* (2014) assumed technological spillovers away and showed that, at the subgame perfect equilibrium, all firms' owners choose to reward managers for intensifying innovation efforts, i.e. θ_i is positive in the entire industry and drives technical progress beyond the levels compatible with pure profit-seeking behaviour. This not only provides a further confirmation that managerial firms must be expected to be more innovative than entrepreneurial ones, but, in line with Hermalin (1994) and Murphy (1999), also constitutes a nice example of a *rationale* for the presence of managerial incentives differing from the standard ones reviewed in Chapter 2.

Veldman and Gaalman (2015) further investigated the properties and implications of this approach by admitting the presence of exogenous information transmission, to find that the equilibrium values of contractual variables θ_i are positive if spillover levels are low ($\beta < 1/2$), and conversely. This reveals that delegation may indeed become restrictive even under quantity competition, because managers are rewarded on the basis of in-house R&D efforts – a net substitute of the managers' preference for output expansion.

6.6 Technology licensing

A relevant question closely related to innovation incentives and the intensity of R&D efforts in any direction is that of technology transfer, which has been investigated in detail in the tradition of industrial organization theory at least since Katz and Shapiro (1985), considering profit-seeking firms. An innovation can be held either by insiders or by outsiders, i.e. by a firm operating in the industry and holding a patent on some relevant innovation, or by an external subject with good ideas but no production facilities. These two alternatives generate different scenarios in terms of licensing the innovation to firms facing consumers in the market place. We are about to see both cases in some detail.

The impact of strategic delegation on the incentives towards technology licensing when the patent holder is an incumbent is the topic modelled by Mukherjee (2001) using the Fershtman and Judd (1987) setup, combined with Basu's (1995) idea that delegation is a costly operation.

Hence, we are in front of a managerialized Cournot duopoly with a homogeneous good whose demand is once again (6.13) but firms are initially endowed with production technologies characterized by different marginal costs, say, $0 < c_i < c_j < a$. The game has a four-stage structure. In the first stage, the owner of firm i decides whether to license its technology to firm j; in the second stage, each owner decides whether to go managerial or not; in the third stage, the contract is set for any manager hired at the previous stage; and the fourth stage is for Cournot–Nash competition to take place once the organizational structure of both firms has been fully shaped.

From the inspection of Basu's (1995) model in Chapter 2, we know that marginal cost asymmetry suffices to ensure the existence of admissible parameter constellations wherein an asymmetric (i.e. mixed) industry structure arises at the subgame perfect equilibrium, even if the cost of hiring managers is symmetric across firms. This allowed Mukherjee (2001) to describe the story emerging from the technology licensing game assuming that the hiring cost is indeed the same, $\Delta_i = \Delta_j = \Delta > 0$, and, as it turns out, the licensing incentive does depend on the size of Δ.

What follows is admissible for all $c_j \in (0, (a + c_i)/2)$. This condition ensures the positivity of firms' equilibrium outputs when the technology transfer does not take place, and therefore also if it has been carried out, in which case firms share the same productive efficiency.

The features of the Cournot–Nash equilibrium at the last stage can be easily reconstructed, as well as those of optimal contracts when at least one firm decides to separate ownership from control. Accordingly, I would like to draw the reader's attention to the characterization of the equilibria which may arise at the second stage, where owners face a binary choice between hiring managers or not. This crucial part of the subgame perfect strategy profile goes as follows (in any strategy pair, the choice of owner i appears first).

For a generic pair of marginal costs, (that is, if the superior technology of firm i has not been licensed to firm j), then:

- (ND, ND) is a Nash equilibrium for all $\Delta > (a - 2c_i + c_j)^2/72$;
- (D, ND) is a Nash equilibrium for all

$$\Delta \in \left(\frac{7(a + 2c_i - 3c_j)^2}{400}, \frac{(a - 2c_i + c_j)^2}{72} \right) \tag{6.64}$$

- (D, D) is a Nash equilibrium for all

$$\Delta \in \left(0, \frac{7(a + 2c_i - 3c_j)^2}{400} \right) \tag{6.65}$$

Conditions (6.64)–(6.65) mean that, intuitively, firm i is willing to hire a manager when the cost of doing so is still quite high, while the less efficient rival cannot do so because it cannot cover the same cost. As a result, the output expansion generated by unilateral delegation couples with that associated with a higher productive efficiency in worsening the position of the pure profit-seeking opponent. In a nutshell, the asymmetric setting describes a situation in which the core of Basu's (1995) idea about the possibility of observing unilateral delegation reproduces itself because technology transfer has not taken place at the first stage.

If instead it has, and the licenser charges a fixed fee to transfer its technology to the licensee, then only symmetric outcomes can be observed at equilibrium. This fact can be easily outlined:

- (ND, ND) is a Nash equilibrium for all $\Delta > (a - c_i)^2/72$;
- (D, D) is a Nash equilibrium for all $\Delta < 7(a - c_i)^2/400$.

On the basis of the above preliminary results, Mukherjee (2001, pp. 351–2) proved the following result.

Proposition 6.8 *Suppose Δ is so high that no firm hires a manager. If so, technology transfer is profitable for firm i and therefore will belong to the subgame perfect strategy profile for all $c_j \in (c_i, (2a + 3c_i)/5)$.*

Its companion is as follows.

Proposition 6.9 *If instead Δ is so low that both firms become managerial, then technology transfer will be observed in equilibrium for all $c_j \in (c_i, (2a + 11c_i)/13)$.*

It is worth observing that

$$\frac{2a + 3c_i}{5} > \frac{2a + 11c_i}{13} \tag{6.66}$$

which implies that the upper bound of the range of c_j creating the room for technology transfer is, as intuition would suggest a priori, shrinking as Δ decreases towards zero. The interpretation is clearcut, and can be fully appreciated keeping in mind that technology transfer accompanied by an exogenous fee makes market competition symmetric whenever both firms have the same organizational structure. Indeed, the case of a prohibitive hiring cost depicts a situation in which the second and third stages fade away and the game has a two-stage structure, involving two Cournot profit-seeking units with initially asymmetric technologies, as in Marjit (1990), which is encompassed by the managerial setup used by Mukherjee (2001) as a special case. Hence, the take-home message of the general case is indeed that managerialization hampers technology transfer.

The second perspective mentioned above is taken in Saracho (2002). At the outset of this chapter, the Arrow vs Schumpeter debate has been presented using a model in which an innovator decides to auction a patent on a non-drastic innovation. However, the possibility of licensing poses the question as to whether one or the other solution is more profitable. Needless to say, this problem has been extensively treated. Kamien and Tauman (1986) used a Cournot model to tackle this issue and found that licensing through an auction or a fixed fee is more convenient to the innovator than licensing through a royalty per unit of output by the licensee(s). Saracho (2002) revisited Kamien and Tauman's (1986) model inserting strategic delegation *à la* Fershtman and Judd (1987) to attain the opposite result, whereby in the presence of managerial firms a royalty scheme may indeed outperform the fixed fee from the innovator's standpoint.

Let the industry be a homogeneous good Cournot duopoly[9] with a linear market demand. Initially, both firms have the same technology characterized by a constant marginal cost c. Hence, the basic layout is the same as in Mukherjee (2001). The innovation takes the form of a lower marginal cost, say, $\widehat{c} = c - \varepsilon$, with $\varepsilon \leq (a - c)/2$, as the innovation is assumed to be non-drastic.

The game consists of four stages. In the first, the innovator chooses either a fixed fee or a royalty. In the second, firms non-cooperatively decide whether to acquire the new technology given the policy chosen by the innovator. In the third stage, owners delegate control to managers endowed with incentives $M_i = \theta_i \pi_i + (1 - \theta_i) p q_i$. In the fourth stage, managers compete in output levels. In stages 2–4, information is complete, symmetric and imperfect. It is instead perfect between any two stages.

If the patent holder chooses a royalty scheme, marginal cost becomes $\tilde{c} = \hat{c} + r = c - \varepsilon + r$, where r is the royalty. Obviously, the royalty must be lower than ε, otherwise neither firm will buy the license. If indeed $r \in (0, \varepsilon)$, both firms will acquire the license; therefore, only this symmetric case is in fact relevant. Given the symmetric solution of the downstream Cournot–Nash equilibrium, the problem of the innovator I is

$$\max_r \pi_I(r) = \frac{4r(a - \tilde{c})}{5} = 2rq^{CN} \qquad (6.67)$$

but since π_I is monotonically increasing in r, we have the corner solution $r^* = \varepsilon$, which extracts from the two firms the entire incremental surplus generated by the innovation. Notice that the aggressiveness of managers generates an expansion of industry output absent in a profit-seeking industry (as in Kamien and Tauman, 1986), enabling the patent holder to achieve higher profits.

In the alternative scenario in which the patent holder opts for a fixed fee F, one has to evaluate firms' incentives to adopt the new technology much the same way as in the initial model on the persistence of monopoly. In the present model, the maximum fee a firm is willing to pay to get the license and obtain the new technology is measured by the following differences:

$$\Delta\pi(2) = \pi(\mathfrak{a}, \mathfrak{a}) - \pi(\mathfrak{n}\mathfrak{a}, \mathfrak{a}) = \frac{6\varepsilon[2(a - c) - \varepsilon]}{25} \qquad (6.68)$$

$$\Delta\pi(1) = \pi(\mathfrak{a}, \mathfrak{n}\mathfrak{a}) - \pi(\mathfrak{n}\mathfrak{a}, \mathfrak{n}\mathfrak{a}) = \frac{6\varepsilon[2(a - c) + 3\varepsilon]}{25} \qquad (6.69)$$

In (6.68)–(6.69), $\mathfrak{a}$ and $\mathfrak{n}\mathfrak{a}$ stand for adopter and non-adopter, respectively. In (6.68), $\Delta\pi(2)$ measures the single firm's incentive to pay for the license when the rival is adopting the new technology; in (6.69), $\Delta\pi(1)$ measures the analogous incentive when the rival is not acquiring the license. On the basis of (6.68)–(6.69), the following holds.

Lemma 6.5 *For all $\varepsilon \in (0, 2(a - c)/5)$, both firms buy the license. For all $\varepsilon \in (2(a - c)/5, (a - c)/2)$, only one firm buys the license.*

In the interval $\varepsilon \in (2(a - c)/5, (a - c)/2)$, mixed strategies become relevant. Leaving this aside, the above lemma implies that the innovator's profits will be

$$\pi_I(F, 1) = \Delta\pi(1) \qquad (6.70)$$

for all $\varepsilon \in (2(a - c)/5, (a - c)/2)$ and

$$\pi_I(F, 2) = 2\Delta\pi(2) \qquad (6.71)$$

for all $\varepsilon \in (0, 2(a-c)/5)$. The number of adopters at equilibrium is lower than, or at most equal to, the number of adopters in Kamien and Tauman (1986), this being due to the presence of managers hindering profits and therefore also the firms' maximum bids.

Now one can compare the performance of the royalty and fixed fee policies from the patent holder's viewpoint. This simple exercise relies on the comparative evaluation of π_I across (6.69)–(6.71), yielding the following.

Proposition 6.10 *The royalty is preferred for all $\varepsilon \in ((a-c)/3, 4(a-c)/9)$. In the remainder of the admissible range of ε, the fixed fee is preferred.*

That is, the patent holder's preferences about the licensing strategy are non-monotone in the size of the patented process innovation: for low values of ε, the fixed fee is optimal, then in correspondence with the intermediate range specified in the proposition, royalty must be used, and finally for large cost reductions the innovator switches again to the fixed fee policy. This is in contrast with the conclusion attained by Kamien and Tauman (1986) under the assumption of pure profit-seeking behaviour, which implies a consistent preference for the fixed fee irrespective of the size of the innovation.

Of course, all of this has welfare consequences, themselves differing from the pure Cournot duopoly benchmark in Kamien and Tauman (1986). Indeed, given that here the number of adopters is, in general, lower than in Kamien and Tauman (1986) – in practice, this means that a single adopter is observed in a wider range of the key parameter values if managers are present – then welfare is higher in the managerialized industry if and only if both firms buy the license and the welfare comparison is carried out under the same licensing policy. Hence, the model illustrated by Saracho (2002) is a dissonant voice in the chorus of contributions reviewed in this chapter, as here managerialization may hinder both the diffusion of an innovation in the industry and the consequent welfare performance of the latter.

6.7 Make or buy?

To conclude this chapter, I illustrate a problem at the intersection between the field of technical progress and that of vertical relations treated in Chapter 5. The topic I am referring to is the choice between outsourcing production or R&D and making it in-house. Globalization through the intensification of intraindustry trade, and the need for firms to be as flexible as possible, render this a crucial decision for firms, no matter whether large or small. And quite naturally, this subject has justly attracted the attention of the modern theory of international trade (McLaren, 2000; Grossman and Helpman, 2002, 2005; Antras and Helpman, 2004) and industrial organization (Garvey and Pitchford, 1995; Tadelis, 2002; Sappington, 2005) alike.

This problem is dealt with in Cellini and Lambertini (2009), once again assuming a Cournot duopoly, this time with an asymmetric organizational choice: firm 1 hires a manager with a contract *à la* Vickers (1985), while firm 2 remains entrepreneurial. Firms sell a homogeneous good whose demand has the standard linear form $p = a - Q$.

The technological landscape looks as follows. Producing one unit of output requires one unit of a certain intermediate input, which can be either produced by the same firms, or bought on the market by an upstream supplier. Input production involves a fixed cost $F \in (0, (a-c)^2/16)$ and a constant marginal cost $c \in (0, a)$, irrespective of whether it is produced in-house or outsourced. In the former case, c and F are paid by either firm 1 or firm 2; in the latter case, these costs are borne by the upstream producer u, which is a monopolist charging a market price $w \in [c, a)$ for each input unit, in order to maximize its profits. The production of the final good entails no costs, except those associated with the production or acquisition of the input.

Four alternative perspectives may arise:

* both downstream firms, 1 and 2, decide to make the input in-house;
* both opt for outsourcing;
* one installs production facilities for the input in-house while the other chooses outsourcing (this of course yields two asymmetric cases).

The timeline of the game is as follows: (i) at the first stage, firms decide whether to outsource the input or produce it in-house; (ii) at the second stage, firm 1's owners design managerial incentives so as to maximize profits; (iii) at the third stage, provided at least one of the two downstream firms is choosing to outsource, firm u sets the input price w; (iv) at the fourth and last stage, firm 1 and 2 compete *à la* Cournot–Nash on the market place. The game is solved by subgame perfection attained through backward induction. Information is complete, symmetric and imperfect at every stage and perfect across stages.

Leaving aside the details of the calculations required in the four cases, one can grasp the essence of this model by looking at Matrix 6.4, which describes the discrete structure of the first stage. Pure strategies *m* and *b* are intuitively mnemonic for *make* and *buy*, respectively, and $A \equiv a - c$. The assumption that $F \in (0, A^2/16)$ ensures the positivity of all payoffs appearing in the matrix. Note that the profits associated with outcome (m, m) coincide with the Stackelberg outcome we know from Chapter 2, being however diminished by the presence of the sunk investment required by the decision to make the input in house.[10]

		2 *m*	2 *b*
1	*m*	$\frac{A^2}{8} - F; \frac{A^2}{16} - F$	$\frac{5A^2}{28} - F; \frac{A^2}{49}$
	b	$\frac{A^2}{36}; \frac{25A^2}{144} - F$	$\frac{A^2}{35}; \frac{A^2}{49}$

Matrix 6.4

The payoffs appearing in the cells of Matrix 6.4 are driven, amongst other things, by the following chain of inequalities describing the optimal extent of delegation specified in the managerial contract by firm 1's owners:

$$\theta^*(m, m) > \theta^*(m, b) > \theta^*(b, b) > \theta^*(b, m) \tag{6.72}$$

This tells us the following.

Lemma 6.6 *Optimal delegation becomes more restrictive as soon as at least one firm (not necessarily the managerial one) opts for outsourcing.*

To understand the lemma, one just needs to keep in mind that the fixed cost F does not affect FOCs and consider what happens if firms switch from (m, m) to (m, b). When playing (m, m), firms bear the same marginal cost c, and therefore, as noted above, they replicate the traditional Cournot–Stackelberg outcome, with the managerial firm striving to achieve a dominant position through delegation. In (m, b), the managerial firm invests to make the input in an internal division of its own, while the entrepreneurial firm is buying it from the upstream supplier u, at the monopolistic price $w^*(m, b) > c$. Hence, in this case the managerial firm is already enjoying a strategic advantage over its rival thanks to $w^*(m, b)$, working as a substitute for the delegation variable, which can therefore be fixed at a lower level.

Having said that, the equilibrium outcome can be characterized on the basis of the following inequalities. For firm 1, we have

$$\frac{A^2}{8} - F > \frac{A^2}{36}; \; \frac{5A^2}{28} > \frac{A^2}{35}; \; \frac{A^2}{8} - F > \frac{A^2}{35} \tag{6.73}$$

for all $F \in (0, A^2/16)$, while for firm 2,

$$\frac{A^2}{16} - F > \frac{A^2}{49}; \; \frac{25A^2}{144} - F > \frac{A^2}{49}; \; \frac{A^2}{16} - F > \frac{A^2}{49} \tag{6.74}$$

for all $F \in (0, 33A^2/784)$, $33A^2/784 < A^2/16$, and

$$\frac{A^2}{16} - F < \frac{A^2}{49}; \; \frac{25A^2}{144} - F > \frac{A^2}{49}; \; \frac{A^2}{16} - F < \frac{A^2}{49} \tag{6.75}$$

for all $F \in (33A^2/784, A^2/16)$, so that (6.74)–(6.75) say that the entrepreneurial firm prefers to outsource (respectively, to make) the input if the managerial rival makes (respectively, buys) it. Jointly, (6.73)–(6.75) yield the following.

Proposition 6.11 *For all $F \in (0, 33A^2/784)$, (m, m) is the unique pure-strategy Nash equilibrium at the first stage. For all $F \in (33A^2/784, A^2/16)$, (m, b) is the unique pure-strategy Nash equilibrium.*

In both cases, the equilibrium is driven by dominance; in particular, (m, b) is attained by iterated dominance, with firm 1 'dropping' strategy b. Additionally, when it is the equilibrium, (m, m) is not the outcome of a prisoners' dilemma. Intuitively, the managerial firm always goes for in-house production, as it enhances the dominant position already engendered by a delegation based on output expansion.

The welfare implications of firms' behaviour are as follows.

Corollary 6.1 *Welfare is maximized in* $(\boldsymbol{m}, \boldsymbol{m})$. *Therefore, private and social incentives are aligned for all* $F \in (0, 33A^2/784)$.

That is, if the sunk costs connected with the 'make' decision are sufficiently low, there emerges a win–win solution: the double marginalization problem along the vertical structure of the industry is fully avoided and the duplication of fixed investment costs is acceptable. This ceases to hold if F becomes larger, in which case the entrepreneurial firm decides to buy the input, thereby generating a surplus loss due to monopoly pricing on the input market, which outweighs the size of the fixed cost. This opens an industrial policy perspective: to avoid this problem and attain the first best, a government should subsidize the profit-seeking firm, using tax income to put it in a position to bear the fixed cost and choose strategy $\boldsymbol{m}$.

Further reading

Interesting variations on the themes discussed in this chapter are available in the literature. Barcena-Ruiz and Olaizola (2006) studied the incentives of managerial firms using revenue-based contracts towards the adoption of technologies with different marginal costs, the more efficient one requiring a sunk investment cost. They found that if the degree of product differentiation is high (low), the incentive to adopt the cost-saving technology is larger under strict profit maximization (strategic delegation). Mahathi *et al.* (2016) illustrated the impact of delegation on the timing of adoption of innovations, showing that under quantity or revenue-based incentives adoption occurs earlier (later) in markets if competition is in quantities (prices) if product differentiation is high (low). Not surprisingly, they also showed that adoption timing is unaffected by the shape of market competition if delegation relies on comparative performance evaluation. On technology transfer in managerialized industries, see Clark and Michalsen (2010). More on the background concerning the theory of technology transfer can be found in Gallini and Wright (1990), Rockett (1990) and Kamien (1992). The paper by Mukherjee (2001) also offers extensions of the baseline model allowing, amongst other things, for precommitment strategies in the form of productive capacity. Saracho (2005) used a conjectural variations approach to further characterize the optimal licensing policy in relation with the intensity of market competition. For more on the theory of R&D with spillovers in oligopoly, see Kamien *et al.* (1992), Suzumura (1992) and Amir (2000), *inter alia*. For additional theoretical and empirical insights on endogenous spillovers, see Lambertini *et al.* (2004). For an empirical evaluation of the relationship between the shape of managerial incentives and risk taking, see Wright *et al.* (2007). An exhaustive overview of the management of innovation is in Tidd *et al.* (2001).

Notes

1 The literature is teeming with contributions dealing with R&D models with and without uncertainty, investigating private and social incentives towards innovation and their policy implications, as well as the pace of technical progress and the optimal extent of patent protection along several dimensions. See, for instance, Tirole (1988), Reinganum (1989), Martin (1993, 2002), Shy (1995), Scotchmer (2004) and Belleflamme and Peitz (2010).

2 The first flight of the A380 took place on April 27, 2005; it started its commercial service in October 2007 with Singapore Airlines. The Boeing 7e7 was to become the 787 Dreamliner, whose prototype flew on December 15, 2009. The first commercial flight of the Dreamliner took place on October 26, 2011, with ANA (All Nippon Airlines).

3 This is traditionally known as the *Schumpeterian hypothesis*. For a comprehensive survey, see Tirole (1988, ch. 10) and Belleflamme and Peitz (2010, ch. 18), *inter alia*.

4 It is also worth noting that in regions III, IV and VI the existence of two pure strategy equilibria makes the mixed strategy solution also relevant.

5 There exists a large literature on R&D with spillovers, which cannot be duly accounted for here. See, e.g., Kamien *et al.* (1992), Suzumura (1992) and Amir (2000).

6 Henceforth, the explicit indication of the hiring cost Δ is omitted for the sake of simplicity, as it obviously never enters FOCs.

7 In this respect, the present model is somewhat similar to the one illustrated in Lambertini (2003), where a portfolio of activities aimed at process and product innovation is investigated in a monopoly market. A similar model is also used by Shaked and Sutton (1990) to discuss the issue of the persistence of monopoly.

8 Profits (6.43) coincide with the leader's and followers' profits, respectively, in a Cournot–Stackelberg game played by entrepreneurial firms. See Vickers (1985, pp. 141–2) and Lambertini (2000, p. 562).

9 Saracho (2002, pp. 237–42) also extended the main results to the case of an oligopoly with n firms. The duopoly model, however, captures the essential features of the general case in a simpler way.

10 It is also worth noting that firm 2's profits when the latter adopts strategy b are invariant with respect to the strategy chosen by the managerial rival. This is due to the fact that $q_2^{CN}(b,b) = q_2^{CN}(m,b) = A/7$, i.e. the entrepreneurial firm produces the same output in both cases. This, in turn, is the consequence of two different strategies on the part of firm 1 and firm u, setting, respectively, $q_1^{CN}(b,b) = A/5$; $w^*(b,b) = (18a + 17c)/35$ and $q_1^{CN}(m,b) = A/2$; $w^*(m,b) = (3a + 11c)/14$.

References

Aggarwal, R.K. and A.A. Samwick (1999), 'Executive Compensation, Strategic Competition, and Relative Performance Evaluation: Theory and Evidence', *Journal of Finance*, **54**, 1999–2043.

Amir, R. (2000), 'Modelling Imperfectly Appropriable R&D via Spillovers', *International Journal of Industrial Organization*, **18**, 1013–32.

Antras, P. and E. Helpman (2004), 'Global Sourcing', *Journal of Political Economy*, **112**, 552–80.

Arrow, K. (1962), 'Economic Welfare and the Allocation of Resources for Invention', in R. Nelson (ed.), *The Rate and Direction of Inventive Activity*, Princeton, CA, Princeton University Press.

Barcena-Ruiz, J. C. and N. Olaizola (2006), 'Cost Saving Production Technology and Strategic Delegation', *Australian Economic Papers*, **45**, 141–57.

Basu, K. (1995), 'Stackelberg Equilibrium in Oligopoly: An Explanation Based on Managerial Incentives', *Economics Letters*, **49**, 459–64.

Belleflamme, P. and M. Peitz (2010), *Industrial Organization: Markets and Strategies*, Cambridge, Cambridge University Press.

Cellini, R. and L. Lambertini (2009), 'The Make-or-Buy Choice in a Mixed Oligopoly: A Theoretical Investigation', in L. Lambertini (ed.), *Firms' Objectives and Internal Organization in a Global Economy: Positive and Normative Analysis*, London, Palgrave-Macmillan.

Chalioti, E. (2015), 'Incentive Contracts under Product Market Competition and R&D Spillovers', *Economic Theory*, **58**, 305–28.

Clark, D.J. and A. Michalsen (2010), 'Managerial Incentives for Technology Transfer', *Economics of Innovation and New Technology*, **19**, 649–68.

Cunat, V. and M. Guadalupe (2006), 'How Does Product Market Competition Shape Incentive Contracts?', *Journal of the European Economic Association*, **3**, 1058–82.

Czarnitzki, D. and K. Kraft (2004), 'Management Control and Innovative Activity', *Review of Industrial Organization*, **24**, 1–24.

d'Aspremont, C. and A. Jacquemin (1988), 'Cooperative and Noncooperative R&D in Duopoly with Spillovers', *American Economic Review*, **78**, 1133–7.

Fershtman, C. (1985), 'Managerial Incentives as a Strategic Variable in a Duopolistic Environment', *International Journal of Industrial Organization*, **3**, 245–53.

Fershtman, C. and K. Judd (1987), 'Equilibrium Incentives in Oligopoly', *American Economic Review*, **77**, 927–40.

Fershtman, C., K. Judd and E. Kalai (1991), 'Observable Contracts: Strategic Delegation and Cooperation', *International Economic Review*, **32**, 551–9.

Galbraith, C.S. and G.B. Merrill (1991), 'The Effect of Compensation Program and Structure on Sbu Competitive Strategy: A Study of Technology-Intensive Firms', *Strategic Management Journal*, **12**, 353–70.

Gallini, N. and B. Wright (1990), 'Technology Transfer under Asymmetric Information', *RAND Journal of Economics*, **21**, 147–60.

Garvey, G.T. and R. Pitchford (1995), 'Input Market Competition and the Make-or-Buy Decision', *Journal of Economics and Management Strategy*, **4**, 491–508.

Gilbert, R. and D. Newbery (1982), 'Preemptive Patenting and the Persistence of Monopoly', *American Economic Review*, **72**, 514–26.

Grossman, G.M. and E. Helpman (2002), 'Integration versus Outsourcing in Industry Equilibrium', *Quarterly Journal of Economics*, **117**, 85–120.

Grossman, G.M. and E. Helpman (2005), 'Outsourcing in a Global Economy', *Review of Economic Studies*, **72**, 135–59.

Hart, O. (1983), 'The Market Mechanism as an Incentive Scheme', *Bell Journal of Economics*, **14**, 366–82.

Hermalin, B. (1992), 'The Effects of Competition on Executive Behavior', *RAND Journal of Economics*, **23**, 350–65.

Hermalin, B.E. (1994), 'Heterogeneity in Organizational Form: Why Otherwise Identical Firms Choose Different Incentives for Their Managers', *RAND Journal of Economics*, **25**, 518–37.

Hutton, W. (2002). *The World We're In*, New York, Little, Brown.

Jaffe, A.B. (1986), 'Technological Opportunity and Spillovers of R&D: Evidence from Firms' Patents, Profits, and Market Value', *American Economic Review*, **76**, 984–1001.

Jansen, T., A. van Lier and A. van Witteloostuijn (2007), 'A Note on Strategic Delegation: The Market Share Case', *International Journal of Industrial Organization*, **25**, 531–9.

Jansen, T., A. van Lier and A. van Witteloostuijn (2009), 'On the Impact of Managerial Bonus Systems on Firm Profit and Market Competition: The Cases of Pure Profit, Sales,

Market Share and Relative Profits Compared', *Managerial and Decision Economics*, **30**, 141–53.

Kamien, M. (1992), 'Patent Licensing', in R.J. Aumann and S. Hart (eds), *Handbook of Game Theory with Economic Applications*, vol. I, Amsterdam, North Holland.

Kamien, M. and Y. Tauman (1986), 'Fees versus Royalties and the Private Value of a Patent', *Quarterly Journal of Economics*, **101**, 471–91.

Kamien, M., E. Muller and I. Zang (1992), 'Research Joint Ventures and R&D Cartels', *American Economic Review*, **82**, 1293–306.

Katz, M. and C. Shapiro (1985), 'On the Licensing of Innovation', *RAND Journal of Economics*, **16**, 504–20.

Kopel, M. and C. Riegler (2006), 'R&D in a Strategic Delegation Game Revisited: A Note', *Managerial and Decision Economics*, **27**, 605–12.

Kopel, M. and C. Riegler (2008), 'Delegation in an R&D Game with Spillovers', in R. Cellini and L. Lambertini (2008, eds), *The Economics of Innovation: Incentives, Cooperation, and R&D Policy*, vol. 286, Contributions to Economic Analysis Series, Bingley, Emerald Publishing.

Kräkel, M. (2004), 'R&D Spillovers and Strategic Delegation in Oligopolistic Contests', *Managerial and Decision Economics*, **25**, 147–56.

Lambertini, L. (2000), 'Strategic Delegation and the Shape of Market Competition', *Scottish Journal of Political Economy*, 47, 550–70.

Lambertini, L. (2003), 'The Monopolist's Optimal R&D Portfolio', *Oxford Economic Papers*, **55**, 561–78.

Lambertini, L. (2004), 'Innovation and Managerial Incentives: A Tale of Two Systems', Working Paper, Department of Economics, University of Bologna.

Lambertini, L. and G. Primavera (2001), 'Delegation vs Cost-Reducing R&D in a Cournot Duopoly', *Rivista Internazionale di Scienze Economiche e Commerciali*, **48**, 163–78.

Lambertini, L., F. Lotti and E. Santarelli (2004), 'Infra-Industry Spillovers and R&D Cooperation: Theory and Evidence', *Economics of Innovation and New Technology*, **13**, 311–28.

McLaren, J. (2000), 'Globalization and Vertical Structure', *American Economic Review*, **90**, 1239–54.

Mahathi, A., R. Pal and V. Ramani (2016), 'Competition, Strategic Delegation and Delay in Technology Adoption', *Economics of Innovation and New Technology*, **25**, 143–71.

Marjit, S. (1990), 'On a Non-cooperative Theory of Technology Transfer', *Economics Letters*, **33**, 293–8.

Martin, S. (1993), *Advanced Industrial Economics*, Oxford, Blackwell.

Martin, S. (2002), *Advanced Industrial Economics. Second Edition*, Oxford, Blackwell.

Miller, N.H. and A.I. Pazgal (2001), 'The Equivalence of Price and Quantity Competition with Delegation', *RAND Journal of Economics*, **32**, 284–301.

Mukherjee, A. (2001), 'Technology Transfer with Commitment', *Economic Theory*, **17**, 345–69.

Murphy, K. (1999), 'Executive Compensation', in O. Ashenfelter and D. Card (eds), *Handbook of Labor Economics*, vol. 3B, Amsterdam, North-Holland.

Overvest, B. and J. Veldman (2008), 'Managerial Incentives for Process Innovation', *Managerial and Decision Economics*, **29**, 539–45.

Reinganum, J. (1983), 'Uncertain Innovation and the Persistence of Monopoly', *American Economic Review*, **73**, 741–8.

Reinganum, J. (1989), 'The Timing of Innovation: Research, Development and Diffusion', in R. Schmalensee and R. Willig (eds), *Handbook of Industrial Organization*, vol. 1, Amsterdam, North-Holland.

Ritz, R.A. (2008), 'Strategic Incentives for Market Share', *International Journal of Industrial Organization*, **26**, 586–97.

Rockett, K. (1990), 'The Quality of Licensed Technology', *International Journal of Industrial Organization*, **8**, 559–74.

Salas Fumas, V. (1992), 'Relative Performance Evaluation of Management: The Effects on Industrial Competition and Risk Sharing', *International Journal of Industrial Organization*, **10**, 473–89.

Sappington, D. (2005), 'On the Irrelevance of Input Prices for Make-or-Buy Decisions', *American Economic Review*, **95**, 1631–8.

Saracho, A.I. (2002), 'Patent Licensing under Strategic Delegation', *Journal of Economics and Management Strategy*, **11**, 225–51.

Saracho, A.I. (2005), 'The Relationship between Patent Licensing and Competitive Behavior', *Manchester School*, **73**, 563–81.

Schumpeter, J. (1942), *Capitalism, Socialism, and Democracy*, London, Allen & Unwin.

Scotchmer, S. (2004), *Innovation and Incentives*, Cambridge, MA, MIT Press.

Shaked, A. and J. Sutton (1990), 'Multiproduct Firms and Market Structure', *RAND Journal of Economics*, **21**, 45–62.

Shy, O. (1995), *Industrial Organization. Theory and Applications*, Cambridge, MA, MIT Press.

Singh, N. and X. Vives (1984), 'Price and Quantity Competition in a Differentiated Duopoly', *RAND Journal of Economics*, **15**, 546–54.

Sklivas, S.D. (1987), 'The Strategic Choice of Managerial Incentives', *RAND Journal of Economics*, **18**, 452–8.

Spagnolo, G. (2000), 'Stock-Related Compensation and Product-Market Competition', *Rand Journal of Economics*, **31**, 22–42.

Spence, A.M. (1976), 'Product Differentiation and Welfare', *American Economic Review*, **66**, 407–14.

Suzumura, K. (1992), 'Cooperative and Noncooperative R&D in an Oligopoly with Spillovers', *American Economic Review*, **82**, 1307–20.

Tadelis, S. (2002), 'Complexity, Flexibility, and the Make-or-Buy Decision', *American Economic Review*, **92**, 433–7.

Tidd, J., J. Bessant and K. Pavitt (2001), *Managing Innovation: Integrating Technological, Market and Organizational Change*, Chichester, Wiley.

Tirole, J. (1988), *The Theory of Industrial Organization*, Cambridge, MA, MIT Press.

Veldman, J, and G. Gaalman (2015), 'Competitive Investments in Cost Reducing Process Improvement: The Role of Managerial Incentives and Spillover Learning', *International Journal of Production Economics*, **170**, 701–9.

Veldman, J., W. Klingenberg, G. Gaalman and R.Teunter (2014), 'Getting What You Pay for – Strategic Process Improvement Compensation', *Production and Operations Management*, **23**, 1387–400.

Vickers, J. (1985), 'Delegation and the Theory of the Firm', *Economic Journal*, **95** (Conference Papers), 138–47.

Wright, P., M. Kroll, J.A. Krug and M. Pettus (2007), 'Influences of Top Management Team Incentives on Firm Risk Taking', *Strategic Management Journal*, **28**, 81–9.

Zhang, Z. and J. Zhang (1997), 'R&D in a Strategic Delegation Game', *Managerial and Decision Economics*, **18**, 391–8.

7 Endogenous product differentiation

While so far product differentiation has appeared here and there in the form of the preference for variety of a representative consumer, this chapter focuses on the bearings of product differentiation formulated from the specific viewpoint of discrete choice theory (Anderson *et al.*, 1992), where a continuum of consumers differ for some specific features (willingness to pay or location in a well behaved preference space) and express unit demands for their preferred variety of a good whose characteristics are endogenously chosen by firms for strategic reasons.

Ever since its early stages, the theory of industrial organization has viewed product differentiation as a means to soften market competition, in particular price competition. Discrete choice theory obviously shares this flavour (see Gabszewicz and Thisse, 1979, 1980, and Shaked and Sutton, 1982), combining it with a renovated attention for the properties of the entry process, in whose connection the so-called finiteness property has been characterized (Shaked and Sutton, 1983).

The relevance of granting differentiation its proper strategic nature deserves a few more words, and perhaps can be best appreciated through a more concrete example. Confining ourselves to the effects of endogenous product differentiation on price competition, it is worth dwelling upon a recurrent idea which may sound sensible to the casual observer but might also haunt the dreams of managers and stockholders (and in fact it has done so several times), namely, that imitating a successful product could be a fruitful strategy, especially if that product relies on secrecy rather than patent protection. Whether this turns out to work or not, essentially depends on consumers' brand loyalty, be that motivated or not by objective considerations. The story of several industries, such as, for instance, that of soft drinks or clothing, provides plenty of examples in either direction, while the seminal debate on the so-called minimum or maximum differentiation principles (Hotelling, 1929; d'Aspremont *et al.*, 1979) decidedly claims that firms should keep off from each other as much as possible in order to soften price competition and increase profits, much the same way as they would by sustaining implicit or explicit cartel behaviour with similar or identical products. In view of the managerial inclinations we have become accustomed to in earlier chapters, this prescription should be expected to apply *a fortiori* for managerial firms.

What follows provides an overview of the available material wherein discrete choice theory overlaps with strategic delegation. As you will see, though quite interesting, this material is still too scant and leaves open questions in many directions which hopefully will be taken up by future research.

7.1 Vertical or horizontal differentiation with convex variable costs

To build up a simple benchmark and fix a few basic ideas, here I will set out using a discrete choice model of vertical product differentiation with hedonic consumer tastes that dates back to Mussa and Rosen (1978) and Gabszewicz and Thisse (1979)[1] and has been extended to the multiproduct firm case by Champsaur and Rochet (1989). A unit mass of consumers is distributed uniformly, with unit density, over the interval $[\overline{m} - 1, \overline{m}]$, with $\overline{m} > 1$. Each consumer is indexed by parameter $m \in [\overline{m} - 1, \overline{m}]$, which measures her/his marginal willingness to pay for quality and is increasing in income.[2]

The industry is a duopoly consisting of single product firms, labelled as H and L, supplying goods characterized by different quality levels, $\xi_H \geq \xi_L$ at different prices, $p_H \geq p_L$. Full market coverage is assumed to hold, with each consumer buying one unit of the good that maximizes her/his net surplus function:

$$U = m\xi_i - p_i \geq 0, i = H, L \tag{7.1}$$

The consumer indifferent between the two varieties is identified by

$$m_{HL} = \frac{p_H - p_L}{\xi_H - \xi_L} \tag{7.2}$$

so that the demand system is

$$q_H = \overline{m} - m_{HL}; \quad q_L = m_{HL} - \overline{m} + 1 \tag{7.3}$$

Quality improvements hinge upon variable costs, $C_i = c\xi_i^2 q_i$, with $c > 0$ (for the alternative version of the same model, envisaging R&D costs convex in product quality, see below). As a result, the profit function of firm i is $\pi_i = (p_i - c\xi_i^2)q_i$. As shown by Cremer and Thisse (1991, 1994), this model encompasses the horizontal differentiation model dating back to Hotelling (1929) in its reformulation based on quadratic transportation costs (d'Aspremont *et al.*, 1979).

7.1.1 Profit incentives

If firms are entrepreneurial, the subgame perfect equilibrium of the two-stage game in qualities and prices (both stages being solved *à la* Nash under simultaneous play) is[3]

$$p_H^N = \frac{(\overline{m} + 1 + 2c\xi_H)\xi_H - \xi_L(\overline{m} + 1 - c\xi_L)}{3}$$
$$p_L^N = \frac{(2 - \overline{m} + c\xi_H)\xi_H - \xi_L(2 - \overline{m} - 2c\xi_L)}{3} \tag{7.4}$$

$$\xi_H^N = \frac{4\overline{m} + 1}{8c}; \quad \xi_L^N = \frac{4\overline{m} - 5}{8c} \tag{7.5}$$

It is worth noting that equilibrium qualities ξ_H^N and ξ_L^N are symmetrically located above and below the preferred quality of the average and median consumer, which corresponds to

$$\xi_{avg}^* = \frac{2\overline{m} - 1}{8c} \tag{7.6}$$

The resulting degree of differentiation

$$\xi_H^N - \xi_L^N = \frac{3}{4c} \tag{7.7}$$

is larger than the degree of differentiation associated with the qualities preferred by the richest and poorest consumer in the market, i.e. those indexed by $\overline{m}$ and $\overline{m} - 1$, respectively. This reveals that the equilibrium is characterized (or affected) by excess product differentiation, resulting from the firms' incentive to use differentiation to soften the intensity of price competition at the second stage of the game.[4] The symmetry of the model is reflected by equilibrium profits $\pi^N = 3/(16c)$ and outputs $q^N = 1/2$.

7.1.2 Managerial incentives

What if firms go managerial? Let us suppose that, if they do so, the delegation contract is written à la Vickers (1985), so that manager i sets p_i to maximize $M_i = \pi_i + \theta_i q_i$. For simplicity, I will consider the case in which qualities are chosen by owners (for more on the opposite possibility, see below).

Proceeding as usual by backward induction to solve this three-stage game, the equilibrium pricing behaviour is now described by the following expressions:

$$p_H^N = \frac{(\overline{m} + 1 + 2c\xi_H)\xi_H - \xi_L(\overline{m} + 1 - c\xi_L) - 2\theta_H - \theta_L}{3}$$

$$p_L^N = \frac{(2 - \overline{m} + c\xi_H)\xi_H - \xi_L(2 - \overline{m} - 2c\xi_L) - \theta_H - 2\theta_L}{3} \tag{7.8}$$

for any vector of contracts and quality levels. The optimal delegation contracts require

$$\theta_H^N = -\frac{(\xi_H - \xi_L)[\overline{m} + 2 - c(\xi_H + \xi_L)]}{5}$$

$$\theta_L^N = -\frac{(\xi_H - \xi_L)[3 - \overline{m} + c(\xi_H + \xi_L)]}{5} \tag{7.9}$$

for any given quality pair, while the Nash equilibrium at the first stage is

$$\xi_H^N = \frac{4\overline{m} + 3}{8c}; \quad \xi_L^N = \frac{4\overline{m} - 7}{8c} \tag{7.10}$$

which, as above, are located symmetrically above and below ξ^*_{avg}, but determine an expansion of the degree of vertical differentiation, which becomes

$$\xi^N_H - \xi^N_L = \frac{5}{4c} > \frac{3}{4c} \tag{7.11}$$

i.e. delegating market behaviour to managers induces owners to increase product differentiation as compared to the one emerging at equilibrium in the purely entrepreneurial setting. This is accompanied by the fact that, in correspondence with (7.11), the equilibrium delegation variables simplify as follows:

$$\theta^N_H = \theta^N_L = -\frac{5}{8c} = -\frac{\xi^N_H - \xi^N_L}{2} \tag{7.12}$$

in line with Fershtman and Judd (1987), whereby delegation must be restrictive under price competition (see Chapter 2). More importantly, it is worth noting that optimal contracts are (inversely) proportional to the degree of quality differentiation.

While the partition of total demand is obviously unaffected by managerialization, profits are, and positively so, as one could anticipate considering that market competition takes place in prices. In fact, $\pi^N = 5/(8c) > 3/(16c)$.

The foregoing discussion can be summarized as in the following proposition.

Proposition 7.1 *If quality hinges upon variable production costs, managerialization intensifies the incentive to differentiate products in order to mitigate price competition. This, combined with restrictive delegation contracts, enhances equilibrium profits.*

It is also worth noting that the above result may have a largely different flavour. By strengthening the incentive to differentiate products, delegation drives the high quality upwards, which means that the widespread presence of managers offers to rich consumers to buy top-notch goods whose hedonic content is higher than that available under pure profit-seeking behaviour. This conclusion, apparently in line with much of the material contained in Chapter 6, emerges however in a setting where quality improvements results from the use of skilled labour rather than by R&D efforts for product innovation, as quality appears in the variable cost function.

7.1.3   Should firms delegate product design?

A natural question triggered by the above model is whether the price decision is the only one which may be delegated to managers, or instead owners might or should also delegate the decision about the quality level. Plenty of real world examples can be mentioned, in opposite directions: in large firms operating in the car industry, short-run decisions are in the hands of managers while those concerning long-run variables remain very much in control of stockholders or even founding family members; the same applies to several well known firms in consumer electronics (typically, in the US) and in fashion (typically, in Italy or France).[5]

This issue has been tackled in Bárcena-Ruiz and Casado-Izaga (2005) using the spatial version of the same model, with quadratic transportation costs *à la* d'Aspremont *et al.* (1979).[6] These authors modelled managerial incentives *à la* Fershtman and Judd (1987) and Sklivas (1987), and investigated a five-stage game with the following structure.

- In stage 1, owners choose whether to delegate quality (location) decisions to managers or not.
- In stage 2, any owner that previously decided to hire a manager writes the optimal contract.
- In stage 3, products are simultaneously defined (along a linear city or the vertical dimension), given the internal organization of firms determined in stage 1. That is, stage 2 may take place among: (i) two entrepreneurial firms, if no manager has been hired; (ii) two managerial firms, if both owners have hired a manager; (iii) a managerial and an entrepreneurial firm if only one firm has separated control from ownership.
- In stage 4, all firms become managerial by delegating control of prices to managers (if either one or both didn't go managerial at stage 1).
- Finally, stage 5 describes Bertrand–Nash competition between managers.

Essentially, the seemingly simplifying assumption defining what happens in stage 4 implies that we must take for granted that pricing behaviour will indeed be delegated, as is surely the case at the subgame perfect equilibrium of the baseline models illustrated in Chapter 2. Honestly, this would need a full proof since the possible presence of delegation upstream (in correspondence of the product design decision might alter the owners' incentive to go managerial downstream), but one may intuitively accept the shortcut proposed by Bárcena-Ruiz and Casado-Izaga (2005), for a reason that will become apparent in a few lines.

Translating their jargon, which is tailored to fit the horizontal differentiation they use, their main result can be spelled out as follows (Bárcena-Ruiz and Casado-Izaga, 2005, p. 220).

Proposition 7.2 *At the subgame perfect equilibrium of the quality-then-price competition game under full market coverage, owners delegate price decisions only, keeping the decision concerning product design in their own hands.*

So, since delegation is a dominant strategy at stage 4, it is indeed true that the price game will be played by managers, confirming the implication of the assumption governing stage 4. Then, by backward induction one finds that long-run decisions about some critical features of products will not be left to managers. Thus, the present model envisages – so to speak – a limited scope for managerial action, in a sense *diminishing the role of delegation*.

This *diminutio* was elegantly amended by Barros and Grilo (2002), where the proper role of managers was fully restored by modelling delegation in an agency problem generated by asymmetric information.

The setup used by Barros and Grilo (2002) is a hybrid combination of the duopoly model of quality competition with zero costs and full market coverage used by Tirole (1988, Chapter 7, Appendix) and Wauthy (1996) and the duopoly with partial market coverage and convex fixed costs of quality improvement illustrated by Motta (1993), i.e. the market is fully covered and quality can be increased by firms bearing fixed costs which increase in the square of the quality level, with the form $C_i = c\xi_i^2$, $i = H, L$, with $c \in \{\underline{c}, \overline{c}\}$, $0 < \underline{c} < \overline{c}$ and probabilities $\Pr(\underline{c}) = p$, $\Pr(\overline{c}) = 1 - p$. Marginal production cost is constant and normalized to zero for the sake of simplicity. Product qualities satisfy $\xi_H, \xi_L \geq \xi \geq 0$.

The most relevant feature of Barros and Grilo's (2002) setup is that managers – if any – operate at the quality stage, while prices are chosen by owners. This is motivated by the presence of uncertainty about the steepness of the R&D curve. If owners retain control of the quality dimension in their hands, they observe the exact value of c (i.e. they know that either $c = \underline{c}$ or $c = \overline{c}$) and choose qualities under perfect certainty. Otherwise, if they delegate the quality decisions to managers, the exact realization of the state of nature determining the steepness of the cost function is known to managers but unobservable for owners.

As a result, a delegating owner must cope with asymmetric information. Barros and Grilo (2002) structured this problem as a three-stage game in which owners decide whether to delegate control or not at the first stage; then, the relevant agents choose quality levels at the second stage; and finally owners compete in prices at the third and final stage, in the market place. Doing so, Barros and Grilo (2002) showed that, in the asymmetric setting in which a firm delegates the quality decision while the other does not, there emerges a multiplicity of equilibria: two equilibria mimic the outcome of the full information game (or, equivalently, the game in which owners keep with themselves the quality decisions), but they are accompanied by two additional ones characterized by lower quality levels than under full information ones (or in the fully entrepreneurial game). That is, asymmetric information about technology may distort quality downwards due to the agents' incentive to exploit the informational rent associated with their exclusive knowledge of the technology in use. Multiple equilibria also arise when the decision to separate control from ownership is taken, as at the first stage literally any configuration can be subgame perfect, with one, both or neither firm delegating.

The demand side is the same as in (7.1)–(7.3). Proceeding by backward induction, one can easily derive the Nash equilibrium prices set by owners at the market stage:[7]

$$p_H^N = \frac{(\overline{m} + 1)(\xi_H - \xi_L)}{3}; \quad p_L^N = \frac{(2 - \overline{m})(\xi_H - \xi_L)}{3} \tag{7.13}$$

which generate revenues

$$R_H^N = p_H^N q_H^N = \frac{(\overline{m} + 1)^2 (\xi_H - \xi_L)}{9}$$

$$R_L^N = p_L^N q_L^N = \frac{(2 - \overline{m})^2 (\xi_H - \xi_L)}{9} \tag{7.14}$$

for any given quality pair (ξ_H, ξ_L). From expressions (7.13)–(7.14), it is evident that, should firms supply identical quality levels, the equilibrium prices would fall to marginal cost, driving profits to zero, reproducing the pure Bertrand competition model with homogeneous goods. On the basis of (7.13)–(7.14), one can investigate the quality choices of firms at the upper stage, in three different scenarios, depending on whether firms operate the separation between ownership and control or not. The first case we encounter is that where neither firm delegates product design to a manager, and therefore the game takes place under full information and has a two-stage structure.

I: Neither firm delegates the quality decision At the quality stage, an owner controlling ξ_i under full information should choose it in order to maximize profits $\pi_i = R_i^N - C_i$. Since $\pi_L = R_L^N - C_L$ is monotonically decreasing in ξ_L, at equilibrium $\xi_L^N = \underline{\xi}$. The high-quality firm, instead, reaches its internal optimum solution at

$$\xi_H^N = \frac{(\overline{m} + 1)^2}{18c} \tag{7.15}$$

where the state of technology, $c \in \{\underline{c}, \overline{c}\}$, is perfectly observed. As a result, the profits associated with the subgame perfect equilibrium of the two-stage game without delegation can be written as

$$\pi_H^N = \frac{(\overline{m} + 1)^2 \left(\xi_H^N - \underline{\xi}\right)}{9} - c \left(\xi_H^N\right)^2$$

$$\pi_L^N = \frac{(2 - \overline{m})^2 \left(\xi_H^N - \underline{\xi}\right)}{9} - c\underline{\xi}^2 \tag{7.16}$$

with equilibrium demands being simultaneously lower than one for all $\overline{m} \in (1, 2)$.

This is the *efficient* equilibrium configuration (as seen from the owners' standpoint), where any quality distortion whatsoever is avoided. The remaining two scenarios will instead be characterized by some positive rents for at least one agent (a manager controlling a firm's quality) and therefore also by some degree of quality distortion generated by the managerial rent-seeking behaviour favoured by the rise of asymmetric information.

If managers are hired, their compensation $\theta_i(\xi_i)$ is based upon the quality level each of them attains, with $\theta_i(\xi_i) = 0$ for all $\xi_i \neq \xi_H^N, \underline{\xi}$. This scenario entails the solution of an agency problem where owners must choose θ_i to meet incentive compatibility and participation constraints, while agents (the managers) choose qualities ξ_i. The outcome can be summarized by defining as ξ_{ic} the quality supplied by firm i's relevant subject (either the owner or the manager) in correspondence with state $c = \underline{c}, \overline{c}$. Since π_L is monotonically decreasing in ξ_L, there are only two relevant cases to be illustrated, both giving rise to multiple equilibria in pure strategies depending on the configuration of parameters and probabilities.

II: Only firm H delegates the quality decision

In this situation, the equilibrium quality configuration is the following:

$$\xi_{H\underline{c}} = \frac{(\overline{m}+1)^2}{18\underline{c}}; \quad \xi_{H\overline{c}} = \frac{(1-\mathfrak{p})(\overline{m}+1)^2}{18(\overline{c}-\mathfrak{p}\underline{c})} \tag{7.17}$$

$$\xi_{L\underline{c}} = \xi_{L\overline{c}} = 0$$

provided that

$$\mathfrak{p} \leq 1 - \frac{(\overline{c}-\underline{c})(\overline{m}+1)^2}{2\left[\overline{c}\left((\overline{m}+1)^2 + (2-\overline{m})^2\right) + \underline{c}(\overline{m}+1)^2\right]}, \tag{7.18}$$

the above condition entailing that as the probability attached to the favourable state increases, the appearance of this equilibrium configuration becomes less likely. As soon as (7.18) is violated, the entrepreneurial firm leapfrogs the managerial rival. Another way of reading (7.18) is that the likelihood of observing the inefficient outcome (7.17) at equilibrium increases as $\overline{c} - \underline{c}$ shrinks. Additionally, the equilibrium quality vector becomes

$$\xi_{H\underline{c}} = \frac{(\overline{m}+1)^2}{18\underline{c}}; \quad \xi_{H\overline{c}} = \frac{(\overline{m}+1)^2}{18\overline{c}} \tag{7.19}$$

$$\xi_{L\underline{c}} = \xi_{L\overline{c}} = 0$$

if the income dispersion (and therefore the dispersion of the marginal willingness to pay) of consumers shrinks as well around the index identifying the average and median consumer. That is, the model offers at least two ways out of the distortion generated by asymmetric information.

When instead firm i delegates and firm j does not (disregarding for a moment the firms' distribution along the quality spectrum), and $\mathfrak{p} \in (\widehat{\mathfrak{p}}, \widetilde{\mathfrak{p}})$, with

$$\widehat{\mathfrak{p}} \equiv \frac{(\overline{m}+1)^2 \left[2\underline{c}\left((\overline{m}+1)^2 + (2-\overline{m})^2\right) - \overline{c}(\overline{m}+1)^2\right]}{2\underline{c}\left((\overline{m}+1)^2 + (2-\overline{m})^2\right)^2}$$

$$\widetilde{\mathfrak{p}} \equiv \frac{1}{2} - \frac{(2-\overline{m})^4}{2\left((\overline{m}+1)^2 + (2-\overline{m})^2\right)^2} \tag{7.20}$$

then the equilibrium configuration becomes

$$\xi_{i\underline{c}} = \xi_{i\overline{c}} = \frac{(1-\mathfrak{p})(\overline{m}+1)^2 - \mathfrak{p}(2-\overline{m})^2}{18\overline{c}}$$

$$\xi_{j\underline{c}} = \frac{(\overline{m}+1)^2}{18\underline{c}}; \quad \xi_{j\overline{c}} = 0 \tag{7.21}$$

which clearly illustrates that firm i can be leapfrogged by the entrepreneurial rival.

III: Both firms delegate quality decisions It turns out that (7.17) remains an equilibrium outcome when both firms delegate control of quality choices to managers, but is not the only one, as also (7.21) is an equilibrium, for all $\mathrm{p} \in (\widehat{\mathrm{p}}, \overline{\mathrm{p}})$, with

$$\overline{\mathrm{p}} \equiv \frac{(\overline{m} + 1)^2}{(\overline{m} + 1)^2 + (2 - \overline{m})^2} \tag{7.22}$$

Relying on the foregoing calculations, Barros and Grilo (2002, p. 179) solved the first stage of the game, where delegation decisions are taken by managers, to formulate the following.

Proposition 7.3 *The first stage has multiple pure-strategy equilibria in which at least one firm hires a manager, and downward quality distortion by at least one firm is observed.*

- *If condition (7.18) holds, then both firms delegate quality control to managers. The high-quality firm's manager enjoys an informational rent driving the high quality below its efficient level.*
- *If the ratio $(2 - \overline{m})^2/(\overline{m} + 1)^2$ is either sufficiently low or sufficiently high, then a single firm delegates quality control to a manager. Here, if $c = \overline{c}$, managerialization induces a downward quality distortion associated with a rent for the agent which is increasing in the size of $\overline{c} - \underline{c}$.*

From the above discussion we also know that the no delegation case or the equivalent configuration with no distortion can arise at the subgame perfect equilibrium. More interesting is discussing in some deeper detail the claim appearing in the second item of the last proposition. Unilateral delegation obtains at equilibrium if either

$$\phi \equiv \frac{(2 - \overline{m})^2}{(\overline{m} + 1)^2} \leq \max \left\{ \frac{\overline{c}(1 - \mathrm{p})}{2(\overline{c} - \mathrm{p}\underline{c})} \equiv \gamma_1, \; \frac{\overline{c}(\overline{c} - \underline{c}) + \underline{c}(1 - \mathrm{p})}{2\overline{c}(\overline{c} - \mathrm{p}\underline{c})} \equiv \gamma_2 \right\} \tag{7.23}$$

or

$$\phi > \frac{\overline{c}\left[\mathrm{p}(\overline{c} - \underline{c}) + \underline{c}(1 - \mathrm{p})\right]}{2(\overline{c} - \mathrm{p}\underline{c})\left[\mathrm{p}\underline{c} + \underline{c}(1 - \mathrm{p})\right]} \equiv \gamma_3 \tag{7.24}$$

where $\gamma_3 \geq \gamma_2$ for all $\mathrm{p} \in (0, 1]$. Conditions (7.23)–(7.24) are drawn in Figure 7.1, where p appears along the horizontal axis, while expressions ϕ, γ_1, γ_2 and γ_3 are measured along the vertical one.

To interpret the graph in Figure 7.1, observe first that ϕ is a flat line with respect to p, being solely determined by the marginal willingness to pay for quality of

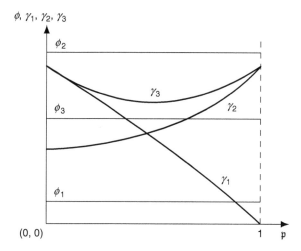

Figure 7.1 Unilateral delegation of quality choice.

consumers. Moreover, ϕ is decreasing and convex in $\overline{m}$. Hence, changing $\overline{m}$ generates infinitely many straight lines parallel to the horizontal axis. Additionally, $\gamma_1 = \gamma_3$ in $\mathfrak{p} = 0$, $\gamma_2 = \gamma_3$ in $\mathfrak{p} = 1$ and $\gamma_3\,(\mathfrak{p} = 0) = \gamma_3\,(\mathfrak{p} = 1)$. Hence, it appears that there are infinitely many lines like ϕ_2, each generated by a single value of $\overline{m}$, satisfying inequality (7.24) for all values of $\mathfrak{p}$, while there are infinitely many lines like ϕ_1 satisfying inequality (7.23) – i.e. lying below the upper envelope of $\{\gamma_1, \gamma_2\}$ – for sufficiently low values of the probability attached to the favourable state of technology. It is worth stressing that lines like ϕ_1 correspond to a high level of consumers' willingness to pay for quality, or income. These results point out that unilateral delegation must be expected to systematically arise in quite extreme cases as far as income distribution is concerned. To conclude the description of Figure 7.1, it is worth observing that intermediate values of $\overline{m}$ engender lines like ϕ_3, intersecting the upper envelope of $\{\gamma_1, \gamma_2\}$ and lying below γ_3, in such a way that for intermediate values of $\mathfrak{p}$ inequalities (7.23)–(7.24) are simultaneously reverted and therefore unilateral delegation cannot arise at equilibrium, leaving room for fully symmetric industry configurations.

What happens if all of the firms' strategies are taken by managers? This brings us to the subject matter of the next subsection, which also involves an additional relevant feature concerning the scope of product differentiation in strategic oligopoly games in general.

7.1.4 Bidimensional product differentiation

Whether or not managers are present, the unidimensional approach to endogenous product differentiation has the obvious merit of providing intuitive results about the firms' incentives to exploit differentiation to soften price competition.

However, one may plausibly argue that a single dimension does not exhaust the entire spectrum of possibilities and most probably is not even representative of it.

The analysis of multidimensional product differentiation dates back at least to Economides (1986) and Neven and Thisse (1990).[8] In the latter paper, Hotelling's linear city is combined with the modelization of consumers' income distribution, generating an incentive towards horizontal and vertical differentiation at the same time. A similar but simpler setup can be found in Ishibashi (2001), where two firms, 1 and 2 are located at the opposite extremes of a city of unit length, and invest to increase product quality before engaging in price competition. Both strategic decisions are delegated to managers, via contracts *à la* Fershtman and Judd (1987) and Sklivas (1987).

A unit mass of consumers is uniformly distributed along the unit segment, each consumer being located at $x \in [0, 1]$. All consumers have the same income, and each of them buys one unit of the good either from firm 1 or from firm 1, receiving a net surplus equal to

$$U = v + \xi_i - p_i - |d_i| \geq 0, \quad i = 1, 2 \tag{7.25}$$

where v is gross surplus (which is assumed to be sufficiently high to ensure (i) full market coverage at any price pair and (ii) the non-negativity of all relevant magnitudes at equilibrium) and $|d_i|$ is the distance separating the consumer at x from firm 1 at 0 or firm 2 at 1. The indifferent consumer is located at

$$\tilde{x} = \frac{p_2 - p_1 + \xi_1 - \xi_2 + 1}{2} \tag{7.26}$$

so that demand functions are $q_1 = \tilde{x}$ and $q_2 = 1 - \tilde{x}$, provided $\tilde{x} \in (0, 1)$.

Let's assume quality improvements hinge upon variable costs, in such a way that the total cost function of firm i is $C_i = c\xi_i^2 q_i$. Then, its profit function is $\pi_i = (p_i - c\xi_i^2)q_i$ and, if this firm delegates control of quality and price decisions to a manager, the latter signs a contract specifying an incentive of the form $M_i = \theta_i \pi_i + (1 - \theta_i)p_i q_i$.

Confining attention to fully symmetric scenarios, one can solve the downstream market stage in the price stage assuming managers have been hired. This yields the following expressions:

$$p_1^N = \frac{\xi_1 - \xi_2 + 3 + 2c\xi_1^2\theta_1 + c\xi_2^2\theta_2}{3}$$

$$p_2^N = \frac{\xi_2 - \xi_1 + 3 + 2c\xi_2^2\theta_2 + c\xi_1^2\theta_1}{3} \tag{7.27}$$

which can be easily simplified to reproduce the equilibrium prices chosen by owners by posing $\theta_1 = \theta_2 = 1$.

The only admissible equilibrium pair at the quality stage is identified by $\xi_i^N = 1/(2c\theta_i)$, $i = 1, 2$.[9] Before completing the backward induction procedure, it is worth dwelling upon the implications of the latter expression, which can be summarized in the following.

Lemma 7.1 *Since $\partial \xi_i^N / \partial \theta_i < 0$ and $\partial \xi_i^N / \partial \theta_j = 0$, (i) delegation involving a revenue-based managerial incentive involves an increase in firm i's product quality and (ii) delegation (or the absence thereof) by the rival firm has no impact on firm i's product quality.*

To grasp the intuition about this result, remember that delegation is *visible* whenever $\theta_i < 1$. This lemma, in a sense, confirms what we have already seen in Chapter 6, i.e. that managers having a taste for sales or output expansion also exhibit an analogous inclination towards innovation or, as is the case here, investments in quality improvements.

As for the first stage, it is not necessary to model the choice of the optimal symmetric contract, for the following reasons. Since $\xi_i^N > 0$ provided $\theta_i > 0$, and

$$\lim_{\theta_i \to \infty} \xi_i^N = +\infty \tag{7.28}$$

one has to confine the analysis to $\theta_i \in (0, 1]$, knowing that if $\theta_i = 1$ then firms remain in the hands of their owners. Relying on this, one can set $\theta_i = \theta_j = \theta$ and simplify the relevant magnitudes associated with the equilibrium prevailing when the industry is fully managerialized, for any symmetric pair of managerial contracts. Intuitively, $\widetilde{x}(D, D) = q^N(D, D) = 1/2$. Moreover, the equilibrium price is

$$p^N (D, D) = 1 + \frac{1}{4c\theta} \tag{7.29}$$

while profits, consumer surplus and welfare are

$$\pi^N (D, D) = \frac{\theta (4c\theta + 1) - 1}{8c\theta^2} \tag{7.30}$$

$$CS^N (D, D) = v + \frac{1}{4}\left(\frac{1}{c\theta} - 5\right) \tag{7.31}$$

and $SW^N(D, D) = CS^N(D, D) + 2\pi^N(D, D)$.

In the opposite case, both firms remain entrepreneurial; therefore, $\theta_1 = \theta_2 = 1$ and equilibrium qualities can be easily calculated anew, obtaining the unique admissible symmetric equilibrium in correspondence with $\xi^N(ND, ND) = 1/(2c) > \xi^N(D, D)$ for all $\theta \in (0, 1)$, which must be used to write the equilibrium values of all relevant variables. It is pretty obvious that $\widetilde{x}(ND, ND) = q^N(ND, ND) = 1/2$. As for the remaining magnitudes, we have

$$p^N (ND, ND) = 1 + \frac{1}{4c} < p^N (D, D) \tag{7.32}$$

$$\pi^N (ND, ND) = \frac{1}{2} > \pi^N (D, D) \tag{7.33}$$

$$CS^{N}(ND, ND) = \frac{1}{4}\left(\frac{1}{4c} - 5\right) < CS^{N}(D, D) \qquad (7.34)$$

and $SW^{N}(ND, ND) > SW^{N}(D, D)$. Hence, the comparison between the fully managerialized industry and its fully entrepreneurial version delivers the following.

Proposition 7.4 *Managerialization increases qualities and prices while decreasing profits, as compared to the outcome generated by a fully entrepreneurial industry. The competitive pressure associated with managerialization increases consumer surplus. On balance, however, welfare is higher when managers are absent.*

The managerial inclination towards quality improvement has, evidently, peculiar effects which one might hardly expect to see. On the one hand, it is reasonable that any quality increase, involving a cost increase, will drive prices upwards. This, in turn, should hamper consumer surplus, which instead goes up because quality increases more than prices and the markup goes down. Combined with the fact that market demand is totally price-inelastic in this model, this lowers profits more than it increases consumer surplus, with the unforeseeable outcome of diminishing social welfare as compared to the fully entrepreneurial setup.

7.2   Process innovation and quality improvements

One last contribution dealing with the impact of managerialization on endogenous investments in product quality is that of Veldman and Gaalman (2014), in which managerial incentives are based on a combination of profits, quality improvements and investments in process (i.e. cost-reducing) innovation efforts, as in Overvest and Veldman (2008), where only the second form of R&D activity is considered.

Their approach must be treated as a separate entity, as it does not make use of hedonic preferences and discrete choices. Instead, it plugs product quality into the standard linear demand structure generated by the traditional constrained maximization of the utility function of a representative consumer buying a basket of all available goods in the market.

The model describes a duopoly consisting of single-product firms, and is constructed upon demand functions specified as in Balasubramanian and Bhardwaj (2004):

$$q_i = 1 - p_i + p_j + \sigma\left(\xi_i - \xi_j\right) \qquad (7.35)$$

so that q_i increases (respectively, decreases) for all $\xi_i > \xi_j$ (respectively, $\xi_i < \xi_j$), via an upward (respectively, downward) shift, leaving its slope with respect to price(s) unmodified. Parameter $\sigma \in (0, 1]$ measures the sensitivity of demand to the existing quality differential, and such sensitivity is assumed to be at most equal to the reaction of q_i to either price.

The profit function of firm i is

$$\pi_i = (p_i - c_i) q_i - C_i (k_i, \xi_i) \tag{7.36}$$

where marginal production cost is $c_i = \bar{c} - k_i$, $\bar{c} \in (0, 1)$, and the total R&D cost function is $C_i (k_i, \xi_i) = bk_i^2 + h\xi_i^2$, where b and h are positive parameters. If a manager is hired, he/she is given the following incentive scheme:

$$M_i = \pi_i + \zeta_i k_i + \theta_i \xi_i \tag{7.37}$$

in which ζ_i and θ_i are chosen by owners.

The structure of the game is as follows. At the first stage, owners decide whether to hire managers or not. At the second, the relevant players (either owners or managers) choose both R&D efforts to optimally adjust marginal production cost and qualities. At the third, the same agents compete in prices. All stages take place under complete, symmetric and imperfect information, and information is perfect between stages. The three subgames arising from the first stage, as usual, are: (i) the symmetric R&D and price two-stage game between owners; (ii) the asymmetric R&D and price two-stage game between a manager and an owner; (iii) the symmetric R&D and price two-stage game between managers.

7.2.1 No delegation

Here the objective of both firms is profit maximization. Solving the two-stage game which is relevant when no managers have been hired, the equilibrium vector of R&D efforts is

$$k^N (ND, ND) = \frac{1}{3b}; \; \xi^N (ND, ND) = \frac{\sigma}{3h} \tag{7.38}$$

in which the expression of $\xi^N (ND, ND)$ immediately implies the following.

Lemma 7.2 *The R&D effort for quality improvement is increasing in σ.*

That is, as the weight of the quality differential in the demand functions (7.35) increases, both qualities also – intuitively – increase; or, as firms become aware that consumers attach a higher relevance to vertical differentiation, owners engage themselves in a quality race whose escalating rate is proportional to the representative consumer's likings.

The associated equilibrium profits are

$$\pi^N(ND, ND) = \frac{h(9b - 1) - b\sigma^2}{9bh} \tag{7.39}$$

7.2.2   *Unilateral delegation*

Here, firm i is entrepreneurial and maximizes (7.36), while firm j is managerial and maximizes (7.37). The subgame perfect R&D efforts are

$$k^N (ND, D) = \frac{9h \left[h (3b - 1) - b\sigma^2 \right]}{\Phi (b, h)}$$

$$\xi^N (ND, D) = \frac{9b\sigma \left[h (3b - 1) - b\sigma^2 \right]}{\Phi (b, h)} \tag{7.40}$$

for the entrepreneurial firm, and

$$k^N (D, ND) = \frac{3h \left[h (9b - 2) - 2b\sigma^2 \right]}{\Phi (b, h)}$$

$$\xi^N (D, ND) = \frac{3b\sigma \left[h (9b - 2) - 2b\sigma^2 \right]}{\Phi (b, h)} \tag{7.41}$$

for the managerial one. In (7.40)–(7.41), $\Phi(b, h)$ is a positive expression. A quick comparison of (7.40) and (7.41) shows that

$$k^N (D, ND) - k^N (ND, D) = \frac{3b \left(h + 3\sigma^2 \right)}{\Phi (b, h)} > 0$$

$$\xi^N (D, ND) - \xi^N (ND, D) = \frac{3b\sigma \left(h + 3\sigma^2 \right)}{\Phi (b, h)} > 0 \tag{7.42}$$

Accordingly, one can formulate the following.

Lemma 7.3 *The managerial firm outperforms the entrepreneurial one along both R&D dimensions.*

This confirms the general intuition about the managerial inclination towards innovation which we have become acquainted with in Chapter 6. The equilibrium profits of the asymmetric case are

$$\pi^N (ND, D) = \frac{81hb \left[h (3b - 1) - b\sigma^2 \right]^2 \left[h (9b - 1) - b\sigma^2 \right]}{\Phi^2 (b, h)} \tag{7.43}$$

$$\pi^N (D, ND) = \frac{\left[h (9b - 2) - 2b\sigma^2 \right]^2}{\Phi (b, h)} \tag{7.44}$$

7.2.3   *Bilateral delegation*

Here both firms delegate R&D and pricing decisions to managers, who are therefore maximizing (7.37).

The resulting equilibrium R&D efforts are

$$k^N(D, D) = \frac{3h}{h(9b-1) - b\sigma^2}$$
$$\xi^N(D, D) = \frac{3b\sigma}{h(9b-1) - b\sigma^2} \tag{7.45}$$

engendering symmetric profits

$$\pi^N(D, D) = \frac{\left[h(9b-1) - b\sigma^2\right]^2 - 81h^2b^2 + 9hb\left[h(9b-1) - b\sigma^2\right]}{\left[h(9b-1) - b\sigma^2\right]^2} \tag{7.46}$$

Before investigating the first stage where the decision to delegate or not is taken by owners, it is worth stressing a result holding here as well as in the previous asymmetric case.

Proposition 7.5 *Irrespective of the rival firm's internal organization, any owner delegating control to a manager provides the latter with positive incentives towards cost reduction and quality improvement, i.e. ζ_i^N and θ_i^N are always positive.*

7.2.4 The delegation decision

The first stage is the familiar 2×2 discrete game appearing in Matrix 7.1, where the relevant payoffs can be reconstructed on the basis of expressions (7.39), (7.43)–(7.44) and (7.46).

		j	
		D	ND
i	D	$\pi^N(D, D)$; $\pi^N(D, D)$	$\pi^N(D, ND)$; $\pi^N(ND, D)$
	ND	$\pi^N(ND, D)$; $\pi^N(D, ND)$	$\pi^N(ND, ND)$; $\pi^N(ND, ND)$

Matrix 7.1

Taking into account the set of non-negativity constraints on profits, outputs and R&D efforts, one obtains the following.

Proposition 7.6 $\pi^N(D, ND) > \pi^N(ND, ND) > \pi^N(D, D) > \pi^N(ND, D)$ *over the admissible parameter region. Hence, (D, D) is the unique equilibrium in dominant strategies, generated by a prisoners' dilemma.*

This means that the increase in R&D expenses hampers firms' profits but, this notwithstanding, the persistent underlying prisoners' dilemma forces owners to delegate, as otherwise the underdog role would be made even more evident because of the resulting technological gap. Of course, given that here individual and aggregate demand functions are indeed price-elastic (unlike what we have seen in the previous model), the equilibrium characterizing Matrix 7.1 is also efficient.[10]

As I anticipated in the introductory remarks, the foregoing material reveals that a lot more could and should be done in this field of IO in order to fully outline the role and scope of strategic delegation when the features of products are strategically determined either by themselves or by their firms' owners. If, on the one hand, this may sound disappointing, on the other, it uncovers plenty of food for thought, looking forward to obtaining a full-fledged picture of managerial firms using differentiation as a proper component of their *panoplia* of strategic tools.

Further reading

Besides Anderson *et al.* (1992), a very accurate account of the theory of product differentiation is contained in Beath and Katsoulacos (1991). An overview of several topics in the economics of vertical differentiation is in Lambertini (2006). The literature using the baseline model of vertical differentiation is very large. In particular, that model has been used to study the effects of minimum quality standards. On this specific aspect, see Ronnen (1991), Crampes and Hollander (1995) and Ecchia and Lambertini (1997). An extension of this debate accommodating strategic delegation would possibly be very fruitful. For more on product development and cost-reducing R&D, see Bonanno and Haworth (1998) and Rosenkranz (2003), proposing models in which, however, delegation to managers is not contemplated. Additional insights on delegation under horizontal product differentiation are in Liang *et al.* (2011).

Notes

1 For a clear and simple treatment of the model, assuming away any production or development costs in order to understand pure profit incentives, see Choia nd Shin (1992) and Wauthy (1996).
2 Indeed, m can be thought of as being inversely related to the marginal utility of income. For more on this interpretation, see Tirole (1988, Chapter 2, p. 96).
3 The FOCs at the quality stage are cubic in ξ_H and ξ_L. The equilibrium quality levels can be easily identified on the basis of second-order conditions for concavity.
4 This feature, as a consequence of the result proved by Cremer and Thisse (1991), emerges as well in the Hotelling model of spatial differentiation with quadratic transportation costs. See Lambertini (1994, 1997) and Tabuchi and Thisse (1995).
5 The fashion industry is a particularly appropriate example, as there the role of skilled labour remains crucial, any technical progress notwithstanding.
6 The bearings of vertical separation on horizontal product differentiation are characterized in a stream of research based on Bonanno and Vickers (1988) and stemming from Pepall and Norman (2001). In a model where retailers choose locations and have private information about their costs, Bassi *et al.* (2015) showed that, for any admissible level of asymmetric information between manufacturers and retailers, the principle of maximum differentiation, in general, does not apply.
7 Expressions (7.13)–(7.14) coincide with those appearing in Tirole (1988, pp. 296–7).
8 Other relevant contributions in the same vein are those of Vandenbosch and Weinberg (1995), Dos Santos Ferreira and Thisse (1996), Irmen and Thisse (1998), Denicolò and Zanchettin (2012) and Garella and Lambertini (2014). It is worth mentioning that Irmen and Thisse (1998) considered a Hotelling problem modelled as a hypercube in n equivalent dimensions, finding out that firms exploit maximum differentiation along one of

these dimensions and then adopt minimum differentiation along the remaining $n-1$ dimensions, implying that, after all, Hotelling was indeed *almost right*.
9 The remaining four pairs can be disregarded as they do not satisfy second-order conditions for at least one of the firms.
10 Veldman and Gaalman (2014, pp. 207–8) also treated the realistic case in which firms offer multiple varieties using the same production technologies, and showed that analogous considerations apply.

References

Anderson, S., A. de Palma and J.-F. Thisse (1992), *Discrete Choice Theory of Product Differentiation*, Cambridge, MA, MIT Press.
Balasubramanian, S. and P. Bhardwaj (2004), 'When not All Conflict Is Bad: Manufacturing-Marketing Conflict and Strategic Incentive Design', *Management Science*, **50**, 489–502.
Bárcena-Ruiz, J.C. and F.J. Casado-Izaga (2005), 'Should Shareholders Delegate Location Decisions?', *Research in Economics*, **59**, 209–22.
Barros, F. and I. Grilo (2002), 'Delegation in a Vertically Differentiated Duopoly', *Manchester School*, **70**, 164–84.
Bassi, M., M. Pagnozzi and S. Piccolo (2015), 'Product Differentiation by Competing Vertical Hierarchies', *Journal of Economics and Management Strategy*, **24**, 904–33.
Beath, J. and Y. Katsoulacos (1991), *The Economic Theory of Product Differentiation*, Cambridge, Cambridge University Press.
Bonanno, G. and B. Haworth (1998), 'Intensity of Competition and the Choice between Product and Process Innovation', *International Journal of Industrial Organization*, **16**, 495–510.
Bonanno, G. and J. Vickers (1988), 'Vertical Separation', *Journal of Industrial Economics*, **36**, 257–65.
Champsaur, P. and J. Rochet (1989), 'Multiproduct Duopolists', *Econometrica*, **57**, 533–57.
Choi, C.J. and H.S. Shin (1992), 'A Comment on a Model of Vertical Product Differentiation', *Journal of Industrial Economics*, **40**, 229–31.
Crampes, C. and A. Hollander (1995), 'Duopoly and Quality Standards', *European Economic Review*, **39**, 71–82.
Cremer, H. and J.-F. Thisse (1991), 'Location Models of Horizontal Differentiation: A Special Case of Vertical Differentiation Models', *Journal of Industrial Economics*, **39**, 383–90.
Cremer, H. and J.-F. Thisse (1994), 'Commodity Taxation in a Differentiated Oligopoly', *International Economic Review*, **35**, 613–33.
d'Aspremont, C., J.J. Gabszewicz and J.-F.Thisse (1979), 'On Hotelling's 'Stability in Competition'', *Econometrica*, **47**, 1145–50.
Denicolò, V. and P. Zanchettin (2012), 'A Dynamic Model of Patent Portfolio Races', *Economics Letters*, **117**, 924–7.
Dos Santos Ferreira, R. and J.-F. Thisse (1996), 'Horizontal and Vertical Differentiation: The Launhardt Model', *International Journal of Industrial Organization*, **14**, 485–506.
Ecchia, G. and L. Lambertini (1997), 'Minimum Quality Standards and Collusion', *Journal of Industrial Economics*, **45**, 101–13.
Economides, N. (1986), 'Nash Equilibrium in Duopoly with Products Defined by Two Characteristics', *RAND Journal of Economics*, **17**, 431–9.
Fershtman, C. and K. Judd (1987), 'Equilibrium Incentives in Oligopoly', *American Economic Review*, **77**, 927–40.

Gabszewicz, J.J. and J.-F. Thisse (1979), 'Price Competition, Quality and Income Dispari-ties', *Journal of Economic Theory*, **20**, 310–59.

Gabszewicz, J.J. and J.-F. Thisse (1980), 'Entry (and Exit) in a Differentiated Industry', *Journal of Economic Theory*, **22**, 327–38.

Garella, P. and L. Lambertini (2014), 'Bidimensional Vertical Differentiation', *International Journal of Industrial Organization*, **32**, 1–10.

Hotelling, H. (1929), 'Stability in Competition', *Economic Journal*, **39**, 41–57.

Irmen, A. and J.-F. Thisse (1998), 'Competition in Multi-characteristics Spaces: Hotelling Was Almost Right', *Journal of Economic Theory*, **78**, 76–102.

Ishibashi, K. (2001), 'Strategic Delegation under Quality Competition', *Journal of Economics*, **73**, 25–56.

Lambertini, L. (1994), 'Equilibrium Locations in the Unconstrained Hotelling Game', *Economic Notes*, **23**, 438–46.

Lambertini, L. (1997), 'Unicity of the Equilibrium in the Unconstrained Hotelling Model', *Regional Science and Urban Economics*, **27**, 785–98.

Lambertini, L. (2006), *The Economics of Vertically Differentiated Markets*, Cheltenham, Edward Elgar.

Liang, W.-J., C.-C. Tseng and K.-C. A. Wang (2011), 'Location Choice with Delegation: Bertrand vs. Cournot Competition', *Economic Modelling*, **28**, 1774–81.

Motta, M. (1993), 'Endogenous Quality Choice: Price vs Quantity Competition', *Journal of Industrial Economics*, **41**, 113–31.

Mussa, M. and S. Rosen (1978), 'Monopoly and Product Quality', *Journal of Economic Theory*, **18**, 301–17.

Neven, D. and J.-F. Thisse (1990), 'On Quality and Variety Competition', in J.J. Gabszewicz, J.-F. Richard and L. Wolsey (eds), *Economic Decision Making: Games, Econometrics, and Optimization. Contributions in Honour of Jacques Drèze*, Amsterdam, North-Holland.

Overvest, B. and J.Veldman (2008), 'Managerial Incentives for Process Innovation', *Managerial and Decision Economics*, **29**, 539–45.

Pepall, L. and G. Norman (2001), 'Product Differentiation and Upstream-Downstream Relations', *Journal of Economics and Management Strategy*, **10**, 201–33.

Ronnen, U. (1991), 'Minimum Quality Standards, Fixed Costs, and Competition', *RAND Journal of Economics*, **22**, 490–504.

Rosenkranz, S. (2003), 'Simultaneous Choice of Process and Product Innovation', *Journal of Economic Behavior and Organization*, **50**, 183–201.

Shaked, A. and J. Sutton (1982), 'Relaxing Price Competition Through Product Differenti-ation', *Review of Economic Studies*, **49**, 3–19.

Shaked, A. and J. Sutton (1983), 'Natural Oligopolies', *Econometrica*, **51**, 1469–83.

Sklivas, S.D. (1987), 'The Strategic Choice of Managerial Incentives', *RAND Journal of Economics*, **18**, 452–8.

Tabuchi, T. and J.-F. Thisse (1995), 'Asymmetric Equilibria in Spatial Competition', *International Journal of Industrial Organization*, **13**, 213–27.

Tirole, J. (1988), *The Theory of Industrial Organization*, Cambridge, MA, MIT Press.

Vandenbosch, M. and C. Weinberg (1995), 'Product and Price Competition in a Two Dimensional Vertical Differentiation Model', *Marketing Science*, **14**, 224–49.

Veldman, J. and G. Gaalman (2014), 'A Model of Strategic Product Quality and Process Improvement Incentives', *International Journal of Production Economics*, **149**, 202–10.

Vickers, J. (1985), 'Delegation and the Theory of the Firm', *Economic Journal*, **95** (Conference Papers), 138–47.

Wauthy, X. (1996), 'Quality Choice in Models of Vertical Differentiation', *Journal of Industrial Economics*, **44**, 345–53.

8 Trade and the environment

This chapter jointly treats two themes closely connected with the globalization of the economic system, although at the moment very few formalized connections exist in the literature on managerial firms between international trade and the environmental effects of production and consumption.[1] As is the case for the topics covered in a few previous chapters, it goes without saying that also in these respects there is much room for relevant extensions.

The revolution in the theory of international trade which is well summarized in Helpman and Krugman (1985, 1989) has produced the so-called *New Trade Theory*, where consumers' preference for variety, product differentiation and imperfect competition combine to produce once and for all a major twist in our understanding of intraindustry trade and the design of related policies. Naturally, this new framework has been conceived thinking of profit-maximizing firms with no hints of separation between ownership and control.

The same holds true in environmental economics, where the bulk of the initial sub-literature in this field using oligopoly models generally assumes pure profit-seeking behaviour (cf. Lambertini, 2013, chapter 2).

So, it was a matter of time for extensions considering strategic delegation to appear. As the following pages are about to illustrate, managerialization has entered the theory of international trade through the main door, revisiting the dominant models of trade dealing with export rivalry and the so-called 'import-competing industry'. Instead, the emergence of strategic delegation in environmental economics via a concept which is specific to the context of environmental economics itself, i.e. Corporate Social Responsibility, whose adoption by firms is quite often implemented by delegating to one or more managers the decisions regarding the preservation of the environment and natural resources.

With the initial remarks of this introduction in mind, the chapter concludes with the exposition of a model containing a mix of trade and environmental themes, being investigated through the lens of the internal organization of firms and industries.

8.1 International trade

The first authors modelling the role of managers in shaping international trade and the related trade policies were Campbell and Vousden (1994) and Horn *et al.*

(1995), using an agency theory approach where the managers' behaviour is unobservable by principals (owners). The strategic delegation approach to international trade was initiated by Das (1997) using the incentive scheme of Fershtman and Judd (1987) and Sklivas (1987), and then by Miller and Pazgal (2005), using – intuitively – the comparative performance criterion as in their own paper (Miller and Pazgal, 2001). As we are about to see, the trade policy implications of adopting sales-based contracts or profit-based contracts are extremely different.

The model in Das (1997) fits into the tradition of international trade under oligopolistic competition dating back to Helpman and Krugman (1985, 1989), and considers both the case of firms based in two different countries competing on the market of a third one (export rivalry) and that of proper intraindustry trade, where firms based in different countries penetrate the other country's market.

8.1.1   Selling on a third country's market: export rivalry

This case is in fact an extension of Brander and Spencer (1985) to encompass the presence of managers. Two firms export a homogeneous good to a third country, whose consumers express the demand function $p = a - Q$, $Q = q_1 + q_2$. The exporting firms use the same technology with a constant marginal cost $c \in (0, a)$. The governments of the exporting countries set export subsidies s_i, $i = 1, 2$, to make their firms more aggressive in the foreign market by reducing marginal cost c. Hence, here trade policy joins delegation in boosting a firm's output expansion.

The game unravels along three stages, the first being for policy making, the other two for delegation and quantity competition, respectively. The relevant welfare function maximized by the government of country i at the first stage is given by firm i's profits net of the amount of subsidies, i.e. $SW_i = \pi_i - s_i q_i$, while the managerial incentive at the second stage is $M_i = \theta_i \pi_i + (1 - \theta_i) p q_i$.

The steps involved in the solution of the familiar delegation-then-Cournot competition two-stage procedure can be skipped to focus on the first stage. The relevant profits to be included in the welfare function can be written as $\pi_i^N = 2A_i/25$, where $A_i \equiv a - c + s_i$, and the FOC of country i's government is

$$\frac{\partial SW_i}{\partial s_i} = a - c - 2\left(6s_i + s_j\right) = 0 \tag{8.1}$$

which, imposing symmetry on policy instruments, yields

$$s^N(D, D) = \frac{a - c}{14} \tag{8.2}$$

which is positive but lower than the optimal subsidy to be adopted should both firms be entrepreneurial units, as in Brander and Spencer (1985):

$$s^N(ND, ND) = \frac{a - c}{5} \tag{8.3}$$

This implies the following.

Proposition 8.1 *The traditional profit-shifting motive for introducing an export subsidy is somewhat reduced in the presence of managers, as delegation is a profit-shifting device itself.*

An analogous conclusion is obtained if firms compete in prices. In this case, the relevant benchmark model is in Eaton and Grossman (1986), where it is shown that the optimal policy takes the form of an export tax, which is partially substituted by a restrictive delegation contract.

8.1.2 Intraindustry trade: import-competing industry

This setting is an extension of Brander (1981) and Brander and Krugman (1983). Here, the driving force is the endogenous behaviour of the terms-of-trade gains generated by the difference between market price and the tariff.

The problem, being symmetric across countries, can be treated by looking at country i, in which the government has to set an import tariff t_i to maximize the domestic welfare function

$$SW_i = \pi_i + CS_i + t_i q_j \tag{8.4}$$

where $CS_i = (q_i + q_j)^2/2$ is consumer surplus. The stage sequence remains the same as above. In this case, the manager of firm j (the foreign one) behaves as if her/his firm where endowed with a less efficient technology than the rival, for all positive levels of t_i.

Leaving aside most of the details of the second and third stage, what matters is that

$$\frac{\partial SW_i}{\partial t_i} = 0 \Leftrightarrow t^N(D, D) = \frac{a - c}{4} \tag{8.5}$$

which is lower than the optimal tariff emerging in the fully entrepreneurial scenario, $t^N(ND, ND) = (a - c)/3$. To interpret this result, we can take a look at the effects of an import tariff on the delegation contracts designed by the owners of the two firms at the second stage:

$$\begin{aligned} \theta_i^N &= \frac{6c - a - 2t_i}{5c} \\ \theta_j^N &= \frac{6c - a + 8t_i}{5(c + t_i)} \end{aligned} \tag{8.6}$$

whereby

$$\begin{aligned} \frac{\partial \theta_i^N}{\partial t_i} &= -\frac{2}{5c} < 0 \\ \frac{\partial \theta_j^N}{\partial t_i} &= \frac{a + 2c}{5(c + t_i)^2} > 0 \end{aligned} \tag{8.7}$$

The partial derivatives in (8.7) imply the following.

Proposition 8.2 *Any import tax adopted by the government of country i reduces (respectively, increases) the profit weight in the managerial objective function as compared to what happens in the presence of pure Cournot profit seekers. As a result, both the optimal tariff and the terms-of-trade gains, measured by $p^N - t^N$, are lower in presence of managerialization.*

It is worth noting that these effects operate *for any θ_i and θ_j different from one*, not only at their equilibrium values: any departure from strict profit maximization suffices to induce a tariff decrease. Quite obviously, the conclusion is reversed under Bertrand competition, which generates a higher import tariff than under pure profit-seeking behaviour (see Eaton and Grossman, 1986).

8.1.3   On the equivalence of tariffs and quotas

The related issue of a restraint on imports is considered by Das (1997). As is well known from trade models based on Cournot behaviour (since Harris, 1985, and Krishna, 1989), it is possible to establish an equivalence theorem between the outcome induced by the introduction of an import quota or a specific tariff on imports, and also to ascertain the *voluntary nature of export restraints* on the part of foreign firms, as a quasi-collusive tool, at least if firms use prices as strategic variables.

As soon as strategic delegation enters the picture, this becomes true under quantity-setting behaviour as well, because the adoption of restrictions imposed on imports (or spontaneously adopted by the foreign firm as an export restraint) at least partially offset the pro-competitive managerial incentives. In particular, identifying again as i the home firm and j the foreign one, if j adopts an export restraint then $\theta_i^N = 1$ and $\theta_j^N < 1$. The presence of a quota *de facto* eliminates quantity competition, thereby inducing the home firm to behave as a pure profit-seeking agent. Equivalently, one could say that the home firm has no incentive whatsoever to hire a manager because the rival's output is, indeed, an exogenous magnitude. To sum up, we have the following.

Proposition 8.3 *Strategic delegation strengthens the pro-collusive nature of voluntary restraints.*

This causes, overall, a decrease in the aggregate output available on the home market and a consequent increase in the equilibrium price, which in turn induces a profit increase for both firms, revealing that quantity restrictions of this kind must be expected to act as collusive devices whenever separation between ownership and control is observed.

The landscape painted by Das (1997), although differing from that delivered by the early literature on oligopoly and trade, leaves us with a general impression of the sensibility of optimal trade policy to the firms' structure and the relevant type of competition, at least as long as delegation is based on output or revenue-based incentives. This impression is bound to fade away as soon as one admits the possibility for owners to rely on managerial incentives based on comparative profits, as in Miller and Pazgal (2001).

8.1.4 Comparative profit performance: ex pluribus unum

This is the topic investigated in Miller and Pazgal (2005), revising the same material as in Das (1997), with delegation contracts defining managerial incentives as $M_i = \pi_i + \theta_i \pi_j$. From the original model (Miller and Pazgal, 2001) encountered in Chapter 2, we are aware that this type of managerial remuneration generates the same outcome irrespective of the nature of market competition (based on prices, outputs or a combination thereof across firms).

Hence, if indeed prices, outputs and profits are the same for any type of competition, this simplifies the task of the policy makers, as the optimal policy becomes insensitive to any switch between price and quantity. In fact, Miller and Pazgal (2005) showed that the only important piece of information is whether goods are demand complements or substitutes. Once this is known, the policy design is immediate, entailing the following (Miller and Pazgal, 2001, p. 221).

Proposition 8.4 *If managers are rewarded on the basis of their comparative profit performance, then the optimal trade policy requires the introduction of a subsidy (respectively, a tariff) if goods are substitutes (respectively, complements). If goods are unrelated, free trade is optimal.*

By 'unrelated', it is meant that there exists no strategic interplay between the goods (as is the case, for instance, of motorbikes and toothbrushes).

To be more precise, the above result is demonstrated looking at the export rivalry case only, but the equivalence between price and quantity competition – as far as the optimal direction trade policy should take – intuitively holds for the scenario involving import competition as well, in view of a crucial condition singled out by Miller and Pazgal (2001, p. 224) and labelled as *output set equivalence*. This concept requires that the set of market outcomes that can be induced by the owners through comparative performance evaluation incentives must be the same irrespective of the market variable set by each manager. Provided this condition is satisfied, then the optimal trade policy is univocally defined by the nature of the goods being traded (as well as the demand and cost conditions) but not by the specific nature of competition, and the policy maker must not even interrogate herself/himself as to which strategic variable is being chosen by firms, as all the resulting outcomes are observationally (and substantively) equivalent.

Das (1997, p. 187) noted that other forms of managerial incentives will exert some influence on trade and trade policy. This is true, as we have just seen, of comparative profit performance, and therefore, intuitively, it must also hold for incentives using market shares, as in Jansen *et al.* (2007, 2009) and Ritz (2008). This is the subject matter considered in the model concluding this section.

8.1.5 The market share case

Wang *et al.* (2009) revisited the two perspectives on export rivalry and an import-competing industry under the assumption that managerial contracts assign a weight to market share, so that the manager of firm i chooses output q_i to maximize $M_i = \pi_i + \theta_i q_i/(q_i + q_j)$. The firms are both managerial. They are identical and sell a homogeneous good, as above, using a technology characterized by constant returns to scale.[2]

Consider first the export rivalry game, where each government strategically tunes export subsidy s_i to maximize welfare $SW_i = \pi_i - s_i q_i$ by enhancing its own firm's ability to extract surplus from the pockets of consumers located in the third country's market.

Given that this is qualitatively equivalent to reducing a firm's marginal cost, the solution of the Cournot–Nash equilibrium in the market case is equivalent to the solution of the baseline market share delegation model in Chapter 2 and can be bypassed. The optimal subsidy turns out to be the following:

$$s^N (D, D) = \frac{\left(12 - 7\sqrt{2}\right)(a - c)}{23} \tag{8.8}$$

which is higher than that derived by Das (1997), cf. expression (8.2) above. So, using market shares instead of output or revenues calls for a more aggressive policy on the part of governments.

In treating the import-competing model, Wang *et al.* (2009) referred to the classical debate about what exactly a government intends to maximize when setting a tariff (cf. Johnson, 1951–1952): the maximand should be the welfare function, but a rent-seeking policy maker would in fact set the tariff to maximize the revenue it generates. Solving both cases, one obtains

$$t_R^N (D, D) = \frac{\left(4 - \sqrt{2}\right)(a - c)}{14} \tag{8.9}$$

if t_i maximizes government i's revenue (thence subscript i), and

$$t_{SW}^N (D, D) = \frac{\left(6 - \sqrt{2}\right)(a - c)}{17} \tag{8.10}$$

when it is chosen to maximize social welfare (the meaning of the subscript being intuitive). While $t_R^N(D, D) < t_{SW}^N(D, D)$, both rank intermediately between those arising when delegation relies on sales incentives and the pure profit-seeking industry. The inequality $t_R^N(D, D) < t_{SW}^N(D, D)$ says that welfare maximization is more demanding than (and therefore not aligned with) tariff revenue maximization, i.e. the import tariff cannot simultaneously strike both targets, the intuitive reason being that in order to expand the revenues one should allow for a higher penetration into the home market by the foreign firm, which has the undesirable effect of draining too much consumer surplus abroad and shrinking the domestic firm's profits at the same time. Or, conversely, one may say that when it comes to maximizing domestic welfare, the balance speaks in favour of the surplus pertaining to domestic agents other than the government itself.

8.2 Polluting emissions and resource exploitation

The role of managers has not been exhaustively treated, at least not explicitly, in oligopoly models where the environmental effects of either production or consumption matters. However, a quick glance at the objectives usually attributed to firms with some environmental concerns reveal that there exists a well defined role for managers, although their presence remains, in some sense, behind the curtains.

An obvious but relevant observation helps to open up this part of the chapter: clearly, any managerial incentive based on magnitudes which make a firm more aggressive than under pure-profit-seeking behaviour is bound to harm the environment, all else equal. Therefore, one has to envisage the possibility for green firms to delegate part of their activities to managers instructed either to explicitly mitigate external effects – so, no output or sales expansion-based contracts should be adopted – or to accompany potentially harmful incentives with countervailing ones, pointing at the attainment of, for example, cleaner technologies.

8.2.1 CSR in mixed oligopolies

The concept of corporate social responsibility (CSR henceforth) holds that firms adopting a CSR stance in their statutes integrate social and environmental matters in their business strategies (see, e.g., the *European Union Paper on Corporate Social Responsibility*).[3] The spectrum of CSR issues is quite wide, ranging from investments in human capital to the social and environmental impact of firms' traditional concerns, such as investments in capacity and R&D, product design, prices and/or quantities and the expansion of market shares. The extant debate on CSR and its consequences on the financial performance of firms is lively and still far from converging to a unanimous view, from both a theoretical and an empirical standpoint (see Baron, 2001, 2008; Benabou and Tirole, 2006, 2010; Cespa and Cestone, 2007; Becchetti and Ciciretti, 2009; Kitzmueller and Shimshack, 2012, *inter alia*).

It can be easily shown that the adoption of CSR, in terms of the focus of the present volume, is formally equivalent to assuming that a firm's owner delegates control to a manager whose objective function is shaped so as to account for CSR objectives, in combination with profits. The material contained in this subsection illustrates this point, broadly following the more detailed analysis appearing in Goering (2007), Kopel and Brand (2012) and Lambertini and Tampieri (2015).

To see this, we may consider a homogeneous-good Cournot duopoly in which firms face a market demand function $p = a - Q$, $Q = q_1 + q_2$ being the sum of firms' individual output levels. Production takes place at constant returns to scale with a marginal cost $c \in (0, a)$, common to both firms, so that firm i's profit function is $\pi_i = (p - c)q_i$.

The production (and/or consumption) of the good implies a negative environmental externality $S = vQ$, with $v > 0$. The consumer surplus is $CS = Q^2/2$ and social welfare is defined as the sum of industry profits and consumer surplus, minus pollution:

$$SW = \pi_1 + \pi_2 + \frac{Q^2}{2} - vQ \qquad (8.11)$$

Here, we may simply consider the volume of CO_2-equivalent emissions instead of the convex environmental damage caused by them, as this simplification does not compromise the qualitative conclusions about the impact of managerialization on the environmental performance of firms.

Consider briefly the reference case where both firms are pure profit seekers. At the Cournot–Nash equilibrium, each of them sells $q^{CN} = t(a-c)/3$, achieving symmetric profits $\pi^{CN} = (a-c)^2/9$. The resulting volume of emissions is $S^{CN} = 2v(a-c)/3$, so that social welfare amounts to

$$SW^{CN} = \frac{2(a-c)[2(a-c)-3v]}{9} \qquad (8.12)$$

Turn now to the scenario in which one of the firms – say, firm 1 – adopts a CSR statute and competes, again simultaneously, with the rival, which has kept its profit-seeking nature unaltered. In order to formalize the social and environmental stance, let's assume the owner of the CSR firm hires a manager whose contract is based upon a combination of profits, the firm's share of polluting emissions and a portion of consumer surplus. In this regard, note that the present setting relies on the notion of the representative consumer, who is supposed to buy the homogeneous good from both firms. Accordingly, it makes sense to think of the CSR firm incorporating in its manager's objective function only a portion of total consumer surplus, but not necessarily in proportion with its market share; the reason will become evident below. As a result, if the manager of firm 1 accepts the contract, she/he has to choose q_1 to maximize

$$M_1 = \pi_1 - vq_1 + \frac{z(q_1+q_2)^2}{2} \qquad (8.13)$$

where parameter $z \in [0,1]$ measures the weight attached to consumer surplus. The inclusion of emissions $s_1 = vq_1$ is observationally equivalent to a situation in which the CSR firm is subject to a tax rate on emissions exactly equal to one. Accordingly, this points to an output restriction as this firm is internalizing an external cost. In turn, assigning a value to consumer surplus (or satisfaction) points in the opposite direction. This dual nature of the CSR stance creates a tradeoff in the manager's mind while thinking about the optimal production decision.

We are now in a position to characterize Cournot competition in this mixed market, and this amounts in fact to investigating the bearings of the CSR components on the two firms' best reply functions in the output space. As far as the profit-seeking firm is concerned, its best reply takes the traditional form:

$$q_2^*(q_1) = \frac{a-c-q_1}{2} \qquad (8.14)$$

while the CSR firm's reaction function is clearly affected by the functional specification of the managerial incentive:

$$q_1^*(q_2) = \frac{a - c - v - (1 - z) q_2}{2 - z} \tag{8.15}$$

In view of the range of parameter z, the above function is flatter than a standard Cournot one, as can be easily ascertained by observing that

$$\left| \frac{\partial q_1^*(q_2)}{\partial q_2} \right| = \frac{1 - z}{2 - z} < \frac{1}{2} \text{ for all } z \in [0, 1) \tag{8.16}$$

and

$$\left| \frac{\partial^2 q_1^*(q_2)}{\partial q_2 \partial z} \right| = -\frac{1}{(2 - z)^2} < 0 \tag{8.17}$$

for all $z \in [0, 1]$. Moreover, the horizontal intercept of $q_1^*(q_2)$ is also affected by the CSR components, since

$$q_1^*(q_2)\big|_{q_2 = 0} = \frac{a - c - v}{2 - z} \gtrless \frac{a - c}{2}, \quad \text{for all} \quad a \gtrless \frac{2v}{z} + c \tag{8.18}$$

These properties can be summarized as follows.

Lemma 8.1 *The CSR firm's output decision becomes less sensitive to the rivals' output choice as z increases.*

That is, the effect of including consumer surplus in the managerial objective is very much like that usually associated with some degree of product differentiation. Moreover, we have the following.

Lemma 8.2 *The reaction function of the CSR firm shifts outward (respectively, inward) because of the inclusion of consumer surplus (respectively, polluting emissions) in the managerial objective function.*

It is now possible to see that, on balance, the implications of adopting a CSR stance are largely analogous to those of a standard unilateral delegation based on output, sales or comparative performance as in Vickers (1985), Fershtman and Judd (1987), Sklivas (1987) and Miller and Pazgal (2001), as long as the other firms remain strictly entrepreneurial.

To his aim, it suffices to take a specific level of z, namely,

$$z = \frac{a - c + 4v}{3 (a - c)} \tag{8.19}$$

which indeed belongs to the unit interval for all $v \in (0, (a - c)/2)$. If the managerial contract specifies z as in (8.19), then the market game between asymmetric firms reproduces the Cournot–Stackelberg equilibrium with the CSR taking the leader's role, which is completely equivalent to the equilibrium of any Cournot–Nash game between a managerial firm and a profit-seeking one, irrespective of the specific shape given to the managerial contract (as we know from chapter 2). That is, as follows.

Proposition 8.5 *The optimal contract offered to a CSR manager is analogous to any optimal delegation contract based on output/revenue expansion or comparative performance.*

In this particular case, the mechanics of the model closely replicate those of the asymmetric delegation game where a delegation contract relies on comparative performance. As in Miller and Pazgal (2001), the Stackelberg outcome is engendered via an outward rotation of the CSR firm's reaction function, which becomes vertical in correspondence with the pure monopoly outcome (or the Stackelberg leader's), as represented in Figure 8.1.

Note that, condition (8.19) being satisfied, the firms' best replies indeed intersect in the same point at which the tangency condition between the CSR firm's highest isoprofit curve and its rival's best reply would occur in the leader–follower game between pure profit seekers.

Hence, the unilateral adoption of a CSR stance (through delegation) ends up implying a higher industry output and therefore also a higher volume of polluting

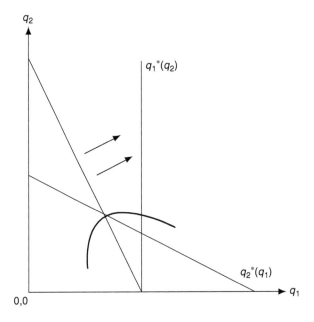

Figure 8.1 Unilateral CSR stance yields Stackelberg leadership.

emissions, with the CSR firm gaining a larger market share and higher profits. All of this, at first sight, suggests that CSR is advantageous for those who adopt it but not socially. Yet, one has to keep in mind that in this simplistic modelization of CSR any environmental policy as well as any green R&D are intentionally left out of the picture in order to convey an intuitive illustration of the fact that the traditional approach to strategic delegation can be easily tailored anew to fit the terms of the debate about the environmental implications of production.

Of course, as is the case in the baseline delegation games reviewed in Chapter 2, also here it is easily shown that the unilateral adoption of a CSR stance is not part of the subgame perfect equilibrium, unless one admits the possible presence of additional costs entailed by delegation, as in Basu (1995). Accordingly, under full symmetry the entire industry must be expected 'to go CSR' as a result of an underlying prisoners' dilemma, with unpleasant consequences for firms' profits.

This theoretical proviso notwithstanding, the most relevant aspect of the analogy between CSR behaviour and strategic delegation is indeed to be found in the fact that CSR firms have a strong incentive to be as transparent as possible concerning their social and environmental performance, being well aware of its positive impact on market shares, revenues and profits thanks to consumers' increasing environmental awareness on the demand side (see, e.g., Mohr *et al.*, 2001).

The related anecdotal evidence is quite large and steadily increasing, with the systematic publication of CSR balance sheets by companies operating in completely different sectors. An evident example is provided by multiutility firms dealing with energy and water supply, and/or waste removal,[4] i.e. utilities with an environmental impact, but casual observation reveals that the same habit is being adopted in other industries where the link between the nature of consumption goods and the environment is less evident (e.g. fashion and consumer electronics).[5]

The toy model illustrated above leaves green R&D out of the picture. Needless to say, this is probably the most relevant component in the *panoplia* of environmentally concerned firms' strategies, as the so-called *dieselgate* – which recently smashed VW-Audi as well as a large part of the German car industry – proves. This is the core topic of the last paper I am going to review in this chapter.

8.2.2 *Managerial incentives and green innovation*

The interplay between managerialization and R&D efforts for cleaner technologies has been investigated by Bárcena-Ruiz and Begoña Garzón (2002),[6] relying on well established Cournot oligopoly models with emission taxation triggering investments in emission abatement (Ulph, 1996; Montero, 2002a,b).

The building blocks are the usual ones. Two Cournot firms supply a homogeneous good with demand function $p = a - Q$, $Q = q_1 + q_2$, produced at a constant marginal cost $c \in (0, a)$. Production pollutes the environment, and the government introduces a tax τ on emissions, the per-firm burden being linear in individual emissions. Hence, to soften the pressure exerted by taxation, each firm may invest in abatement technologies via an R&D effort $k_i > 0$, the cost of the project being $\Gamma_i = bk_i^2/2$. Firm i's profit function writes

$$\pi_i = (p - c) q_i - \tau e_i - \Gamma_i \qquad (8.20)$$

where $e_i = q_i - k_i$ is the level of emissions, net of the abatement effort.

If firm i delegates control over output and green R&D to a manager, her/his objective function is

$$M_i = \theta_i \pi_i + (1 - \theta_i) pq_i \qquad (8.21)$$

as in Fershtman and Judd (1987) and Sklivas (1987).

The welfare function adopted by the policy maker is

$$SW = \sum_{i=1}^{2} \pi_i + CS + T - D \qquad (8.22)$$

where $CS = (q_1 + q_2)^2/2$ is consumer surplus, $T = \sum_{i=1}^{2} \tau e_i$ is the tax revenue and

$$D = \frac{d (e_1 + e_2)^2}{2} \qquad (8.23)$$

is the environmental damage due to unabated emissions.

The game has a three-stage structure. In the first stage, the government sets the tax rate on polluting emissions to maximize social welfare (8.22); in the second, owners decide whether to hire managers or not (and, if they do so, they also choose the optimal value of θ_i); in the third and last stage, owners or managers simultaneously choose both the R&D effort and the output level, using the relevant objective function. As usual, each stage takes place under complete, symmetric and imperfect information, and variables chosen at the first two stages become immediately common knowledge.

Assume for the moment that both firms are managerial. Observing the FOCs at the third stage,

$$\frac{\partial M_i}{\partial q_i} = a - 2q_i - q_j - \theta_i (c + \tau) = 0 \qquad (8.24)$$

$$\frac{\partial M_i}{\partial k_i} = \theta_i (\tau - bk_i) = 0 \qquad (8.25)$$

one sees that (i) taxation enhances the well known shift in the best reply in the output space for any $\tau > 0$, as the tax rate (as long as it is indeed a tax and not a subsidy) has the obvious effect of increasing the marginal production cost and (ii) for any given τ, delegation has no effect on the optimal R&D effort, which is $k^N = \tau/b$. This poses a lower bound to τ, which must be strictly positive to stimulate investments in abatement technologies.[7]

Confining their attention to the two symmetric settings where both firms share the same organizational structure (an assumption entailing that it suffices to set both θ_i to zero in order to switch to the fully entrepreneurial game), Bárcena-Ruiz and Begoña Garzón (2002, p. 308) proved the following.

Proposition 8.6 *When both firms are managerial entities, the equilibrium levels of social welfare, environmental damage, emission taxation and consumer surplus are higher than under pure profit-seeking behaviour. The opposite holds for firms' profits.*

The second part of the proposition is obvious. The first part, instead, deserves a few comments, as it results from the tradeoff between the standard output expansion associated with the managerial contract based on output or sales and the opposite push generated by taxation (or a marginal cost increase). Also note that being subject to a higher tax rate means that managerial firms invest more than profit-seeking ones in abatement technologies, since $k^N = \tau/b$. Overall, the outcome described in the proposition tells that the balance between the managerial preference for output expansion and a higher R&D effort driven by a higher tax pressure on emissions speaks in favour (if one may say so) of the former, with the somewhat undesirable consequence of increasing welfare as compared to the fully entrepreneurial industry performance through an increase in consumer surplus, the presence of a greener R&D notwithstanding. By the way, the latter aspect also contributes to curtailing managerial firms' profits by increasing the R&D costs, adding up to the output expansion effect.

In view of the foregoing illustration of CSR incentives, the impact of strategic delegation based on any of the standard contracts based upon output, sales or comparative profits, as well as CSR delegation aiming at resource preservation, can be intuitively and quickly appreciated – for opposite reasons, of course. Keep considering output competition: a delegation contract *à la* Vickers (1985) generates an output expansion and therefore implies a higher pressure on resources, with undesirable consequences; if instead a CSR stance is adopted, then the firm, say, firm i, instructs its manager to maximize a modified version of (8.13), which may look as follows:

$$M_i = \pi_i + \theta_i X \tag{8.26}$$

where X is the size of the existing resource pool. A straightforward implication of (8.26) is that when CSR takes this form then the impact of a managerial firm on natural resources is milder than that of pure profit-seeking entities. In a way, this seems too trivial to deserve more than a quick glance.

However, the issue of natural resource exploitation does not lend itself to be modelled as a static game so easily, for two orders of reasons. The first is that the activity of resource extraction is intrinsically dynamic, and the time dimension not only matters but plays a crucial role in shaping firms' behaviour and ultimately also the fate of the resource itself. This of course is true for environmental damages as well, but natural resources have also a second feature, that of being sometimes renewable and sometimes not. This dichotomy draws a line which a static game does not allow us to identify. Hence, an alternative approach based on dynamic games becomes necessary, about which I will tell you more in the next chapter.

For the moment, however, we can dwell upon a model relying on Bonanno and Vickers (1988) to investigate the impact of vertical relations on trade in a model where the environmental damage generated by production is also accounted for.

8.3   Supply chains, trade, and pollution

The joint analysis of trade flows and environmental policy is motivated by the possibility for governments to distort environmental regulation, using it as a subsidiary trade policy to obtain some strategic advantage. This is the topic taken up by Hamilton and Requate (2004), who formalized this problem as an extension of the vertical relations setup introduced by Bonanno and Vickers (1988), and treated in Chapter 5.[8] There, we have seen that the vertical contract governing the behaviour of a supply chain operates as a credible commitment device, as much as any observable managerial contract in this book. In particular, an optimal two-part tariff must induce the downstream firm to act more (respectively, less) aggressively if market variables are strategic substitutes (respectively, complements). Hence, this intuitively implies that it must produce the same effects of a subsidy (respectively, tax) *all else equal.*

The scenario is as follows. There are two firms, one upstream and one downstream, in each of two countries. Exclusive contracts are assumed, with each downstream firm buying from the upstream firm based in the same country an essential input to produce the final good, which is homogeneous and traded in the international market made up by those of both countries. So, here the relevant case is that of import competition, with simultaneous play, either in quantities or in prices. For the sake of simplicity, we may assume any production costs away for all the firms involved.

Polluting emissions enter the picture via the technology used by both upstream firms to supply the input, for instance, because such a technology relies on fossil fuels. This involves an amount of emissions which is linear in the final output level, say, $e_i = q_i$. Pollution is not transboundary, with the environmental damage $D_i(e_i)$ being increasing and convex in the emissions caused by the activity of the domestic upstream firm. Hence, both governments adopt an emission tax τ_i per unit of emissions, to be paid by the domestic input supplier.

The timing is structured as follows. At the first stage, governments simultaneously set their respective emission taxes on the polluting input. At the second stage, the optimal contract along each vertical channel is designed, on the basis of a wholesale price w_i and a fixed fee F_i. If it is signed, then at the third stage downstream firms engage in market competition. Otherwise, if input suppliers have rejected the contract at the second stage, the downstream firms proceed towards market competition after having acquired the input on the spot market at a price $w_i(t_i)$ incorporating the the full burden of the emission tax, which is then transferred upon consumers via the resulting market price.

The essential results of the analysis carried out by Hamilton and Requate (2004) are the following. First of all, under Cournot competition the equilibrium vertical contract is structured as follows.

Proposition 8.7 *If downstream firms are quantity-setters, the optimal wholesale price and fixed fee are $w_i^* \in (0, w_i(t_i))$ and $F_i^* \in (0, \pi_{id}^N(w_i(t_i)))$, respectively.*

In the above proposition, $\pi_{id}^N(w_i(t_i))$ is the Nash equilibrium profit of the downstream firm based in country i. The proposition says that in order for the contract to be signed, it has to ensure positive profits to both partners along the vertical channel.[9]

What matters here is that w_i^* is lower than $w_i(t_i)$. This makes the downstream firm more aggressive on the international market than it would be if resorting to the spot market. Of course, the opposite applies under Bertrand competition.

Proposition 8.8 *If downstream firms are price setters, the optimal wholesale price and fixed fee are $w_i^* > w_i(t_i)$ and $F_i^* < 0$, respectively.*

Again fully in line with the original results found by Bonanno and Vickers (1988), under strategic complementarity between market variables the contract must mimic a marginal cost increase, and indeed goes above the spot market price, inducing downstream firms to increase prices, which take a quasi-collusive flavour.

As far as environmental policy is concerned, the equilibrium between governments at the first stage is portrayed in the following.

Proposition 8.9 *Under both Cournot and Bertrand competition preceded by the respective optimal two-part tariffs, the optimal strategy of governments consists of adopting the Pigouvian tax rate $\tau_i^N = \partial D_i / \partial q_i$.*

That is, efficient vertical relations governed by optimal contracts cancel any risk of (or opportunity for) the adoption of an inefficient emission policy motivated by a form of rent-seeking behaviour on the part of governments, as instead there emerges in setups in which, optimal contracts being absent and firms being forced to buy on the input market at a price incorporating the emission tax, environmental regulation falls short of its proper target. Indeed, strategic trade reasons cause the emission tax to be too low (with a consequent underinternalization of the externality by firms) in Conrad (1993), Barrett (1994), Simpson and Bradford (1996) and Ulph (1996), *inter alia*.

Further reading

For more on voluntary export restraints, see Pomfret (1989), Berry *et al.* (1999) and Mai and Hwang (1988). The interplay between trade, industrial policy and delegation is illustrated in Chang (2007), while Wang and Wang (2011) focused on trade, delegation and vertical differentiation. For cross-border mergers with managerial firms, see Dragone (2007) and Heywood and McGinty (2011). The impact of delegation with observable contracts on foreign direct investments (FDIs) is considered in Mukherjee and Suetrong (2013). A benchmark on delegation in environmental policy making (where, however, managers are being delegated this role by public authorities) is Roelfsema (2007). On the asymmetric treatment of symmetric polluting firms, see Anderson and Jensen (2005) and Long and Soubeyran (2005). The baseline model of green R&D in Cournot industries can be found in Chiou and Hu (2001), Requate and Unold (2003) and Poyago-Theotoky (2007). Concerning the growing discussion on CSR, see Hillman and Keim (2001), Hay *et al.* (2005), Baron (2007, 2009) and Bian *et al.* (2016). On the empirical evidence of the impact of CSR on firms' performance, see McWilliams and Siegel (2000), Mahoney and Thorne (2006), Paul and Siegel (2006), Siegel and Vitaliano (2007) and Becchetti *et al.* (2008), *inter alia.* For other extensions about managerial incentives, CSR and the environment, see Van Witteloostuijn *et al.* (2003) and Goering (2010, 2014).

Notes

1 While of course there exists a number of contributions at the intersection between environmental economics and trade theory. See Copeland and Taylor (1994, 1995a,b, 2003, 2004).
2 Wang *et al.* (2009) derive all of their results under constant but asymmetric marginal production costs.
3 One may visit the web page https://protect-us.mimecast.com/s/1drmB5u2DNnJhZ? domain=ec.europa.eu to fully appreciate the EU view of CSR.
4 This is the case, in Italy, of Gruppo Hera, who have a specific CSR management and whose CSR balance sheet is publicly accessible on line (https://protect-us.mimecast.com/s/VAz4BRU5DodNTe?domain=gruppohera.it_sostenibilita/).
5 The firms' widespread interest towards the CSR phenomenon is also triggering the creation of intersectoral networks of companies operating in different industries, in order to create a shared view of CSR and common guidelines to implement it. Again in Italy, this is the case of Impronta Etica, a voluntary association of firms based in Emilia Romagna (https://protect-us.mimecast.com/s/5JZeB3fXDRW1um).
6 On the same topic, see also Pal (2012).
7 More explicitly, if $\tau < 0$ we find ourselves in the unrealistic situation in which production and pollution are being subsidized. In addition to being hardly acceptable in line of principle, the adoption of a pollution subsid entails that $k^N < 0$, which is economically nonsensical. Hence, if indeed $\tau < 0$, then necessarily $k = 0$.
8 As usual throughout the volume, I focus on partial equilibrium models of managerial firms belonging to the mainstream of the IO literature. However, this is admittedly not the only possible approach to the modelization of managerial behaviour and its impact on firms and markets. Indeed, a joint modelization of firms' internal structures, outsourcing and foreign direct investments (FDIs) in the presence of agency problems connected with principals' limited ability of monitoring their contractors (suppliers or subsidiaries) can be found in Grossman and Helpman (2004). As is typical of trade theory, this is done in a general equilibrium framework. Grossman and Helpman (2004) showed that cost heterogeneity causes firms to sort themselves out in terms of different organization structures, in such a way that the choice of the internal organization is non-monotone in revenues, with vertical integration emerging only in an intermediate range. Then, they

also show that (i) in the group of those choosing vertical integration, the firms bearing lower total transportation costs enjoy higher revenues than those adopting FDI strategies, and (ii) any fall in trade costs favours the adoption of FDIs and/or outsourcing.

9 A few additional words are in order here. Actually, what appears in the proposition is not the standard two-part tariff, as the tradition of vertical relations establishes that in order to reproduce the profits which would accrue to an integrated firm including both partners as internal divisions, the tariff should be composed by $w_i^* = 0$ (wholesale pricing at marginal cost) and $F_i^* = \pi_{id}^N(w_i(t_i))$. This is known as the fully extracting two-part tariff. See, for instance, Tirole (1988, chapter 3).

References

Andersen, P. and F. Jensen (2005), 'Unequal Treatment of Identical Polluters in Cournot Equilibrium', *Journal of Institutional and Theoretical Economics*, **161**, 729–34.

Bárcena-Ruiz, J.C. and M. Begoña Garzón (2002), 'Environmental Taxes and Strategic Delegation', *Spanish Economic Review*, **4**, 301–10.

Baron, D.P. (2001), 'Private Politics, Corporate Social Responsibility, and Integrated Strategy', *Journal of Economics and Management Strategy*, **10**, 7–45.

Baron, D.P. (2007), 'Corporate Social Responsibility and Social Entrepreneurship', *Journal of Economics and Management Strategy*, **16**, 683–717.

Baron, D.P. (2008), 'Managerial Contracting and Corporate Social Responsibility', *Journal of Public Economics*, **92**, 268–88.

Baron, D.P. (2009), 'A Positive Theory of Moral Management, Social Pressure, and Corporate Social Performance', *Journal of Economics and Management Strategy*, **18**, 7–43.

Barrett, S. (1994), 'Strategic Environmental Policy and International Trade', *Journal of Public Economics*, **54**, 325–38.

Basu, K. (1995), 'Stackelberg Equilibrium in Oligopoly: An Explanation Based on Managerial Incentives', *Economics Letters*, **49**, 459–64.

Becchetti, L. and R. Ciciretti (2009), 'Corporate Social Responsibility and Stock Market Performance', *Applied Financial Economics*, **19**, 1283–93.

Becchetti, L., S. Di Giacomo and D. Pinnacchio (2008), 'The Impact of Social Responsibility on Productivity and Efficiency of US Listed Companies', *Applied Economics*, **40**, 1–27.

Benabou, R. and J. Tirole (2006), 'Incentives and Prosocial Behavior', *American Economic Review*, **96**, 1652–78.

Benabou, R. and J. Tirole (2010), 'Individual and Corporate Social Responsibility', *Economica*, **77**, 1–19.

Berry, S., J. Levinsohn and A. Pakes (1999), 'Voluntary Export Restraints on Automobiles: Evaluating a Trade Policy', *American Economic Review*, **89**, 400–30.

Bian, J., K.W. Li and X. Guo (2016), 'A Strategic Analysis of Incorporating CSR into Managerial Incentive Design', *Transportation Research Part E*, **86**, 83–93.

Bonanno, G. and J. Vickers (1988), 'Vertical Separation', *Journal of Industrial Economics*, **36**, 257–65.

Brander, J. (1981), 'Intra-Industry Trade in Identical Commodities', *Journal of International Economics*, **11**, 1–14.

Brander, J. and P. Krugman (1983), 'A 'Reciprocal Dumping' Model of International Trade', *Journal of International Economics*, **15**, 311–21.

Brander, J. and B. Spencer (1985), 'Export Subsidies and International Market Share Rivalry', *Journal of International Economics*, **18**, 83–100.

Campbell, N. and N. Vousden (1994), 'The Organizational Cost of Protection', *Journal of International Economics*, **37**, 219–38.

Cespa, G. and G. Cestone (2007), 'Corporate Social Responsibility and Managerial Entrenchment', *Journal of Economics and Management Strategy*, **16**, 741–71.

Chang, W. (2007), 'Optimal Trade, Industrial, and Privatization Policies in a Mixed Duopoly with Strategic Managerial Incentives', *Journal of International Trade and Economic Development*, **16**, 31–52.

Chiou, J.-R. and J.-L. Hu (2001), 'Environmental Research Joint Ventures under Emission Taxes', *Environmental and Resource Economics*, **20**, 129–46.

Conrad, K. (1993), 'Taxes and Subsidies for Pollution-Intensive Industries as Trade Policy', *Journal of Environmental Economics and Management*, **25**, 121–35.

Copeland, B.R. and M.S. Taylor (1994), 'North-South Trade and the Environment', *Quarterly Journal of Economics*, **109**, 755–87.

Copeland, B.R. and M.S. Taylor (1995a), 'Trade and Transboundary Pollution', *American Economic Review*, **85**, 716–37.

Copeland, B.R. and M.S. Taylor (1995b), 'Trade and the Environment: A Partial Synthesis', *American Journal of Agricultural Economics*, **77**, 765–71.

Copeland, B.R. and M.S. Taylor (2003), *Trade and the Environment: Theory and Evidence*, Princeton, NJ, Princeton University Press.

Copeland, B.R. and M.S. Taylor (2004), 'Trade, Growth, and the Environment', *Journal of Economic Literature*, **42**, 7–71.

Das, S. (1997), 'Strategic Managerial Delegation and Trade Policy', *Journal of International Economics*, **43**, 173–88.

Dragone, D. (2007), 'Should One Sell Domestic Firms to Foreign Ones? A Tale of Delegation, Acquisition and Collusion', in L. Lambertini (ed.), *Firms' Objectives and Internal Organisation in a Global Economy: Positive and Normative Analysis*, Basingstoke, Palgrave Macmillan.

Eaton, J. and G. Grossman (1986), 'Optimal Trade and Industrial Policy with Oligopoly', *Quarterly Journal of Economics*, **101**, 383–406.

Fershtman, C. and K. Judd (1987), 'Equilibrium Incentives in Oligopoly', *American Economic Review*, **77**, 927–40.

Goering, G.E. (2007), 'The Strategic Use of Managerial Incentives in a Non-Profit Firm Mixed Duopoly', *Managerial and Decision Economics*, **28**, 83–91.

Goering, G.E. (2010), 'Corporate Social Responsibility, Durable-Goods and Firm Profitability', *Managerial and Decision Economics*, **31**, 489–96.

Goering, G.E. (2014), 'The Profit-Maximizing Case for Corporate Social Responsibility in a Bilateral Monopoly', *Managerial and Decision Economics*, **35**, 493–9.

Grossman, G.M. and E. Helpman (2004), 'Managerial Incentives and the International Organization of Production', *Journal of International Economics*, **63**, 237–62.

Hamilton, S.F. and T. Requate (2004), 'Vertical Structure and Strategic Environmental Trade Policy', *Journal of Environmental Economics and Management*, **47**, 260–9.

Harris, R. (1985), 'Why Voluntary Export Restraints are 'Voluntary'', *Canadian Journal of Economics*, **63**, 799–809.

Hay, B.L., R.N. Stavins and R.H.K. Vietor (2005, eds), *Environmental Protection and the Social Responsibility of Firms*, Washington, DC, Resources for the Future.

Helpman, E. and P. Krugman (1985), *Market Structure and Foreign Trade: Increasing Returns, Imperfect Competition, and the International Economy*, Cambridge, MA, MIT Press.

Helpman, E. and P. Krugman (1989), *Trade Policy and Market Structure*, Cambridge, MA, MIT Press.

Heywood, J. and M. McGinty (2011), 'Cross-Border Mergers in a Mixed Oligopoly', *Economic Modelling*, **28**, 382–9.

Hillman, A.J. and G.D. Keim (2001), 'Shareholder Value, Stakeholder Management, and Social Issues: What's the Bottom Line?', *Strategic Management Journal*, 22, 125–39.

Horn, H., H. Lang and S. Lundgren (1995), 'Managerial Effort Incentives, X-Inefficiency and International Trade', *European Economic Review*, 39, 117–38.

Jansen, T., A. Van Lier and A. Van Witteloostuijn (2007), 'A Note on Strategic Delegation: The Market Share Case', *International Journal of Industrial Organization*, 25, 531–9.

Jansen, T., A. Van Lier and A. Van Witteloostuijn (2009), 'On the Impact of Managerial Bonus Systems on Firm Profit and Market Competition: The Cases of Pure Profit, Sales, Market Share and Relative Profits Compared', *Managerial and Decision Economics*, 30, 141–53.

Johnson, H. (1951–1952), 'Optimum Welfare and Maximum Revenue Tariff', *Review of Economic Studies*, 19, 28–35.

Kitzmueller, M. and J. Shimshack (2012), 'Economic Perspectives on Corporate Social Responsibility', *Journal of Economic Literature*, 50, 51–84.

Kopel, M. and B. Brand (2012), 'Socially Responsible Firms and Endogenous Choice of Strategic Incentives', *Economic Modelling*, 29, 982–9.

Krishna, K. (1989), 'Trade Restrictions as Facilitating Practices', *Journal of International Economics*, 26, 251–70.

Lambertini, L. (2013), *Oligopoly, the Environment and Natural Resources*, London, Routledge.

Lambertini, L. and A. Tampieri (2015), 'Incentive, Performance and Desirability of Socially Responsible Firms in a Cournot Oligopoly', *Economic Modelling*, 50, 40–8.

Long, N.V. and A. Soubeyran (2005), 'Selective Penalization of Polluters: an Inf-Convolution Approach', *Economic Theory*, 25, 421–54.

McWilliams, A. and D. Siegel (2000), 'Corporate Social Responsibility and Financial Performance: Correlation or Misspecification?', *Strategic Management Journal*, 21, 603-9.

Mahoney, L.S. and L. Thorne (2006), 'An Examination of the Structure of Executive Compensation and Corporate Social Responsibility: A Canadian Investigation', *Journal of Business Ethics*, 69, 149–62.

Mai, C. and H. Hwang (1988), 'Why Voluntary Export Restraints Are Voluntary: An Extension', *Canadian Journal of Economics*, 21, 877-82.

Miller, N. and A. Pazgal (2001), 'The Equivalence of Price and Quantity Competition with Delegation', *RAND Journal of Economics*, 32, 284–301.

Miller, N. and A. Pazgal (2005), 'Strategic Trade and Delegated Competition', *Journal of International Economics*, 66, 215–31.

Mohr, L.A., D.J. Webb and K.E. Harris (2001), 'Do Consumers Expect Companies to Be Socially Responsible? The Impact of Corporate Social Responsibility on Buying Behavior', *Journal of Consumer Affairs*, 35, 45–72.

Montero, J.-P. (2002a), 'Permits, Standards, and Technology Innovation', *Journal of Environmental Econonomics and Management*, 44, 23–44.

Montero, J.-P. (2002b), 'Market Structure and Environmental Innovation', *Journal of Applied Economics*, 5, 293–325.

Mukherjee, A. and K. Suetrong (2013), 'Privatization, Incentive Delegation and Foreign Direct Investment', *Open Economies Review*, 24, 657–76.

Pal, R. (2012), 'Delegation and Emission Tax in a Differentiated Oligopoly', *Manchester School*, 6, 650–70.

Paul, C. M. and D. Siegel (2006), 'Corporate Social Responsibility and Economic Performance', *Journal of Productivity Analysis*, 26, 207–11.

Pomfret, R. (1989), 'The Economics of Voluntary Export Restraint Agreements', *Journal of Economic Surveys*, **3**, 199–211.

Poyago-Theotoky, J. (2007), 'The Organization of R&D and Environmental Policy', *Journal of Economic Behaviour and Organization*, **62**, 63–75.

Requate, T. and W. Unold (2003), 'Environmental Policy Incentives to Adopt Advanced Abatement Technology - Will the True Ranking Please Stand up?', *European Economic Review*, **47**, 125–46.

Ritz, R.A. (2008), 'Strategic Incentives for Market Share', *International Journal of Industrial Organization*, **26**, 586–97.

Roelfsema, H. (2007), 'Strategic Delegation of Environmental Policy Making', *Journal of Environmental Economics and Management*, 53, 270–5.

Siegel, D. and D. Vitaliano (2007), 'An Empirical Analysis of the Strategic Use of Corporate Social Responsibility', *Journal of Economics and Management Strategy*, **16**, 773–92.

Simpson, R. and R. Bradford (1996), 'Taxing Variable Cost: Environmental Regulation as Industrial Policy', *Journal of Environmental Economics and Management*, 30, 282–300.

Sklivas, S.D. (1987), 'The Strategic Choice of Managerial Incentives', *RAND Journal of Economics*, **18**, 452–8.

Tirole, J. (1988), *The Theory of Industrial Organization*, Cambridge, MA, MIT Press.

Ulph, A. (1996), 'Environmental Policy and International Trade when Governments and Producers Act Strategically', *Journal of Environmental Economics and Management*, **30**, 265–81.

Van Witteloostuijn, A., C. Boone and A. Van Lier (2003), 'Toward a Game Theory of Organizational Ecology: Production Adjustment Costs and Managerial Growth Preferences', *Strategic Organization*, **1**, 259–300.

Vickers, J. (1985), 'Delegation and the Theory of the Firm', *Economic Journal*, **95** (Conference Papers), 138–47.

Wang, L.F.S., Y.-C. Wang and L. Zhao (2009), 'Market Share Delegation and Strategic Trade Policy', *Journal of International Trade and Economic Development*, **9**, 49–56.

Wang, Y.-C. and L.F.S. Wang (2011), 'Strategic Trade and Delegated Competition with Endogenous Quality Choice: Is Export Policy Needed?', *Pacific Economic Review*, **16**, 489–503.

9 Strategic delegation in differential games

While the early debate on managerial firms examined in Chapter 1 gave a considerable amount of space and attention to the dynamic aspects of a firm's life, because the focus of that discussion was on the impact of managerialization on growth – think of the Penrose (1959) model, for instance – the current literature on strategic delegation commonly adopts a static game approach and therefore the applications of dynamic games in this field are quite rare. However, the few existing ones – which are just scratching the surface of an ocean-wide volume of applications – deliver relevant hints enriching our understanding of the incentives and strategies of modern corporations, and, most probably, this strand of research is bound to be boosted in several directions in the near future.

Indeed, the material already available illustrates the dynamics of some core issues, such as: (i) the impact of managerial inputs on growth, revisiting Penrose (1959); (ii) capacity accumulation; (iii) investment in process and product innovation; (iv) the exploitation of renewable natural resources, reinterpreting the tragedy of commons (Gordon, 1954; Hardin, 1968) as a dynamic oligopoly game. The ensuing models are, in a sense, no more than an appetizer suggesting and inviting for a much wider range of potential applications of optimal control and differential game theory in this field. The survey of applications is preceded by a brief exposition of the building blocks of dynamic optimization and differential games.

9.1 Elements of differential game theory

The easiest approach to a differential game probably consists of considering it as the strategic version of an optimal control problem, with many agents (at least two) instead of a single one. Conversely, an optimal control problem with a single agent taking decisions can be viewed as the collapse of a differential game where the set of players shrinks to a singleton.

Hence, suppose n players strategically interact over continuous time $t \in [0, T]$, with the time horizon possibly extending itself to doomsday if $T \to \infty$. Each agent i has a strategy, which in dynamic games is known as a *control variable*, and identify it as $u_i(t) \in \mathcal{U}$, where $\mathcal{U} \subseteq \mathbb{R}^n$ is the control domain, which is assumed here to be common to all players, for simplicity. Define as $\mathbf{u}(t)$ the vector of controls at any time t. Then, suppose there exists a single state variable $x(t)$ common to all players, and let $\pi_i(x(t), u(t), t)$ and $\dot{x} = dx(t)/dt = f(x(t), u(t), t)$ identify the instantaneous payoff of agent i controlling $u_i(t)$ and the differential equation describing the kinematics of the state $x(t)$, respectively; the latter is known as the *state equation*.

If all players share the same intertemporal preferences, measured by the common discount rate $\rho \geq 0$, each of them has to solve the following problem:[1]

$$\max_{u_i(t)} \Pi_i = \int_0^T \pi_i(x(t), u(t), t) e^{-\rho t} \, dt \qquad (9.1)$$

subject to the dynamic constraint posed by the state equation $dx(t)/dt$, the initial condition $x_0 = x(0)$ and the appropriate set of transversality conditions. This is equivalent to saying that player i must choose $u_i(t)$ so as to maximize the following Hamiltonian function:

$$\mathcal{H}_i(x(t), u(t), \mu(t), t) = \pi_i(x(t), u(t), t) e^{-\rho t} + \mu_i(t) f(x(t), u(t), t) \qquad (9.2)$$

where $\mu_i(t)$ is the costate variable associated by player i to the state variable $x(t)$. Alternatively, the above Hamiltonian function can be rewritten in its *current value* form:

$$\mathcal{H}_i(x(t), u(t), \lambda(t), t) = e^{-\rho t} [\pi_i(x(t), u(t), t) + \lambda_i(t) f(x(t), u(t), t)] \qquad (9.3)$$

in which $\lambda_i(t) = \mu_i(t) e^{\rho t}$ is the *capitalized costate variable* of player i, $\mu_i(t)$ being the costate variable.

The solution of this problem relies on the *Maximum Principle* (Pontryagin *et al.*, 1962; Pontryagin, 1966), which can be formulated as follows.[2]

The maximum principle (finite horizon) If $(x^*(t), u^*(t))$ is an equilibrium vector, then there exists a trajectory for each $\lambda_i : [t_0, T] \to \mathbb{R}$, not identically equal to zero, such that

$$\dot{\lambda}_i = -\frac{\partial \mathcal{H}_i(\cdot)}{\partial x} + \rho \lambda_i \qquad (9.4)$$

provided the following set of transversality conditions

$$\mu_i(T) \geq 0; \ \mu_i(T) x^*(T) = 0 \qquad (9.5)$$

is satisfied, for all $i = 1, 2, 3, \ldots, n$.

Equation (9.4) is the *costate* or *adjoint equation* of player i. A cautionary note is in order concerning the costate $\lambda_i(t)$, which is commonly interpreted as a 'shadow price', in analogy with the interpretation of the Lagrange multiplier in static constrained optimization problems. This is generally not true in differential games, unless a condition I will put in evidence below is satisfied.

If the time horizon of the game is infinite, the Maximum principle must be reformulated as follows.

The maximum principle (infinite horizon) If $(x^*(t), u^*(t))$ is an equilibrium vector, then there exists a trajectory for each $\lambda_i : [t_0, T] \to \mathbb{R}$, not identically equal to zero, such that

$$\dot{\lambda}_i = -\frac{\partial \mathcal{H}_i(\cdot)}{\partial x} + \rho \lambda_i \tag{9.6}$$

provided the following set of transversality conditions

$$\lim_{t \to \infty} \mu_i(t) x^*(t) = 0 \tag{9.7}$$

is satisfied, for all $i = 1, 2, 3, \ldots, n$.

9.1.1 The state-control system and its properties

Each player i derives the following necessary conditions:

$$\frac{\partial \mathcal{H}_i(\cdot)}{\partial u_i} = 0 \tag{9.8}$$

$$\dot{\lambda}_i = -\frac{\partial \mathcal{H}_i(\cdot)}{\partial x} + \rho \lambda_i \tag{9.9}$$

which can be manipulated to yield the dynamics of each individual control,

$$\dot{u}_i = g(x(t), u(t)) \tag{9.10}$$

known as the *control equation*. The system made up by the n control equations and the state equation defines the so-called *state-control system*. If one can assume players, and therefore their controls, to be symmetric, the state control system reduces to

$$\begin{cases} \dot{x} = f(x(t), u(t)) \\ \dot{u} = g(x(t), u(t)) \end{cases} \tag{9.11}$$

The solutions of (9.11) give the trajectories of state and control variables in the phase plane, and the stability of its steady state solution(s) can be studied by linearizing the system around the steady state(s), and look at the properties of the 2×2 *Jacobian matrix*,

$$J = \begin{bmatrix} \dfrac{\partial f(\cdot)}{\partial x} & \dfrac{\partial f(\cdot)}{\partial u} \\ \dfrac{\partial g(\cdot)}{\partial x} & \dfrac{\partial g(\cdot)}{\partial u} \end{bmatrix} \tag{9.12}$$

which depend on the sign and size of the trace $\mathcal{T}(J)$ and determinant $\Delta(J)$ of the Jacobian matrix itself. In particular, if

$$\Delta(J) = \frac{\partial f(\cdot)}{\partial x} \cdot \frac{\partial g(\cdot)}{\partial u} - \frac{\partial f(\cdot)}{\partial u} \cdot \frac{\partial g(\cdot)}{\partial x} < 0 \tag{9.13}$$

then the system produces *saddle point stability* independently of the sign of the trace of the Jacobian matrix,

$$\mathcal{T}(J) = \frac{\partial f(\cdot)}{\partial x} + \frac{\partial g(\cdot)}{\partial u} \tag{9.14}$$

If instead the determinant is positive, we have four alternative cases:

- a stable node, if $\mathcal{T}(J) < 0$ and $\Delta(J) \in (0, \mathcal{T}^2(J)/4]$;
- an unstable node, if $\mathcal{T}(J) > 0$ and $\Delta(J) \in (0, \mathcal{T}^2(J)/4]$;
- a stable focus, if $\mathcal{T}(J) < 0$ and $\Delta(J) > \mathcal{T}^2(J)/4$;
- an unstable focus, if $\mathcal{T}(J) > 0$ and $\Delta(J) > \mathcal{T}^2(J)/4$.

9.1.2   The Hamilton–Jacobi–Bellman equation

The solution based upon the Hamiltonian function typically depends on initial condition(s). The main problem with it is that it relies on *open-loop information*, whereby each player chooses a plan at the initial time, once and for all, determining the trajectory of her/his control variable over the entire time horizon of the game. Note that the instantaneous strategy may well be a function of the state(s), but this does not imply that the player is properly accounting for the effects (called loop or, more properly, feedback effects) of the state(s) on the controls of all players alike. This entails that the open-loop equilibrium is not subgame perfect or, equivalently, strongly time consistent (in the technical jargon of differential game theory), but only weakly so.

An alternative approach is based on *dynamic programming* and the *optimality principle* (Bellman, 1957), which establishes that if a dynamic problem is originally defined for all $t \in [0, T]$, and one drops off a portion $[0, \bar{t}]$, with $\bar{t} < T$, what remains of the solution identified on the original time horizon $[0, T]$, when reconsidered for $t \in [\bar{t}, T]$ must remain optimal from $\bar{t}$ to the terminal time. This means that the control path selected by the optimality principle must be optimal independently of specific initial conditions and be robust to changes in the latter. Intuitively, this is an obvious candidate as a solution method for differential games.

The building blocks (players, state and control variables, state dynamics and payoffs) are the same as above, plus the value function $V_i(x)$ of player i, which, in maximum problems, must be concave with respect to x. The optimal value function $V^*(x)$ must solve the HJB (Hamilton–Jacobi–Bellman) – or, simply, Bellman – equation

$$\rho V_i(\cdot) = \max_{u_i \in \mathcal{U}} \left\{ \pi_i(\cdot) + \frac{\partial V_i(\cdot)}{\partial x} \cdot f(\cdot) \right\} \tag{9.15}$$

The analytic solution of the problem defined in (9.15) can be attained in those cases (indeed, very few) where one can guess a form for the value function and then verify that it is indeed a correct guess by using it to solve (9.15) explicitly. A well known case in which this is possible is that of linear-quadratic games, defined in this way in view of the fact that the payoffs are quadratic in state(s) and controls and the state equation is linear in the same variables. Accordingly, in linear-quadratic games the value function can be specified in a linear-quadratic form as well, as $V_i(x) = \epsilon_{i1} x^2 + \epsilon_{i2} x + \epsilon_{i3}$ (in this section I am assuming the problem to be autonomous and therefore omit the time argument). The solution of the Bellman equation (9.15) yields a *feedback Nash equilibrium* which is strongly time consistent and therefore can be labelled as subgame (or Markov) perfect.

Some classes of differential games have been identified as producing strongly time consistent equilibria under open-loop information.[3] Indeed, in the remainder of this chapter we will see one game structure endowed with this property.

An additional remark is in order. As to the desirability or necessity of using feedback information to produce strongly time consistent equilibria, one should take into account that assuming that firms use feedback rules amounts to imposing upon them a very strong requirement, since they must shape their plans so as to incorporate the loops between state(s) and control(s) at every instant. This may or may not be realistic or even feasible, depending on the nature of controls. If firms are adjusting market variables only, then it is at least admissible. If instead they are controlling several types of investments (in capacity or technology), it may not, and the open-loop solution may represent a more plausible tool in such circumstances.[4]

9.1.3   Closed-loop memoryless information

To enrich this brief and necessarily incomplete exposition of the essential elements of differential game theory, it remains to illustrate the so-called memoryless closed-loop solution, which relies on the Hamiltonian function (9.2) but features loops among state(s) and controls in the adjoint equations.

As a result, the set of necessary conditions becomes

$$\frac{\partial \mathcal{H}_i}{\partial u_i} = 0 \tag{9.16}$$

$$-\frac{\partial \mathcal{H}_i(\cdot)}{\partial x} - \sum_{j \neq i} \frac{\partial \mathcal{H}_i(\cdot)}{\partial u_j} \cdot \frac{\partial u_j^*}{\partial x} = \frac{d\lambda_i(t)}{dt} - \rho \lambda_i \tag{9.17}$$

where $\partial \mathcal{H}_i(\cdot)/\partial u_j \cdot \partial u_j^*/\partial x$ is the instantaneous loop measuring the effect of the state x on the control of player j, as the product of the partial derivative of i's Hamiltonian function with respect to u_j times the partial derivative of the optimal control of player j with respect to the state variable at any time t. Note that (9.17) contains $n - 1$ loops of this type, since the i-th term, $\partial \mathcal{H}_i(\cdot)/\partial u_i \cdot \partial u_i^*/\partial x$ is enveloped out by virtue of the FOC (9.16).

It is also worth stressing that, in general, the closed-loop solution sketched here does not coincide with the solution of the Bellman equation (9.15), and therefore is not strongly time consistent.[5] However, it has the desirable property of allowing for feedback effects describing the impact of state on controls and therefore on players' optimal intertemporal strategies which cannot be grasped, by definition, in an open-loop information structure. We will also encounter an example of such a solution in the remainder.

9.2   A dynamic model of managerial firms' growth *à la* Penrose

The first model I illustrate in this chapter is not a game but rather an optimal control model. It offers a reformulation of Slater (1980), revisiting the theory of the growth of managerial firms which took shape in the 1960s thanks to the works of Penrose (1959), Baumol (1962) and Marris (1964), *inter alia*. As we know from Chapter 1, that is a theory about the managerial limits to firms' growth, and this *leitmotiv* emerges once again in the setup proposed by Slater (1980), assuming a properly dynamic nature.

The market exists over time $t \in [0, \infty)$. The model rules out the usual demand externality operating in oligopoly by assuming a constant price p – admittedly, a strong assumption but quite common in the early days of this literature and maintained here – and this is the reason for the lack of strategic interaction with any other firms in the industry, whereby this setup identifies a pure optimal control model and not a game.[6]

Production of the final good requires two inputs, labour and managerial skills. For the sake of simplicity, I assume that all magnitudes are normalized with respect to the labour input (as is common practice in the growth models reviewed in the next section), and pose the unit labour wage equal to zero.

Let $m(t)$ measure the total managerial input operating in a firm at any time t. Part of this amount, $m_1(t)$, must be employed as a productive input in a Cobb–Douglas technology yielding the final output $q(t) = \sqrt{m_1(t)}$ at every instant, while the rest, $m_2(t) = m(t) - m_1(t)$, is used to train new managers, generating a dynamic behaviour of the stock of managerial skills inside the firm, which is described by the kinematic equation:

$$\dot{m} = \sqrt{m_1(t)m_2(t)} - \delta m(t) \tag{9.18}$$

where $\delta > 0$ is the constant decay rate of the managerial stock (due to retirement, for instance).

Now define $m_1(t) = [1 - \alpha(t)]m(t)$ and $m_2(t) = \alpha(t)m(t)$. Variable $\alpha(t) \in [0, 1]$ is the control in the hands of owners, who must choose it so as to maximize the discounted profit flow

$$\Pi = \int_0^\infty \pi(t)e^{-\rho t}dt = \int_0^\infty [pq(t) - wm(t)]e^{-\rho t}dt \tag{9.19}$$

where $w \in (0, p)$ is the managerial wage and $\rho > 0$ is the discount rate, under the dynamic constraint represented by the state equation (9.18), and the initial condition $m(0) = m_0 > 0$. In fact, $\alpha(t)$ is an endogenous weight determining the fractions of the managerial stock working in the production division and in the training division, respectively. Hence, one could see the present model as the description of a specific multidivisional firm, resembling those considered in Chapter 5.

The current value Hamiltonian function of the firm is

$$\mathcal{H}(\cdot) = e^{-\rho t} \left\{ pq(t) - wm(t) + \lambda \left[\sqrt{m_1(t)m_2(t)} - \delta m(t) \right] \right\} \qquad (9.20)$$

with $\lambda(t) = \mu(t)e^{\rho t}$ is the capitalized costate variable.

The FOC on the control variable is[7]

$$\frac{\partial \mathcal{H}(\cdot)}{\partial \alpha(t)} = \frac{m(t)}{2} \left[\frac{(1 - 2\alpha(t))\lambda(t)}{\sqrt{\alpha(t)(1 - \alpha(t))}} - \frac{p}{\sqrt{m(t)(1 - \alpha(t))}} \right] = 0 \qquad (9.21)$$

and the costate equation is

$$\dot{\lambda} = -\frac{\partial \mathcal{H}(\cdot)}{\partial m(t)} + \rho \lambda(t) \Leftrightarrow \qquad (9.22)$$

$$\dot{\lambda} = w - \frac{p\sqrt{m(t)(1 - \alpha(t))}}{2m} - \left[\sqrt{\alpha(t)(1 - \alpha(t))} - \delta - \rho \right] \lambda(t)$$

Now, the equilibrium expression of the costate variable $\lambda(t)$ and the dynamics of $\alpha(t)$ can be easily obtained by solving (9.21) and using (9.22). The resulting control equation reads as follows:

$$\dot{\alpha} = \frac{\alpha[2\alpha - 1]\left\{2w[2\alpha - 1]\sqrt{m(1 - \alpha)} + p\left[1 - \alpha(2 - \alpha) - (\delta + 2\rho)\sqrt{\alpha(1 - \alpha)}\right]\right\}}{p(1 + 2\alpha)\sqrt{\alpha(1 - \alpha)}} \qquad (9.23)$$

where the time argument is omitted for simplicity.

Although the state-control system formed by (9.18) and (9.23) may indeed appear cumbersome, it produces two steady state solutions whose coordinates can be written quite easily (subscript ss stands for *steady state*):

$$m_{ss} = \frac{p^2\left[1 + \alpha_{ss}^2(3 - \alpha_{ss}) - 2(\delta + 2\rho)\sqrt{\alpha_{ss}(1 - \alpha_{ss})} + \alpha_{ss}\Phi\right]}{4w(1 - 2\alpha_{ss}^2)} \qquad (9.24)$$

$$\Phi \equiv (\delta + 2\rho)\left[\delta + 2(\rho + \sqrt{\alpha_{ss}(1 - \alpha_{ss})})\right] - 3$$

$$\alpha_{ss}^{\pm} = \frac{1 \pm \sqrt{1 - 4\delta^2}}{2} \qquad (9.25)$$

These solutions are real and positive, with $\alpha_{ss}^{\pm} \in [0, 1]$, provided that $\delta \in [0, 1/2]$. Observe that this is not too demanding a condition, as it says that the steady state equilibria are plausible if and only if the fraction of managerial skills leaving the firm at any instant is at most 50% of the extant stock. It is also worth noting that

$$\alpha_{ss}^{-} \in \left[0, \frac{1}{2} \right] \quad \text{and} \quad \alpha_{ss}^{+} \in \left[\frac{1}{2}, 1 \right] \tag{9.26}$$

for all $\delta \in [0, 1/2]$. This means that, should α_{ss}^{-} identify a stable solution, the fraction of managers assigned to productive activity would be lower than that assigned to training newcomers (the opposite would obviously apply if α_{ss}^{+} were a stable root).

To ascertain what's going to happen in the long run equilibrium, one may just use the pair $(m_{ss}, \alpha_{ss}^{-})$ to simplify the determinant of the 2×2 Jacobian matrix associated with the state-control system, thereby obtaining the following expression:

$$
\begin{aligned}
\Delta(J) &= \frac{\partial \dot{m}}{\partial m} \cdot \frac{\partial \dot{\alpha}}{\partial \alpha} - \frac{\partial \dot{m}}{\partial \alpha} \cdot \frac{\partial \dot{\alpha}}{\partial m} \\
&= -\frac{wm_{ss}(1 - 4\delta^2)(2\sqrt{1 - 4\delta^2} - 1 + 4\delta^2)}{p(\sqrt{1 - 4\delta^2} - 2)^2 \sqrt{2m_{ss} \left(1 + \sqrt{1 - 4\delta^2} \right)}}
\end{aligned}
\tag{9.27}
$$

Here, the denominator is positive and therefore the determinant $\Delta(J)$ has the sign of

$$-\left(2\sqrt{1 - 4\delta^2} - 1 + 4\delta^2 \right) \tag{9.28}$$

which is negative for all $\delta \in [0, 1/2]$. The opposite is true for $(m_{ss}, \alpha_{ss}^{+})$. Hence, one may formulate the following.

Proposition 9.1 *The steady state $(m_{ss}, \alpha_{ss}^{-})$ is a saddle point equilibrium where at least 50% of the managerial stock working in the firm is assigned to training newcomers.*

The other side of the coin being that less than 50% of m_{ss} enters the Cobb–Douglas production function, this proposition offers a clear picture of the managerial limits posed by the dynamics of the managerial input to the growth of the firm. A quintessential ingredient this early class of models lacks is productive capacity. After all (or better, to begin with), this is the driver of growth, together with technical progress. These two factors, and the role of managers in determining both of them, are modelled in the remainder of the chapter.

9.3 Capacity accumulation games

Quite intuitively, firms need to install capacity to supply goods. This is a major subject in applications of differential game theory to IO models, both in monopoly and in oligopoly settings, and overlaps with a vast literature belonging to the theory of growth. Here I am about to illustrate the impact of managerialization on the growth of firms, a theme which we have already dealt with in Chapter 1, using two alternative models of capacity accumulation commonly used in macroeconomics, i.e. those dating back to Ramsey (1928), Solow (1956) and Swan (1956).

9.3.1 The Solow–Swan game

To the best of my knowledge, the material contained in this section is entirely new. It consists of a very simple extension of a model investigated by Reynolds (1987, 1991), first in the duopoly case and then in an *n*-firm oligopoly setting, under the assumption of pure profit-maximizing behaviour.

Two firms, 1 and 2, interact for all $t \in [0, \infty)$, investing instant by instant to accumulate productive capacity. Firm i's state and control variables are the capacity endowment $k_i(t)$ and the instantaneous investment $I_i(t)$, respectively, and the state equation is

$$\dot{k}_i(t) = I_i(t) - \delta k_i(t) \tag{9.29}$$

where $\delta \geq 0$ is the common and constant decay rate of capacity.

Firms operate at full capacity at every instant, $q_i(t) = k_i(t)$ for all i and t, and sell a homogeneous good, whose inverse market demand function is

$$p(t) = a - k_1(t) - k_2(t) \tag{9.30}$$

The investment activity involves a linear-quadratic instantaneous cost $C_i(t) = cI_i(t) + bI_i^2(t)$, with $b > 0$ and $c \in [0, a)$. The marginal production cost associated with the production of the consumption good is constant, identical for both firms and normalized to zero for the sake of simplicity. Hence, the instantaneous profit function of firm $i = 1, 2$ is

$$\pi_i(t) = [a - k_i(t) - k_j(t)]\,k_i(t) - cI_i(t) - bI_i^2(t),\ i, j = 1, 2;\ j \neq i \tag{9.31}$$

In the original Reynolds' (1987, 1991) model, firm i chooses $I_i(t) \geq 0$ so as to maximize the discounted profit flow

$$\Pi_i(t) = \int_0^\infty \pi_i(t)e^{-\rho t}dt \tag{9.32}$$

subject to the set of dynamic constraints (9.29) and initial conditions $k_i(0) = k_{i0} > 0$. The discount rate $\rho > 0$ is constant and common to all firms.

Here, I suppose that firms delegate control of their respective investment plans to managers hired with contracts based on Vickers (1985), whereby the instantaneous maximand of the manager of firm i becomes

$$M_i(t) = \pi_i(t) + \theta_i k_i(t) \tag{9.33}$$

and the same manager has to choose $I_i(t)$ to maximize

$$\mathbf{M}_i(t) = \int_0^\infty M_i(t) e^{-\rho t} dt \tag{9.34}$$

under the aforementioned constraints. I am posing that θ_i is a constant throughout the time horizon. Although one could argue that a contract delegating the control of a firm to a manager for an arbitrarily long time span should be a function of time and possibly also of the state(s), this assumption is acceptable in view of the results I intend to derive from the analysis of the present model.

To make my point, I will rely on open-loop rules. Firm i's Hamiltonian function is the following

$$\mathcal{H}_i(t) = e^{-\rho t} \left[M_i(t) + \lambda_{ii}(t) \dot{k}_i(t) + \lambda_{ij}(t) \dot{k}_j(t) \right] \tag{9.35}$$

where $\lambda_{ij}(t)$ is the costate variable associated with the state $k_j(t)$. The necessary conditions are

$$\frac{\partial \mathcal{H}_i(t)}{\partial I_i(t)} = -2b I_i(t) - c + \lambda_{ii}(t) = 0 \tag{9.36}$$

$$-\frac{\partial \mathcal{H}_i(t)}{\partial k_i(t)} = \dot{\lambda}_{ii}(t) - \rho \lambda_{ii}(t) \Leftrightarrow \tag{9.37}$$

$$\dot{\lambda}_{ii}(t) = \lambda_{ii}(t)(\delta + \rho) - a - \theta_i + 2k_i(t) + k_j(t)$$

$$-\frac{\partial \mathcal{H}_i(t)}{\partial k_j(t)} = \dot{\lambda}_{ij}(t) - \rho \lambda_{ij}(t) \tag{9.38}$$

where (9.38) can be disregarded as the rivals' capacities do not enter (9.36)–(9.37).

Differentiating (9.36) with respect to time and solving, one derives the following control equation:

$$\dot{I}(t) = \frac{\dot{\lambda}_{ii}(t)}{2b} \tag{9.39}$$

which, using (9.36)–(9.37) and imposing the symmetry conditions $I_i(t) = I_j(t) = I(t)$, $k_i(t) = k_j(t) = k(t)$ and $\theta_i(t) = \theta_j(t) = \theta$, can be rewritten in its final formulation:[8]

$$\dot{I} = \frac{(\delta + \rho)(2bI + c) - a - \theta + 3k}{2b} \tag{9.40}$$

whereby the steady state equilibrium point of the open-loop Nash game is

$$k_{OL} = \frac{a + \theta - c(\delta + \rho)}{3 + 2b\delta(\delta + \rho)}; \quad I_{OL} = \delta k_{OL}. \tag{9.41}$$

The following can be shown to hold.

Proposition 9.2 *The steady state* (k_{OL}, I_{OL}) *is a saddle point equilibrium.*

The proof relies on the fact that the determinant of the Jacobian matrix of the state-control system formed by (9.29) and (9.40),

$$\Delta(J(k, I)) = \frac{\partial \dot{k}}{\partial k} \cdot \frac{\partial \dot{I}}{\partial I} - \frac{\partial \dot{k}}{\partial I} \cdot \frac{\partial \dot{I}}{\partial k}$$

$$= -\delta(\delta + \rho) - \frac{3}{2b} \tag{9.42}$$

is negative everywhere. The saddle path is drawn in the phase diagram appearing in Figure 9.1.

As to the influence of delegation on $I^N(t, \cdot)$ and $k^N(t, \cdot)$, a neat result can be outlined in a fully analytical way. One has to solve the state-control system made up by (9.29) and (9.40), to obtain the expressions of the optimal instantaneous investment $I^N(t, \cdot)$ and installed capacity $k^N(t, \cdot)$ at any instant, as a function of time and the vector of parameters (whose long list is replaced by a dot). Additionally, the solutions of the two differential equations obviously contain two integration constants, C_k and C_I, and the the expressions of $I^N(t, \cdot)$ and $k^N(t, \cdot)$ are decidedly too long to be reported here. However, their partial derivatives with respect

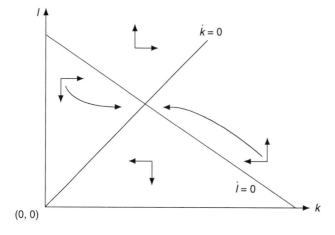

Figure 9.1 The Solow–Swan game: phase diagram.

to θ are

$$\frac{\partial I^N(t,\cdot)}{\partial \theta} = \frac{\delta}{3 + 2b\delta(\delta + \rho)} \qquad (9.43)$$

$$\frac{\partial k^N(t,\cdot)}{\partial \theta} = \frac{1}{3 + 2b\delta(\delta + \rho)} \qquad (9.44)$$

and therefore

$$\frac{\partial I^N(t,\cdot)}{\partial \theta} \bigg/ \frac{\partial k^N(t,\cdot)}{\partial \theta} = \delta = \frac{I_{OL}}{k_{OL}} \qquad (9.45)$$

This amounts to saying the following.

Proposition 9.3 *Under time-invariant managerial contracts, the optimal instantaneous investment and capacity are linear in (and positively related to) the extent of delegation. The ratio between the marginal impacts of delegation on state and control at any instant coincides with the ratio between state and control at the steady state.*

The intuitive reason behind this result is that the same applies if one works out the equivalent of (9.43)–(9.45) using parameter a. Now, keeping in mind that any exogenous increase in a can be equivalently simulated by increasing the extent of delegation θ, the above claim appears entirely obvious.

9.3.2   The Cournot–Ramsey game

The Solow–Swan game is a partial equilibrium model, independent of the assumptions about the behaviour of firms, which in the original macroeconomic approach are supposed to be perfectly competitive agents while in the foregoing game are assumed to behave as strategic players. Conversely, and again irrespective of the presence of strategic interplay or the lack thereof, the Ramsey (1928) model describes the growth process through capital accumulation using a general equilibrium approach. This change in the flavour of the analysis is entirely driven by the fact that the Ramsey model is a *corn–corn* one, i.e. capital (or productive capacity) accumulates through unsold output – or the difference between production and consumption, which is reinserted into the production process at no cost other than the opportunity cost associated with consumption postponement.

What follows summarizes the analysis of Cournot behaviour in a managerialized oligopoly in which firms' profits are being taxed at a constant rate throughout the time horizon of the game, and relies on Baldini and Lambertini (2011), which in turn builds on Cellini and Lambertini (1998, 2008a).

Assume the quantity-setting oligopoly operates over $t \in [0, \infty)$, being made up by $n \geq 1$ firms supplying a homogeneous good, whose instantaneous market demand function is

$$p(t) = a - Q(t), \quad Q(t) \equiv \sum_{i=1}^{n} q_i(t) \tag{9.46}$$

Marginal production cost c is constant and common to all firms. Each firm i accumulates productive capacity $k_i(t)$ over time, according to the following dynamics:

$$\dot{k}_i = f(k_i(t)) - q_i(t) - \delta k_i(t) \tag{9.47}$$

where $f(k_i(t)) = y_i(t)$ is individual production at time t and $\delta > 0$ is the instantaneous and constant decay rate of installed capacity. As in the macroeconomic version of the model, all magnitudes are normalized with respect to the labour input, and it is assumed that $f' \equiv \partial f(k_i(t))/\partial k_i(t) > 0$ and $f'' \equiv \partial^2 f(k_i(t))/\partial k_i(t)^2 < 0$, i.e. production takes place at decreasing returns with respect to capital (cf. Blanchard and Fischer, 1989, chapter 2). Capital accumulates whenever $y_i(t) - q_i(t) > \delta k_i(t)$, and conversely.

The control variable $q_i(t)$ is in the hands of managers rewarded *à la* Vickers (1985) or Fershtman and Judd (1987),

$$M_i(t) = \pi_i(t) + \theta q_i(t) \tag{9.48}$$

and their behaviour impacts on the evolution of the state variable is $k_i(t)$. In (9.48), θ is taken to be constant and identical across firms.

The government levies a constant tax τ on the profits of all firms, so that firm i's instantaneous profit function writes

$$\pi_i(t) = [a - q_i(t) - Q_{-i}(t) - c](1 - \tau)q_i(t) \tag{9.49}$$

and manager i's objective function is

$$\begin{aligned}
\boldsymbol{M}_i(t) &= \int_0^{\infty} M_i(t)e^{-\rho t}dt \\
&= \int_0^{\infty} \{[(a - q_i(t) - Q_{-i}(t) - c)(1 - \tau) + \theta]q_i(t)\}e^{-\rho t}dt
\end{aligned} \tag{9.50}$$

to be maximized with respect to $q_i(t)$ under the set of n dynamic constraints (9.47) and the vector of initial conditions concerning the state variables, $k_i(0) = k_{i0}$, $i = 1, 2, 3, \ldots n$.

Profit taxation is intentionally inserted in the model to put into question a well established result coming from the static analyses of this instrument in imperfectly competitive settings, from which we are accustomed to think of profit taxation as a neutral policy tool (see Levin, 1985; Delipalla and Keen, 1992; Denicolò and Matteuzzi, 2000, *inter alia*).

Now observe that since we are assuming to know only the first and second derivatives of the production function, this setup does not identify a linear-quadratic game. Hence, we have to rely on open-loop rules to attain an explicit solution. However, as we are about to discover, this game is a state-redundant one and therefore yields a subgame perfect (or strongly time consistent equilibrium) under open-loop information.[9]

The Hamiltonian of firm i is

$$\mathcal{H}_i(t) = e^{-\rho t}\{[(a - q_i(t) - Q_{-i}(t) - c)(1 - \tau) + \theta]q_i(t) +$$
$$+ \lambda_{ii}(t)[f(k_i(t)) - q_i(t) - \delta k_i(t)] + \sum_{j \neq i}\lambda_{ij}(t)[f(k_j(t)) - q_j(t) - \delta k_j(t)]\}$$

$$\text{(9.51)}$$

On the basis of the FOC on the control variable,

$$\frac{\partial \mathcal{H}_i(t)}{\partial q_i(t)} = \left[a - 2q_i(t) - Q_{-i}(t) - c\right](1 - \tau) + \theta - \lambda_{ii}(t) = 0 \qquad \text{(9.52)}$$

and the set of costate equations,

$$-\frac{\partial \mathcal{H}_i(t)}{\partial k_i(t)} = \dot{\lambda}_{ii}(t) - \rho\lambda_{ii}(t) \Leftrightarrow$$
$$\frac{d\lambda_{ii}(t)}{dt} = \lambda_{ii}(t)\left[\rho + \delta - f'(k_i(t))\right] \qquad \text{(9.53)}$$
$$-\frac{\partial \mathcal{H}_i(t)}{\partial k_j(t)} = \dot{\lambda}_{ij}(t) - \rho\lambda_{ij}(t) \Leftrightarrow$$
$$\dot{\lambda}_{ij}(t) = \lambda_{ij}(t)\left[\rho + \delta - f'(k_j(t))\right] \qquad \text{(9.54)}$$

one can establish a number of relevant results. The first comes from (9.53).

Lemma 9.1 $\dot{\lambda}_{ii}(t) = 0$ *in correspondence with the Ramsey golden rule and in* $\lambda_{ii}(t) = 0$.

More explicitly, the costate becomes stationary at the Ramsey capacity, say, k_R, which solves $f'(k_i(t)) = \delta + \rho$. Here, as in the original growth model, the marginal productivity of capital equals the sum of discounting and depreciation.

The second result is a direct consequence of the above lemma.

Proposition 9.4 *The Cournot–Ramsey differential game is state-redundant. Therefore, its open-loop solution is strongly time consistent.*

This is because the alternative solution to $\dot{\lambda}_{ii}(t) = 0$, i.e. $\lambda_{ii}(t) = 0$, makes the Cournot game described by the set of FOCs (9.52) entirely independent of the state dynamics, although the game itself is not linear in state variables.

The third result emerges from the inspection of (9.54).

Remark 9.1 *Since $\mathcal{H}_i(t)$ is additively separable in state variables, the loops between any $k_j(t)$ and $q_i(t)$ are nil, for all $j \neq i$.*

Moreover, (9.54) also shows that $\lambda_{ij}(t) = 0$ is an admissible solution at any t, which implies that firm i is allowed not to care about the rivals' accumulation processes at all. This is also true of (9.53), which has the share features with (9.54) except for a change in indices. However, an alternative solution comes from (9.52):

$$\lambda_{ii}(t) = (1 - \tau)[a - 2q_i(t) - Q_{-j}(t) - c] + \theta \tag{9.55}$$

or from (9.53):

$$\lambda_{ii}(t) = \alpha \exp \left\{ \int_0^t [\delta + \rho - f'(k_i(s))]ds \right\}, \quad \text{with } \alpha > 0. \tag{9.56}$$

and neither of these, in general, will be identically equal to zero at any generic instant; the second, indeed, is always strictly positive.

In either case, the FOC on the control variable implies (i) a distortion induced by taxation in the choice of the output level and therefore also (ii) a distortion again induced by taxation on the capital accumulation dynamics, whenever $\lambda_{ii}(t)$ and θ are not simultaneously nil forever. In itself, the notion that profit taxation distorts a firm's investment path is not new, as we have been aware of that since Hall and Jorgenson (1967). Yet, these authors investigated the dynamic performance of a profit-seeking monopolist, while here this consideration arises in a managerialized oligopoly, entailing the following.

Lemma 9.2 *The presence of either managerialization or taxation in isolation suffices to distort the path of capacity accumulation.*

Suppose $\lambda_{ii}(t) \neq 0$ and solve the FOC to get (dropping the time argument)

$$q_i^* = \frac{(a - Q_{-i} - c)(1 - \tau) + \theta - \lambda_{ii}}{2(1 - \tau)} \tag{9.57}$$

and then differentiate q_i^* with respect to τ and impose full symmetry, to get

$$\frac{\partial q^*}{\partial \tau} = \frac{\theta - \lambda}{2(n + 1)(1 - \tau)^2} \tag{9.58}$$

The sign of $\partial q^*/\partial \tau$ is the sign of $\theta - \lambda$, and this has a straightforward implication.

Proposition 9.5 *Pure profit-seeking firms (for which $\theta = 0$) restrict their sales as the tax pressure on profits increases. The reaction of managerial firms to a tax increase is, in principle, ambiguous. In the special case in which $\theta = \lambda(t)$, delegation fully offsets profit taxation and the latter turns out to be neutral.*

The last claim appearing in the above proposition says profit taxation retrieves its neutrality provided that the extent of delegation be specified in managerial contracts so as to equal the shadow price attached to an additional unit of installed capacity at every instant.

Now we are ready for the characterization of the state-control system, steady state equilibria and their stability properties. The control equation is obtained by differentiating (9.57) with respect to time, using expression (9.55) for the costate and imposing symmetry across firms' outputs, in such a way that

$$\text{sign}(\dot{q}) = \text{sign}\left\{\left[(1-\tau)(a-c-(n+1)q)+\theta\right]\left[f'(k)-\rho-\delta\right]\right\} \qquad (9.59)$$

which is equal to zero in correspondence with

$$q_{ss} = \frac{(a-c)(1-\tau)+\theta}{(n+1)(1-\tau)}; \quad f'(k)=\rho+\delta \qquad (9.60)$$

The phase diagram of the game, drawn in the space $\{k,q\}$, appears in Figure 9.2. The locus $\dot{q}\equiv dq/dt=0$ is given by the solutions in (9.60). The two loci partition the space $\{k,q\}$ into four regions, the dynamics of output being summarized by the vertical arrows. From (9.47) one obtains the concave locus $\dot{k}\equiv dk/dt=0$ as well as the dynamics of k, described by horizontal arrows. Steady state equilibria generated by the horizontal Cournot output are $E1$ and $E2$, while R is the steady state associated with the golden rule. The saddle path leading to steady state $E1$ is also represented.

The scenario depicted in Figure 9.2 describes only one out of a total of five possible situations, each of which is univocally determined by the position of the locus horizontal $q_{ss}=[(a-c)(1-\tau)+\theta]/[(n+1)(1-\tau)]$, which shifts upwards (respectively, downwards) as market size $(a-c)$ and/or the extent of delegation θ

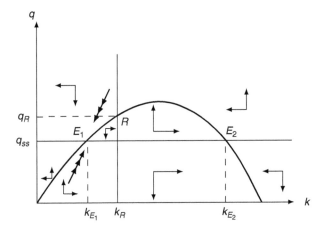

Figure 9.2 The phase diagram of the Cournot–Ramsey game.

increase (respectively, decrease), or the number of firms n decreases (respectively, increases). Conversely, the Ramsey equilibrium R identified along the vertical line $f'(k) = \rho + \delta$ is independent of demand parameters. Therefore, we obtain one out of five possible regimes.

- There exist three steady state points, with $k_{E1} < k_R < k_{E3}$ (this corresponds to Figure 9.2).
- There exist two steady state points, with $k_{E1} = k_R < k_{E3}$.
- There exist three steady state points, with $k_R < k_{E1} < k_{E3}$.
- There exist two steady state points, with $k_R < k_{E1} = k_{E3}$.
- There exists a unique steady state equilibrium point, corresponding to R.

The details about the stability analysis are omitted (see Cellini and Lambertini, 1998, 2003). However, taking into account the effects of changes in parameters on the position of q_{ss}, it is easily seen that the market-driven Cournot solution generates a saddle point equilibrium in E_1 provided q_{ss} intersects the concave locus of $\dot{k} = 0$ to the left of point R, in which case the capital accumulation process falls short of the golden rule and R is not a saddle point. This is one of the most valuable conclusions of the foregoing analysis, and can be properly spelled out as follows.

Proposition 9.6 *If the values of parameters are such that $k_{E1} < k_R < k_{E3}$, managerialization prevents the industry from attaining the Ramsey golden rule.*

Yet, also the opposite may apply. To see this, suppose firms are strict profit-seeking units and $a - c$ is low enough to prevent the attainment of the golden rule. Hiring managers and granting them a sufficient freedom of action may solve the problem and drive the industry into the efficient equilibrium. As soon as $k_{E1} > k_R$, the Ramsey solution is attained and qualifies itself as a saddle point equilibrium. That is, as follows.

Proposition 9.7 *Managerialization may deliver the Ramsey golden rule in situations where a fully entrepreneurial industry would fall short of it.*

The model also allows for a description of the interplay between delegation, capital accumulation and the tax policy. Looking at (9.60), there clearly emerges that, in steady state, while the golden rule is unaffected by τ, profit taxation is distortionary provided firms are managerial and the market-driven equilibrium is a saddle point, i.e. $k_{E1} < k_R$. However, it is also true that fine-tuning the tax pressure may favour the attainment of the golden rule, and once the steady state corresponding to the latter is reached, taxation becomes neutral, having accomplished a most desirable task. This can be appreciated through the following derivative taken on the market-driven solution,

$$\frac{\partial q_{ss}}{\partial \tau} = \frac{\theta}{(n+1)(1-\tau)^2} \tag{9.61}$$

which is positive for all $\theta > 0$. Given that installed capacity at equilibrium is increasing in the level of sales (because the horizontal locus shifts upwards as τ increases and therefore its intersection with $\dot{k} = 0$ shifts rightwards) then also $\partial k_{E1}/\partial \tau > 0$, while $\partial k_R/\partial \tau = 0$. Therefore, any increase in τ exerted on the Cournot solution brings it closer to the Ramsey golden rule, and there exists a finite τ solving $q_{ss} = q_R$. This yields the final result.

Corollary 9.1 *There exists a finite tax rate τ_R such that $k_{E1} = k_R$. In correspondence of τ_R, a managerialized industry which otherwise would have been unable to reproduce the golden rule is driven into it by a fine-tuned policy measure.*

The oligopolistic version of the Ramsey (1928) model has also been used in Lambertini *et al.* (2016) to produce the dynamic version of the Cournot duopoly with CSR investigated in Lambertini and Tampieri (2015), showing that, provided market size is sufficiently large, a CSR firm internalizing polluting emissions and consumer surplus sells more, installs a larger productive capacity and earns higher profits than its profit-seeking rival in the market-driven steady state equilibrium. This and several other extensions of the setup illustrated above (sometimes not explicitly admitting a role for managers) show that the IO reinterpretation of a classical macroeconomic growth model is very versatile, and is most likely to hide additional routes for research, still unexplored.

9.4   R&D games

In this section we come to the dynamic analysis of innovation, whose static counterpart was discussed in Chapter 6. The ensuing models extend those appearing in Cellini and Lambertini (2002, 2004b, 2005, 2009), in which strict profit-seeking behaviour is considered. The material you are about to see relies on Cellini and Lambertini (2008b), where product and process innovations are the outcome of differential games played by managerial firms adopting delegation contracts of the Vickers (1985) type. In both cases, n firms operate in the industry, the instantaneous market demand function encompasses product differentiation *à la* Singh and Vives (1984),

$$p_i(t) = a - q_i(t) - \sigma(t) \sum_{j \neq i} q_j(t) \qquad (9.62)$$

and market competition takes place in the space of quantities. In (9.62), the degree of product substitutability $\sigma(t) \in [0, 1]$ is a function of time $t \in [0, \infty)$ because the first game is for product innovation in the form of investments aimed at decreasing substitutability to soften competition. The output is produced at constant returns to scale and, if process innovation is pursued, it is permanently equal to $c \in (0, a)$ for all firms alike. In both cases, all firms are assumed to discount future magnitudes at a common and constant discount rate $\rho > 0$.

Both games nicely lend themselves to a revisitation of the traditional debate between Schumpeter (1942) and Arrow (1962) about the relationship between the intensity of competition and R&D incentives.

9.4.1 Product innovation

Take as a departure point the initial condition on the state variable $\sigma(t)$, $\sigma(0) = 1$, which says that firms initially supply a homogeneous good. The value of $\sigma(t)$ may decrease over time, thereby increasing product differentiation, according to the state equation

$$\dot{\sigma} = -\frac{K(t)\sigma(t)}{1+K(t)} = -\frac{\left[k_i(t)+\sum_{j\neq i}k_j(t)\right]\sigma(t)}{1+\left[k_i(t)+\sum_{j\neq i}k_j(t)\right]} \qquad (9.63)$$

where $k_i(t)$ is firm i's instantaneous R&D effort. Note that $\sigma(t)$ is the same for all firms – or for any pair of varieties – at all times, so that product innovation is indeed comparable to a public good. The investment carried out by every single firm immediately produces a positive spillover to any other firm via the system of demand functions (9.62).

The shape of (9.63) implies the presence of decreasing returns to scale in product innovation, while the instantaneous individual cost of R&D is linear in the effort $k_i(t)$, and the profit function of firm i can be written as $\pi_i(t) = [p_i(t) - c]q_i(t) - k_i(t)$. Every firm controls two variables (its output and R&D effort), while the single state variable $\sigma(t)$ is common to all firms.

To facilitate the exposition of calculations, here I will use the variable $\widehat{A} = a - \widehat{c} = a - (c - \theta)$ used in Chapter 1, to stress that the model defines a game where managers behave as if their firms had access marginal production costs lowered by an amount corresponding to the extent of delegation θ.

The current Hamiltonian value of firm i is

$$\mathcal{H}_i(t) = e^{-\rho t} \cdot \left\{ \left[\widehat{A} - q_i^2(t) - \sigma(t)\sum_{j\neq i}q_j(t) \right]q_i(t) - k_i(t) + \right.$$
$$\left. - \lambda_i(t)\left[\frac{\left[k_i(t)+\sum_{j\neq i}k_j(t)\right]\sigma(t)}{1+\left[k_i(t)+\sum_{j\neq i}k_j(t)\right]} \right] \right\} \qquad (9.64)$$

where $\lambda_i(t) = \mu_i(t)e^{\rho t}$, $\mu_i(t)$ being the costate variable associated to $\sigma(t)$.

Manager i must choose $q_i(t)$ and $k_i(t)$ to maximize (9.64). The game is non-cooperative and moves are simultaneous forever. Let's set out considering the open-loop solution. The set of necessary conditions is the following:

$$\frac{\partial \mathcal{H}_i(t)}{\partial q_i(t)} = \widehat{A} - 2q_i(t) - \sigma(t)\sum_{j\neq i}q_j(t) = 0 \qquad (9.65)$$

$$\frac{\partial \mathcal{H}_i(t)}{\partial k_i(t)} = -1 - \frac{\lambda_i(t)\sigma(t)}{\left[1 + k_i(t) + \sum_{j \neq i} k_j(t)\right]^2} = 0 \tag{9.66}$$

$$\dot{\lambda}_i = q_i(t)\sum_{j \neq i} q_j(t) + \lambda_i(t)\left[\frac{k_i(t) + \sum_{j \neq i} k_j(t)}{1 + k_i(t) + \sum_{j \neq i} k_j(t)} + \rho\right] \tag{9.67}$$

$$\lim_{t \to \infty} \mu_i(t)\sigma(t) = 0 \tag{9.68}$$

Through the usual procedure based on appropriate manipulations of (9.65)–(9.67), dropping the time argument and imposing symmetry, one obtains a quasi-static solution for the Cournot–Nash output

$$q = \frac{\widehat{A}}{2 + \sigma(n-1)} \tag{9.69}$$

and the control equation describing the dynamics of the R&D effort

$$\dot{k} = \frac{1}{2n(1+nk)}\left[\frac{\rho}{\sigma}(1+nk)^2 - (n-1)q^2\right] \tag{9.70}$$

which is admissible iff $\sigma \in (0, 1]$. If $\sigma = 0$, then $k = 0$ because here, by assumption, product differentiation does not decay.

In view of the economic interpretation of σ and k, we must restrict our analysis of the state-control system made up by (9.63) and (9.70) to the first quadrant of the space of the space (σ, k), as neither the state nor the control variable may become negative. This can be done by looking at the phase diagram appearing in Figure 9.3, in which the locus

$$\dot{k} = 0 \Leftrightarrow k_{ss}^{OL} = \frac{1}{n}\left[\frac{\widehat{A}\sqrt{(n-1)\sigma}}{[2+\sigma(n-1)]\sqrt{\rho}} - 1\right] \tag{9.71}$$

draws a positively sloped and concave curve. Superscript OL intuitively mnemonics for *open-loop*.

If locus k_{ss}^{OL} does cross the horizontal axis at some $\sigma \in (0, 1]$, the resulting degree of substitutability at the steady state is identified by the following expression:

$$\sigma_{ss}^{OL} = \frac{\widehat{A}\left(\widehat{A} - \sqrt{\widehat{A}^2 - 8\rho}\right) - 4\rho}{2(n-1)\rho} \tag{9.72}$$

which is indeed internal to the unit interval for all

$$\widehat{A} > (n+1)\sqrt{\frac{\rho}{n-1}} \tag{9.73}$$

Since $\widehat{A} > a - c$ for all $\theta > 0$, condition (9.73) establishes the following.

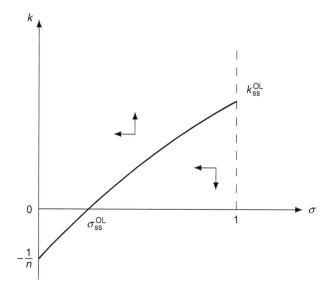

Figure 9.3 Phase diagram in the space (σ, k) under open-loop rules.

Lemma 9.3 *Under open-loop information, the industry-wide adoption of a sales-based delegation contract facilitates the attainment of an inner steady state solution of the product innovation game.*

Studying stability is an easy task, as the arrows appearing in Figure 9.3 illustrate that, whenever the inner solution exists, it is a saddle being reached along the north-east arm of the saddle path. Concerning instead the Arrow (1962) vs Schumpeter (1942) debate, it is evident that σ_{ss}^{OL} is decreasing in n in a hyperbolic way, a fact which, given the dual interpretation of σ, yields the following.

Proposition 9.8 *The degree of product differentiation in steady state is increasing in the intensity of competition, as measured by the numerosity of firms in the industry.*

This has a decidedly Arrovian flavour and suggests that as competition increases because the industry becomes progressively more fragmented, firms strive to preserve profit margins by increasing the amount of differentiation, which is monotonically increasing in the number of firms, since $\partial\sigma_{ss}^{OL}/\partial n < 0$ always.

Instead, as to the impact of managerialization on product differentiation, we know from Cellini and Lambertini (2002) that σ_{ss}^{OL} is increasing in market size when managers are absent, the reason being that any increase in market size is a net substitute of product differentiation as far as profits are concerned. A fortiori this applies in the present setting where the presence of managers implies that firms perceive market size as being increased artificially by delegation. As a result,[10] we have the following.

Proposition 9.9 *Managerialization brings about a decrease in the R&D efforts and a consequent decrease in the equilibrium level of product differentiation.*

The game has not a linear-quadratic form, and this prevents the characterization of the solution of the Bellman equation of the i-th firm. However, one is not necessarily confined to open-loop information, as the present setup can also be solved under closed-loop memoryless rules.

These require firms to account for the loops between the state and all controls at any instant, and these effects must appear in the costate equation derived from the Hamiltonian of every single firm. The consequence is that, while the FOCs on controls are still given by (9.65)–(9.66), the adjoint equation of firm i becomes

$$\dot{\mu}_i = -\frac{\partial \mathcal{H}_i(t)}{\partial \sigma(t)} - \sum_{j \neq i} \frac{\partial \mathcal{H}_i(t)}{\partial q_j(t)} \frac{\partial q_j^*(t)}{\partial \sigma(t)} - \sum_{j \neq i} \frac{\partial \mathcal{H}_i(t)}{\partial k_j(t)} \frac{\partial k_j^*(t)}{\partial \sigma(t)} \Rightarrow$$

$$\dot{\lambda}_i = q_i(t) \sum_{j \neq i} q_j(t) - \left[\sum_{j \neq i} \sigma(t) q_j(t) \sum_{\ell \neq j} \frac{q_m(t)}{2} \right.$$

$$\left. + \sum_{j \neq i} \frac{\lambda_i(t) \sqrt{\lambda_i(t) \sigma(t)}}{2 \left[1 + k_i(t) + \sum_{j \neq i} k_j(t) \right]^2} \right] + \lambda_i(t) \left(\frac{k_i(t) + \sum_{j \neq i} k_j(t)}{1 + \left[k_i(t) + \sum_{j \neq i} k_j(t) \right]} + \rho \right)$$

$$(9.74)$$

and consequently

$$\text{sign}(\dot{k}) = \text{sign} \left\{ [1 + nk(t)] [2\rho(1 + nk(t)) + n - 1] + \right.$$
$$\left. - \sigma(t)(n-1)[q(t)]^2 [2 - \sigma(t)(n-1)] \right\} \quad (9.75)$$

We may drop the time argument and note that, since $\dot{\sigma} = -nk\sigma(t)/(1 + nk) < 0$ for all $k, \sigma > 0$, if there exists an economically admissible steady state, this is necessarily identified by a value of σ belonging to the unit interval and such that the value of k solving $\dot{k} = 0$ is nil. This, in turn, amounts to requiring the expression in (9.75) to be nil as well, which happens in correspondence with

$$k_{ss}^{CL\pm} = \frac{-[2 + (n-1)\sigma](4\rho + n - 1) \pm \sqrt{\Omega}}{4n[2 + (n-1)\sigma]\rho} \quad (9.76)$$

$$\Omega \equiv 8\widehat{A}^2 \sigma [2 + (n-1)\sigma] \rho - (n-1)(2-\sigma)^2$$
$$+ n \left\{ 4[1 + (n-2)\sigma] + \sigma^2 [n^2 - 3(n-1)] \right\}$$

where superscript CL stands for *closed-loop*. The smaller root, k_{ss}^{CL-}, is negative and can be disregarded. Hence, we may focus our attention on k_{ss}^{CL+}, which draws a concave curve that may or may not cross the horizontal axis of the first quadrant of the space (σ, k) at some $\sigma \in (0, 1]$. If it does, then the candidate degrees of steady state substitutability are

$$\sigma_{ss}^{CL\pm} = \frac{\widehat{A}\left[\widehat{A} - 2(2\rho + n - 1) \pm \sqrt{\widehat{A}^2 - 8(2\rho + n - 1)}\right]}{(n-1)\left(\widehat{A}^2 + 2\rho + n - 1\right)} \tag{9.77}$$

A little algebra is needed to ascertain that, depending on the size of $\widehat{A}$ (and therefore also on the extent of delegation, θ), (i) only $\sigma_{ss}^{CL-} \in (0, 1)$ (if $\widehat{A}$ is large enough) or (ii) both σ_{ss}^{CL-} and σ_{ss}^{CL+} belong to $(0, 1)$ (if $\widehat{A}$ is low enough).[11] The first case gives rise to a phase diagram qualitatively analogous to Figure 9.3. The phase diagram pertaining instead to the second scenario appears in Figure 9.4.

The dynamics of the system, illustrated by the arrows in Figure 9.4, tells that the steady state $(\sigma_{ss}^{CL-}, 0)$ is always a saddle point, while the other solution, $(\sigma_{ss}^{CL+}, 0)$, if admissible, is unstable. The properties emerging from comparative statics are analogous to those highlighted in the open-loop case, although the related calculations are more cumbersome.

Again, even with closed-loop memoryless strategies the equilibrium has an Arrovian flavour, and it is possible to compare the steady state outcome generated by the two different information structures, to find that $\sigma_{ss}^{OL} > \sigma_{ss}^{CL-}$ everywhere. This is a consequence of the intensification of strategic interaction generated by closed-loop rules, with firms investing more than in the open-loop game to increase product differentiation at any finite t. This last finding is summarized in the following.

Corollary 9.2 *The industry-wide incentive to increase product differentiation is larger under closed-loop rules than under open-loop ones.*

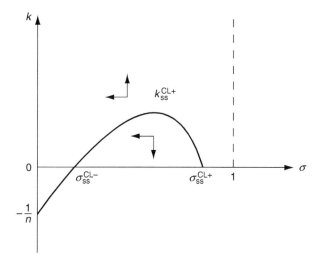

Figure 9.4 Phase diagram in the space (σ, k) under closed-loop rules for $\widehat{A}$ 'low enough'.

Then, as it turns out from this exercise, one may say that intensifying strategic interaction among firms, by switching from open-loop to closed-loop information, induces them to follow more closely the invitation explicitly conveyed by the representative consumer's preference for variety.

9.4.2   Process innovation

This section relies on Cellini and Lambertini (2005, 2008b, 2009), a dynamic revisitation of the d'Aspremont and Jacquemin (1988) model,[12] in which Cournot firms engage in R&D projects for marginal cost reductions, their activities being positively affected by symmetric technological spillovers. Both R&D and quantity strategies are in the hands of managers characterized by a taste for output expansion. Hence, the following may be considered as a differential game broadly inspired by the static multistage games exposed in chapter 6 (Zhang and Zhang, 1997; Kräkel, 2004; Kopel and Riegler, 2006, 2008). The ensuing game revisits the idea that, delegation mimicking a decrease in marginal cost, one could use managers in place of costly R&D projects. Or, since managerialization implies an output expansion, perhaps we might expect managers to shrink R&D efforts. Conversely, several models reviewed in Chapter 6 convey the opposite message. Hence, what should we expect to see at the equilibrium of a dynamic game?

Here, firm i's marginal cost is the relevant state variable, whose dynamics obey the following differential equation:

$$\dot{c}_i = c_i(t)\left[-k_i(t) - \beta\sum_{j\neq i} k_j(t) + \delta\right] \tag{9.78}$$

In (9.78), $k_i(t)$ is the R&D effort exerted by firm i at time t, while the technological spillover received by firm i from the R&D activity of its rivals is measured by parameter $\beta \in [0, 1/(n-1)]$. Parameter $\delta > 0$ represents the constant depreciation rate of in-house production technology, or its *ageing*. The instantaneous cost function associated with the R&D lab of firm i is $\Gamma_i(k_i(t)) = b[k_i(t)]^2$, where $b > 0$ is a constant.

The instantaneous profit function is $\pi_i(t) = [p(t) - c_i(t)]q_i(t) - \Gamma_i(k_i(t))$, and each firm hires a manager who is being assigned the objective function $M_i(t) = \pi_i(t) + \theta q_i(t)$, whose discounted integral is to be maximized with respect to $k_i(t)$ and $q_i(t)$. The Hamiltonian function of manager i is therefore

$$\mathcal{H}_i(t) = e^{-\rho t}\left\{\left[a + \theta - q_i(t) - \sigma\sum_{j\neq i} q_j(t) - c_i(t)\right]q_i(t) - b[k_i(t)]^2 + \right.$$
$$\left. -\lambda_{ii}(t)c_i(t)\left[k_i(t) + \beta\sum_{j\neq i} k_j(t) - \delta\right] - \sum_{j\neq i}\lambda_{ij}(t)c_j(t)\left[k_j(t) + \beta\sum_{\ell\neq j} k_\ell(t) - \delta\right]\right\}$$

$$\tag{9.79}$$

The relevant FOCs on controls are

$$\frac{\partial \mathcal{H}_i(\cdot)}{\partial q_i(t)} = a + \theta - 2q_i(t) - \sigma \sum_{j \neq i} q_j(t) - c_i(t) = 0 \tag{9.80}$$

$$\frac{\partial \mathcal{H}_i(\cdot)}{\partial k_i(t)} = -2bk_i(t) - \lambda_{ii}(t)c_i(t) - \beta \sum_{j \neq i} \lambda_{ij}(t)c_j(t) = 0 \tag{9.81}$$

while the adjoint or costate equations are

$$-\frac{\partial \mathcal{H}_i(\cdot)}{\partial c_i(t)} = \frac{\partial \lambda_{ii}(t)}{\partial t} - \rho \lambda_{ii}(t) \tag{9.82}$$

$$-\frac{\partial \mathcal{H}_i(\cdot)}{\partial c_j(t)} = \frac{\partial \lambda_{ij}(t)}{\partial t} - \rho \lambda_{ij}(t) \tag{9.83}$$

The system (9.80)–(9.83) must be evaluated together with the set of initial conditions $c_i(0) = c_{i0} \in (0, a)$ and transversality conditions $\lim_{t \to \infty} \mu_{ij}(t)c_j(t) = 0$, where $\mu_{ij} = \lambda_{ij}(t)e^{-\rho t}$, for all i and j.

All costate equations (9.83) admit $\lambda_{ij}(t) = 0$ as a solution at all times. This fact, combined with a little algebra I will skip as it follows the same line as in the previous models, yields (again dropping the time argument)

$$\lambda_{ii} = -\frac{2bk_i}{c_i} \tag{9.84}$$

and

$$\dot{k}_i = -\frac{1}{2b}(c_i \dot{\lambda}_{ii} + \lambda_{ii}\dot{c}_i)$$

$$\dot{k}_i(t) = -\frac{\lambda_{ii}(t)c_i(t)}{2b} \tag{9.85}$$

while (9.80) is quasi-static, and imposing symmetry delivers

$$q = \frac{a - c + \theta}{2 + \sigma(n - 1)} \tag{9.86}$$

Then, using (9.84) and (9.86), one may write the control equation in its final form:

$$\dot{k} = \rho k - \frac{c(a - c + \theta)}{2b[2 + \sigma(n - 1)]} \tag{9.87}$$

The above differential equation, with the state equation rewritten under symmetry,

$$\dot{c} = c[-k(1 + \beta(n - 1)) + \delta] \tag{9.88}$$

forms the state-control system of this game, under open-loop rules. Its stationary points – excluding the pair $(0, 0)$, unstable – are identified by the following coordinates:

$$k_{ss}^{OL} = \frac{\delta}{1 + \beta(n - 1)}$$

$$c_{ss}^{OL\pm} = \frac{(a + \theta) \pm \sqrt{(a + \theta)^2 - 4\Phi k_{ss}^{OL}}}{2} \tag{9.89}$$

in which $\Phi = 2b\rho[2 + \sigma(n - 1)]$. Such pairs are admissible provided that $(a + \theta)^2 > 4\Phi k_{ss}^{OL}$. The stability analysis reveals that while $(c_{ss}^{OL-}, k_{ss}^{OL})$ identifies a saddle point, $(c_{ss}^{OL+}, k_{ss}^{OL})$ is an unstable focus. Then, looking at the effects of delegation on $(c_{ss}^{OL-}, k_{ss}^{OL})$, it is obvious that $\partial k_{ss}^{OL}/\partial\theta = 0$ and it is easy to see that, instead,

$$\frac{\partial c_{ss}^{OL-}}{\partial\theta} = \frac{\sqrt{(a + \theta)^2 - 4\Phi k_{ss}^{OL}} - (a + \theta)}{2\sqrt{(a + \theta)^2 - 4\Phi k_{ss}^{OL}}} < 0 \tag{9.90}$$

This implies the following.

Proposition 9.10 *The steady state R&D effort is independent of delegation. However, the steady state marginal cost is monotonically decreasing in the extent of delegation.*

That is, keeping managerial bridles loose favours technical progress, as in the previous game. In the present case, the intuition appears to be that managers invest more in process innovation than owners would do, because of their inclination to expanding output, a task which becomes easier and easier as marginal cost shrinks, all else equal.

9.5   Natural resource extraction

The game, which mainly refers to Lambertini (2016), nests into a relatively large literature (Benchekroun, 2003, 2008; Fujiwara, 2008; Colombo and Labrecciosa, 2015; Lambertini and Mantovani, 2014, 2016), where a common property productive asset exploited by Cournot oligopolists is investigated as a differential game. The market is supplied time $t \in [0, \infty)$ by $n \geq 2$ firms which produce a homogeneous good, whose inverse demand function is $p = a - Q$ at any t, $Q = \sum_{i=1}^{n} q_i$. I will omit the time argument from the very outset, as this shouldn't cause any misunderstanding at this point. Firms share the same marginal cost $c \in (0, a)$, constant over time, and extract a renewable natural resource stock S, whose state equation is

$$\dot{S} = F(S) - Q \tag{9.91}$$

with

$$F(S) = \begin{cases} \delta S \, \forall \, S \in (0, S_{msy}] \\ \delta S_y \left(\dfrac{S_{cc} - S}{S_{cc} - S_{msy}} \right) \forall \, S \in (Sms_y, S_{cc}] \end{cases} \tag{9.92}$$

where $\delta > 0$ is the *implicit* growth rate of the resource when the stock is at most equal to S_{msy}, so that δS_{msy} is the *maximum sustainable yield*. Hence, if the stock is small enough, the size of the resource grows at an exponential rate, while for any $S > S_{msy}$, the resource grows at a decreasing rate. S_{cc} is the *carrying capacity* of the habitat, above which the resource decreases, having reached the upper bound posed by available food and/or space. In order to build up a linear-quadratic game, the extant literature confines itself to the case $F(S) = \delta S$, so that the state equation is

$$\dot{S} = \delta S - Q \tag{9.93}$$

As in the entire chapter, firms play non-cooperatively over an infinite horizon and adopt time-invariant managerial contracts *à la* Vickers (1985). Manager i must

$$\max_{q_i} M_i = \int_0^\infty M_i e^{-\rho t} dt \tag{9.94}$$

subject to (9.93). Let the initial condition be $S_0 \in (0, S_y]$.

Given the linear-quadratic form of the game, and its linearity with respect to the single state variable, the HJB equation

$$\rho V_i(S) = \max_{q_i} \left[(a - Q - c + \theta) q_i + V_i'(S)(\delta S - Q) \right] \tag{9.95}$$

can be solved to find the pair of feedback solutions, one of which is in fact the open-loop equilibrium. In (9.95), $V_i(S)$ is firm i's value function and $V_i'(S) = \partial V_i(S)/\partial S$. The FOC is

$$\widehat{A} - 2q_i - \sum_{j \neq i} q_j - V_i'(S) = 0 \tag{9.96}$$

which, after imposing symmetry, yields

$$q^F(S) = \max \left\{ 0, \frac{\widehat{A} - V'(S)}{n + 1} \right\} \tag{9.97}$$

where superscript F stands for *feedback*. If $\widehat{A} - V'(S) > 0$, $q^F(S) = (\widehat{A} - V'(S))/(n + 1)$ may be plugged into (9.95), which simplifies as follows:

$$\frac{\widehat{A} \left[(n^2 + 1)V'(S) - \widehat{A} \right] + (n + 1)^2 \left[\rho V(S) - \delta S V'(S) \right] - n^2 V'(S)^2}{(n + 1)^2} = 0 \tag{9.98}$$

The next step consists of conjecturing $V(S) = \epsilon_1 S^2 + \epsilon_2 S + \epsilon_3$, whereby $V'(S) = 2\varphi_1 S + \varphi_2$, in such a way that solving (9.98) is equivalent to solving with respect to parameters ϵ_i the system

$$\epsilon_1 \left[(n+1)^2 (\rho - 2\delta) - 4n^2 \epsilon_1 \right] = 0 \tag{9.99}$$

$$2\epsilon_1 (n^2 + 1)\widehat{A} + \epsilon_2 \left[(n+1)^2 (\rho - \delta) - 4n^2 \epsilon_1 \right] = 0 \tag{9.100}$$

$$\epsilon_3 (n+1)^2 \rho + \epsilon_2 \left[(n^2 + 1)\widehat{A} - n^2 \epsilon_2 \right] - \widehat{A}^2 = 0 \tag{9.101}$$

Equations (9.100)–(9.99) are solved by

$$
\begin{aligned}
\epsilon_3 &= \frac{\widehat{A}^2 - \epsilon_2 \left[(n^2 + 1)\widehat{A} - n^2 \epsilon_2 \right]}{(n+1)^2 \rho} \\
\epsilon_2 &= \frac{\epsilon_3 (n+1)^2 \rho}{(n+1)^2 (\delta - \rho) + 4n^2 \epsilon_1}
\end{aligned}
\tag{9.102}
$$

and

$$\epsilon_{11} = 0; \quad \epsilon_{12} = \frac{(n+1)^2 (\rho - 2\delta)}{4n^2} \tag{9.103}$$

Choosing $\epsilon_1 = \epsilon_{11}$, one obtains the open-loop output

$$q^{OL} = \frac{\widehat{A}}{n+1} \tag{9.104}$$

which is a *degenerate* feedback solution in view of the fact that the Bellman equation is linear in S if $\epsilon_1 = 0$, and therefore the control is independent of S at all times. Instead, $\epsilon_1 = \epsilon_{12}$ delivers the following output level,

$$q^F(S) = \frac{\widehat{A}\left[\rho(n^2 + 1) - 2\delta \right] + (n+1)^2 (2\delta - \rho)\delta S}{2\delta(n+1)n^2} \tag{9.105}$$

which is a 'proper' feedback control and, as such is a (linear) function of the state, while q^{OL} is independent of S and involves a perpetual repetition of the static Cournot strategy.

The phase diagram drawn in Figure 9.5 illustrates the dynamic properties of the two equilibria. In particular, the arrows appearing along q^{OL} and $q^F(S)$ show that the open-loop (or degenerate feedback) harvesting strategy is unstable, while the proper feedback one is stable. Observing that $S^{OL} > S^F$ one is easily induced to say that this is due to feedback information intensifying strategic interaction and therefore resource extraction. While this is true as it reflects our usual understanding of the consequences of adopting feedback rather than open-loop rules, there is more to it, as (S^{OL}, q^{OL}) is unstable and we can not expect firms – and the resource stock – to stay put. The unstable nature of the open-loop solution is eventful, as it

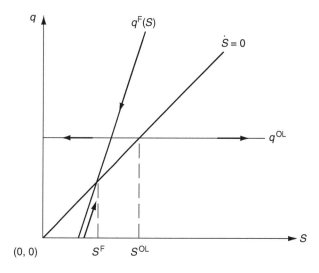

Figure 9.5 Open-loop and linear feedback strategies in the (S, q) space.

implies that if the initial stock of the resource is low (more precisely, lower than S^{OL}), then the resource is going to disappear completely even if the industry is monopolistic. That is, as follows.

Proposition 9.11 *Excess exploitation, caused by the carelessness embodied in open-loop rules and ultimately leading to resource extinction, is independent of industry structure.*

Linear strategies do not exhaust the set of feedback solutions. In fact, there are infinitely many others whose characterization requires the adoption of non-linear feedback rules. Concerning the technique involved, I refer the interested reader to Tsutsui and Mino (1990) and especially to Rowat (2007). The full details of what follows are in Lambertini (2016) and Lambertini and Mantovani (2016), so here I will strip down the exposition to a few essential elements.

Impose symmetry on controls and solve (9.96) with respect to $V'(S)$, and then substitute $V'(S) = \sigma - (n + 1)q(S)$ in (9.95), which can be differentiated with respect to S and rewritten in the following form:

$$q'(S) = \frac{(\delta - \rho)\left[\widehat{A} - (n+1)q(S)\right]}{\widehat{A}(n - 1) + \delta(n + 1)S - 2n^2 q(S)} \tag{9.106}$$

From (9.106), one gets the so-called *non-invertibility condition*,

$$q'(S) \to \pm\infty \Leftrightarrow q_\infty(S) = \frac{\sigma(n - 1) + (n + 1)\delta S}{2n^2} \tag{9.107}$$

establishing that the ensuing analysis is valid for all $q(S) \in (0, q_\infty(S))$.

Then, the continuum of non-linear feedback solutions can be characterized observing that, in the set of the representative firm's isoclines defined in the state-control space, there exists a single isocline which is tangential to the steady state locus $\dot{S} = 0$ and fulfils the requirement posed by (9.107). This particular isocline and the tangency point can be singled out by imposing the tangency condition

$$\frac{(\delta - \rho)\left[\widehat{A} - (n+1)q(S)\right]}{\widehat{A}(n-1) + \delta(n+1)S - 2n^2q(S)} = \frac{\delta}{n} \tag{9.108}$$

in which the expression on the left-hand side is the slope of the isocline, $q'(S)$, resulting from (9.106), and that on the right-hand side results from differentiating with respect to S the stationarity condition $q(S) = \delta S/n$ generated by $\dot{S} = 0$. The resulting coordinates of the tangency point are

$$S^T = \frac{\widehat{A}(\delta - \rho n)}{\delta\left[2\delta - n(1+\rho)\right]}; \; q^T = \frac{\delta S^T}{n} = \frac{\widehat{A}(\delta - \rho n)\delta}{n\delta\left[2\delta - n(1+\rho)\right]} \tag{9.109}$$

The tangency point appears in Figure 9.6, together with the linear solutions and the non-invertibility condition. Form the arrows appearing along the isocline tangential to the steady state locus, we learn that the tangency solution is the first of a set of unstable feedback equilibria, the other extremal of this set being the open-loop solution. The remaining equilibria identified by all points belonging to the segment identified along $\dot{S} = 0$ by points LF and T are instead stable non-linear solutions. The size of this set (call it $SNLE$, for *stable non-linear*

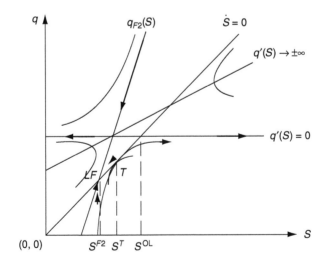

Figure 9.6 Linear and non-linear feedback strategies in the (S, q) space.

equilibria) depends on the extent of delegation θ, which also determines $q^F(S)$ and the exact position of T. It is easily established that $\partial SNLE/\partial\theta$ and $\partial S^T/\partial\theta$ are both positive. These properties jointly entail the following.

Proposition 9.12 *Managerialization expands the set of stable non-linear equilibria and increases its upper bound.*

That is, the tangency point T shifts up along the steady state locus as θ increases, showing that the maximum stock of the resource surviving in stable steady states generated by feedback rules is monotonically increasing in the extent of delegation *à la* Vickers (1985).

This finding, combined with the fact that $\partial S^F/\partial\delta < 0$ for all

$$\delta > \frac{\rho\left[n^2 + 1 + \sqrt{(n^2+1)(2+n(n+1))}\right]}{2} \qquad (9.110)$$

means that delegation can mitigate the so-called *voracity effect* (Lane and Tornell, 1996; Tornell and Lane, 1999) appearing in correspondence with sufficiently high rates of reproduction of the natural resource.[13]

Further reading

For extensive expositions of optimal control theory, see Chiang (1967, 1992), Intriligator (1971) and Kamien and Schwartz (1981, 1991[2]). For more on differential game theory and its applications to oligopoly, see Başar and Olsder (1982, 1995[2]), Mehlmann (1988), Clemhout and Wan (1994), Dockner *et al.* (2000), Cellini and Lambertini (2003), Jørgensen and Zaccour (2007) and Long (2010). Concerning the rise of feedback equilibria under open-loop information, see Clemhout and Wan (1974), Reinganum (1982), Mehlmann and Willing (1983), Dockner *et al.* (1985), Fershtman (1987), Fershtman *et al.* (1992) and Cellini *et al.* (2005). Accounts of the debate on the Schumpeterian hypothesis can be found in Tirole (1988), Reinganum (1989) and Martin (2002). For more on the tragedy of commons, see Tornell and Velasco (1992), among several others.

Notes

1 Here I am confining myself to the case in which agents are maximizers (for instance, because their objectives are measured by profits). If these agents are perfectly competitive firms, then they can be supposed to be aiming at cost minimization. If so, one needs just to replace max with min in (9.1).
2 Rufus Isaacs (1954, 1965) obtained the equivalent *tenet of transition* while working at RAND Corporation.
3 For an exhaustive exposition of differential games whose open-loop solution is strongly time consistent or subgame perfect, see Mehlmann (1988, chapter 4) and Dockner *et al.* (2000, chapter 7), *inter alia.*
4 I am surely not the first to bring this argument forward. See, for instance, Clemhout and Wan (1994).

5 For a classical differential oligopoly game where open-loop, closed-loop memoryless and feedback equilibria differ from one another, see the sticky price game analysed in Simaan and Takayama (1978), Fershtman and Kamien (1987), Tsutsui and Mino (1990) and Cellini and Lambertini (2004a).

6 One plausible interpretation of the fixed-price assumption would be that this firm operates in a perfectly competitive industry, but then one should justify why it should hire any managers, to begin with.

7 Exponential discounting is omitted for brevity, as it is immaterial to the solution of necessary conditions.

8 In the remainder, I omit the explicit indication of the time argument for the sake of brevity.

9 For more on state-redundancy in the Ramsey oligopoly game, see Calzolari and Lambertini (2006, 2007), Cellini and Lambertini (2008a) and Haurie *et al.* (2012, pp. 263–4).

10 It is worth stressing that this is a delicate and possibly not robust conclusion, as θ is being treated as an exogenous parameter while in static games it is common place to treat it as an endogenous strategy in the owners' hands, as we know from the foregoing chapters.

11 The related calculations are overlong and can be omitted. It suffices to note the following. The solutions of $\partial \sigma_{CL+}/\partial \widehat{A} = 0$ are $\widehat{A}_{\pm} = \pm\sqrt{1 - n - 2\rho} \notin \mathbb{R}$ for all $n \geq 1$ and $\rho > 0$. Hence, the sign of $\partial \sigma_{CL+}/\partial \widehat{A}$ necessarily coincides with the sign of the coefficient of $\widehat{A}^2$ in $\partial \sigma_{CL+}/\partial \widehat{A}$ itself, and it's easily checked that such coefficient is positive. The immediate implication is that σ_{CL+} increases monotonically in $\widehat{A}$ and becomes larger than one for sufficiently high values of $\widehat{A}$ (and θ).

12 See also Kamien *et al.* (1992) and Suzumura (1992), *inter alia*.

13 In a nutshell, the voracity effect consists in the following phenomenon. A priori, one would expect to see that the surviving stock is increasing in its rate of reproduction. Yet, this may not happen because, observing an increase in δ, firms may increase their individual and aggregate extraction rates, causing the residual stock in steady state to be *decreasing* in δ. For a more detailed analysis of the arising of voracity in dynamic games of resource exploitation with this structure, see Benchekroun (2008) and Lambertini and Mantovani (2014).

References

Arrow, K.J. (1962), 'Economic Welfare and the Allocation of Resources for Invention', in R. Nelson (ed.), *The Rate and Direction of Industrial Activity*, Princeton, NJ, Princeton University Press.

Baldini, M. and L. Lambertini (2011), 'Profit Taxation and Capital Accumulation in A Dynamic Oligopoly Model', *Japan and the World Economy*, **23**, 13–18.

Başar, T., and Olsder, G.J. (1982, 1995²), *Dynamic Noncooperative Game Theory*, San Diego, CA, Academic Press.

Baumol, W. (1962), 'On the Theory of the Expansion of the Firm', *American Economic Review*, **52**, 1078–87.

Bellman, R.E. (1957), *Dynamic Programming*, Princeton, NJ, Princeton University Press.

Benchekroun, H. (2003), 'Unilateral Production Restrictions in a Dynamic Duopoly', *Journal of Economic Theory*, **111**, 214–39.

Benchekroun, H. (2008), 'Comparative Dynamics in a Productive Asset Oligopoly', *Journal of Economic Theory*, **138**, 237–61.

Blanchard, O.J. and S. Fischer (1989), *Lectures on Macroeconomics*, Cambridge, MA, MIT Press.

Calzolari, G. and L. Lambertini (2006), 'Tariffs vs Quotas in a Trade Model with Capital Accumulation', *Review of International Economics*, **14**, 632–44.

Calzolari, G. and L. Lambertini (2007), 'Export Restraints in a Model of Trade with Capital Accumulation', *Journal of Economic Dynamics and Control*, **31**, 3822–42.

Cellini, R. and L. Lambertini (1998), 'A Dynamic Model of Differentiated Oligopoly with Capital Accumulation', *Journal of Economic Theory*, **83**, 145–55.

Cellini, R., and L. Lambertini (2002), 'A Differential Game Approach to Investment in Product Differentiation', *Journal of Economic Dynamics and Control*, **27**, 51–62.

Cellini, R. and L. Lambertini (2003), 'Differential Oligopoly Games', in R. Bianchi and L. Lambertini (eds), *Technology, Information and Market Dynamics: Topics in Advanced Industrial Organization*, Cheltenham, Edward Elgar, 173–207.

Cellini, R. and L. Lambertini (2004a), 'Dynamic Oligopoly with Sticky Prices: Closed-Loop, Feedback and Open-Loop Solutions', *Journal of Dynamical and Control Systems*, **10**, 303–14.

Cellini, R. and L. Lambertini (2004b), 'Private and Social Incentives Towards Investment in Product Differentiation', *International Game Theory Review*, **6**, 493–508.

Cellini, R., and L. Lambertini (2005) 'R&D Incentives and Market Structure: Dynamic Analysis', *Journal of Optimisation Theory and Applications*, **126**, 85–96.

Cellini, R. and L. Lambertini (2008a), 'Weak and Strong Time Consistency in a Differential Oligopoly Game with Capital Accumulation', *Journal of Optimization Theory and Applications*, **138**, 17–26.

Cellini, R. and L. Lambertini (2008b), 'Product and Process Innovation in Differential Games with Managerial Firms', in R. Cellini and L. Lambertini (eds), *The Economics of Innovation: Incentives, Cooperation, and R&D Policy*, Bingley, Emerald Publishing, 159–76.

Cellini, R. and L. Lambertini (2009), 'Dynamic R&D with Spillovers: Competition vs Cooperation', *Journal of Economic Dynamics and Control*, **33**, 568–82.

Cellini, R., L. Lambertini and G. Leitmann (2005), 'Degenerate Feedback and Time Consistency in Differential Games', in E.P. Hofer and E. Reithmeier (eds), *Modeling and Control of Autonomous Decision Support Based Systems. Proceedings of the 13th Workshop on Dynamics & Control*, Aachen, Shaker Verlag, 185–92.

Chiang, A.C. (1967), *Fundamental Methods of Mathematical Economics*, New York, McGraw-Hill.

Chiang, A.C. (1992), *Elements of Dynamic Optimization*, New York, McGraw-Hill.

Clemhout, S. and H.Y. Wan, Jr. (1974), 'A Class of Trilinear Differential Games', *Journal of Optimization Theory and Applications*, **14**, 419–24.

Clemhout, S. and H.Y. Wan, Jr. (1994), 'Differential Games: Economic Applications', in R. Aumann and S. Hart (eds), *Handbook of Game Theory with Economic Applications*, Amsterdam, North-Holland.

Colombo, L. and Labrecciosa, P. (2015), 'On the Markovian Efficiency of Bertrand and Cournot Equilibria', *Journal of Economic Theory*, **155**, 322–58.

d'Aspremont, C. and A. Jacquemin (1988), 'Cooperative and Noncooperative R&D in Duopoly with Spillovers', *American Economic Review*, **78**, 1133–7.

Delipalla, S. and M. Keen (1992), 'The Comparison between *Ad Valorem* and Specific Taxation under Imperfect Competition', *Journal of Public Economics*, **49**, 351–67.

Denicolò, V. and M. Matteuzzi (2000), 'Specific and Ad Valorem Taxation in Asymmetric Cournot Oligopolies', *International Tax and Public Finance*, **7**, 335–42.

Dockner, E.J., G. Feichtinger and S. Jørgensen (1985), 'Tractable Classes of Nonzero-Sum Open-Loop Nash Differential Games: Theory and Examples', *Journal of Optimization Theory and Applications*, **45**, 179–97.

Dockner, E.J, S. Jørgensen, N.V. Long and G. Sorger (2000), *Differential Games in Economics and Management Science*, Cambridge, Cambridge University Press.

Fershtman, C. (1987), 'Identification of Classes of Differential Games for Which the Open-Loop Is a Degenerate Feedback Nash Equilibrium', *Journal of Optimization Theory and Applications*, **55**, 217–31.

Fershtman, C. and K. Judd (1987), 'Equilibrium Incentives in Oligopoly', *American Economic Review*, **77**, 927–40.

Fershtman, C. and M.I. Kamien (1987), 'Dynamic Duopolistic Competition with Sticky Prices', *Econometrica*, **55**, 1151–64.

Fershtman, C., M. Kamien and E. Muller (1992), 'Integral Games: Theory and Applications', in G. Feichtinger (ed.), *Dynamic Economic Models and Optimal Control*, Amsterdam, North-Holland.

Fujiwara, K. (2008), 'Duopoly Can Be More Anti-Competitive than Monopoly', *Economics Letters*, **101**, 217–19.

Gordon, H.S. (1954), 'The Economic Theory of a Common-Property Resource: The Fishery', *Journal of Political Economy*, **62**, 124–42.

Hall, R.E. and D.W. Jorgenson (1967), 'Tax Policy and Investment Behaviour', *American Economic Review*, **57**, 391–414.

Hardin, G. (1968), 'The Tragedy of the Commons', *Science*, **162**, 1243–8.

Haurie, A., J.B. Krawczyk and G. Zaccour (2012), *Games and Dynamic Games*, Singapore, World Scientific.

Intriligator, M.D. (1971, 2002), *Mathematical Optimization and Economic Theory*, SIAM Classics in Applied Mathematics, vol. 39, Philadelpia, PA.

Isaacs, R. (1954), 'Differential Games, I, II, III, IV', Reports RM-1391, 1399, 1411, 1486, RAND Corporation.

Isaacs, R. (1965), *Differential Games*, New York, Wiley.

Jørgensen, S. and G. Zaccour (2007), 'Developments in Differential Game Theory and Numerical Methods: Economic and Management Applications', *Computational Management Science*, **4**, 159–82.

Kamien, M.I. and N.L. Schwartz (1981, 1991^2), *Dynamic optimization: The Calculus of Variations and Optimal Control in Economics and Management*, Amsterdam, North-Holland.

Kamien, M.I., E. Muller and I. Zang (1992), 'Cooperative Joint Ventures and R&D Cartels', *American Economic Review*, **82**, 1293–306.

Kopel, M. and C. Riegler (2006), 'R&D in a Strategic Delegation Game Revisited: A Note', *Managerial and Decision Economics*, **27**, 605–12.

Kopel, M. and C. Riegler (2008), 'Delegation in an R&D Game with Spillovers', in R. Cellini and L. Lambertini (2008, eds), *The Economics of Innovation: Incentives, Cooperation, and R&D Policy*, vol. 286, Contributions to Economic Analysis Series, Bingley, Emerald Publishing.

Kräkel, M. (2004), 'R&D Spillovers and Strategic Delegation in Oligopolistic Contests', *Managerial and Decision Economics*, **25**, 147–56.

Lambertini, L. (2016), 'Managerial Delegation in a Dynamic Renewable Resource Oligopoly', in H. Dawid, K. Doerner, G. Feichtinger, P. Kort and A. Seidl (eds), *Dynamic Perspectives on Managerial Decision Making: Essays in Honor of Richard F. Hartl*, Heidelberg, Springer.

Lambertini, L. and Mantovani, A. (2014), 'Feedback Equilibria in a Dynamic Renewable Resource Oligopoly: Pre-Emption, Voracity and Exhaustion', *Journal of Economic Dynamics and Control*, **47**, 115–22.

Lambertini, L. and A. Tampieri (2015), 'Incentive, Performance and Desirability of Socially Responsible Firms in a Cournot Oligopoly', *Economic Modelling*, **50**, 40–8.

Lambertini, L. and A. Mantovani (2016), 'On the (In)stability of Nonlinear Feedback Solutions in a Dynamic Duopoly with Renewable Resource Exploitation', *Economics Letters*, **143**, 9–12.

Lambertini, L., A. Palestini and A. Tampieri (2016), 'CSR in Asymmetric Duopoly with Environmental Externality', *Southern Economic Journal*, **83**, 236–52.

Lane, P.R. and Tornell, A. (1996), 'Power, Growth, and the Voracity Effect', *Journal of Economic Growth*, **1**, 213–41.

Levin, D. (1985), 'Taxation within Cournot Oligopoly', *Journal of Public Economics*, **27**, 281–90.

Long, N.V. (2010), *A Survey of Dynamic Games in Economics*, Singapore, World Scientific.

Marris, R. (1964), *The Economic Theory of Managerial Capitalism*, New York, Fee Press.

Martin, S. (2002), *Advanced Industrial Economics. Second Edition*, Oxford, Blackwell.

Mehlmann, A. (1988), *Applied Differential Games*, New York, Plenum Press.

Mehlmann, A. and R. Willing (1983), 'On Nonunique Closed-Loop Nash Equilibria for a Class of Differential Games with a Unique and Degenerate Feedback Solution', *Journal of Optimization Theory and Applications*, **41**, 463–72.

Penrose, E. (1959), *The Theory of the Growth of the Firm*, Oxford, Wiley.

Pontryagin, L.S. (1966), 'On the Theory of Differential Games', *Uspekhi Matematicheskikh Nauk*, **21**, 219–74.

Pontryagin, L.S., V.G. Boltyanskii, R.V. Gamkrelidze and E.F. Mishchenko (1962), *The Mathematical Theory of Optimal Processes*, New York, Interscience.

Ramsey, F.P. (1928), 'A Mathematical Theory of Saving', *Economic Journal*, **38**, 543–59.

Reinganum, J. (1982), 'A Class of Differential Games for Which the Closed Loop and Open Loop Nash Equilibria Coincide', *Journal of Optimization Theory and Applications*, **36**, 253–62.

Reinganum, J. (1989), 'The Timing of Innovation: Research, Development and Diffusion', in Schmalensee, R. and R. Willig (eds), *Handbook of Industrial Organization*, vol. 1, Amsterdam, North-Holland.

Reynolds, S.S. (1987), 'Capacity Investment, Preemption and Commitment in an Infinite Horizon Model', *International Economic Review*, **28**, 69–88.

Reynolds, S. (1991), 'Dynamic Oligopoly with Capacity Adjustment Costs', *Journal of Economic Dynamics and Control*, **15**, 491–514.

Rowat, C. (2007), 'Non-Linear Strategies in a Linear Quadratic Differential Game', *Journal of Economic Dynamics and Control*, **31**, 3179–202.

Schumpeter, J.A. (1942), *Capitalism, Socialism and Democracy*, London, Allen & Unwin.

Simaan, M. and T. Takayama (1978), 'Game Theory Applied to Dynamic Duopoly Problems with Production Constraints', *Automatica*, **14**, 161–6.

Singh, N. and X. Vives (1984), 'Price and Quantity Competition in a Differentiated Duopoly', *RAND Journal of Economics*, **15**, 546–54.

Slater, M. (1980), 'The Managerial Limitation to the Growth of Firms', *Economic Journal*, **90**, 520–8.

Solow, R. (1956), 'A Contribution to the Theory of Economic Growth', *Quarterly Journal of Economics*, **70**, 65–94.

Suzumura, K. (1992), 'Cooperative and Noncooperative R&D in Duopoly with Spillovers', *American Economics Review*, **82**, 1307–20.

Swan, T.W. (1956), 'Economic Growth and Capital Accumulation', *Economic Record*, **32**, 334–61.

Tirole, J. (1988), *The Theory of Industrial Organization*, Cambridge, MA, MIT Press.

Tornell, A. and Lane, P.R. (1999), 'The Voracity Effect', *American Economic Review*, **89**, 22–46.

Tornell, A. and Velasco, A. (1992), 'The Tragedy of the Commons and Economic Growth: Why Does Capital Flow from Poor to Rich Countries?', *Journal of Political Economy*, **100**, 1208–31.

Tsutsui, S. and Mino, K. (1990), 'Nonlinear Strategies in Dynamic Duopolistic Competition with Sticky Prices', *Journal of Economic Theory*, **52**, 136–61.

Vickers, J. (1985), 'Delegation and the Theory of the Firm', *Economic Journal*, **95** (Conference Papers), 138–47.

Zhang, J. and Z. Zhang (1997), 'R&D in a Strategic Delegation Game', *Managerial and Decision Economics*, **18**, 391–8.

Index

For Product Safety Concerns and Information please contact our EU
representative GPSR@taylorandfrancis.com
Taylor & Francis Verlag GmbH, Kaufingerstraße 24, 80331 München, Germany

www.ingramcontent.com/pod-product-compliance
Ingram Content Group UK Ltd.
Pitfield, Milton Keynes, MK11 3LW, UK
UKHW021002180425
457613UK00019B/782